THE WORLD BANK
ANNUAL REPORT 1994

The World Bank
Washington, D.C. 20433

Photo Credits

Cover: François Charton
Page 10: Antonia Macedo
Page 78: François Charton
Page 81: Jan Post
Page 92: Antonia Macedo
Page 97: François Charton
Page 103: Ephim Schluger
Page 109: Jan Post
Page 120: Peter Muncie

Cover:
This girl lives near the Guatemala high-country village of Solala near Lake Atitlan. Known as the "jewel of the highlands," the lake has generated income from tourism and allowed the villagers to become relatively prosperous. The child has traveled to the market with her parents and is waiting at the bus plaza to travel home.

Cover design by Joyce C. Petruzzelli

ISSN: 0252–2942
ISBN: 0–8213–2545–0

Letter of Transmittal

This Annual Report, which covers the period July 1, 1993, to June 30, 1994, has been prepared by the executive directors of both the International Bank for Reconstruction and Development (IBRD) and the International Development Association (IDA) in accordance with the respective by-laws of the two institutions. Lewis T. Preston, president of the IBRD and IDA and chairman of the boards of executive directors, has submitted this Report, together with accompanying administrative budgets and audited financial statements, to the board of governors.

During this, the Fiftieth Anniversary year of the founding of the Bank, the directors wish to pay tribute to the dedication of Bank staff, who for five decades have served to make the world a better place in which to live. Enormous development challenges remain; the directors are confident that they will be addressed with enthusiasm and professionalism equal to that given in the past.

Annual Reports for the International Finance Corporation (IFC), the Multilateral Investment Guarantee Agency (MIGA), and the International Centre for Settlement of Investment Disputes (ICSID) are published separately.

EXECUTIVE DIRECTORS

Ibrahim A. Al-Assaf
Faisal A. Al-Khaled
Aris Othman
Marc-Antoine Autheman
Mohamed Benhocine
Andrei Bugrov
John H. Cosgrove
Robert R. de Cotret
Marcos Caramuru de Paiva
Huw Evans
Fritz Fischer
Nicolas Flaño
Jean-Daniel Gerber
Enzo Grilli
Eveline Herfkens
Ruth Jacoby
Bimal Jalan
Yasuyuki Kawahara
Jean-Pierre Le Bouder
O.K. Matambo
Jan Piercy
Walter Rill
Angel Torres
Wang Liansheng

ALTERNATES

Ibrahim M. Al-Mofleh
Mohamed W. Hosny
Jannes Hutagalung
Jérôme Haas
Abdul Karim Lodhi
Alexander N. Doumnov
Bong-Hee Won
Hubert Dean
Marcela Cartagena
David Stanton
Harald Rehm
Julio Nogues
Jan Sulmicki
Helena Cordeiro
Ileana Ionescu
Helga Jonsdottir
M.A. Syed
Rintaro Tamaki
Ali Bourhane
Hary M. Mapondo
(vacant)
Nurcan Akturk
Gabriel Castellanos
Zhang Shengman

August 2, 1994

The World Bank, the IFC, and MIGA

The World Bank is a multilateral development institution whose purpose is to assist its developing member countries further their economic and social progress so that their people may live better and fuller lives. The term "World Bank" refers to two legally and financially distinct entities: the International Bank for Reconstruction and Development (IBRD) and the International Development Association (IDA). The IBRD and IDA have three related functions: to lend funds, to provide economic advice and technical assistance, and to serve as a catalyst to investment by others.

The IBRD finances its lending operations primarily from borrowings in the world capital markets. IDA extends assistance to the poorest countries on easier terms, largely from resources provided by its wealthier members. Funds from such other sources as governments, commercial banks, export-credit agencies, and other multilateral institutions are increasingly being paired with World Bank funds to cofinance projects. The World Bank also provides loans to help developing countries adjust their economic policies and structures in the face of structural problems that threaten continuing development.

The International Finance Corporation (IFC), an affiliate of the World Bank, seeks to promote growth in the private sector of developing countries by mobilizing foreign and domestic capital to invest alongside its own funds in commercial enterprises.

The Multilateral Investment Guarantee Agency (MIGA), also an affiliate of the World Bank, was established in 1988 to encourage direct foreign investment in developing countries by protecting investors from noncommercial risk, especially risk of war or repatriation.

Contents

Glossary

Agenda 21 The main operational product of the United Nations Conference on Environment and Development (UNCED), Agenda 21 is an ambitious action plan covering over 100 program areas (climate, desertification, sustainable agriculture, for example) integrating environment and development, to be supported by new and additional financial resources, improved access on favorable terms to environmentally sound technology, and strengthened institutional capacity in developing countries. States were called upon to prepare national sustainable development plans outlining their own environmental problems as well as their strategies, programs, and priorities for implementing Agenda 21. UNCED agreed that financing should be assembled to support these programs through a variety of existing, rather than new, funding mechanisms.

"Brady" operations Named after a March 1989 initiative by then-U.S. Secretary of the Treasury Nicholas Brady who proposed that countries with sound adjustment problems should get access to debt- and debt-service reduction facilities supported by international financial institutions and official creditors. It represented a shift in the international community's debt strategy from supporting adjustment with concerted new lending to supporting adjustment with debt- and debt-service reduction.

"Brown" environmental agenda Refers to the immediate and most critical environmental problems facing cities and includes three main areas—energy use and efficiency, urban and industrial pollution control, and urban environmental management.

Central bank facility A facility used by the IBRD to raise short-term United States-dollar debt by offering to central banks and other government organizations of member countries a one-year, United States-dollar denominated variable-rate instrument. The interest rate is adjusted monthly on the yield of the one-year U.S. Treasury bill plus a spread.

Committee of the Whole The Committee of the Whole is a committee made up of all exec-

utive directors; it has traditionally served as a forum in which preliminary discussion of issues takes place before they are taken up by the executive board. It is also the forum in which the executive directors act as a preparatory body for the work of the Development Committee.

Currency swaps Currency swaps are used by the Bank as a liability-management tool and essentially involve an exchange of a stream of principal and interest payments in one currency for a stream in another currency. The Bank uses currency swaps to obtain borrowings in the ultimately desired "target" currency at below cost of a market borrowing in that currency.

Development Committee This committee is known formally as the Joint Ministerial Committee of the Boards of Governors of the World Bank and the International Monetary Fund on the Transfer of Real Resources to Developing Countries. Established in October 1974, the committee currently consists of twenty-four members, generally Ministers of Finance, appointed for periods of two years by one of the countries or a group of countries that designates a member of the Bank's or the International Monetary Fund's board of executive directors. The committee is required to advise and report to the boards of governors of the two institutions on all aspects of the broad question of the transfer of real resources to developing countries and to make suggestions for their implementation.

"Enhanced" Toronto terms A menu of Paris Club concessions for low-income countries, initiated in 1991, comprises two options providing for deeper debt reduction plus the nonconcessional option from the old Toronto terms. The concessional options amount to 50 percent forgiveness in present-value terms on debt-service payments falling due during the consolidation period. Enhanced Toronto terms also provide for a third nonconcessional option: consolidation at market rates, with a repayment period of twenty-five years, including a fourteen-year grace period. This option was adopted by the United States and some smaller creditor countries that were, at the time, unable to adopt debt cancellation for non-ODA debt.

Forward foreign exchange market   Allows for the sale or purchase of foreign currency for deferred rather than immediate delivery.

G-7 countries   Canada, France, Germany, Italy, Japan, the United Kingdom, and the United States

"Green" environmental agenda   Refers to the promotion of sustainable natural resource management and the reduction of resource degradation, and includes agriculture and land management, forest management, water-resource and watershed management, marine and coastal zone management, and biodiversity conservation.

ICOR (incremental capital-output ratio)   An aggregate measure of the efficiency of investment. It shows the amount of investment required to produce an annual income stream of one dollar. The lower the ICOR, the more efficient the investment.

LIBOR (London Interbank Offered Rate)   LIBOR is the rate at which major banks in London are willing to lend in a specific currency or currency unit to other banks. It is used as a base rate for many international interest-rate transactions.

Low-income countries   Are those countries with a GNP per capita of $675 or less in 1992 United States-dollar terms.

Mezzanine financing   Has two separate meanings, one having to do with the type of finance, the other with the stage a company has reached. It is the second sense that applies to mezzanine finance funds supported by the IFC: risk capital made available to unlisted companies to support development and expansion programs, in anticipation of the companies' being listed.

Middle-income countries   Are those countries with a GNP per capita of more than $675 but less than $8,356 in 1992 United States-dollar terms.

Negative-pledge clause   Negative-pledge clauses are concerned with the granting of security interests by a borrower over its assets to its creditors. By the terms of such a clause, the borrower agrees with a creditor or group of creditors to restrictions on its granting, or otherwise permitting to exist, security interests in favor of other creditors. Negative-pledge clauses are usually standard in Bank loan documents. They may be waived on a case-by-case basis, however.

Official development assistance (ODA)   Financial aid to developing countries and multilateral institutions provided by official agencies, or by their executive agencies. ODA is administered with the promotion of the economic development and welfare of developing countries as its main objective, is concessional in character, and contains a grant element of at least 25 percent.

Panel data set   Is one composed of both time series and cross-section observations. The resulting data base is a gold mine of analytical information relative to the much more common cross-sectional base.

Paris Club   The Paris Club is the name given to the *ad hoc* meetings of creditor governments that, since 1956, have arranged, when necessary, for the renegotiation of debt owed to official creditors or guaranteed by them. (Debts to commercial banks are renegotiated with committees of the banks involved.) The World Bank is not a member of the Paris Club.

Social-action programs   Social-action programs and social funds consist of multisectoral operations that mobilize several sources of financing to fund special interventions and targeted projects seeking to alleviate the social costs of adjustment, as well as poverty in general. The project components that typically get financed include public works, severance payments, retraining, and schemes in nutrition, primary health, and primary education. While the objectives and project content of social-action programs and social funds are similar, they differ in their institutional set-up. Social funds finance small, demand-driven subprojects and often bypass existing bureaucratic systems and procedures; funding commitments are often based on the evaluation of project proposals prepared according to predetermined selection criteria. Social-action program subprojects are typically appraised by the World Bank. Whereas social funds are most often parastatal quasi-financial institutions, social-action programs generally cover a broader array of institutional arrangements, such as quasi-autonomous project units or integration into sectoral ministries.

Social fund   (See social-action programs)

SPA-eligible country   Country eligibility is determined on the basis of poverty (countries cannot be eligible for IBRD loans), indebtedness (countries have to have projected debt-service ratios of 30 percent or more, and efforts to adjust (countries have to be currently implementing a policy-reform program that is endorsed and normally supported by the Bank and the International Monetary Fund, and agreement has to be reached on a policy framework paper).

Special drawing rights (SDRs)   The special drawing right is a reserve asset created in 1968 by the International Monetary Fund for use by its members and certain prescribed institutions, among which are multilateral development banks and the Bank for International Settlements. Its value is calculated daily by using a weighted basket of the currencies of the G-5 countries (France, Germany, Japan, the United Kingdom, and the United States).

Structured notes   Those for which the returns are linked to interest and/or exchange rate indices.

Toronto terms   Toronto terms refer to a menu of options that can be chosen to reduce official debt in low-income, debt-distressed countries. The terms, agreed upon in September 1988 (following agreement in principle at the economic summit held in Toronto three months earlier), include reduced interest, very long grace and repayment periods (at commercial rates), or partial write-offs of debt-service obligations during the consolidation period (with the rest rescheduled at commercial rates and shorter maturities), or a combination of these options.

Vehicle currency   A currency in which the Bank borrows and simultaneously enters into a currency swap in order to convert the "vehicle" currency liability into a liability denominated in another currency (a so-called "target" currency").

School children in Guiling, a city in the southern province of Guangxi. In China, equal education is provided to girls from the earliest age.

Overview of World Bank Activities in Fiscal 1994

The fundamental objective of the World Bank is to support the reduction of poverty in its member countries. During fiscal 1994, the Bank continued to make progress—through its lending operations and a strengthened policy dialogue—in implementing the poverty-reduction strategies first outlined in *World Development Report 1990* and subsequently elaborated in a policy paper and associated operational documents.

A report on poverty reduction, discussed by the executive board in April 1994, concluded that progress was being made in implementing the Bank's poverty-reduction strategy—in the Bank's lending operations, in country-assistance strategies and the policy dialogue, and in strengthening poverty analyses. The report noted, however, that several challenges had to be addressed in the Bank's future poverty-reduction work. They include ensur-

ing an integrated poverty-reduction effort in country-assistance strategies; completion of, and improvements to, poverty assessments for all borrowers; and development of poverty-monitoring systems and expansion of countries' capacity to implement them.

Most recently, the Bank has placed less emphasis on the growth of its portfolio and more on its quality. This shift grew out of the 1992 report of the Task Force on Portfolio Management, which identified certain aspects of Bank practice that either may have contributed to portfolio-management problems or were insufficiently effective in resolving them. Steps were taken in fiscal 1994 to incorporate the task force's recommendations so as to make the Bank more effective in pursuing its basic goal of reducing poverty in borrowing countries.

As the core of its action plan, the Bank introduced a country-by-country approach,

Operational and Financial Overview, Fiscal 1990–94
(millions of US dollars unless otherwise noted; fiscal years)

Item	1990	1991	1992	1993	1994
IBRD					
Commitments	15,180	16,392	15,156	16,945	14,244
Disbursements	13,859	11,431	11,666	12,942	10,447
Net disbursements[a]	5,726	2,109	1,833	2,331	−731
New medium- to long-term borrowings	11,481	10,883	11,789	12,676	8,908
Net income	1,046	1,200	1,645	1,130	1,051
Subscribed capital	125,262	139,120	152,248	165,589	170,003
Statutory lending limit	137,046	152,327	168,369	183,312	189,189
Loans outstanding	89,052	90,638	100,810	104,451	109,291
Keys ratios					
Loans outstanding as a percentage of lending limit	65	59	60	57	58
Interest coverage ratio	1.17	1.17	1.24	1.16	1.16
Liquidity ratio (percent)	47	51	48	48	51
Reserves-to-loans ratio[b]	10.8	11.2	11.7	11.7	13.9
IDA					
Commitments	5,549	6,293	6,550	6,751	6,592
Disbursements	3,931	4,549	4,765	4,947	5,532
Net disbursements[a]	3,713	4,274	4,441	4,581	5,110

a. Amounts include disbursements, repayments, and prepayments to/from all members, including third party repayments.
b. Includes amount allocated to reserves for prefunding of interest waivers.

rather than a project-by-project approach, into the management of its ongoing lending operations. To complement the changes it made in its own policies and practices, the Bank is collaborating with the authorities in borrowing countries to review the performance of the portfolio in each country and resolve systemic problems. These and other measures are helping the Bank take a much more strategic view of its $148 billion loan portfolio ($107 billion, 982 projects, IBRD; $41 billion, 915 projects, IDA). According to a report on the progress of activities designed to improve the management of the development programs and projects the Bank finances, steady and substantial progress has been made during the past year towards sharpening the focus on implementation and on a performing portfolio. The report adds, however, that more remains to be done, for the action plan is not a set of one-time activities; rather, it is a process that is expected to take years before it is satisfactorily completed.

The Bank is also devoting more energy and resources to fostering stakeholder participation during project preparation. In June 1993, a Participation Fund was established to finance extra expenditures incurred in involving beneficiaries in project preparation and in economic and sector work. The initial monies allocated to the fund were fully committed by November, and additional amounts were allocated in March 1994. Involving beneficiaries in project preparation is now beginning to become normal Bank procedure.

Cooperation between the Bank and nongovernmental organizations (NGOs) continued to expand in terms of both lending operations and the policy dialogue throughout the year. Increased collaboration was clearly exhibited at the Conference on Actions to Reduce Hunger Worldwide that was convened by the Bank in November 1993. In addition to participating in presentations and discussion, NGOs assisted in the conference's preparatory and follow-up work.

During the year, steps were taken to increase the Bank's accountability and openness:

In September 1993, the executive board of the Bank established an independent Inspection Panel, which will receive and investigate complaints that the Bank has not followed its own policies and procedures with respect to

---

The Bank, Age 50, Looks to the Next Century

Fifty years ago, in July 1944, the World Bank was conceived at the United Nations Monetary and Financial Conference held in Bretton Woods, New Hampshire, United States of America.

Representatives of forty-four nations assembled there established two complementary financial institutions—the Bank and the International Monetary Fund.

This is what the report of Commission II (International Bank for Reconstruction and Development) to the Executive Plenary Session (United Nations Monetary and Financial Conference) wrote about the Bank in that summer of 1944:

"The creation of the Bank was an entirely new venture. . . . So novel was it, that no name could be found for it. Insofar as we can talk of capital subscriptions, loans, guarantees, issue of bonds, the new financial institution may have some apparent claim to the name of Bank. But the type of shareholders, the nature of subscriptions, the exclusion of all deposits and short-term loans, the non-profit basis, are quite foreign to the accepted nature of a Bank. However, it was accidentally born with the name Bank, and Bank it remains, mainly because no satisfactory name could be found in the dictionary for this unprecedented institution."

Reflection on the experience of the past fifty years highlights how far the world has progressed economically and socially and how far it still has to go.

In the developing countries, average life expectancy has increased by about 50 percent; the proportion of children attending school has risen from less than half to more than three quarters; and average income per person has more than doubled. The Bank—through its support for more than 5,000 projects in about 140 countries—has contributed to this progress.

Enormous challenges remain, however. They include reducing poverty for the more than 1 billion people who struggle to survive on about a dollar a day and providing basic sanitation, clean water, health care, and schooling for those lacking access to these basic services. Most countries in sub-Saharan Africa have been mired in lackluster or declining rates of growth for more than a decade. The problems associated with economic transformation in Central and Eastern Europe and the former Soviet Union have proved to be extremely complex. And new challenges are coming to the fore, in South Africa and the West Bank and Gaza, for example.

In a number of ways, the Bank is uniquely placed to help address these challenges. Most important is its fifty years of experience in working on almost every kind of development issue in almost every developing country. From that experience has come lessons learned over the years:

the design, appraisal, and/or implementation of a development project that it supports. The panel will be functionally independent and will report directly to the board. In April 1994, the three members of the panel were appointed.

In January 1994, the Bank expanded public access to operational information by opening a Public Information Center at the Bank's headquarters in Washington, D.C. that aims to provide timely and relevant information about the Bank's present and future plans by allowing public access to previously restricted documents. The information is also available through Bank offices in London, Paris, Tokyo, and through the institution's many field offices. The public can also use the Internet computer network to access project information documents and to view (and order) the titles of all Bank documents available on request, as well as the abstracts and entire text of selected documents. Greater transparency is essential to explain the Bank's work to the various stakeholders and thereby increase understanding of and support for Bank-supported activities.

Resources devoted to the many types of non-lending activities that serve to underpin future lending operations continued to be significant. In fiscal 1994, resources spent on economic and sector work were about 19 percent of the total. On an ongoing basis for all borrowers, the Bank is engaged in preparing or updating poverty assessments, private sector assessments, environmental assessments, national environmental action plans, and country-assistance strategies for discussion by the executive directors.

These and other economic and sector analyses are designed to deepen the Bank's understanding on development issues, improve the impact of its operations, and enhance policy-reform efforts. They are particularly important for the Bank's newest member countries, where there continues to be a need for considerable investment in analytical work prior to expanding technical assistance and lending programs. Furthermore, through the three new thematic vice presidencies, the Bank is evaluating best practices in human resources development, environmentally sustainable development, and financial and private sector development and is disseminating them to both staff and external audiences.

---

that people are both the means and ends of development; that sustained commitment to sound macroeconomic policy is vital; that institutional capacity is a major determinant of progress; and that economic growth should be broad-based and environmentally sustainable to reduce poverty effectively.

Of fundamental importance, through decades of experience in designing and implementing investment projects, the Bank has become a trusted adviser on development—sharing its global experience of what does and does not work—and helping its member countries apply those lessons.

In assisting its member countries to meet current and future challenges, the Bank is committed to build on and enhance its roles as a supplier of development finance/provider of advice, and, in special cases, as a resource for helping address strategic development issues that transcend national boundaries.

Given the scale and scope of the development agenda, the Bank is aware that it must avoid stretching itself too thin. It is focusing, therefore, on doing what it does best and is encouraging a division of labor with its partners. It is doing this by following six guiding principles:

Being selective in choosing which strategic actions to pursue; embracing partnerships with other participants—multilateral, bilateral, governmental, nongovernmental, the private sector; responding to borrower needs and facilitating their participation in the design and implementation of Bank-supported programs; looking beyond lending commitments and concentrating on results in the field; ensuring that scarce development resources are spent wisely and efficiently; and maintaining its high standing in the financial markets.

The Bank's record in fostering economic development over the past half century has been aided in no small part by its ability to respond quickly and flexibly to the ever-changing environment in which it works. One fundamental point, however, has endured and will not change:

The Bank remains the only development institution in the world with a long-term partnership with virtually every developing country, a wealth of cross-country experience, and a product mix that combines finance, policy advice, and in-depth research. This unique capacity and the fifty-year experience with development make the Bank a major global asset in the effort to reduce poverty and improve the human condition—an asset that is just as needed today as it was fifty years ago.

The Bank calls on its partners to work with it in meeting the challenges of the twenty-first century.

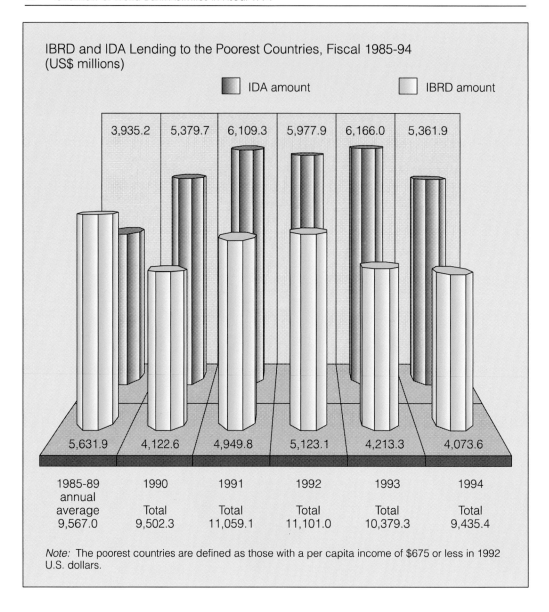

IBRD and IDA Lending to the Poorest Countries, Fiscal 1985-94 (US$ millions)

■ IDA amount   □ IBRD amount

| 3,935.2 | 5,379.7 | 6,109.3 | 5,977.9 | 6,166.0 | 5,361.9 |

| 5,631.9 | 4,122.6 | 4,949.8 | 5,123.1 | 4,213.3 | 4,073.6 |

| 1985-89 annual average 9,567.0 | 1990 Total 9,502.3 | 1991 Total 11,059.1 | 1992 Total 11,101.0 | 1993 Total 10,379.3 | 1994 Total 9,435.4 |

Note: The poorest countries are defined as those with a per capita income of $675 or less in 1992 U.S. dollars.

In various parts of the Bank, changes in business practices are being explored. Experimentation is under way to help define means of delivering Bank products of higher quality with reduced costs. Most of these efforts are currently directed to process simplification, although more ambitious ''redesigning'' or process-innovation pilot programs are also under review. In addition, more focused priority setting is fostering greater partnerships with the private sector and other multilateral and bilateral donors. A greater role for the private sector is being promoted explicitly as the Bank moves to support and catalyze private sector activities. Collaboration with the International

Finance Corporation at the operational level has been intensified, including review of programs in support of the telecommunications sector and private sector development activities.

Private flows represent an increasingly important source of finance for developing countries, with net flows reaching a ten-year high in 1993 of $113 billion, an increase of more than 150 percent of the level of 1990. Although levels of flows in the future are unpredictable, clearly today the private sector is playing a major role in those countries where reform programs are well established or the potential exists for large gains. Countries in East Asia,

Latin America, and Central and Eastern Europe have been the largest recipients of private capital, enabling the Bank to address more basic social and environmental issues that are not covered by other lenders.

In summary, the operational context was one of changing business products and processes in an environment containing many country uncertainties, making it all the more important that the Bank be well positioned to deliver work programs that are appropriate to current country circumstances and be able to respond quickly to changing conditions as they arise.

In fiscal 1994, lending by the Bank to all borrowers amounted to $20,836 million: $14,243.9 million by the IBRD and $6,592.1 million by IDA.

Specific investment loans and credits was, by far, the most favored lending instrument employed during the year. Commitments for this type of instrument totaled $14.1 billion (68 percent of the total).

Adjustment lending has been declining since 1989. In fiscal 1994, adjustment lending amounted to $2.4 billion, representing 12 percent of the total, compared with $6.2 billion in fiscal 1989, an amount that represented 29 percent of total lending. This decline is due to the relative maturity of the reform process in many countries and to constraints and uncertainties that impede progress in others.

Assistance to the poorest countries—those with a per capita gross national product of $675 or less (in terms of 1992 United States dollars) totaled $9,435.4 million: $4,073.6 million from the IBRD and $5,361.9 million from IDA (see accompanying figure). One loan of $30 million, on IDA-like terms, from resources provided by the Trust Fund for Gaza was approved for the Occupied Territories.

Net disbursements from the IBRD to member countries were a negative $731 million. IDA's net disbursements were $5,110 million.

During the year, the tenth replenishment of IDA's resources (IDA-10) became effective, and the Debt-reduction Facility for IDA-only Countries was extended until July 31, 1995. In July 1993, the executive board agreed to allocate $100 million from the IBRD's net income earned during fiscal 1993 to the facility.

The IBRD borrowed the equivalent of $8,908 million in the world's financial markets. Net income was $1,051 million.

During the fiscal year, the former Yugoslav Republic of Macedonia fulfilled the required formalities to succeed to the membership of the former Socialist Federal Republic of Yugoslavia, bringing the total membership of the IBRD to 177. At the end of the fiscal year, action was pending on membership in the IBRD for Bosnia-Herzegovina, Eritrea, and the Federal Republic of Yugoslavia.

The former Yugoslav Republic of Macedonia also fulfilled the required formalities to succeed to the membership of the former Socialist Federal Republic of Yugoslavia as a member of IDA. Armenia became a member of IDA on August 25, 1993, Georgia became a member on August 31, 1993, and Moldova became a member on June 14, 1994, bringing the total membership of IDA to 156. At the end of the fiscal year, action was pending on membership in IDA for Bosnia-Herzegovina, Eritrea, Turkemenistan, Ukraine, and the Federal Republic of Yugoslavia.

Section One
The Executive Board

The executive directors are responsible for the conduct of the general operations of the Bank, which includes deciding on Bank policy in the framework of the Articles of Agreement and approving all loan and credit proposals. The president of the Bank is the chairman of the executive directors. The president is also the chief of the operating staff of the Bank and conducts, under the direction of the executive directors, the ordinary business of the Bank.

The executive directors are also responsible for presenting to the board of governors an audit of accounts, an administrative budget, the *Annual Report* on the operations and policies of the World Bank, and any other matters that, in their judgment, require submission to the board of governors. Matters may be submitted to the board of governors at its annual meetings or at any time during the year.

The executive board exercises its authority, under the Articles of Agreement, in three general areas. First, through its annual oversight of the financial and operating programs, and administrative budgets, the board determines the allocation of financial and staff resources for the coming year. Second, through its review of evaluations of completed Bank projects and the Bank's experience in individual sectors and with particular policies, as well as through its participation in the annual review of portfolio performance, the board is actively involved in auditing development effectiveness, thereby ensuring that the Bank and member countries can benefit from the lessons of experience. Through its review of specific policy proposals (for example, the Bank's financial policies, operational policies, lending terms, sectoral priorities), the board determines the direction of Bank policies. Through its approval of lending operations and its review of the Bank's country-assistance strategies, the board oversees the Bank's lending program.

Exercise of executive board authority in these three areas results in continuous dialogue between the board and the management of the Bank. The quality of that dialogue was further enhanced throughout the fiscal year on those occasions of broad discussion on key issues such as emergency assistance to the Occupied Territories and the countries of the CFA Zone, poverty reduction, portfolio management, establishment of an independent inspection panel, and the Bank at age fifty as it looks towards its work and role in the Twenty-first Century.

Oversight of Financial and Operating Programs

In fulfilling its responsibilities to oversee the IBRD and IDA financial and operating programs, the executive directors authorized a program of borrowings and liability management in the context of a borrowing plan for fiscal 1994 of $12.0 billion equivalent. This program, which the board monitored on a quarterly basis through regular market briefings, was carried out according to agreed broad parameters. In accordance with the simplified budget review cycle endorsed by the board in fiscal 1992, the executive directors were involved in the formulation of the Bank's medium-term planning directions (fiscal 1995–97) and in setting the fiscal 1995 operating budget. In this framework, they approved indicative IBRD lending for the year at between $15.5 billion and $17.5 billion, with an indicative IDA lending program of 5.3 billion in special drawing rights (about $7.5 billion). The board also approved the allocation of fiscal 1993's net income and the plan for fiscal 1994.

Operations Evaluation and Project Implementation

In order to fulfill its responsibility to review project evaluations and proposals for future evaluation activities, the board continued to give particular attention to the Operations Evaluation Department (OED). The OED, under the management of the director general, is linked administratively to the Bank president but is directly responsible to the executive directors. The board approved OED's work program and staff budget for fiscal 1994 and reviewed the status of the department's work and its report on operations evaluation. The executive board also agreed that, following its discussion of OED's annual review of evaluation results, the review should be published and made available outside the Bank.

In addition, the executive directors endorsed steps for strengthening portfolio-performance management, including the internal processes used by the Bank to oversee portfolio performance. In turn, they held discussions with management and staff on the "Annual Report on Portfolio Performance," which covered the results of fiscal 1993. This report noted that the greater attention to portfolio-performance management, particularly the "cleaning up" of the operations portfolio, had helped in the short term to avoid a further deterioration in the Bank's quantitative measures of portfolio performance. The board will continue to monitor progress and review the next steps in this ongoing process.

Review of Policy Proposals

In the course of the fiscal year, the executive board reviewed policy proposals and made decisions that affected the operations in many areas of Bank activities, including finance, lending operations, sector policies, development economics, and administration.

Finance. In fiscal year 1994, IDA policies and operations continued to receive the attention of the directors. Early in the fiscal year, the board reviewed IDA's policies, operations, and finances during the ninth replenishment period (fiscal 1991–93).[1] With respect to IDA reflows, the board set the use of advance commitment authority from future reflows amounting to SDR800 million (about $1,126 million) annually for the period fiscal 1994–96 and further annual allocations in fiscal 1994 of SDR190 million (about $265 million) for the "fifth dimension" program. This program provides supplementary IDA resources to those IDA-only countries that have outstanding debt to the IBRD, are current in their debt-service payments to both the IBRD and IDA, and have in place IDA-supported adjustment programs. Such supplementary resources, therefore, take into account the debt impact arising from IBRD interest payments.

Following the launch of a pilot program of single-currency loans to respond to some borrowers' needs in fiscal 1993 for a choice of terms to help reduce the currency and interest rate risks in their IBRD loans, the board held an interim review to assess the target ratios for the composition of the currency pools.[2] The executive directors also approved a structured bond borrowings and liquidity arrangement that, by applying the existing debt buyback and borrowing authority, would permit the IBRD to exchange outstanding structured bonds denominated in any currency for floating rate notes or new structured bonds with different embedded derivatives. In order to facilitate such exchanges, and structured borrowings generally, the executive directors also authorized short-term borrowings to be conducted in any currency by amending the short-term United States dollar borrowing authorization and the exclusion of such exchanges from the volume limit approved by the board applicable to the IBRD's regular repurchases of debt securities.

In fiscal 1989 the board had approved a joint resolution establishing the Debt-reduction Facility for IDA-only Countries. Subsequent extensions were made to the facility, and in fiscal 1994 the board assessed progress under the facility and approved its extension until July 31, 1995.

Operations. In fiscal year 1994 the board interacted with Bank management and staff to set policies fundamental to the Bank's operational priorities and strategies. Establishing an inspection function at the Bank was one of the board's major concerns in the fiscal year. As a result of its intensive discussions of the issues and options in both formal and informal settings, the executive directors established the objectives, mandate, and operating procedures for an inspection panel. This panel would provide an independent review mechanism for affected parties of an action or omission by the Bank resulting from its failure to follow its operational policies and procedures.[3] The three members of the panel were named in April 1994. The members of the panel accepted their appointments, effective August 1, and the panel was expected to open for business in early September.

A similar process was followed by the executive directors in expanding access to Bank information through revisions to the Bank's policies on disclosure of information, which provided, among other things, access by the public to a number of previously restricted documents and the establishment of a Public Information Center at the Bank's headquarters.[4]

The board reaffirmed the importance of poverty reduction as an integrating theme in nearly all Bank assistance. The executive directors assessed the progress that had been made in supporting poverty reduction in the Bank's activities in fiscal year 1993 and reviewed the adequacy of the steps taken by the Bank to improve the way it addresses poverty issues.[5]

---

[1] For details, see page 170.
[2] For details, see page 167.
[3] For details, see page 74.
[4] For details, see page 75.
[5] For details, see page 36.

In fiscal 1993, the board approved a policy under which countries in transition could be granted a temporary waiver of the negative-pledge clause under certain conditions. The negative-pledge clause is a standard feature of all IBRD loan agreements. Its basic purpose is to protect the Bank by prohibiting, among other things, member-country borrowers from establishing liens on public assets that would create a preference for other creditors on foreign exchange loans over the debt owed to the Bank. For countries in transition to market economies, however, most of their important assets are still publicly owned, and, therefore, the negative-pledge clause makes it extremely difficult for public sector enterprises to enter into much-needed financial relationships with private creditors without either requesting a waiver of the negative-pledge clause or granting equal and ratable security to the IBRD.

As a result of the eligibility requirements established under the fiscal 1993 policy, however, no waivers of the negative pledge were granted. Therefore, substantial investments were pending in several countries because of the continued application of the negative-pledge clause. To address this problem, the board approved in fiscal 1994 a modification to the negative-pledge waiver that would allow the country-eligibility decision to be based on the Bank's judgment that the country was making progress in privatization, was moving toward a market economy and experiencing improvement in its macroeconomic situation, and that the waiver of the negative pledge would further contribute to the attainment of these goals. In the wake of this modification, the board approved country waivers for Russia, Uzbekistan, and Kazakhstan.

The board continued to monitor the Bank's role in providing technical assistance. They reviewed the first year of experience with the Institutional Development Fund,[6] recommended to the board of governors the establishment of the Joint Vienna Institute, and discussed the board's report on technical assistance activities in fiscal year 1993. In addition, the board provided guidance to staff on revising the Bank's policies as they relate to procurement activities, outreach, and supervision.

The importance placed by the board on environmental sustainability in the Bank's operations was reflected in the directors' discussions of the annual report on the Bank and the environment, in their major review of Bank projects involving involuntary resettlement in the period 1986–93,[7] and in their substantial involvement with the negotiations, replenishment, and restructuring of the Global Environment Facility.[8]

The board carefully followed developments in the international economic and political environment, often in forums such as seminars and briefings, which allowed for a more informal debate with management and staff. Major issues included the establishment of a donors' group for the Occupied Territories and a transfer from surplus to fund an emergency rehabilitation program for Gaza,[9] specific issues related to development in Africa, such as the adjustment experience,[10] better health,[11] and the Bank's role in the development of South Africa; Latin America, a decade after the debt crisis; the East Asian economic "miracle";[12] and the international conference on hunger.[13] The executive directors were also participants in a colloquium with outside experts on the recent economic developments in China.

The board reviewed the Bank's development in the context of the country-assistance strategies (CAS) of sixty IBRD and IDA borrowers. To ensure that these reviews provided appropriate coverage of the key issues affecting the Bank's strategy and that individual lending operations were consistent with the overall strategy, the board considered the role and nature of the CAS and set guidelines for their preparation. The executive directors also kept abreast of the activities and progress of the increasing number of consultative and aid groups chaired by the Bank at the request of the recipient countries (see Table 1-1).

In addition to approving all IBRD loans and IDA credits, the board monitored the progress of the Bank's overall lending program through regular briefings with senior management. In addition, to gauge the impact of the Bank's work "on the ground" and to discuss priority development issues with senior policymakers in member countries, selected groups of executive directors and alternate executive directors travelled to a number of borrowing countries. In fiscal 1994, there were four such missions: to Indonesia and Fiji; the Czech Republic, Hungary and Slovakia; Egypt, Lebanon, and Morocco; and Benin, Côte d'Ivoire, and Ghana.

Sector Policies and Development Economics

In regular board sessions, committees of the whole, seminars, and informal briefings, a

---

6   For details, see page 68.
7   For details, see page 44.
8   For details, see page 47.
9   For details, see page 116.
10 For details, see page 82.
11 For details, see page 85.
12 For details, see page 89.
13 For details, see page 49.

Table 1-1. **Aid Coordination Group Meetings Chaired by the World Bank in Fiscal 1994**
(consortia, consultative groups, and aid groups)

Date	Country	Location
1993		
July 1–2	India consortium	Paris
July 12–13	Tanzania consultative group	Paris
October 26	Moldova consultative group	Paris
October 27	Belarus consultative group	Paris
November 22–23	Kenya consultative group	Paris
December 6–8	Mozambique consultative group	Paris
December 8–10	Zambia consultative group	Paris
December 9–10	Bolivia consultative group	Washington, D.C.
December 12–14	Zimbabwe consultative group	Paris
December 16	West Bank and Gaza Strip consultative group	Paris
December 19–21	Malawi consultative group	Paris
1994		
January 14	Kazakhstan consultative group	Paris
January 25–26	Egypt consultative group	Paris
January 27–28	Caribbean sub-group for Guyana	Guyana
February 24–25	Pakistan consortium	Paris
March 7–8	Ethiopia consultative group	Paris
March 17–18	Sierra Leone consultative group	Paris
March 22–23	Zambia consultative group	Paris
April 19–20	Bangladesh aid group	Paris
April 21–22	Caribbean Group for Cooperation in Economic Development (meeting of donors)	Washington, D.C.
May 5–6	Mauritania consultative group	Paris
May 10–11	Peru consultative group	Paris
May 17	Jordan consultative group	Paris
June 2	Kyrgyz Republic consultative group	Paris
June 6–7	Romania consultative group	Paris
June 6–10	Caribbean Group for Cooperation in Economic Development	Washington, D.C.
June 9–10	Bulgaria consultative group	Paris
June 16	Nicaragua consultative group	Paris
June 27–28	FYR Macedonia consultative group	Paris
June 30–July 1	India Development Forum 1994	Paris

NOTE: The meeting of the Nepal aid group, originally scheduled for April 28–29, 1994 was postponed.

number of sector policies, their implementation, and "best practices" were reviewed. In the area of human resources development, the executive directors discussed the lessons of experience with higher education[14] and, on several occasions, debated the issues of gender and development, which culminated in a policy paper on enhancing women's participation in economic development.[15] In the area of trade, the board considered a preliminary assessment of the completed Uruguay Round of GATT talks, as well as the emergence of "new regionalism" and its consequences.[16]

Other important sector reviews included Bank Group issues with regard to telecommunications, transport policies, and financial and private sector development. The board also considered the outline and final draft of *World Development Report 1994*, which examined the interplay between infrastructure and development.[17]

Administration

The board also dealt at some length with the Bank Group's administrative policies and practices. In fiscal year 1994, it was involved in issues of staff benefits, including the quadrennial review of benefits and eligibility for expatriate benefits. They also reviewed their own

[14] For details, see page 34.
[15] For details, see page 37.
[16] For details, see page 31.
[17] For details, see page 43.

operational travel policies and made modifications that aligned these policies with those of the staff. As it does each year, the executive directors considered the issues affecting staff compensation and approved a salary adjustment. They made a recommendation to the governors on the remuneration of the Bank's president.

In a number of meetings, the board followed the implementation of the rehabilitation of the Bank's main complex building. They also reviewed the arrangements for the Bank's annual meetings.

As the fiftieth anniversary of the founding of the Bretton Woods institutions approached, the executive directors extensively involved themselves in the planning for commemorating the anniversary and in collaborating with Bank management and staff on the drafting of the Bank's current and future agenda.

Development Committee

As in previous years, the executive directors were actively involved with the Development Committee, assisting committee members in preparing for their meetings, considering the draft provisional agenda, and discussing the president's reports and background papers that were the basis for the ministers' discussions. In addition, several months prior to each Development Committee meeting, the executive directors convened as a committee of the whole to review the preliminary agenda and the outlines for the background papers in order to ensure that the main issues and concerns of committee members were well reflected in the documentation.

In preparing for the committee's semiannual meetings, the board discussed a range of papers and reports that touched on many issues of importance to the Bank's member countries, including the adjustment experience in, and implications for, low-income countries; social security reforms and social safety nets in reforming transition economies; reports on population in developing countries[18] and migration flows, and Bank activities in women in development.[19] The executive directors' Steering Committee reviewed the communiqués released by the Development Committee following its semiannual meetings and made suggestions to ensure that the board's work program was responsive to the directions set by the committee.

Board Committees

Joint Audit Committee. Established in 1970, the Joint Audit Committee (JAC) represents shareholders in overseeing the soundness of the Bank's financial practices and the ade-

quacy of the work of the operations evaluation and internal audit units. The committee provides a channel through which the internal and external auditors can communicate with the executive directors.

In pursuing its responsibilities during fiscal 1994 the committee nominated a firm of private, independent, internationally established accountants to conduct the annual audits of the Bank. The committee reviewed the scope of the independent accountants' examination and their annual audited financial statements. It also held in-depth discussions with the external auditors on the scope of their work on special audits, particularly those carried out on the main complex rehabilitation project. The committee reiterated the importance of maintaining a close working relationship with the external auditors. Several meetings were held in the course of the year to this effect. In addition, through regular meetings with the Bank's senior financial officers, the committee helped to provide assurance to the executive board that the financial affairs of the Bank were properly conducted. In this regard, the committee reviewed and endorsed recommendations pertaining to the fiscal 1994 implementation of the IBRD's policy for loan-loss provisioning. It was also briefed on the status of the current Bank loan portfolio. In addition, the committee reviewed the situation of countries in arrears and heard reports on recent developments in nonaccrual countries. The committee also reviewed and endorsed preliminary recommendations regarding the annual allocation of the IBRD's net income. Another area examined was the adequacy of the Bank's internal control systems. As part of its oversight function, the committee undertook its annual review of the work programs of the Operations Evaluation Department (OED) and Internal Auditing Department (IAD). Two subcommittees of alternate executive directors were appointed to assist the committee in carrying out its mandate with regard to the OED and the IAD. In addition, the committee reviewed numerous papers by the OED as part of an ongoing effort to identify problems or policy issues for consideration by the executive directors.

The committee consists of eight executive directors. Marc-Antoine Autheman has served as chairman of the committee since March 1994.

Committee on Cost Effectiveness and Budget Practices. The Committee on Cost Effectiveness and Budget Practices (CEBP) was established in 1986 to examine aspects of the

---

[18] For details, see page 37.
[19] For details, see page 36.

Bank's business processes, administrative policies, business standards, and budget practices that significantly affect the cost effectiveness of its operations.

Fiscal year 1994 was the first year that the committee's mandate was expanded to include the review of all the major papers in the Bank's budget cycle—the fiscal 1993 retrospective review, IBRD/IDA planning directions for fiscal years 1995–97, the fiscal 1994 mid year review, and the IBRD programs and fiscal 1995 budget. Following meetings to consider the relevant papers, the committee prepared reports to the board conveying its views on the planning directions paper and on the budget for fiscal 1995. The discussion of the latter was added to the committee's work program as a follow-up to the fiscal 1994 budget discussion during which the importance of the committee's active involvement in the planning and budgeting process was strongly encouraged.

The committee devoted a number of meetings to considering cost-saving issues that covered a wide range of Bank activities, from improvements in the efficiency with which work is carried out to systematic and incentive changes in processes and procedures. As a part of this exercise, the committee requested and was given a presentation on the work of the staff Committee on Business Innovation and Simplification (BIAS). Thereafter, the BIAS Committee sought the advice and views of the CEBP on the streamlining of some board documentation.

The committee consists of eight executive directors. Angel Torres has served as chairman of the committee since December 1992.

Committee on Personnel Policy Issues. The committee, which was established in 1980, is charged with keeping under continuing review and, where appropriate, advising the executive directors on, staff compensation and other significant personnel policy issues. It also maintains close liaison with the executive directors of the International Monetary Fund (IMF) on these issues, bearing in mind the general parallelism of the two institutions.

One of the main undertakings of the committee during the year was the continuing examination of the complex subject of expatriate benefits. The board subsequently took up the matter, first, on the basis of the committee's report and recommendation, and then, on the basis of a paper from management. The board finally decided not to change the current policy.

The committee reviewed the Bank's and the International Finance Corporation's (IFC) personnel policies and practices, results of the 1993 staff attitude survey, issues related to skills mix (that is, how the Bank identifies and recruits people with the skills needed to carry out its changing work program), and possible changes in the local currency option of the staff retirement plan. Two of the major actions undertaken by the committee were to review the results of the quadrennial benefits survey and of the 1994 review of staff compensation. Following the committee's endorsement, the board approved management's recommendations with respect to both items. The role of the Bank's field offices was also a focus of the committee's scrutiny.

The committee consists of eight executive directors. Jean-Pierre Le Bouder has served as chairman of the committee since January 1993.

Committee on Directors' Administrative Matters. The Committee on Directors' Administrative Matters (CODAM) was established in 1968 to consider administrative matters relating to executive directors and their alternates, advisers, and staff. The committee recommends to the executive board the formulation and implementation of new administrative policies and changes in existing policies.

Major issues taken up by the committee in the fiscal year included remuneration of advisers and executive directors' assistants; executive directors' travel to member countries outside of their constituencies (group travel); travel policy for executive directors; and consideration of executive directors' administrative expenses.

The committee coordinates many of its recommendations with a similar committee established by the executive board of the IMF.

The committee consists of six executive directors. John Cosgrove has served as chairman of the committee since January 1993.

The Ad Hoc Committee on Review of Board Committees. The Ad Hoc Committee on Review of Board Committees was established in December 1993 to review the function, structure, and terms of reference of standing committees of executive directors, including criteria for appointments to committees. It completed its work in April 1994. The committee's recommendations will be implemented following the 1994 regular election of executive directors.

The conclusions and recommendations in the committee's report, which was approved by the executive directors in May 1994, aim to improve and strengthen, rather than fundamentally change, existing arrangements for executive directors' committees. The main conclusions and recommendations are summarized below.

Functions and structure of committees. It was agreed that the overall objective of committees should be to strengthen the efficiency and effectiveness of the board in discharging its responsibilities. To meet this overall objective, committees need to carry out work programs that facilitate the process of consensus building and decisionmaking in the board and assist the board in discharging its oversight responsibilities. Generally, committees need to focus on a limited number of clearly defined priority issues.

In view of the overall workload of committees and the steadily growing importance and need for review of operations evaluation and development-effectiveness issues in the context of the Bank Group's operational activities, it was further agreed that (a) the mandate of the Joint Audit Committee should focus on external and internal audit and financial policy issues and (b) a new committee of eight executive directors should be established to review operations evaluation and development-effectiveness issues.

It was agreed that the mandates of all committees should apply uniformly to the IFC.

Interaction between committees, Bank management, and the board. New procedures were approved to strengthen interaction between committees, management, and the board. These procedures cover reporting requirements of committees and management to the board and are designed to facilitate board discussion of formal management proposals (including, in some cases, management option papers) submitted to committees for prior review.

A number of recommendations aimed at improving efficiency in the conduct of committee business were also approved, including, for example, recommendations for building consensus among executive directors on controversial issues, for identifying priority issues for board consideration, and for board approval of committee recommendations on an absence-of-objection basis.

Composition and guidelines for appointment to committees. It was further agreed that appointments to committees should be governed by general principles that can be applied flexibly, the two most important of which are consultation among executive directors and balanced representation from the board. Specifically, appointments to committees should reflect economic and geographic diversity of the Bank's member countries with a view to ensuring balanced representation between borrowing and nonborrowing member countries.

The committee consisted of four executive directors. Jorunn Maehlum served as chairman of the committee.

Executive Directors' Steering Committee. The Executive Directors' Steering Committee, an informal advisory body of executive directors composed of the dean and the co-dean of the board, as well as the chairpersons of the other standing board committees, meets monthly to consult on, and review with the Bank's vice president and secretary, the executive directors' work program. The committee also provides a consultative framework for various board issues. In addition, the committee reviews the Development Committee's communiqués to ensure that the implications for the executive directors' work program are fully considered. The steering committee has also taken a leadership role in ensuring the implementation of the new board policies and procedures, including, among others, the determination of the scheduling of country-assistance strategies and periodic reviews of sector policies. The committee consists of six executive directors. The dean of the board, Ibrahim Al-Assaf, has served as chairman since September 1993.

The meetings of committees of the executive board are open to participation by all executive directors.

Section Two
The Economic Scene: A Global Perspective

Economic activity in the industrialized countries slowed further in 1993, to 1.2 percent, as a result of sluggish growth in Japan and recession in continental Europe (see Table 2-1). Recovery in the United States was well under way by the fourth quarter of 1993, when output expanded by 7 percent on an annual basis. Canada and the United Kingdom experienced a modest recovery in 1993. The slow pace of overall growth in 1993 was associated with rising unemployment, which reached 8.2 percent in the industrial countries as a group, topping out at 10 percent of the labor force in several European countries.

Reflecting the significant gap between actual and potential output in most industrial countries, inflation continued to ease, as growth in the GDP deflator fell to 3.3 percent, down from 4 percent in 1992.[1]

The developing countries—excluding the countries in transition in Central and Eastern Europe and the former Soviet Union (FSU)— grew by an estimated 4.5 percent in 1993, up from 3.6 percent in 1992, thereby exceeding industrial-country growth by more than three percentage points for the third straight year (see Table 2-2). Underlying these aggregates, however, were widely differing trends between the countries in transition and the traditional universe of developing countries. Output in Central and Eastern European countries and in the republics of the FSU fell by an estimated 7.4 percent in 1993. Although the rate of decline slowed from 12.7 percent in 1992, it was the fourth straight year of diminishing output.

The continued robust growth in the traditional developing countries in the face of recession in the industrialized countries can be attributed to several factors. These include the effects of increasingly widespread and sustained policy reforms in many countries; low international interest rates (that partly offset the depressing effect on commodity exporters of falling export prices); and, associated with these two factors, the enormous continued surge in private capital flows to developing countries.

Growth performance among the main developing country regions continued to diverge widely. Growth in East Asia and the Pacific, of 9.2 percent, continued to outpace that in every other developing region by at least five percentage points. China remained the fastest growing economy in the region—and the world. Growth has averaged 13 percent in the past two years, as the government continued to implement market-based reforms and as transnational corporations continued to commit record amounts of investment. In July 1993, the Chinese authorities undertook measures to slow the torrid pace of growth and ease rising inflationary pressures. Malaysia and Thailand, two other prime recipients of foreign direct investment, once again displayed outstanding growth performance. These countries began to show strains resulting from shortages of skilled labor and adequate infrastructure, as well as from the need to address longer-term issues, such as upgrading production to higher value-added sectors as competition in the labor-intensive sectors increases from countries such as China, India, and Indonesia.

Latin American and the Caribbean once again experienced gains in output as reforms in many countries continued to take root and show results. Growth for the region as a whole, supported by large inflows of foreign private capital flows, rose to 3.5 percent, up from 2.8 percent in 1992. Individual country performance was mixed, however. Although Brazil's economy grew by an estimated 4.9 percent (up from a decline of close to 1 percent in the previous year), the inflation rate increased dramatically. Political uncertainty, lower oil prices, and policy weaknesses moved Venezuela into recession during the year. Growth, which slowed in Mexico to about 2 percent in 1992 after several years of more robust gains, was stagnant in 1993, as tighter credit conditions aimed at curbing a bulging external deficit slowed activity. The signing of the North American Free Trade Agreement (NAFTA),

---

[1] Although inflationary pressures remained in check, the strength of the recovery in the United States moved the Federal Reserve Board to increase short-term dollar interest rates in the first quarter of 1994. European and Japanese rates, however, remain low.

Table 2-1. **G-7 Countries: Output, Inflation, Investment, and Unemployment, 1983–93**
(average annual percentage change; unemployment rates in percent)

G-7 country	1983–93	1992	1993[a]	1983–93	1992	1993[a]
	Real GDP			GDP deflator		
Canada	2.7	0.7	2.4	3.3	1.1	1.8
France	2.1	1.4	−1.0	4.2	2.3	1.5
Germany[b]	2.6	1.2	−1.9	2.9	4.4	3.8
Italy	2.2	0.9	−0.7	7.7	4.7	3.8
Japan	3.7	1.2	1.1	1.5	1.8	1.4
United Kingdom	2.2	−0.5	1.9	5.3	4.3	2.5
United States	2.8	2.6	3.0	3.7	2.9	2.8
G-7 average	2.8	1.7	1.3	3.7	3.0	2.6
Total OECD	2.8	1.7	1.2	5.1	4.0	3.3
	Gross fixed investment			Unemployment rate		
Canada	3.3	−2.1	0.5	9.8	11.3	11.2
France	1.1	−3.1	−6.5	9.9	10.4	11.7
Germany[b]	2.9	0.3	−5.1	7.3	5.9	7.4
Italy	1.4	−1.5	−9.1	11.0	11.5	10.4
Japan	5.3	−4.3	−7.4	2.5	2.2	2.5
United Kingdom	3.2	−3.3	−2.9	9.2	9.8	10.3
United States	3.4	6.2	10.9	6.8	7.4	6.8
G-7 average	3.3	1.3	1.6	6.8	7.1	7.1
Total OECD	3.6	1.9	1.9	7.5	7.8	8.2

a. Preliminary.

b. German data refer to western Länder only.

SOURCE: Organisation for Economic Co-operation and Development (OECD), International Monetary Fund (IMF).

however, bolstered the positive longer-term outlook for the economy. Argentina, Chile, and Colombia experienced growth of more than 5 percent.

Sub-Saharan Africa (excluding South Africa) posted a modest increase in GDP of 1.4 percent; the region was helped by recovery from the most severe drought to hit Eastern and Southern Africa in this century, as well as by gradually improving performance in countries that have persisted with adjustment and reform policies. Although overall growth remained low, some hopeful signs also emerged: Civil war came to an end in Ethiopia and Mozambique, beverage prices moved higher during the year, and expectations for at least a stabilization in nonoil commodity prices became somewhat firmer. The 50 percent devaluation of the CFA franc and the subsequent prompt support from multilateral lenders and the French government substantially improved prospects for the revitalization of the adjustment process in the CFA Zone countries. Finally, the South African economy began its recovery from prolonged recession with the passing of drought, rising gold prices, and the ending of international sanctions, thereby providing a more favorable backdrop for the country's transition to multiracial democracy. That process has brought to the fore both hopes for substantial future economic progress, as well as recogni-

tion of the deep social and structural challenges facing a new administration.

Growth in South Asia slowed to 3.8 percent, in part the result of devastating floods in Pakistan towards the end of 1992 and weak industrial growth in India. Nevertheless, countries in the region showed improvements in their external account performance, with increased exports and private capital inflows. The new government in Pakistan confirmed its adherence to the reform policies of the previous transitional administration. India continued its moderately paced but steady economic reform policies. Although inflows of foreign capital to that country were small by comparison with leading East Asian and Latin American economies, they were nonetheless far greater than at any time in the past.

A fall in world oil prices of more than 10 percent contributed to a marked decline in growth, to an estimated 1.9 percent, in the Middle East and North Africa. Output fell almost 2 percent in Algeria as the country's political crisis deepened. Growth was almost negligible in Egypt, where the process of adjusting fiscal imbalances continued.

As a group, the transitional economies in Central and Eastern Europe and the FSU suffered a further decline in output of more than 7 percent. The republics of the FSU contributed the most to this decline, as their output fell 13

Table 2-2. **Low- and Middle-income Economies: Growth of GDP and GDP per Capita, 1982–93**
(average annual percentage change unless otherwise noted)

Region or income group	GDP					GDP per capita				
	1982–90	1991–93	1991	1992	1993[a]	1982–90	1991–93	1991	1992	1993[a]
Low- and middle-income economies	3.4	0.7	0.2	0.3	2.1	1.4	−1.1	−1.6	−1.5	0.2
By regional group										
Sub-Saharan Africa[b]	2.4	1.4	1.5	1.2	1.4	−0.7	−1.3	−1.5	−1.8	−1.7
East Asia and Pacific[c]	8.1	8.5	7.0	8.7	9.2	6.4	6.9	5.5	7.2	7.5
South Asia[d]	5.7	4.0	2.0	4.6	3.8	3.4	1.5	−0.2	2.5	1.8
Middle East and North Africa[e]	0.0	2.7	3.1	4.0	1.9	−3.1	−0.3	−0.2	1.1	−1.1
Europe and Central Asia[f]	1.9	−10.0	−9.3	−12.7	−7.4	1.1	−10.6	−9.8	−13.2	−8.0
Latin America and the Caribbean[g]	2.3	3.1	3.4	2.8	3.5	0.3	1.2	1.6	1.0	1.6
By income group										
Low- and middle-income economies, excluding transition economies in Europe and Central Asia	3.8	4.5	4.1	3.6	4.5	1.7	2.5	2.0	1.7	2.9

a. Estimated.

b. Excludes South Africa.

c. American Samoa, Cambodia, China, Fiji, Guam, Indonesia, Kiribati, Republic of Korea, Lao People's Democratic Republic, Macao, Malaysia, Mongolia, Myanmar, New Caladonia and Pacific Islands' Trust Territory, Papua New Guinea, the Philippines, Solomon Islands, Thailand, Tonga, Vanuatu, Viet Nam, and Western Samoa.

d. Afghanistan, Bangladesh, Bhutan, India, Maldives, Nepal, Pakistan, and Sri Lanka.

e. Algeria, Bahrain, Egypt, Islamic Republic of Iran, Iraq, Jordan, Lebanon, Libya, Morocco, Oman, Saudi Arabia, Syrian Arab Republic, Tunisia, and Yemen.

f. Albania, Bulgaria, Czechoslovakia (through 1992; the Czech Republic and the Slovak Republic thereafter), Gibraltar, Greece, Hungary, Isle of Man, Malta, Poland, Portugal, Romania, Turkey, republics of the former Soviet Union, and republics of the former Yugoslavia.

g. All American and Caribbean economies south of the United States, except Cuba.

SOURCE: World Bank.

percent on top of a 20 percent drop in 1992. Political uncertainty and macroeconomic instability in Russia continued throughout the year. Nonetheless, the government maintained progress on the structural reform agenda, albeit at a halting pace. The privatization program maintained momentum; by the end of 1993, two thirds of all small service enterprises had been privatized. Output in Poland grew for a second year in a row, while economic contraction in Hungary and the Czech Republic appeared to be drawing to a close. There is evidence, especially in those three countries, that "new" largely private sector activity (concentrated in services, construction, and the trades) is beginning to account for a significant share of output (approaching 50 percent in some cases) and is providing support for growth.

Recent Trends in External Debt and Debt Strategies

The total external debt of all developing countries, including short-term debt, was esti-

mated at $1,700 billion at the end of 1993, an increase of 6.5 percent in nominal terms, or about $108 billion, over the previous year. Of this amount, long-term debt outstanding stood at $1,411 billion, an increase of 7.9 percent ($103 billion) (see Table 2-3). The increase in long-term debt is accounted for principally by net inflows of around $72 billion and a currency-valuation factor of over $20 billion resulting from the fall of the United States dollar against the yen in 1993. In addition, capitalization of interest through debt reschedulings added $15 billion to long-term debt (though much of this was offset by reduction in short-term debt, in which interest arrears are classified for debt-accounting purposes), while voluntary debt reductions (buybacks, debt exchanges, equity swaps, and so forth) were expected to have reduced debt by $9 billion.

Private creditors provided 61 percent, or $44 billion, of the overall $72 billion net flow of long-term debt to the developing countries, an increase of $2 billion from 1992. For the second

Table 2-3. **Low- and Middle-income Economies: Long-term Debt and Debt Service, Selected Years, 1988–93**
(billions of US dollars; percentages)

Item	All low- and middle-income economies			Severely indebted middle-income economies			Sub-Saharan Africa		
	1988	1992	1993[a]	1988	1992	1993[a]	1988	1992	1993[a]
Debt outstanding	1,128.1	1,308.2	1,410.9	440.0	456.9	475.2	135.0	155.5	156.4
Official (%)	46.0	50.9	51.0	38.4	47.0	46.4	60.6	73.0	74.0
Private (%)	54.0	49.1	49.0	61.6	53.0	53.6	39.4	27.0	26.0
Debt as % of GNP	29.1	29.6	31.7	38.8	36.4	37.2	57.1	55.8	53.7
Debt service	154.2	155.3	161.1	51.8	51.0	53.6	11.2	12.0	9.8
Interest payments	66.1	57.1	61.5	28.4	18.2	20.2	5.1	5.6	4.8
Official (%)	27.6	39.3	40.8	18.9	42.4	42.4	42.7	32.9	36.6
Private (%)	72.4	60.7	59.2	81.1	57.6	57.6	57.3	67.1	63.4
Principal payments	88.0	98.2	99.6	23.4	32.8	33.4	6.1	6.4	5.0
Official (%)	28.4	30.3	33.1	31.2	31.2	36.4	31.5	30.3	42.2
Private (%)	71.6	69.7	66.9	68.8	68.8	63.6	68.5	69.7	57.8
Debt-service ratio (%)[b]	19.9	16.3	16.3	31.5	27.1	26.7	16.4	14.5	11.7
Average interest rate on new commitments (%)[c]	6.6	6.1	n.a.	7.5	6.7	n.a.	4.1	2.9	n.a.
Official (%)	5.0	5.4	n.a.	6.3	6.9	n.a.	3.4	2.8	n.a.
Private (%)	8.0	6.8	n.a.	8.2	6.6	n.a.	7.1	4.9	n.a.
Disbursements	121.5	160.0	171.2	34.1	37.9	44.9	10.5	8.5	7.7
Official (%)	39.1	31.2	35.6	38.1	31.1	38.0	61.9	77.2	81.9
Private (%)	60.9	68.8	64.4	61.9	68.9	62.0	38.1	22.8	18.1
Net resource flows on long-term lending[d]	33.5	61.8	71.1	10.7	5.1	11.6	4.4	2.1	2.8
Net transfers on long-term lending[e]	−32.6	4.7	10.2	−17.7	−13.1	−8.6	−0.7	−3.5	−2.1

NOTE: Stock, flow, and economic data cover 148 countries of which 129 report to the World Bank Debtor Reporting System.
n.a. Not available.
a. Preliminary.
b. Debt service as a percentage of exports of goods and services.
c. Covers the countries reporting to the World Bank Debtor Reporting System.
d. Disbursements minus (actual) principal repayments.
e. Net resource flows minus (actual) interest payments.
SOURCE: World Bank.

year in succession, private net flows exceeded official ones, an occurrence otherwise not experienced since the onset of the debt crisis of the early 1980s. East Asian and Latin American countries continued to borrow actively in financial markets, as falling short-term and long-term international interest rates and an intense (if temporary) vogue for emerging market debt facilitated a substantial increase in bond issuance. Ten countries—Argentina, Brazil, Mexico, and Venezuela in Latin America; China, Korea, and Thailand in East Asia; and the Czech Republic, Hungary, and Turkey in Europe—are estimated to have raised over $34 billion in public and private bond placements.

Official net flows increased sharply by $8 billion, to $28 billion. Net flows from multilateral sources, including the World Bank, are estimated to have risen to around $18 billion, up from $12 billion in 1992 (see Table 2-4). Bilateral lending was estimated to have risen by 22 percent, to almost $10 billion. The share of concessionality in official debt is also estimated to have risen, reflecting the restructuring of nonconcessional debt on concessional terms in Egypt, Poland, and those countries benefiting

Table 2-4. **Long-term Financial Flows to Developing Countries, 1986–93**
(billions of US dollars)

Item	1986	1987	1988	1989	1990	1991	1992	1993[a]
Long-term aggregate net resource flows	64.0	67.8	74.1	79.4	102.2	121.2	156.6	176.6
Official development finance	44.0	43.9	40.8	41.1	59.2	63.0	54.6	63.4
Official grants	16.0	16.7	18.3	19.0	28.5	32.9	34.5	35.5
Net official loans	28.0	27.2	22.5	22.1	30.7	30.1	20.1	27.9
Bilateral	12.8	12.2	11.4	10.4	15.9	15.2	7.9	9.6
Multilateral	15.2	15.0	11.1	11.7	14.8	14.9	12.2	18.3
Net private loans	9.2	8.6	11.0	10.1	12.9	13.8	41.7	43.7
Commercial banks	1.8	1.1	7.9	3.9	−2.5	5.4	18.5	n.a.
Bonds	0.8	1.0	2.9	4.2	2.3	7.4	6.3	n.a.
Others	6.7	6.5	0.2	2.0	13.1	1.0	16.8	n.a.
Foreign direct investment	10.1	14.5	21.2	24.7	26.3	36.9	47.3	56.3
Portfolio equity investment[b]	0.6	0.8	1.1	3.5	3.8	7.6	13.1	13.2
Long-term aggregate net transfers[c]	−5.0	−3.0	−5.4	2.2	25.6	44.5	79.6	91.5
Interest on long-term debt	57.6	58.3	66.1	60.2	59.1	59.6	57.1	61.5
Profit remittances on FDI	11.4	12.4	13.4	17.0	17.6	17.0	19.9	23.6

n.a. Not available.

a. Preliminary.

b. World Bank staff estimates available since 1990 only.

c. Long-term aggregate net resource flows minus interest payments and reinvested and remitted profits.

SOURCE: World Bank.

from enhanced Toronto terms, as well as new concessional flows to sub-Saharan Africa, the Central Asian republics, and Viet Nam.

Voluntary debt-reduction operations, including official debt forgiveness by key Arab creditors to countries in the Middle East, are estimated to have reduced debt by about $9 billion in 1993, bringing the total of such reductions since 1988 to almost $100 billion. The "Brady" type of debt and debt-service reduction operation carried out by Argentina in April 1993 reduced the face value of its debt by close to $3.3 billion. Jordan came to an agreement with its commercial creditors in December 1993 to restructure an estimated $900 million of principal and arrears. The Dominican Republic, after reaching agreement in principle with bank creditors in May 1993 to restructure $1.1 billion of principal and arrears, continued to make progress towards a final agreement, while Bulgaria reached an agreement in principle with its creditor banks on restructuring $9.3 billion of commercial bank debt. Brazil also continued discussions on a restructuring of about $50 billion of obligations.[2]

Use of the other main venue for commercial debt reduction, the Debt- reduction Facility for IDA-only Countries, also increased. This facility, created in 1989, provides grants to eligible IDA members to reduce their commercial debt. Significant bilateral official cofinancing support has also been made available for facility-supported operations. By the end of 1993, five operations had been completed: Niger and

Mozambique in 1991, Guyana in 1992, and Uganda and Bolivia in 1993. These operations extinguished $623 million of principal in commercial debt at an average price of 14 cents on the dollar. Similar buyback operations were in preparation for another ten countries: Albania, Ethiopia, Guinea, Mali, Mauritania, Nicaragua, São Tomé and Principe, Sierra Leone, Tanzania, and Zambia.

Restructuring of official bilateral debt under Paris Club auspices also contributed to debt reduction. During 1993, agreement was reached with eleven countries to reschedule or restructure $1.2 billion in debts. Six of the agreements—with Benin, Burkina Faso, Guyana, Mauritania, Mozambique, and Viet Nam—were reached under enhanced Toronto terms. In November 1993 the French government canceled F800 million of the debt of four CFA countries, and, in the wake of the devaluation of the CFA franc in January 1994, France proposed canceling another F25 billion owed by the CFA Zone countries affected by the exchange-rate adjustments. The focus of the debt strategy, especially for the severely indebted low-income countries, continues to shift from repeated reschedulings to the maintenance of a positive cash flow as a means of accelerating the resumption of these countries' external viability.

---

[2] In April 1994, Brazil implemented the deal with its commercial creditors and exchanged old debt for new long-term bonds. The debt collateralized by the zero-coupon bonds amounts to $17.8 billion.

Accumulated interest arrears were reduced by about $10 billion in 1993, the second year in succession that arrears fell rather than increased. A large portion of this reduction came from clearance of arrears in Latin America, especially Peru, and the former Soviet Union. Rescheduled interest payments in 1993 were estimated at $15 billion, up slightly from the previous year's $14.2 billion.

Despite the increase in developing country debt stocks, key debt ratios did not worsen as economic and trade conditions improved. Although the ratio of developing countries' long-term debt to GNP rose to 31.7 percent from 29.6 percent in 1992, the increase partly reflected large currency devaluations that reduced the dollar value of GNP in some Middle Eastern, European, and Central Asian countries. Significant increases in the outstanding debt of East Asian and South Asian countries, as well as of the FSU, also contributed to the rise. The long-term debt service-to-exports ratio remained constant at 16.3 percent. This ratio has hovered around the 16 percent mark for four years in a row.

Capital Flows on the Increase

Aggregate long-term net resource flows to developing countries—defined as net flows of long-term debt, grants (excluding technical assistance), and equity investment (foreign direct and portfolio-equity investment)—are estimated to have increased by $20 billion to $177 billion in 1993 (see Table 2-4). Net flows of long-term debt of $72 billion were the largest single component of aggregate resource flows. Of these debt flows, $28 billion was from official creditors. Official creditors also provided grants of $36 billion, up $1 billion from 1992; official finance, therefore, amounted to $63 billion, up $9 billion from the previous year.

Net foreign direct investment (FDI) rose 19 percent, or $9 billion, to $56 billion. Equity-portfolio investment, which reached $13 billion in 1992, stayed at that level. In addition to FDI and portfolio investment, private flows in the form of long-term debt amounted to $44 billion. Private sources, therefore, are estimated to have been responsible for 64 percent of overall net resource flows to the developing countries, an increase of more than 150 percent since 1990. This amount, in constant dollars, matches the level attained in the early 1980s before the onset of the debt crisis.

Aggregate long-term net transfers to developing countries—defined as net resource flows less interest payments on long-term debt and profits on FDI—increased by $12 billion to $92 billion, as increased net flows more than offset the increase in interest and profits. Net trans-fers to developing countries were positive for the fifth consecutive year. They were also substantial, amounting to 2.1 percent of developing country GDP, an increase from 1.8 percent in 1992.

Because the flow of FDI to industrial countries declined, developing countries are estimated to have increased their share of global FDI from 31 percent in 1992 to around 35 percent. An improved economic climate has made foreign investment attractive in many countries; privatization of state-owned enterprises has also boosted inflows, especially in Latin America and Eastern Europe. China, by far, was the largest recipient of FDI, with $15 billion flowing into the country in 1993, up $4 billion over the 1992 total.[3] In general, FDI continues to be concentrated in a limited number of developing countries: Five countries—in order of FDI amounts, China, Mexico, Argentina, Malaysia, and Thailand—received 59 percent of FDI flows. Regionally, FDI favored East Asia ($25 billion), Latin America ($18 billion), and Europe and Central Asia ($9 billion). Flows to most low-income countries were stagnant, however, reflecting the slow growth of official flows and the lack of access of most of these countries to private capital markets. In some instances, low-income countries have suffered from a lack of enthusiasm by the private sector—for example, commercial banks in sub-Saharan Africa.

Portfolio-equity flows appear to have been similarly concentrated, with three quarters of the $13 billion total going to East Asia and Latin America. Developing country securities are currently underrepresented in the portfolios of industrial country investors, given their big diversification benefits and higher risk-adjusted returns. If countries persist with their policy reforms, a gradual rebalancing of these growing portfolios is likely to increase private flows to developing countries significantly. At the same time, such flows are likely to be more volatile than FDI because they are more sensitive to global interest-rate movements and to positive or negative "bandwagon" effects.[4]

Primary Commodity Developments

Primary commodity market trends in 1993 were mixed, with nonoil commodity prices rising modestly and oil prices falling sharply once again. The dollar index of nonoil commodity-

---

[3] These figures may be inflated by Chinese capital that is rerouted through Hong Kong back into China and then recorded as FDI.

[4] The turbulence early in 1994 in the emerging country bond markets is a testament to the volatility of such flows.

Table 2-5. **Commodity Prices, 1986–93**
(average annual percentage change)

Commodity price	1986–91	1991	1992	1993
In current-dollar terms				
Food and beverages	−4.4	−2.1	−6.6	0.7
Nonfood agriculture	4.6	−0.8	−4.9	−5.4
Metals and minerals	6.1	−8.1	−1.4	−14.6
Total nonoil	−0.9	−3.0	−4.1	1.4
Petroleum	7.7	−18.4	−0.5	−11.6
In real terms[a]				
Total nonoil	−5.5	−5.1	−8.2	1.0
Petroleum	2.7	−20.2	−4.6	−12.1
In special drawing rights (SDRs)				
Total nonoil	−3.8	−3.8	−6.9	2.3
Petroleum	4.3	−19.1	−3.3	−10.8

NOTE: Weights in the commodity price indexes are commodity exports of all developing countries.
a. Deflated by unit-value index of manufactures exports from the G-5 countries (France, Germany, Japan, the United Kingdom, and the United States) to the developing countries.
SOURCE: World Bank.

prices was 1.4 percent higher than in 1992, supported by gradually reviving growth in the industrialized countries, continued growth in the developing countries, and lower international interest rates (see Table 2-5). In terms of constant 1990 dollars (using the unit-value index of exports of manufactured goods from the five largest industrialized countries to the developing countries as the deflator) nonoil prices were up 1 percent. By either measure, the slight increase in 1993 was the first in five years and followed a 27 percent fall (in constant dollar terms) during the period 1988–92. Indeed, constant dollar prices in 1993 were almost 50 percent below their postwar average. If the rise in the nonoil commodity price index was mild, it was at least fairly steady over the course of the year; by the fourth quarter, prices were 3.7 percent above the cyclical low reached in the same period of 1992. On a fourth quarter-to-fourth quarter basis, the largest contributions to the pick-up in prices were made by beverages, grains, and timber.

Metals and minerals suffered the steepest price decline of any commodity group in 1993, averaging 14.6 percent lower than in 1992. In constant dollar terms, the price index of this group fell to its lowest level in the whole postwar period. Prices for all the main industrial metals (copper, tin, nickel, aluminum, lead, zinc, iron ore) fell sharply; only precious metals prices moved higher. Overall world demand for industrial metals was broadly flat or lower than in the previous year, as increased demand in the United States and in the developing countries was offset by weakness in Europe, Japan, and the transitional economies of Central and Eastern Europe and the FSU. Surplus

output capacity and higher world production added to the downward pressure on prices in aluminum and iron ore. Increased exports from Russia affected the aluminum and nickel markets. Late in the year, lead, zinc, and nickel prices rallied to varying degrees, reflecting the more substantial production cutbacks that have taken place in these industries.

Crude-oil prices fell by $2 a barrel, or 11.6 percent, to $15.30. Much of the decline occurred in the second half of the year. The pressure on oil prices derived from several sources. A weak increase in demand by the industrialized countries was more than offset by higher output from the North Sea and Canada. Although production fell steeply in the FSU and Eastern Europe, consumption fell a little more steeply yet, releasing more oil to the market. Finally, although demand for oil increased in the developing countries (by about 1 million barrels a day), output in these countries increased even more (by about 1.2 million barrels a day). OPEC countries were responsible for two thirds of the production increase.

World Trade Growth Slows

The rate of growth in the volume of world merchandise exports slowed to an estimated 2.6 percent in 1993 (see Table 2-6). The two most important reasons for the slowdown were the recession in Europe (which curbed intra-Europe trade, the largest part of the trade of individual European countries,[5] as well as imports from the rest of the world) and sluggish

---

[5] Because of the merger in trade-accounting procedures in the European Union, it is generally thought that intra-European trade was underreported.

Table 2-6. **Selected Trade-performance Indicators, 1970–93**
(average annual percentage change)

Country group and indicator	1970–80	1980–90	1991	1992	1993[a]
Low and middle-income countries[b]					
Import volume	3.5	0.8	11.3	8.6	6.5
Export volume	2.7	3.6	11.1	5.6	3.8
Terms of trade	0.7	−3.3	−5.5	−0.8	−1.7
Sub-Saharan Africa[c]					
Import volume	−0.5	−4.9	8.8	−1.0	4.0
Export volume	−0.7	2.1	2.3	1.9	2.4
Terms of trade	−0.1	−5.8	−8.7	−4.2	−9.0
Asia					
Import volume	7.3	7.0	16.4	9.4	11.2
Export volume	8.5	9.6	16.2	12.5	7.4
Terms of trade	−0.8	−1.7	−0.2	−0.3	1.7
Europe and Central Asia					
Import volume	2.4	3.5	2.4	−1.0	0.8
Export volume	4.0	3.0	13.3	−1.4	−4.0
Terms of trade	−0.9	1.2	−9.8	−0.5	−0.3
Middle East and North Africa					
Import volume	5.7	−4.5	3.6	10.2	1.0
Export volume	−2.4	−1.6	9.3	−0.4	1.2
Terms of trade	4.6	−7.2	−12.9	−0.2	−7.2
Latin America and the Caribbean					
Import volume	0.1	−2.5	21.0	19.0	7.6
Export volume	2.5	2.7	5.0	6.3	5.6
Terms of trade	−0.3	−2.8	−3.7	−3.3	−3.7
Memorandum item					
World export volume	4.2	4.6	6.1	3.5	2.6

NOTE: Trade volumes measured in constant 1987 prices and exchange rates. Terms of trade are calculated as the ratio of export price to import price.
a. Estimated.
b. Including republics of the former Soviet Union.
c. Excluding South Africa.
SOURCE: World Bank.

growth in Japan. The recovery in the United States, which caused demand for imports to rise, was not sufficient to offset the dampening effect on world trade of the adverse conditions in Europe and Japan. Estimates by the GATT suggest that trade in commercial services may have increased by only 3 percent in nominal terms to reach $1,030 billion, as against a 12 percent rise in 1992.

Reflecting these conditions, the growth of merchandise export volumes from the low-income and middle-income countries decelerated to an estimated 3.8 percent. Export growth in Asia slowed from 12.5 percent to a still robust 7.4 percent, while Latin American export growth slowed from 6.3 percent to 5.6 percent. Exports from the Europe and Central Asia region, with their greater focus on Western European markets, fell 4 percent.

Two developments in 1993—the conclusion of the Uruguay Round of the GATT and of the NAFTA among Canada, Mexico, and the United States—underlined the importance for the future of two coexisting trends, one towards broad multilateral trading arrangements under the GATT and the other towards regional integration arrangements (RIAs).

According to the GATT Secretariat, the Uruguay Round is expected to generate an increase in merchandise trade of 12 percent by the year 2005 (or roughly $745 billion in 1992 dollars) over the level that would have existed by then had trade grown only at its average for the period 1980–91 (4.1 percent). The largest increases are expected in clothing (60 percent); textiles (34 percent); agricultural, forestry, and fisheries products (20 percent); and processed food and beverages (19 percent). Estimates suggest that world income could increase by at least 1 percent, or some $212 billion to $270 billion annually (1992 dollars). Of that amount, $80 billion is expected to accrue to developing countries. The regional effects on exports and real incomes are likely to vary significantly, depending largely on the market-access provisions of the round (see Box 2-1).

Gains for Asia will be substantial. Quota-constrained exporters of textiles and clothing (mainly in Southeast Asia and East Asia, including China) will benefit greatly from the slow phaseout (over a ten-year period) of the Multi-Fibre Arrangement, with quotas increas-

ing about 50 percent over seven years. Latin America will also gain, but proportionately less. Its food exporters (Argentina, Chile, and Uruguay, in particular) will benefit from reductions in agricultural subsidies. Latin American economies are also likely to benefit from reductions in tariffs on metals and minerals, and they have little to lose on preferences. Sub-Saharan Africa's gains from the Uruguay Round will be limited by the low proportion of manufactures in its exports. Nevertheless, faster world growth resulting from the round's partial liberalization of trade would provide additional support at the margin for prices of, and

---

Box 2-1. The Uruguay Round, Market Access, and the Developing Countries

For each of the 118 participants in the Uruguay Round, the increase in national income resulting from the successful conclusion of the round will come from two principal sources: first, more efficient use of domestic resources when domestic distortions, such as trade barriers, are reduced or removed; and second, increased access to markets of trading partners.

It is estimated that implementation of the market-access provisions of the round could add between $200 billion and $300 billion (in 1992 dollars) annually to world income. These figures are probably an underestimate; they do not include services, and no attempt has yet been made to capture the effects on productivity growth of greater openness in trade. Even at the "underestimated" level, full implementation of the Uruguay Round could boost the GDP of developing economies by almost $80 billion (in 1992 dollars) a year. Developing country gains from agricultural liberalization alone are estimated at between $20 billion and $60 billion a year, depending on the extent of each economy's liberalization.

Improved market access for agricultural and industrial products will result primarily from broad reductions in tariffs and more control of quantitative restrictions and subsidies. In contrast to the situation for industrial products, increased market access for agricultural products will involve limiting the use of domestic support policies. Reduction of export subsidies by industrial countries will boost the competitiveness of exports from developing countries.

The effect of the reduction in most-favored-nation (MFN) tariffs on individual suppliers depends on whether the importing country gives the product MFN, preferential, or free-trade treatment. For MFN imports there is an unambiguous increase in the volume of sales in the importing country following a tariff reduction. In the case of imports already receiving preferential or free-trade-area treatment, the reduction in MFN tariff rates can reduce margins of preference, inducing buyers to switch to competing suppliers. Analyses suggest that the trade gains from reductions in

MFN tariff rates are likely to outweigh the losses from preference erosion, even for exporters receiving preferences.

The reduction in duties that apply to developing countries is estimated at 34 percent—less than the 38 percent reduction on industrial products from all sources—and the figures for clothing and footwear (of particular interest to developing countries) are even lower. Nevertheless, the effects on trade creation will be large even for such products because existing tariff rates on them are the highest, and the percentage decline in the tariff-inclusive price in importing countries will be substantial. Moreover, where a quantitative restriction (rather than the tariff) is the binding restraint under the Multi-Fibre Arrangement, the extent of the increase in market access may be larger than the cut in the tariff alone would indicate.

A disappointing result of the agreement is that tariff escalation will continue for agricultural products. It was hoped that discrimination against processed commodities would be reduced, thus enhancing strategies for natural resource-based industrialization. But the agreed reductions in tariffs, whether viewed in absolute or percentage terms, do not clearly rise or fall with the level of processing.

Considerable progress has been made in the latest agreement toward the goal of increasing the proportion of tariffs that are bound (subject to commitments not to raise the tariff rate). This will significantly reduce exporter risk. For industrial products, virtually all tariffs in developed and transition economies are bound under current offers, and developing countries have offered to increase the proportion of bound tariffs to 65 percent. For agricultural products there is a substantial increase in the proportion of tariff lines subject to bindings, especially in the developing economies, where there is a fivefold increase (from 17 to 89 percent). For the first time in the GATT's history the proportion of bound tariff lines will be broadly the same for agricultural and nonagricultural products.

volume demands for, primary commodities of significance to the region. A point of concern to African countries is that reductions in tariffs will reduce the margin of preference enjoyed by the exports from African countries under current unilateral preferential arrangements such as the Lomé Convention. However, the limited nature of these preferences and the gradual phasing-in period of the new provisions are likely to limit adverse effects.

Over the next fifteen years, the NAFTA will remove barriers to trade and investment flows within North America; it also sets the stage for reforms in domestic policies to foster trade and competition within an area rivaling the European Union in economic size. The NAFTA's main effect will be to improve the growth prospects of Mexico, which is required by the agreement to liberalize its policies the most and which should consequently experience a significant boost in its exports. Economic models estimate that in the short term, the NAFTA will be responsible for increased exports to the United States of 11 percent and 9 percent from Mexico and Canada, respectively, while exports to the United States from elsewhere could fall by small amounts. One drawback is that the NAFTA's domestic content regulations could prevent the agreement's three member countries from relying on some low-cost (non-NAFTA) sources of production inputs—a factor that would restrict the ability of members to use their NAFTA tariff and nontariff preferences.

The passage of the NAFTA and the deepening of the European Union under its single-market program are illustrative of the renewed interest in RIAs, a trend referred to as the "new regionalism."

RIAs, which entail reciprocal negotiation of trade preferences among participants, can take several forms. These extend from preferential trading arrangements and free trade arrangements (under which participants levy lower, or eliminate, respectively, tariffs on imports from each other while maintaining independent trade policies toward third parties) to customs unions. In a customs union, members not only reduce tariffs among themselves; they also adopt a common foreign trade policy against nonmembers. Common markets, in turn, expand the parameters of a customs union by allowing free movement of labor and capital among members; in an economic union, members further expand those parameters by explicitly pursuing harmonization of their microeconomic and macroeconomic policies ("deep integration").

The trend towards increased regionalization of world trade is long standing. A recent GATT study shows that the amount of world trade occurring within regions as a share of world GDP rose from 7 percent in 1948 to 17 percent in 1990, driven mainly by the performance of Western Europe. However, this rise did not choke off trade between regions, as the amount of intraregional trade as a share of GDP has remained fairly stable at between 15 percent and 16 percent.

The future of "benign regionalism," which minimizes harm to outsiders and contributes to world trade and welfare, depends critically on a commitment to maintaining and furthering openness and multilateral cooperation among trading blocs. In this regard, the successful completion of the Uruguay Round has helped to alleviate concern that the "new regionalism" might substitute for multilateral trade liberalization. In recognition of the potential threat posed by RIAs, the Uruguay Round strengthens existing GATT rules that forbid barriers against third parties from rising through the creation of an RIA. Further, the round will strengthen surveillance of RIAs, an effort that will undoubtedly be pursued by the new World Trade Organization (WTO), which will succeed the GATT in 1995. The WTO, designed by the Uruguay Round participants to enforce the GATT's free trade rules, will have the power to levy trade penalties against countries by a semijudicial disputes procedure that will no longer allow countries to ignore findings against them.

Section Three
Major World Bank Programs: Fiscal Year 1994

World Development Report 1990 outlined a strategy for reducing poverty based on experiences from developing countries across the world. How this strategy should be implemented in the World Bank's operations was subsequently spelled out in three documents: the policy paper, *Assistance Strategies to Reduce Poverty,* the *Poverty Reduction Handbook,* and a World Bank Operational Directive on poverty reduction. The yardstick to evaluate the Bank's progress in implementing the poverty-reduction strategy is the extent to which the Bank is implementing the strategies articulated in the three documents.

During fiscal 1994, the Bank continued to make progress in implementing its poverty-reduction strategy both through its lending operations and a strengthened policy dialogue. Analysis is also being strengthened to ensure that the Bank's country-specific assistance strategies develop the most relevant mix of lending for each country, as well as to improve the targeting and design of its operations. The Bank, in both the central and regional vice presidencies, now systematically monitors how it supports government efforts to reduce poverty. At the planning stage, each adjustment operation is classified as to whether or not it is poverty focused, and each investment project is classified as to whether or not it is in the program of targeted interventions (PTI). Each region periodically outlines what progress is being made in implementing the Bank's poverty-reduction strategy and what special initiatives are being undertaken to strengthen these efforts. To strengthen both the technical and analytical tools being used in the Bank's operations, the central vice presidencies are supporting the regions by refining methodologies for analyzing policy issues, disseminating best-practice analysis and project design, and providing training.

Human Resources Development

Developing countries are turning to the Bank for intellectual leadership and financial assistance for investments in the human resources area. Aid donors are increasingly channeling their assistance to this area and are asking the Bank to coordinate the aid flows.

The Human Resources Development and Operations (HRO) vice presidency is the focal point of the Bank's human resources and poverty operations. Operational relevance and client orientation are the main criteria used for selecting tasks in the human resources development sectors.

During the past year, demand was also heavy for HRO's analytical services. The executive directors of the Bank, as well as the six operational regions, requested a number of analytical papers on several critical issues: higher education (see Box 3-1), gender policy, and population. The dissemination of information through the vice presidency's Working Papers series and Dissemination Notes, as well as through population and health/nutrition newsletters and the electronic network, has proven popular with task managers and external audiences alike.

Tools for Reducing Poverty. By a variety of measurements—through its lending program, development of country-assistance strategies and the policy dialogue, and analysis of poverty issues—the Bank continued to advance during the year in its work to reduce poverty.

The lending program for human resources development (comprising lending to education; population, health, and nutrition; and the social sector) continued to be robust during fiscal 1994, attracting $3,104 million in commitments (15 percent of total Bank commitments). Eighteen percent of all new IDA commitments—some $1,198 million—were directed toward human resources development. Lending for the agriculture and water supply and sanitation sectors, which play an important role in supporting the Bank's poverty-reduction efforts, increased by more than $400 million.

Lending for projects in the PTI was 25 percent of total investment lending (see Table 3-1). IDA commitments for the PTI, as a share of IDA investment lending, increased to 43 per-

Box 3-1. Higher Education—Lessons of Experience

Higher education is in crisis in all parts of the world, both developed and developing, a study by the World Bank finds. And, as might be expected, the crisis is most acute in the developing world, where fiscal constraints are tighter and pressures for expansion of enrollment are greater.

The study—the third in a series on education subsectors[1]—analyzes recent lessons of developing-country experience in higher education reform at both the national and institutional level to show how countries contemplating reform, or just starting on its path, might realize the goals of greater efficiency, quality, and equity in higher education. The study also charts the probable course of World Bank lending to the subsector in the years to come.

Based on a review of experience across countries, the study suggests—without trying to provide a blueprint for each country—that higher education reform might best be directed at (a) expanding the menu of higher education choice in terms of types of institutions and modes of delivery (which, concomitantly, would stimulate the development of private institutions); (b) providing incentives for public institutions to diversify sources of funding; (c) linking public funding closely to performance; (d) redefining the role of government in higher education; and (e) introducing policies explicitly designed to increase the quality and equity of higher education.

An expanded menu of tertiary education would find universities being complemented by other types of institutions such as polytechnics, short-cycle professional technical institutes, community colleges, and "distance" and "open-learning" programs. Typically, these higher-education supplements are often less costly to set up and operate and are therefore attractive to private entrepreneurs.

To relieve the financial burden imposed on public institutions by increasing enrollments, the World Bank study advocates sweeping reforms in the ways such institutions are funded. For example, students should be required to pay a greater share of their education costs;[2] public subsidies for noninstructional expenses—housing and meals, for instance—should be sharply reduced if not eliminated altogether; tax codes should be modified to encourage philanthropy by alumni and private industry; and public higher-education institutions should be encouraged to pursue income-generating activities. At the very least, governments should stop penalizing entrepreneurial activities as they do, for example, when they reduce budget allocations by the same amounts as public institutions make on "non-core" activities.

The study reports that, as a result of the crisis in publicly funded higher education, government's role in the subsector is being redefined.

cent.[1] Projects are included in the PTI if they include a specific mechanism for reaching the poor or if the participation of the poor significantly exceeds the proportion of the population as a whole.[2]

Of the twenty-three adjustment operations approved during the year, seventeen, or three of every four, were poverty focused.[3]

It is now widely acknowledged that participation by beneficiaries in the design and implementation of projects can often be an important determinant of project effectiveness. As a result, the Bank's use of participatory methodologies—including beneficiary assessments, participatory rural assessments, and participatory workshops to fine-tune project design—is on the rise. A preliminary review of fiscal 1994 operations shows that ninety-six out of the total of 228 projects included participation by primary stakeholders (individual beneficiaries, people affected in one way or another by the project, community organizations, user groups, and others such as producer groups and cooperatives).[4]

The salutary effect of beneficiary participation is now becoming clearer. A study of 121 rural water supply and sanitation projects,[5] supported by eighteen development agencies

(including the Bank), throughout Asia, Africa, and Latin America, has revealed beneficiary

---

[1] The Bank takes very seriously its commitment to increase the shares of poverty-targeted investments and social-sector lending during the three-year period encompassed by the tenth replenishment of IDA resources (fiscal 1994–96). Care should be taken, however, not to use the PTI as the sole measure of the Bank's poverty-reduction efforts. In some cases, the greatest contribution to poverty reduction in a given country could come from the implementation of a well-designed adjustment program. In addition, many PTI projects are experimental and, as a result, loan amounts can be expected to be small. For these reasons, there may be natural fluctuations in the size of the PTI from year to year, although the trend line should be an increasing one.

[2] A description of each project in the PTI that was approved during fiscal 1994 can be found in the project summaries in Section Five of this *Annual Report*. The PTI projects are marked by an asterisk.

[3] A description of each poverty-focused adjustment operation that was approved during fiscal 1994 can be found in the project summaries in Section Five of this *Annual Report*. These operations are marked by a pound sign (#).

[4] A description of each project approved during fiscal 1994 with participation by primary stakeholders can be found in the project summaries in Section Five of this report. The projects are marked with a "†."

[5] Deepa Narayan. 1994. *The Contribution of People's Participation: 121 Rural Water Supply Projects.* The World Bank: Washington, D.C.

Rather than aiming at direct control of the entire subsector, a government's main responsibility is becoming that of providing an enabling policy environment—for private as well as public institutions—and of using the leverage of public funding to stimulate institutions of higher learning to meet national training and research needs more efficiently.

Encouraging an expanded menu of opportunities for higher education, providing incentives for diversifying funding sources, and relaxing governmental control are necessary elements for improving higher education. By themselves, however, they are insufficient. The Bank study goes on to say that the final element of the reform process must be implementation of policies that increase the quality of higher education and improve the access of traditionally disadvantaged groups. Greater equity of participation is important not only for economic efficiency but for social justice as well.

The Bank's latest examination of an education subsector points to the conclusion that higher education investments have lower social rates of return than do investments in primary and secondary education and that investments in basic education have a more direct impact on poverty reduction. As a result, the Bank will continue to give priority to lending for primary and lower secondary education.

Lending in support of higher-education reform, however, can be justified, as Bank financing helps countries free up some of the incremental public resources needed to improve quality and access at the primary and secondary levels. Properly designed projects also allow the subsector to operate more efficiently and at lower public cost. Higher education lending will be directed to countries prepared to adopt an education policy framework that stresses a differentiated institutional structure and a diversified resource base, with greater emphasis on private provision of services and private funding. In these countries, Bank lending is supporting, and will continue to support, sector-policy reforms, institutional development, and improvements in quality.

---

[1] The first study, on primary education, was discussed by the executive board in fiscal 1990, while policies for vocational and technical education and training were the subject of a board discussion in fiscal 1991.
[2] Cost-sharing cannot be implemented equitably, however, without scholarship programs that guarantee necessary financial support to academically qualified poor students unable to absorb the direct and indirect (foregone earnings) costs of higher education and without a functioning student-loan program to assist students who need to borrow for their education.

participation as the single most important element in determining the overall quality of implementation. Similarly, the Operation Evaluation Department's *Annual Report of Evaluation Results 1992* listed beneficiary participation and borrower ownership as two important features of the twenty-four operations classified as outstanding.

Fiscal 1994 marked the culmination of a three-year Bankwide learning process on participation, which has sought to review the

Bank's experience in participatory approaches and to identify ways to support participation in borrower countries. The result—a report to the Bank's management, developed by a learning group of some fifty Bank staff involved in participatory work—has been widely reviewed by Bank staff and outside experts in participation. The report puts forward a number of recommendations, including ensuring that all projects under preparation include (a) a provision for systematically identifying and seeking the par-

Table 3-1. **Program of Targeted Interventions, 1992–94**
(millions of US dollars; fiscal years)

	1992	1993	1994
Total World Bank PTI lending	3,837	4,674	4,441
As share of investment lending (%)	24	27	25
As share of all Bank lending (%)	18	20	21
Total number of PTI projects	57	72	63
IDA PTI lending	1,828	2,137	1,853
As share of IDA investment lending (%)	43	41	43
As share of all IDA lending (%)	28	32	28
Number of IDA PTI projects	35	44	35

NOTE: Investment lending is defined as all lending except for adjustment, debt and debt-service reduction operations, and emergency-reconstruction operations. Data for FY92 and FY93 have been revised to reflect this definition.

ticipation of relevant stakeholders and (b) sharing responsibility for economic and sector work with a wide range of stakeholders. The report was a focus of discussions at a May 1994 workshop on participatory development, hosted by the Bank, which included sixty nongovernmental organization (NGO) representatives, staff from donor agencies, and academics. The workshop discussions helped prioritize the Bank's next steps in this area as it begins to mainstream participatory approaches in its work.

As a further means of encouraging a mainstreaming of participatory approaches, a $300,000 Participation Fund was established during the year to support a wide range of participatory initiatives in the Bank's lending and nonlending operations. The fund proved so popular among task managers that a $200,000 replenishment was approved to meet the heavy demand.

Activities financed by the Participation Fund included several workshops during project preparation involving beneficiaries, NGOs, and government staff in discussions about project design; workshops were also funded that involved local communities in the evaluation of participatory components of ongoing projects. Building on this precedent, a $2 million Fund for Innovative Approaches in Human and Social Development was set up toward the end of the fiscal year. The fund will support efforts to promote participatory approaches and will finance a limited number of social assessments of the potential impacts of proposed projects.

Country-assistance strategies and the policy dialogue increasingly address poverty in a wide context. In particular, poverty issues are being addressed comprehensively, both within the context of human resources development and more fully within the overall country-assistance strategy (including macroeconomic and sector policies) in the more than three dozen countries for which poverty assessments or other poverty analyses have been completed. In the policy dialogue on country-assistance strategies, poverty reduction is high on the agenda. In particular, Bank staff are discussing poverty reduction more frequently than before with finance and planning ministries in the context of macroeconomic and sectoral policies. In several countries (Belarus, Ecuador, and Sierra Leone, for example), special units have been created within those ministries to integrate the goal of poverty reduction more explicitly into economic planning.

In the area of analysis of poverty issues, significant progress was made in preparing poverty assessments and other analytical work in

fiscal 1994.[6] Eleven assessments were completed, bringing the number of completed assessments to thirty-nine. By the end of fiscal 1995, ninety-four assessments for eighty-three countries are scheduled to be completed. Strides were also made during the year toward overcoming the lack of good household data on poverty, although this remains a problem in many countries. The most progress in data collection and analysis has been made in the Africa region, where acquisition of recent household data has accelerated.

In a report to the Bank's executive directors that was later made public,[7] several lessons from the Bank's past poverty-reduction work, as well as challenges for the future, were highlighted.

• The challenge for future country-assistance strategies is to ensure that they address the main poverty problems in each country, that they complement efforts by government and donors to reduce poverty, and that the appropriate mix of broad-based and targeted lending instruments evolves for each country.

• Clearly the Bank is challenged to complete poverty assessments for all borrowing member countries, to continue to improve their quality, to enhance the quality of analysis through greater coordination among donors, and to ensure that assessment findings are fully integrated into country-assistance strategies.

• Development of poverty-monitoring systems and expansion of countries' capacity to implement them is a priority. To date, only a few poverty assessments have evaluated a country's statistical system for monitoring poverty; even less attention has been given to developing action plans for implementing poverty-monitoring systems over time.

Activities on Women in Development (WID). According to a report written for the September 1993 meeting of the Development Committee, the Bank has made progress in implementing its operational strategy on WID. That strategy aims to reduce gender disparities and enhance women's participation in the eco-

---

[6] Poverty assessments are crucial to the Bank's poverty-reduction efforts. A poverty assessment provides the basis for a collaborative approach to poverty reduction by country officials and the Bank. It also helps to establish the agenda of issues for the policy dialogue between the government and the Bank and between the government and agencies of the international donor community. The process of completing assessments for all IDA borrowers has taken longer than originally planned. This is mainly because of the time-consuming process of overcoming data constraints, developing appropriate analytical approaches, and increasing government involvement in the process.

[7] World Bank. 1994. *Poverty Reduction and the World Bank: Progress in Fiscal 1993.* Washington, D.C.

nomic development of their countries by integrating gender consideration in country-assistance programs. Of all projects approved by the Bank in fiscal 1993, about one in three included gender-targeted interventions.

The integration of WID issues into the Bank's economic and sector work continues. Almost half of the Bank's economic and sector reports contain WID-related analytical work. Gender issues are also increasingly addressed in poverty assessments, particularly in countries where the number of female-headed households is disproportionately high and where there are significant disparities in social indicators between males and females.

According to the 1993 progress report, various lessons have already been learned from the preparation by the Bank of best-practice papers on education, agriculture, safe motherhood, and enterprise development and financial services. In agriculture, for example, it has been found that targeting special services to women does not guarantee success. Rather, it is more effective to ensure that women's programs become part of the mainstream extension services and to encourage women farmers to participate in the services' design. Projects also need to be tailored to specific country or regional circumstances so that women's roles and needs can be properly taken into account.

Lessons learned by the Bank, by other donors, and NGOs suggest some promising approaches to overcoming the barriers to improving the status and productivity of women. That combined experience points unambiguously to five operational strategies that are key to improving the status and productivity of women: expanding the enrollment of girls in school, improving the health of women, increasing their participation in the formal labor force, expanding their options in agriculture, and providing financial services to them.

Until quite recently, WID programs, including those of the Bank, tended to treat women as a special target group of beneficiaries in projects and programs. According to a recent Bank policy paper,[8] development organizations have begun to recognize, however, that the best way to ensure that women are not left at the margin of the development process is to analyze the relative roles and responsibilities of both men and women and to apply the insights gained from this analysis to the design of projects and programs. This new approach, which focuses on gender relations in the family and in the community rather than on women in isolation, constitutes the "gender and development" approach. This is the focus that the Bank is now promoting to enhance women's participation in development.

The policy paper outlined the rationale and strategy for integrating gender in Bank operations. Addressing gender issues is essential for the realization of the Bank's goal of reducing poverty. In addition, reducing gender disparities and enhancing women's participation in economic development are entirely compatible with the promotion of growth as well as with environmentally sustainable development. The Bank is committed, therefore, to integrating gender issues into the mainstream of its operational, as well as its analytical, activities.

A new operational policy directive, issued in April 1994, states that it is the Bank's intention to reduce gender disparities and enhance women's participation in economic development by integrating gender issues into country-assistance strategies. These issues will be identified through the use of various instruments (poverty assessments, country WID assessments, public expenditure reviews, and other economic and sector work). Objectives and interventions for carrying out gender strategies are then to be reflected in the Bank's lending program and the design of lending operations. Implementation is to be monitored as part of the country-implementation review.

The Bank is only one contributor on the international scene that seeks to advance women's status and participation in economic development. Other donors, as well as international, national, and local institutions are also playing important roles in closing the gender gap. The Bank will continue to learn from, and collaborate with, other agencies and capitalize on a wide range of expertise that exists in advancing gender issues on the development agenda. All these efforts, however, will be fruitful only with governments' leadership, commitment, and collaboration.

Population, Health, and Nutrition. Rapid population growth in the world's poorest countries is a matter of considerable concern because of its possible negative effects on efforts to reduce poverty, generate economic growth, and preserve the environment.

Although the global picture is one of continued growth, rates of growth have begun to slow in many developing countries. The slowing of growth reflects a pervasive shift in reproductive attitudes and behaviors in those countries. The pace of change varies by region, but fertility declines are widespread.

Over the past three decades, the percentage of married women in developing countries using some method of contraception has in-

---

[8] World Bank. 1994. *Enhancing Women's Participation in Economic Development*. A World Bank Policy Paper. Washington, D.C.

creased from 10 percent to 51 percent—from 40 million users in 1960 to some 365 million in 1990. Because of the large increase in the number of women of reproductive age, however, the total number of women not using contraception has declined little, leaving an estimated 350 million still to be served.

During the 1990s, an additional 170 million individuals will move into their reproductive ages in developing countries; another 180 million are projected for the following decade. Just to maintain the current level of coverage, services will have to be expanded to accommodate 80 million to 90 million more contraceptive users during each of these two decades. That still leaves the challenge of providing services for at least 100 million married couples and at least 20 million unmarried individuals, many of whom are at risk of contracting sexually transmitted diseases, as well, because needed contraceptive services are not available or are of poor quality.

As the number of potential clients increases, the definition of what constitutes a population program is expanding. It is now widely accepted that programs must meet a wide range of the reproductive health needs of women and men.[9] In addition, they are increasingly addressing other health concerns related to sexual activity and reproduction—the AIDS epidemic and other sexually transmitted diseases, for example. Similarly, the scope of programs is also expanding to include such groups as unmarried adolescents and males, particularly those who engage in high-risk sexual behavior, whose needs have not been served by traditional modes of service provision.[10]

The Bank's role in population has been shaped by its comparative advantage in a number of areas: It brings strength in sector and economic analysis, which together provide a basis for policy dialogue between the Bank and borrowing countries. This strength is particularly relevant in the current population-policy environment, in which fertility reduction is increasingly being pursued as part of a broad range of social policies, particularly those that improve the status of women, such as education.

The Bank has been an active player in the population field for the past twenty-five years, lending more than $1.7 billion to support population activities through more than 100 projects. The value of the current portfolio stands at slightly more than $1 billion, representing seventy-three projects under Bank supervision. Many Bank projects include family planning within larger health and nutrition projects, leading to mutually reinforcing effects for both better health and increased demand for family planning. Commitments in fiscal 1994 totaled $199 million for family-planning and population-policy components in fourteen health and social development projects. New commitments vary considerably from year to year, but the trend has been steadily upward.

The increasing complexity of population projects offers particular challenges when it comes time for project supervision. Some of the Bank's more successful population and health projects—in Bangladesh and Kenya, for example—have included provision for resident management staff to strengthen supervision capacity. The experience of other donors also suggests a strong relationship between the intensity of in-country management effort and project effectiveness. The Bank has been making a special effort to improve supervision and strengthen its skill mix in needed technical areas and to assure that it is responsive to borrower needs.

Health sector reform is a high priority. Since the publication in July 1993 of *World Development Report 1993*, which was devoted to the issues of health reform, assistance has been requested by more than three dozen countries for assessing the burden of disease. Guidelines for health-sector reform are now being prepared; they will be published in fiscal 1995 as a companion volume to *World Development Report 1993*. Also under study are managed-care arrangements in both developing and industrialized countries, the efficacy of differing systems of health care, and pharmaceutical policies in a number of countries. The goal of the last-named study is to assist borrowing member countries in formulating and enforcing policies that improve the access to, and quality of, essential drugs.

The upward momentum that has characterized recent lending trends for nutrition within Bank projects continues, assisted, in part, by

---

[9] The Development Committee, for example, in its April 1994 communiqué following its spring meeting, noted that an integrated population policy must recognize the links between economic growth, population, poverty reduction, health, investment in human resources, and environmental degradation. "Family planning," the communiqué went on to say, "is only one of the available instruments and needs to be seen in the broader context of changing social patterns and the increased awareness of women's role."

[10] The changing nature of population programs and the challenging population issues of this decade and beyond will be the subject of the 1994 International Conference on Population and Development—the third in a series of United Nations conferences that started in Bucharest in 1974 and continued in Mexico City in 1984. These meetings produced and refined the World Population Plan of Action, which has provided donors and developing countries with a framework for population policies and action programs over the past two decades. The 1994 conference will be held in September in Cairo.

the recommendations for cost-effective interventions in *World Development Report 1993*. An additional focus within the Bank was generated by the convening in late November of the Bank's first major conference on hunger, "Overcoming Global Hunger—A Conference on Actions to Reduce Hunger Worldwide."

Children three years old and younger and pregnant and lactating women remain the primary target of nutrition operations in Bank projects. Several recent projects, however, such as fiscal 1994's Maternal and Child Health Project in Argentina, include integrated early childhood-development components that address the full range of health, nutritional, and educational needs of young children in their most critical years of development.

Overall lending for population, health, and nutrition has increased substantially, from an annual average of $103 million in new commitments during the four-year period fiscal 1981–84 to an annual average of $1,307 million during the period fiscal 1991–94.[11]

Bank investments in education (which amounted to $2,068 million in fiscal 1994) are increasingly targeted toward getting girls into school and eliminating existing gender disparities in participation, achievement, and attainment; the objective is to empower women as producers, reduce their dependence on husbands and sons, and lower the fertility rate.

The HRO vice presidency is actively involved in improving the design and implementation of the Bank's education projects. During the past year, for example, senior staff were actively involved in the implementation of a complex and comprehensive primary education project in Uttar Pradesh—one of the most educationally deprived states of India. The project, supported in fiscal 1993 by a $165 million IDA credit, focuses on the education of girls and disadvantaged ethnic minorities. The project design and its implementation reflect a deep government commitment to the concept of education for all, both at the central government and at the grassroots level. This commitment has manifested itself in the ways that staff and other resources have been assigned to the project, in the interest of top-level civil servants and grassroots-level NGOs in its implementation, and in the exceptionally fast pace with which project baseline studies and infrastructure are being carried out, facilitating subsequent evaluation and measurements of project achievements. The results of this project are now being replicated in a much larger, countrywide project.

At the other end of the education spectrum, HRO staff have been involved in the design and implementation of higher education projects in countries that are changing from centrally planned economies to market-responsive ones. One such project is in Hungary, which has introduced reform to its higher education system by promoting the concept that participating institutions must compete for investment funds by submitting funding proposals to an impartial national agency. This agency assesses the submitted proposals on their educational and economic merits through well-understood and transparent criteria and procedures that emphasize economy and efficiency in the use of public resources. A recent midterm review of the results has been encouraging; the new procedures are being expanded to replace the entire higher education funding mechanism, and neighboring countries have shown interest in replicating the system.

In July 1992, Lewis Preston, in a letter to 1,400 parliamentarians from twenty-six countries about future lending by the Bank, wrote that the Bank would increase its support for education projects in the period fiscal 1993–95 over levels of the preceding three-year period. Commitments in fiscal 1993 and 1994 totaled $4,074 million, $336 million higher than in the period fiscal 1990–91. Mr. Preston also said that support by the Bank for basic education during fiscal 1993–95 would rise above the 42 percent mark achieved in fiscal 1992. Such support amounted to 45.7 percent and 30.2 percent of total lending for education in fiscal 1993 and 1994, respectively.

External Relations. The Bank is a partner with numerous United Nations organizations and a variety of other international and bilateral agencies, as well as with major NGOs. The HRO vice presidency pays close attention to nurturing these relationships, to listening, to sharing understanding of the problems being faced, and to building collaborative relationships.

During the past year, the Bank shared the podium in United Nations' fora to address development issues of global reach. The Bank's follow-up to environmental activities after the

---

[11] In July 1992, Lewis Preston, president of the World Bank, said that the Bank planned to substantially increase lending for population, health, and nutrition—in both dollar-volume terms and as a percentage of total commitments—during the period fiscal 1993–95 as compared with the three previous years. During fiscal 1990–92, lending to the sector averaged $1,154 million annually and represented 5 percent of total Bank lending. During fiscal 1993–94, lending for population, health, and nutrition averaged $1,349 million and amounted to 6 percent of total commitments. Mr. Preston also projected that lending for primary health would be more than 5 percent of total lending over the same period. In fiscal 1993 and 1994, commitments in support of primary health amounted to 6 percent and 4 percent of the total, respectively.

United Nations Conference on Environment and Development was discussed in the UN's Inter-Agency Committee on Sustainable Development and in the Commission on Sustainable Development. The Bank also addressed environmental issues at such UN gatherings as the Small Island Economies Conference (held in Barbados) and the Disaster Reduction Conference (held in Japan).

The Bank actively participated in all phases of the preparations for the Third Population and Development Conference, scheduled for September 1994 in Cairo. The Bank provided travel grants to developing country NGOs to ensure their full participation in the conference and its preparation. It also participated in the preparations (including provision of background papers on social and human resources development and grant funds to ensure NGO participation) for the Social Summit that will be held in Copenhagen in 1995. The Bank also cosponsored, with the summit's secretariat and the government of the Netherlands, a meeting held in June 1994 in Zambia of a preparatory expert group on poverty. The Bank's contribution to the Conference on Women and Development—to be held in Beijing in 1995—included a special study on the economic potential of women, while the Second (Economic and Financial) and Third (Social, Humanitarian, and Cultural) Committees of the UN General Assembly provided a forum for presenting updates on major Bank activities.

The Bank continues to coordinate project-focused work with UN agencies in areas of mutual involvement, including food security with the Food and Agriculture Organization of the UN; health and education with the United Nations Children's Fund (UNICEF); employment with the International Labour Office; AIDS and other health interventions with the World Health Organization; environmental issues with the United Nations Environment Programme (UNEP); basic education with the United Nations Educational, Scientific, and Cultural Organization, UNICEF, and the United Nations Development Programme (UNDP); and water and sanitation and technical assistance with the UNDP. The Bank remains a cosponsor (with the UNDP) of the Energy Sector Management Assistance Programme (ESMAP), designed to assist countries in developing environmentally sound energy strategies and investments.

Cooperation with Nongovernmental Organizations. Cooperation with NGOs continued to expand in terms of both lending operations (see Tables 3-2 and 3-3) and the policy dialogue. Some 50 percent of all Bank-approved projects involved NGOs.

In the realm of lending operations, NGOs increasingly are designing, preparing, implementing, and evaluating subprojects financed through Bank-assisted projects, while the expansion of the policy dialogue has led to increased beneficiary ownership of Bank-assisted projects. Social-fund projects worldwide and food-security and nutrition projects in Africa have benefited from NGO involvement, while Pakistan's Social Action Program is an example of the Bank's increasing commitment in support of participatory development. In the Pakistan program, the Bank created a $10 million Participatory Development Program Fund to support various implementing organizations in their efforts to involve communities in the delivery of basic social services, such as primary education and health care and rural water supply.

One of the Bank's main goals in collaborating with NGOs has been to increase the institutional capacity of project-implementing organizations. To this end, the Bank has provided, or has made arrangements with other organizations (very often NGOs) to provide, capacity-building assistance to various NGOs and communities. One such example is the capacity-building exercise for indigenous NGOs that has been launched in several Latin American countries with grants from the Bank's Institutional Development Fund. This exercise stemmed directly from requests from indigenous NGO leaders who attended the Latin American Second Interagency Workshop on Indigenous Development, held in Washington, D.C. in September 1993.

The Bank is also helping governments analyze their relationship with NGOs with a view to constructing a more enabling environment for NGO activities. For example, it convened a workshop in Uganda that brought together NGOs, government officials, and donors to discuss specially prepared reports on the country's NGOs and the policy environment in which they operate and to formulate a national action plan to promote the role of NGOs in poverty reduction.

In the twice-yearly meetings of the Bank-NGO Committee, topics such as popular participation and the social effects of structural adjustment programs were discussed. The Bank also consulted on an *ad hoc* basis with NGOs on issues of particular concern. In May 1994, for example, discussions with NGO representatives were held on the implementation experience of the Bank's forest policy in preparation for a review in fiscal 1995 of the policy by the Bank's executive directors. A separate consultation with NGOs in May 1994 helped the Bank evolve strengthened indicators of development impact. Consultations were also

Table 3-2. **Patterns in World Bank-NGO Operational Collaboration, Fiscal Years 1974–94**

	Total 1974–91		1992		1993		1994	
	No.	%	No.	%	No.	%	No.	%
By region (number of projects)								
Africa	204	n.a.	32	42*	31	41*	38	63*
East Asia and Pacific	45	n.a.	8	17*	12	27*	22	51*
South Asia	59	n.a.	9	39*	11	42*	15	79*
Europe and Central Asia	6	n.a.	4	29*	2	7*	10	24*
Latin America and the Caribbean	59	n.a.	12	27*	14	28*	24	50*
Middle East and North Africa	18	n.a.	3	18*	3	16*	5	31*
Total	391	10*	68	31*	73	30*	114	50*
By sector (number of projects)								
Adjustment related (incl/social funds)	27	7	8	12	5	7	12	11
Agriculture/rural development	150	38	22	32	14	19	36	32
Education	41	10	6	9	6	8	10	9
Environment	12	3	13	19	13	18	5	4
Industry/energy	35	9	6	9	8	11	13	11
Infrastructure/urban development	63	16	4	6	8	11	24	21
Population, health, and nutrition	57	15	7	10	16	22	14	12
Rehabilitation/reconstruction	6	2	2	3	3	4	—	—
Total	391	100	68	100	73	100	114	100

* Refers to percentage of NGO-involved projects in all World Bank-approved projects; n.a. = not available.

Table 3-3. **Type and Function of NGOs in NGO-associated Projects, Fiscal Years 1991–94**

	1991		1992		1993		1994	
	No.	%	No.	%	No.	%	No.	%
Total projects involving NGOs	**89**		**68**		**73**		**114**	
By type of NGO (number of NGOs)								
Grassroots	49	55	37	54	21	29	46	40
Indigenous	66	74	52	76	58	79	80	70
International	23	26	33	49	16	22	11	10
Unclassified	—	—	—	—	1	1	19	17
By function (number of functions)								
Advice	40	45	37	54	35	48	14	12
Design	39	44	31	46	17	23	60	53
Implementation	85	96	59	87	57	78	99	87
Monitoring/evaluation	15	17	26	38	33	45	38	33
Cofinancing	23	26	10	15	1	1	11	10

NOTE: The numbers in this table are estimates of the ways NGOs may be involved in each project. Regardless of the actual number of NGOs involved in each project, projects are counted only once for each type/function of NGOs. For these reasons, numbers under "By type of NGO" and "By function" exceed the total number of projects involving NGOs.

held with NGOs in Paris and Washington on the draft of *World Development Report 1994: Infrastructure for Development.*

In addition to formal consultations, an increasing number of meetings between senior Bank officials and NGO representatives around the world have been held. A series of meetings took place with NGOs during the past year on issues such as the disclosure of information, creation of an inspection panel, and follow-up to the report of the Bank's Task Force on Portfolio Management. Another series of meetings focused on environmental sustainability, resettlement issues, specific project concerns, and the environmental effects of macroeconomic policies.

The changing nature of the Bank-NGO relationship was clearly exhibited at the Conference on Actions to Reduce Hunger Worldwide that was convened by the Bank in November 1993. In addition to participating in presentations and discussions, NGO representatives assisted in the conference's preparatory and follow-up work. Discussions at the country level on hunger issues are currently being planned by the Bank and NGOs in various countries.

NGOs are also playing a role in the Global Environment Facility (GEF), especially in the areas of project design, implementation, and monitoring. The twice-yearly meetings of GEF "participants" (members) are routinely preceded by GEF-NGO consultations.

The instrument for the Establishment of the Restructured Global Environment Facility, adopted in March 1994 at the GEF Participants Meeting in Geneva, included several provisions that relate to NGOs' concerns: In the restructured facility, NGOs will have important roles to play in proposing, preparing, and implementing projects, and local communities will be consulted throughout the project cycle.

The facility's three implementing agencies are moving to modify their procedures as needed to assure consultation with affected communities, increased participation by NGOs in GEF projects, public access to GEF project information, and regular monitoring and evaluation of project implementation and results.

Environmentally Sustainable Development

Achieving environmentally sustainable development is a major challenge of the 1990s. The June 1992 UNCED succeeded in raising the consciousness of the world to the urgency of this task. The World Bank, as the largest multilateral source of development finance for developing countries, has a special responsibility to ensure that the programs and projects it supports are consistent with the objective of sustainable development. The mandate of the Environmentally Sustainable Development (ESD) vice presidency is to develop an effective Bank response to this challenge.

At all times, people and the capacities of ecosystems to support life are the center of ESD's focus. The existence of acute poverty in the world and the degradation and contamination of ecosystems are related critical issues and essential concerns in environmentally sustainable development. The Bank must provide leadership in accelerating the improvement of living standards while incorporating the objectives of environmentally appropriate management and sustainability into the design of development policies and projects.

In carrying out its mandate, ESD engages in six types of activities:
• improving the Bank's understanding of the meaning of, and requirements for, achieving environmentally sustainable and equitable development;
• formulating sound environmental, agricultural, and infrastructural policies, projects, and programs—through its own studies and by drawing on the best work wherever it is being done—that promote sustainability;
• providing guidance and technical support to the Bank's six regional offices in devising operations consistent with the object of sustainability;[12]
• helping to address global issues related to the environment, agriculture, and infrastructure and urban development—in partnership with bilateral agencies, other multilateral institutions, and NGOs;
• exchanging and disseminating the findings of policy and "best practices" work with its external partners and within the Bank; and
• developing the Bank's technical capabilities through selective recruitment and training of staff to become more alert to environmental issues and more proficient in elaborating and managing environmentally sound programs.

Policy and Best-practice Work. The ESD vice presidency is responsible for advancing appropriate sustainable development policies in the Bank and monitoring progress in the field of environment, agriculture, and infrastructure. Recent policy papers have addressed urban development (fiscal 1991), forestry (fiscal 1992), housing (fiscal 1993), and water-resource management (fiscal 1993) issues.

During the past fiscal year, the vice presidency promoted the acceptance of the Bank's water-resource management policies, which call for treating water as an economic good, involving stakeholders in its management, and fostering institutional environments that encourage efficient, effective, and equitable water use. The importance of a comprehensive framework that takes into account cross-sectoral considerations was also stressed.

These concerns were pursued in countries worldwide. In the Africa region, for example, staff have been assisting the government of Malawi to develop a water-resources management policy to guide the sustainable use of water resources and the planning and provision of services, accompanied by substantial sector re-

---

[12] The 1987 report of the World Commission on Environment and Development (the Brundtland Commission) defined sustainable development as development that meets "the needs of the present generation without compromising the needs of future generations."

form. In China, work has focused on water issues and policy reforms as they relate to urban environmental management; and in the Brazilian states of Paraná, Minas Gerais, and São Paulo, the principles of water-resources management at the basin level, including consideration of the use of economic instruments for water allocations and pollution control, are being implemented.

In the second half of the fiscal year, ESD undertook a review of the degree of acceptance and implementation of the findings of the 1991 paper on forest policy.[13] The ongoing review—it had not been completed by the end of the fiscal year—is concentrating on the degree to which changes are being made at the country level to sector work and project design. Consultations on an early draft of the review were held in Libreville (capital of timber-rich Gabon), London, and Washington, D.C. Participants included NGOs from both developed and developing countries, members of the Forestry Advisers Group (which includes the forestry advisers of the principal donor agencies), representatives of the timber industry, and academicians.

Fiscal 1994 saw the publication of *World Development Report 1994: Infrastructure for Development*,[14] which examines the links between infrastructure and development and explores ways in which developing countries can improve both the provision and the quality of infrastructure services (transportation, telecommunications, water and sanitation, power and gas, and major water works).

World Development Report 1994 presents new strategies for developing infrastructure in more effective, less wasteful ways. The report shows that the quantity of investment cannot be the exclusive focus of policy. It is also vital that the quality of infrastructure service be improved. To promote more efficient and responsive delivery of infrastructure service, the report points to the need to change incentives through the application of three instruments —commercial management, competition (directly if feasible, indirectly if not), and stakeholder involvement.

The report also identifies trends that will facilitate improvements in the performance of infrastructure. These include innovation in technology and regulatory management, the new willingness of governments to involve the private sector, and increased concern about social and environmental sustainability.

World Development Report 1994 benefited from analysis initiated in ESD and published in the Bank's Discussion Papers series. Papers on "Railways, Energy, and the Environment" and "Rural Road Maintenance and Improve-

ment" were also completed during the past year.

Four major parallel reviews—the second review of environmental assessments, the implementation review of the Bank's active portfolio of environmental projects, a review of national environmental action plans (NEAPs), and a review of projects involving involuntary resettlement—were the focus of environmental activities during fiscal 1994. The resettlement review, rather than being carried out as a deskbound and static stock-taking exercise, was deliberately designed as a broad process of resettlement analysis in the field, carried out by the Bank's relevant regional and central units jointly with borrowers (see Box 3-2).

Central to integrating environmental concerns into the Bank's activities is the "Operational Directive on Environmental Assessment," which was issued in October 1989. The directive mandates an environmental assessment (EA) for all projects that may have a significant negative effect on the environment. Those expected to have significant, sensitive, irreversible, or diverse effects are classified as "Category A" and require a full EA. Less sensitive "Category B" projects undergo a more limited environmental analysis.

A first review of EA procedures, conducted in fiscal 1992, found that although they were realistic, workable, and instrumental in improving development planning and environmental management, problems remained. More effort was needed, the review concluded, to strengthen borrowers' capacity to conduct effective EAs. The review recommended, therefore, that EA training in borrowing countries be made a priority. The review also recommended that the Bank seek to move the EA process to earlier stages in borrower project planning before major decisions—for example, siting and technology—are made.

---

[13] The paper set forth a fourfold strategy to check deforestation. First, although general economic development is necessary for a longer-term solution to the problem of deforestation, priority should be given in the interim to increasing agricultural productivity in poor, densely populated areas—especially those adjacent to forested areas or those from where most forest encroachers originate—and to expanding nonfarm employment opportunities in these targeted areas. Second, forest protection will need to be ensured through specific legislation and regulatory measures, especially in tropical moist forests. Third, private incentives need to be changed, for enforcement of zoning and other regulations is likely to be ineffective unless they are. Fourth, public investments need to be preceded by much more careful environmental assessments.

[14] World Bank. 1994. *World Development Report 1994: Infrastructure for Development*. New York: Oxford University Press.

Box 3-2. Review of Projects Involving Involuntary Resettlement

In the wake of the Bank's experience with its involvement in the Sardar Sarovar projects in India, a task force was formed in 1993 to carry out an analysis of 146 projects approved between 1986 and 1993 with resettlement components to ensure that project implementation was being carried out consistent with loan and credit agreements and with Bank guidelines and policy.[1] Nearly 2 million people were in various stages of resettlement in the 146 projects, which represented 8 percent of the Bank's active portfolio of projects (and 15 percent by worth).

The main product of the review was not simply its final report,[2] but the process that the review triggered throughout 1993 across the Bank and on the ground. The review process consisted of intensified field supervision; analysis of project preparation, appraisal, supervision, and implementation; on-site consultations with nongovernmental organizations; sectoral resettlement studies; development of new technical tools for resettlement planning; and a considerable number of remedial actions initiated by the Bank and borrowers for those projects that were failing to meet set objectives.

Although task force members found that the Bank had made significant progress between 1986 and 1993 in some areas, they also discovered that when projects were not consistent with policy and processing guidelines, resettlers ended up worse off in some cases.

The single most important message of their review was that good resettlement can prevent impoverishment and even reduce poverty by rebuilding sustainable livelihoods. Socially responsible resettlement is also economically beneficial because the heavy costs of poorly handled resettlement extend well beyond the immediately affected population—to the regional economy and to the host population in relocation areas. Inadequate resettlement induces local resistance, increases political tensions, entails extensive project delays, and postpones project benefits for all concerned; the benefits lost because of such unavoidable project delays sometimes far exceed the marginal cost of a good resettlement package. Ensuring that involuntary resettlement is minimized—and when unavoidable, is carried out without impoverishing the people displaced—is fully justified, therefore, on both economic and ethical grounds.

The review showed, once again, that resettlement is nearly always more difficult, more expensive, and more time consuming than generally realized. The largest resettlement operations move tens of thousands of people—often very poor people—long distances in a very short time, and reestablishing their standard of living is a hard task. The inherent difficulty in reestablishing standards of living and community services is compounded by the limited technical and institutional resettlement capacity of most borrowers, as well as by weak commitment from some executing agencies.

During the review period, the Bank tripled its resources for resettlement supervision, and more supervision missions of projects with resettlement components were launched than in the previous three years put together. Remedial actions—they included increasing participation of affected people, finding ways to reduce displacement, provision of additional financial resources, and adjusting resettlement timetables—had the effect of considerably improving the Bank's overall portfolio. In-house analytical work and training offered to country officials also contributed during 1993 to improving portfolio management. In fact, the entire review process proved to be an exceptional opportunity for learning how to do resettlement better, for identifying good practices, adjusting general approaches to particular circumstances, building institutional capacity for

---

The second EA review found that Bank support to activities aimed at building and strengthening EA capacity in borrowing countries did significantly expand in the two intervening years. Support came mainly in the form of environmental institution-building projects aimed specifically at this and related objectives; technical assistance components, aimed at developing EA capacity, in regular investment projects; in-country training spearheaded by the Bank's Economic Development Institute and the Bank's regional environmental divisions; and advice on EA legislation and procedures. The Bank has also been successful in moving EA "upstream" in borrowers' planning processes, as evidenced by the growing number of "sectoral" EAs.

These efforts are beginning to bear fruit. Quality has improved considerably in important areas such as impact identification and analysis; public consultation, especially in the context of resettlement; and mitigation, monitoring, and management planning for projects. In addition, and even more important, the Bank has witnessed a diversification of EA approaches into newer areas, both in terms of sectoral spread (tourism and solid waste management, for example) and types of lending operations (privatization and onlending, for example).

Progress has been particularly significant as concerns the preventive dimension of EA—minimizing the negative environmental effects of a given project. But progress was also made

resettlement, and refining analytical and evaluation methodologies.

In the end, the Bank will be judged on how well the lessons learned from the review process will be integrated into its future activities. Important weaknesses in past Bank practice have been revealed, and actions to improve Bank resettlement work are under way. Thus:

• The Bank will not finance projects involving large-scale resettlement operations unless the government concerned adopts policies and legal frameworks that are conducive to resettlement with income restoration.

• The Bank will help borrowers build their institutional capacity to implement review before displacement starts with a view to protecting people's rights.

• Bank-assisted projects will avoid or reduce displacement as much as possible through technical and social studies for project design and execution.

• The active participation of would-be resettlers in the preparation, planning, and implementation of resettlement will be required.

• All projects will internalize the full cost of resettlement and of the investments required for income restoration within total project costs so as to prevent impoverishment.

• Twin-project approaches for large-scale civil works causing resettlement will be considered. This approach was used in fiscal 1994, when a $460 million loan in support of China's Xiaolangdi Multipurpose Project was coupled with a $110 million IDA credit to help resettle and restore and improve the livelihoods of 154,000 people (directly) and 300,000 people (indirectly) affected by the multipurpose project.

• The Bank's own institutional capacity will be strengthened, primarily through the better use of existing staff skills and by adding staff capacity in critical fields.

• Remedial and retrofitting actions will continue for all active projects that fall short of policy and legal provisions.

• Full compliance with procedures and established safeguards for ensuring project quality will be insisted upon. While full implementation responsibility rests with borrowing governments, the Bank has a responsibility to follow up carefully on performance, impacts, and outcomes.

• The content and frequency of resettlement supervision will be further improved, and regular and adequately staffed supervision missions will take place at least every twelve months, including on-the-ground visits to places where displacement and relocation occur.

• To sustain progress achieved and to monitor continued compliance with Bank guidelines and procedures, regional units will prepare annual reports on projects with resettlement in their portfolio as part of the annual review of portfolio performance.

By setting such exacting norms for the operations it assists and promoting resettlers' reestablishment at comparable or improved income levels, the Bank will continue to work to narrow the gap between resettlement goals and past entrenched practice in many countries.

---

[1] The Bank's resettlement policy has evolved steadily since 1980. Basic elements of that policy include avoidance or minimization of involuntary displacement whenever feasible; assistance to displaced persons in their efforts to improve, or at least restore, former living standards and earning capacity; compensation to displaced persons for their losses at replacement cost; promotion of resettlers' and hosts' participation in planning resettlement; and provision of adequate land, infrastructure, and other compensation for groups that may have informal customary rights to the land or resources taken for the project.

[2] World Bank. 1994. *Resettlement and Development: The Bankwide Review of Projects Involving Involuntary Resettlement, 1986–93.* Washington, D.C.

---

on the "proactive" front in terms of helping design individual projects and larger investment programs that actively enhance environmental quality.

The implementation review of environmental projects covered ninety-three projects—4.2 percent of all projects under implementation at the end of fiscal 1993 and entailing commitments of $6.4 billion—that had been identified as having primarily environmental objectives. These operations were approved between fiscal 1986 and fiscal 1993, with the majority coming after fiscal 1990. The operations, therefore, comprised a rather "young" segment of the total active portfolio.

On the basis of supervision ratings, environmental projects were found to be performing slightly better than the average for the portfolio as a whole at the end of fiscal 1993. Part of the explanation of the apparent above-average performance is the aforementioned "youth" of the projects in relation to the portfolio as a whole. Thus, controlling for project "age," it is probably more accurate to conclude that environmental projects are performing about the same as the Bank's active portfolio as a whole.

As in the case for the Bank's portfolio generally, there also appears to be a clear positive correlation between country income level and environmental project performance. Only one "problem project" was found in an upper-middle-income country, compared with the much larger number found in lower-middle and low-income countries.

It does appear, however, that certain types of environmental projects are performing better than others ("brown" projects are doing better than "green" and "institutional" ones). Furthermore, as a comparatively recent area of Bank lending, there are the inevitable number of start-up costs associated with new and often weak national and sectoral institutions. Other problems include the relative unfamiliarity of executing agencies with Bank requirements; a tendency in some cases to try to "pack too much" into single operations; and, in some cases, less than full borrower commitment to project objectives and components, especially those not involving physical investment.

Bank assistance in elaborating and implementing national environmental action plans (NEAPs) plays a critical role in helping member countries improve their environmental management. NEAPs provide a basis for the Bank's dialogue with borrowers on environmental issues, describe a country's major environmental concerns and problems, and formulate policies and actions to address whatever problems are identified. The responsibility for NEAP preparation and implementation rests with the borrower. By the end of fiscal 1994, most active IDA borrowers had completed NEAPs or equivalent documents, and several non-IDA countries had completed them or were in advanced stages of preparation.

A study of country environmental strategies is currently under way in the Bank; it has been designed to provide guidance to governments in preparing such strategies. The study— "National Environmental Strategies and Action Plans—Key Elements and Best Practice"—is expected to be completed by the middle of fiscal 1995. Its findings will be directed to governments of developing countries, particularly ministries that are primarily responsible for environmental planning and implementation.

The study is finding that the experience with preparing NEAPs has varied considerable from country to country. NEAPs need to be country driven and participatory, involving all segments of society and the government. At the same time, as strategies, national plans become more feasible to implement when there are clear priorities. Achieving both objectives has sometimes proved difficult, the study shows.

Making Development Sustainable: The World Bank Group and the Environment, a detailed review of World Bank environmental activities in fiscal 1994, was published in early fiscal 1995.

An important element of the support ESD provides the Bank's operational departments in delivering assistance of good quality to the Bank's borrowers is the promotion of "best practices." Best-practices papers, which build on completed policy papers, are drawn from ESD's operational support work and from rapidly accumulating experience as developing countries endeavor to put policies into practice. They are brief, practical, and driven by real-world successes and failures. During fiscal 1994, examples include the initiation of the Agricultural Technology News series—consisting of four-page notes written specifically for operational task managers on recent technological developments in specific branches of agriculture—and the continuation and expansion of the Infrastructure Notes series. Technical papers on topics as diverse as air pollution from motor vehicles, experience with lending for railways, urban infrastructure and productivity, and sectoral indicators for housing were also completed.

The sectoral indicators for housing have been developed collaboratively with the United Nations Centre for Human Settlements under the Housing Indicators Programs (HIP). The indicators reflect the interests of all key stakeholders in the sector (end users, suppliers, financiers, and governments) and cover factors as diverse as the price of housing, homelessness, quality, production, investment, interest rates for mortgages, the importance of housing finance within the overall financial system, subsidies, and taxes. They have been collected in fifty-three countries at every level of economic development and have been used within the Bank to evaluate priorities for policy reform and lending in a number of countries. Several borrower countries (Hungary and the Philippines, for example), with assistance from the HIP, have developed housing indicators as a tool for evaluating housing policies and programs at both the local and national level and for monitoring the performance of the sector on a continuing basis. Drawing on the successful experience of the HIP, sectoral performance indicators are now being extended to other urban subsectors, including local government finance and services, water supply and sanitation, urban environment, and urban transport.

Evidence exists that the failure to pay sufficient attention to social factors in development can jeopardize the effectiveness of Bank-supported programs and projects. The social dimensions of development are especially important in dealing with environmental and social issues. It is increasingly recognized that problems can be diagnosed and solutions implemented only through the development and application of the tools of social analysis. To bridge the social-dimension gap, preparation of a Participation Sourcebook was begun during the past year.

The sourcebook, which builds on the findings of a three-year learning program funded by the Swedish International Development Authority, is being prepared in a participatory manner, drawing upon contributions of more than 200 Bank staff and external advisers. The sourcebook will be a loose-leaf action guide, providing Bank operational staff with key questions they should ask; best-practice answers to tackle these questions; brief case studies; and available resources. In addition to the sourcebook, ESD has also prepared a document providing guidance on social assessment (SA). The SA draws on best practice from a number of areas. Its objectives are to (a) identify key stakeholders and provide an appropriate framework for their participation in Bank-assisted operations; (b) ensure that project objectives and incentives for change are acceptable to those the project is intended to benefit; (c) assess the social impact of projects and minimize adverse impacts, if any; and (d) develop capacity at the appropriate level to enable participation and to carry out proposed activities. Both the guidelines and sourcebook will be elaborated upon and improved as practical experience is gained.

Training and Seminars. A key element of the work program of the ESD vice presidency is the training that it provides Bank staff on a range of topics to support operational work and help improve project implementation. During the past year forty-eight training courses were given. In addition, seminars, workshops, and study tours were organized, with participation by experts in their fields from outside the Bank. Thus, the Bank cosponsored—with the United Nations Development Programme (UNDP) and the Rockefeller Foundation—a workshop (held in Bangkok) on integrated pest management and biotechnology. Similarly, an irrigation seminar/study tour in Mexico, concentrating on the successful experience there with promotion of water-users' associations, brought together Bank staff with irrigation specialists from both developed and developing countries.

Direct Operational Support. A central objective of the Environmentally Sustainable Development vice presidency is to help the Bank's operational departments achieve the full integration of environmental considerations—with state-of-the-art technical, social, and economic approaches—in their project designs (appropriate to local ecosystems and country conditions) with the objective of long-term sustainability. Operational support activities are viewed as opportunities to explore systematically new

approaches and build up knowledge step-by-step in a process of structured learning.

For example, the Russia Farm Transformation Study involved setting up an apparatus for farm surveys to monitor changes in farm organization; training of staff of the collaborating local institution in farm-survey techniques, data processing, and analytical methods; and producing an up-to-date picture of the situation in the farm sector. The capacity-building aspects of this task are already bearing fruit, as the collaborating institution is now conducting a follow-up survey with very little supervision. Furthermore, the work served as a model for a similar study under way that deals with Ukraine.

Protecting the Global Environment. The ESD vice presidency leads the Bank's efforts to address critical global issues affecting the environment, agriculture, and infrastructure and to follow up on the strategic agenda that emerged from UNCED. A part of this work emerges from the Global Environment Facility (GEF).

The GEF was established as a pilot program in 1991 to act as a mechanism for international cooperation for the purpose of providing new and additional grant and concessional funding to meet the incremental costs of measures to achieve agreed global environmental benefits in four focal areas: climate change, biological diversity, international waters, and ozone-layer depletion. The agreed incremental costs of activities concerning land degradation, primarily desertification and deforestation, as they relate to the four focal areas, are also eligible for funding. Day-to-day operation of the facility is shared among the UNDP, UNEP, and the Bank. In addition to providing administrative support to the GEF secretariat, the Bank performs two principal functions: as trustee of a new trust fund and as one of the implementing agencies.

During its pilot phase, 115 projects, valued at more than $733 million, had been endorsed by GEF participants, of which sixty-eight (worth $471 million) had received final clearance. Forty-two percent of the facility's resources had been allocated to biodiversity projects, 40 percent to climate-change projects, 17 percent to international waters projects, and 1 percent to ozone projects.

In March 1994, more than eighty industrialized and developing countries agreed to restructure and replenish the GEF. Twenty-six countries, including several developing countries, pledged more than $2 billion to the GEF's core fund (the GEF Trust Fund) over the next three years. The eight principles that serve as the basis for the restructured facility may be found on page 51 of the World Bank's *Annual Report* for fiscal year 1993.

After fifteen months of negotiations, the participants settled on a "double majority" voting system in a thirty-two-member council to protect the interests of both donor and recipient countries. This requires approval by a 60 percent majority of all member countries, as well as approval by donors representing at least 60 percent of contributions. The council will operate by consensus, using votes only in exceptional circumstances. The restructured and replenished GEF represents an innovative mechanism for international cooperation. As one of the GEF implementing agencies, the Bank has a special responsibility to assist countries in integrating their actions to protect the global environment with their national development strategies. One aspect of this is for the Bank to ensure that where it is responsible for GEF-financed activities linked to Bank-assisted projects, the GEF component is fully integrated with the project and is not seen simply as an add-on.

In December 1992, GEF participants requested an independent evaluation of the pilot phase of the facility to guide future planning. Reflecting the organizational structure of the GEF, the evaluation was conducted under the oversight of senior evaluation managers from each of the implementing agencies, with the Bank's Operations Evaluation Department providing the secretariat. An independent panel of experts provided strategic guidance and validated the methodology and approach used for the evaluation.

The resulting evaluation study, *The Global Environment Facility: Independent Evaluation of the Pilot Phase*, published jointly by the UNDP, UNEP, and the Bank in May 1994, advocated some fundamental changes. These include articulating more clearly the GEF's mandate, goals, and strategies; addressing deficiencies in meeting the GEF's global focus; improving the capacities and procedures of implementing agencies for managing the portfolio; and increasing NGO, country, and community-level participation.

The vice president for ESD also serves as chairman of the Consultative Group on International Agricultural Research (CGIAR), an informal association of forty-two public and private sector donors that supports a network of eighteen international agricultural research centers.[15] The Bank is a cosponsor of the together with the Food and Agricul- nization of the UN (FAO) and the

ters pursue a research agenda agreed he donors on the recommendations of

an independent Technical Advisory Committee, after a careful review of the global challenges, the work of other institutions, and the centers' proposed programs. The CGIAR is widely considered as an outstanding success. The past contribution of its research centers to reducing hunger and poverty is demonstrable. Following a recent realignment of research programs, the centers are committed to grappling with today's challenges to sustainable agriculture, food security, and poverty reduction.

At the mid term meeting that took place in New Delhi in late May 1994, proposals for revitalizing the CGIAR system were endorsed. The proposals aim at stabilizing the system's financial system and halting the erosion of its scientific capacity; refocusing the research agenda on approved programs; improving governance and reforming management with a view to ensuring predictability, transparency, and accountability; linking the CGIAR's programs with participatory programs at the farm level; and developing an action plan and an eighteen-month timetable designed to secure government endorsement of the new strategy.

In the area of finances, members of the group stressed their commitment in support of the $270 million core research agenda. To this end, it was decided to redirect funding of activities in the complementary program to the core program, and a proposal by the three cosponsors to launch a one-time financial supplement brought indications of support of at least $10 million in additional pledges for 1994. The World Bank is considering matching additional donor core funding with an extra contribution on a 1:2 basis, up to a maximum of $10 million annually, for both 1994 and 1995.

To ensure transparency, accountability, and predictability of finances, the CGIAR will move toward a new program-budgeting system. The system will clearly identify the relative role of CGIAR centers in undertaking research programs within the context of a global research agenda implemented by industrialized countries, international agricultural research centers, the national agricultural research systems of developing countries, and nongovernmental organizations. The 1995 program and budgets will be presented in a form that facilitates the move towards the new approach.

---

[15] There will be sixteen centers in 1995 following the creation of a new single institutional entity for livestock research, which would comprise the existing International Livestock Centre for Africa and the International Laboratory for Research on Animal Diseases, and the merger of the International Network for the Improvement of Banana and Plantain with the International Board on Plant Genetic Resources.

The Russian Federation became the forty-second member of the group at the New Delhi meeting, and South Africa attended for the first time as an observer.

Outreach. Reliance on policy studies, best-practices papers, and other reports and studies for the dissemination of ESD's intellectual output is increasingly being supplemented by briefer specialized newsletters that are circulated widely ("Urban Age," "ENV Dissemination Notes," and "Forestry Newsletter," for example), as well as by informal workshops, seminars, and symposia aimed at enhancing collaboration with other agencies. Examples of the latter included involvement in the Dutch Ministerial Conference on "Drinking Water and Environmental Sanitation: Implementing Agenda 21" and continuing collaboration with the bilateral aid agencies of Denmark and Sweden on water resources-management issues.

The First Annual ESD Conference (September 30–October 1, 1993), convened at the Bank's headquarters, focused mainly on the question of properly identifying the costs and benefits of alternative uses of natural resources. The hundreds of experts attending the talks also looked at the growing need for better management in the face of worsening shortages and increasing pollution.

The conference yielded a rich discussion of some of today's cutting-edge environmental challenges. Its purpose was not, however, to look for a perfect solution to the world's environmental problems; instead, it set out to change the processes by which solutions are identified by involving people and focusing on the environment while promoting economic development.

ESD also organized a Conference on Actions to Reduce Hunger Worldwide (November 30–December 1, 1993). The inspiration for the conference came from a twenty-three-day fast earlier in the year by United States Congressman Tony Hall to raise public awareness about the growing scourge of hunger. The conference, which was planned in collaboration with other multilateral development agencies and NGOs from both the developing and industrialized world, aimed at strengthening global efforts to reduce hunger.

The Bank announced at the conference its willingness to work with other donors to fund credit organizations that offer very small loans to the very poor as part of an overall program to empower them to take control of their lives. The program is similar to several successful programs in the developing world such as the Grameen Bank of Bangladesh, the Badan Kredit Kecamatan of Indonesia, the micro-

enterprise credit programs sponsored by the International Fund for Agricultural Development (IFAD), and the Freedom from Hunger Campaign. An immediate grant of $2 million was extended by the Bank to the Grameen Bank to help cover the start-up costs of the Grameen Trust for the first year of its operations. The grant is separate from the World Bank's normal loans and credits, which are made only to governments or involve a government guarantee.

The $2 million allocation to the Grameen Trust is indicative of the Bank's commitment to directly support action-oriented programs that target the reduction of poverty and the alleviation of hunger. Other agencies have already contributed to the trust, and the Bank's modest contribution reinforces the institution's intent to join donors and other partners to explore programs that address the credit and savings needs of the self-employed poor and to support institutions whose aim is to help those who are in the greatest need. The Grameen Trust was founded by the president of the Grameen Bank, Mohammed Yunus, one of the speakers at the conference.

Other speakers included Boutros Boutros-Ghali, secretary general of the United Nations; Ketumile Masire, president of Botswana; former United States president Jimmy Carter (in his capacity as a leader of the Carter Center, a nongovernmental organization); World Bank president Lewis Preston; and Congressman Hall.

Lending operations. In fiscal 1994, lending in support of environmentally sustainable development totaled $10,203 million, or 49 percent of total Bank lending. Some $6,835 million of the investments were supported by IBRD loans, while $3,368 million were supported by IDA credits.

Eight projects with primarily environmental objectives, involving commitments of $748 million, were approved. Seventeen projects contained significant environmental components that advanced the green agenda (ten projects, $742 million) and the brown agenda (seven projects, $913.6 million).[16]

Lending in support of agriculture and natural-resource development totaled $3,907 million for forty-six projects; transportation lending amounted to $3,293 million (twenty-five projects); fifteen investments in the urban

---

[16] In fiscal 1994, "environment" was formally included as a sector. To be so classified, a project must primarily address one of four concerns: environmental institutional development, natural resources management, pollution control/waste management, and resettlement.

development sector amounted to $1,279 million; and commitments totaling $975 million (ten projects) were made in the water supply and sewerage sector.

Financial and Private Sector Development

During fiscal 1994, the World Bank Group— the World Bank, the International Finance Corporation (IFC), and the Multilateral Investment Guarantee Agency (MIGA)—stepped up its support to developing countries to expand their private sectors and build up their financial sectors. The objective is to enhance their prospects for growth and to make their economies responsive enough to compete in today's fast-moving global economy. The Bank Group's support for private sector development and privatization also helped governments reduce their responsibilities and fiscal burdens— freeing them to focus on poverty and the environment.

As last year's *Annual Report* noted, the Bank Group is looking for ways to understand the dynamics of the environment affecting private sector development. It is also forging links among local institutions critical to creating a vibrant environment for business. And it is learning from—and disseminating—successful country experiences in implementing reforms.

Contributing to much of this work is the Bank's new central vice presidency for finance and private sector development (FPD), which, during fiscal 1994, completed its staffing and organizational set-up. Bank Group operations and activities in support of private sector development focused on three main areas:

• effectively supporting private sector development through an increasing range of actions;

• better dissemination of knowledge; and

• experimenting with innovative ideas.

Supporting Private Sector Development. The Bank is fostering the private sector throughout the developing world in a variety of ways. World Bank adjustment loans and credits, for example, help produce a competitive and attractive business environment, as well as help reform in the financial sector. In addition, the Bank Group is supporting about $25 billion worth of private investment annually. The Bank's financial intermediation loans of about $1.5 billion a year support $4 billion in private sector investment; the IFC—through its loans, equity, and credit lines—provides about $2.5 billion a year, and with a much bigger multiplier of about 7 to 1, supports approximately $18 billion worth of investment; and MIGA's guarantee operations are currently running at about $400 million a year, supporting about $3 billion in private sector investments. That $25 billion represents about 10 percent of private investment by enterprises in developing countries.

Support for operations. In its efforts to help develop more vibrant and competitive private sectors, a central concern of FPD has been to improve the quality and effectiveness of Bank operations—the focus of more than two thirds of FPD's resources. Activities during the past year have included support to country teams for better design and execution of projects, more and better staff training, better programs of technical assistance, increased networking with "best-practice" innovators throughout the world, and enhanced dissemination of knowledge and best practices to Bank staff and borrowers.

As was highlighted at a seminar on finance and private sector development for the Bank's executive board in March 1994, with governments everywhere reexamining their role in development and reorienting public sector activities to maximize efficiency, the private sector is increasingly being asked to help meet their development priorities. At the same time, today's worldwide trade and business patterns imply a higher competitiveness threshold and much higher standards of responsiveness for government institutions and firms alike.

Accepting this reality requires a fundamental change in what governments do and in the way they relate to the private sector. It means that governments have to move away from controlled, inward-looking economies to competitive, outward-looking ones. And it means that firms have to move from courting the state for special privileges to courting the markets for profits.

Governments thus have to establish a competitive environment, a legal and regulatory system that can support the market, and institutions that can help firms upgrade their capabilities. They have to move from being owners and operators to being competent regulators and partners.

During fiscal 1994 the Bank Group continued to help its borrowing countries intensify their efforts in privatizing publicly owned enterprises, redesigning regulatory frameworks, and, more generally, developing an attractive business environment. By the end of the fiscal year the Bank and the IFC jointly had virtually completed seventeen private sector assessments. Their findings have been disseminated through seminars and workshops with a view to assisting governments develop solutions in consultation with the private sector. The reports themselves, however, have typically presented the Bank Group's own diagnosis and recommendations to the governments concerned as a means of assisting them in their policy formulation on private sector development-related issues. The recommendations of these assessments have helped the Bank's country-assistance strategy and lending program (see Box 3-3). Over the past few years, almost three of every four Bank-supported adjustment operations have included components that helped establish competitive markets and an environment to support the development of a successful private sector. There has also been an increasing effort to generate the institutions fundamental to the development of competitive and responsive markets—customs and tax, technology, technical education, and standards and patents institutions, for example.

Privatization remained a central focus of the Bank Group's and FPD's assistance to a geographical cross-section of member countries during fiscal year 1994. Many initiatives were aimed at establishing the institutional framework for privatization in such a way as to facilitate efficient, timely, and transparent divestitures. Major programs were undertaken in a range of economies, from larger (Turkey) to smaller (Bolivia and Fiji). The targets for divestiture included the sale of small businesses and shops, medium-sized and large enterprises in the tradable sector, and public utilities. The IFC has taken an active role in technical assistance for privatization in Russia, helping to develop suitable methods built around an easily

---

Box 3-3. Private Sector Assessments

To sharpen the focus of its work on private sector development, the Bank introduced in fiscal 1992 a new element in its program of economic and sector work—the private sector assessment. As of June 30, 1994, seventeen assessments had been completed (of which ten were completed during the past year). Six additional assessments are currently under preparation, and fourteen more are expected to be started and completed during the next two years.

These assessments differ from other Bank economic and sector work in that they involve the formal cooperation of the IFC. This cooperation has had several beneficial effects: It helps focus assessments tightly on those elements of the business environment that directly affect private business activity, and it permits the Bank to take advantage of the IFC's considerable transactions experience in the private sector. Cooperation also helps ensure that the Bank and the IFC pursue consistent private sector development strategies and that the country dialogue, economic and sector work, and lending operations reflect joint Bank/IFC concerns.

In general, a well-formulated private sector assessment describes the structure of the private sector in a given country, identifies the key constraints to its development, and lays out economically efficient ways for the country to remove those constraints.

The exact content of a private sector assessment depends largely on other economic and sector work that has been prepared for a country. Typically, this work would:

• set out the major macroeconomic issues facing the private sector and discuss how trade barriers and price distortions might lead the private sector to make investments that are not conducive to growth;

• discuss the merits of different public investments and expenditures, suggesting economically efficient changes in spending and raising possibil-

ities for the private provision of infrastructure and services that are currently being provided by the government; and

• report on the entities in the financial sector and explore how well the sector offers access to credit to the business community.

When these areas are not covered in economic and sector work, they are covered by a private sector assessment. Typically, however, a private sector assessment focuses more on the business environment. How is business regulated? What are the costs of excessive regulation? Are monopolies and anti-competitive practices properly regulated? Does the state supply its public services efficiently? Does the legal system permit the writing of loan contracts that cover important economic transactions? Does it permit these contracts to be enforced?

Private sector assessments have turned up several broad areas of interest.

• Many high-payoff returns have come from small and uncontroversial changes in practice that, nonetheless, have caused private sector activity to take off.

• Private sector assessments have helped focus the Bank's other economic and sector work more sharply on private sector development concerns.

• Recently completed surveys of private enterprises that assess the institutional and policy framework that governs private sector activity indicate that among the regulatory constraints that businesses face, tax and labor regulations are the most burdensome. Surveys have found regulatory compliance costs to be high—in one instance, taking up as much as 26 percent of senior management time.

• Failure of public infrastructure is a large problem. Infrastructure problems tend to be sector specific, although larger firms in any sector are better able to bear the costs of infrastructure failure than smaller firms.

replicated open voucher process. The IFC's assistance began with model approaches for privatizing small-scale enterprises and then truck transport, followed by voucher privatization of medium and large-scale enterprises. The Bank Group has also continued to play a central role in the design and implementation of mass privatization schemes aimed at introducing sweeping ownership changes in such transition economies as Kazakhstan, the Kyrgyz Republic, Moldova, Russia, and Ukraine. Work is also under way—in many of these transition economies and in Latin America—to devise and implement programs to support the growth and sustainability of recently privatized enterprises.

The Bank's traditional agenda in dealing with state infrastructure monopolies was to expand the network, introduce new technology, and strengthen operating entities. The emphasis was on least-cost design, efficient procurement, and the financial and managerial autonomy of operating entities. For this, the main instruments were Bank investment loans and the use of the ECO—expanded cofinancing operations—program.

In today's world, the move toward increasing private participation in infrastructure is driven by dissatisfaction with the performance of state-owned and state-operated infrastructure enterprises. At the same time, government finances are precarious, while investment needs are on the order of $200 billion a year. And technical change is making it possible for smaller scales to be economical—and private.

Seeking greater efficiency and better value for money, regulatory reforms can facilitate competition by unbundling potentially competitive activities (electric power generation and distribution) from less competitive activities (power transmission).

Where full-fledged competition is absent, complementary regulation aimed at protecting the public interest can improve efficiency. New approaches to regulation are evolving, too—aimed at improving incentives for cost control and technical innovation. The choice of the right regulatory approach is complex, and while some are better than others, there is no best scheme for all circumstances. Much depends on each industry's structure and each country's institutional and civil service capacity.

Private sector financing of infrastructure is growing fast, although it is still fairly small. Both the number of countries and subsectors involved have expanded significantly. Apart from power and telecommunications, private participation in infrastructure is entering areas such as airports, railways, ports, toll roads, and water supply and treatment. The IFC's investments in this sector have risen sharply in recent years. The corporation's infrastructure operations for fiscal 1994 were in excess of $550 million in terms of net financing ($1.29 billion gross), for about $5 billion worth of projects. These figures represent an increase of 80 percent to 90 percent over fiscal 1993 figures.

Telecommunications is a good example. As was highlighted at a joint Bank-IFC seminar on telecommunications for the executive board in February 1994, developing countries must invest about $30 billion a year just to provide the basic infrastructure to sustain economic growth and meet current demand. Even with the support of the Bank Group and other official lenders, there is at least a $20 billion gap in financing—a gap that only the private sector can fill.

To mobilize such amounts of private capital, more and more developing countries are undertaking broad reforms in telecommunications. The time for this is propitious. Rapid technological change, declining costs, and good potential for fast growth—unparalleled in other sectors—open the way to a range of ownership and management structures.

The Bank Group is supporting these reforms by acting as agent of change and using a widening range of Bank, IFC, and MIGA instruments to attract private capital and management. Under joint approaches of the three institutions, flexible packages of technical assistance, lending, investment, and guarantees are being tailored to individual country situations.

The Bank's work on energy during fiscal 1994 focused on energy efficiency, energy sector restructuring and regulation, private sector involvement, gas trade, rural energy, household fuels, and renewable energy sources—with particular emphasis on the analysis and mitigation of environmental impacts. FPD continued its analysis of success factors in energy-efficiency programs—with a view to designing better country-specific and market-based approaches for improving energy efficiency on both the supply and demand sides. Various initiatives assisted sectoral reforms in key countries. The Bank encouraged cross-fertilization through technical assistance, seminars, and workshops for policymakers, notably in Brazil, China, India, and several countries of Central and Eastern Europe and the former Soviet Union.

The Bank strengthened its work on natural gas, which is abundant and environmentally clean. The challenges have to do with the distance of many gas fields from the market and

---

Box 3-4. Managing Energy

The joint UNDP/Bank Energy Sector Management Assistance Programme (ESMAP) was established in the early 1980s to assess the effects in developing countries of dramatic changes in energy prices. With the help of more than a dozen donors, it now focuses mainly on sector restructuring, regulation, energy efficiency, and household fuels, as well as on institution building and policy advice in selected countries. ESMAP's activities, integrated into the Bank's Industry and Energy Department, are often vital complements or preconditions to Bank operations and bilateral aid programs.

In fiscal 1994, ESMAP focused on assisting developing countries as they embark on "second generation" energy strategies, often linked to broad economic reforms. During this phase, traditional technical assistance activities take place in conjunction with the implementation of major economic reforms—including restructuring and regulatory adjustments, price and tariff revisions—and new investment programs that increasingly embody environmental concerns.

During the past year, ESMAP assisted countries such as Bolivia, India, Morocco, and Poland in planning and carrying out a restructuring of key segments of their energy sector. ESMAP household and rural energy activities, one of the program's long-term strengths, continued vigorously in Bolivia, Chad, India, Jamaica, Mali, Rwanda, and Viet Nam. Similarly, energy efficiency and conservation efforts, including institution and local capacity-building work and training in demand-side management, have been a major feature of ESMAP work in Brazil, China, Pakistan, Tanzania, Zimbabwe, and elsewhere. Oil and gas activities remained important in countries such as Mozambique and Morocco, as well as in several Central and Eastern European countries that have substantially underused capacities and an urgent need for reliable and clean energy sources. In this respect, trade issues associated with the development and use of natural gas resources are an area of particular emphasis for ESMAP's present and future activities.

---

the difficulty of transporting the gas. During the year, Bank work focused on improving the regulatory framework and on supporting new projects for transporting gas to the markets—in such countries as Argentina, Bolivia, and Pakistan.

FPD continued to administer the joint UNDP/World Bank Energy Sector Management Assistance Programme (ESMAP), now supported by fifteen bilateral donors. The program provides technical assistance to help developing countries implement key policy reforms for making the energy sector more efficient and ensuring that investments in the sector make the most use of scarce domestic and external resources (see Box 3-4).

In the realm of financial systems and capital markets, experience shows that when a banking system is in crisis, strong measures are required at several levels. At the broader level of the banks' business environment, three types of action are necessary. First, the macroeconomic environment has to be improved, and enterprises restructured so they become healthy, productive borrowers. Second, the interest-rate regime and the schemes that provide targeted, subsidized credit need reform. Third, the financial infrastructure, including the legal, accounting, and regulatory framework, needs to be upgraded.

Because the financial health of banks determines the quality of resource allocation in an economy, a principal focus of the World Bank has been to help strengthen banking institu-

tions and their environments. Through financial sector adjustment loans and similar operations, the Bank is working with borrowing countries to build better systems of prudential bank regulation and transparent accounting. Supervision has been strengthened to ensure that reasonable standards of bank capital are maintained—along with the management capacity necessary to see that it is effectively deployed. Assistance has also been delivered directly to banks, through capacity-building operations and financial restructuring to strengthen their ability to respond to effective enterprise demand for investment capital.

Bank restructuring has become a frequent component of Bank operations. It aims at isolating and tackling the nonperforming assets of the banking sector. Bank management and procedures also need reform to prevent the reemergence of subsequent asset problems. Once the banks are overhauled, it is vital to strengthen durably the institutions and processes of bank supervision and regulation so that a recurrence of asset problems is forestalled. Because the process of bank restructuring is long and arduous, it is vital that Bank supervision of associated loans be intensive for several years. Without intensive supervision, it is unlikely the process of reform will maintain sufficient momentum and avoid a relapse.

If banking intermediaries are in good health, the Bank and the IFC can usefully lend through them. Financial intermediary lending, an important instrument for the Bank in achieving its developmental objectives, can be very effective in reaching several classes of borrowers (small industry, farmers, the housing market, municipalities, and infrastructure developers). This lending is a means for the Bank Group to deliver to borrowers the benefit of its excellent credit standing in global financial markets. And as the reform and restructuring efforts of financial sector adjustment loans bear fruit—and financial intermediaries begin to function efficiently in a sound business environment—financial intermediation lending may well again emerge as an important part of the Bank's lending activities, complementing the IFC's successful credit line activities. Market pricing of such financial intermediation loans is essential in all cases.

The Bank and the IFC are also engaged in a variety of capital-market development activities. Complementing the IFC's long-standing work with capital markets in developing countries, the Bank is concentrating on the broader issues—such as regulation, institutional investment capacity, and contractual saving schemes. This work typically includes the promotion of credit transparency through such channels as independent rating agencies and the development of simple, standardized securities, such as bank debentures. The Bank and the IFC have collaborated closely in capital-market development in Mexico, where a joint Bank-IFC-Inter-American Development Bank team worked on the design of promising structures for a private infrastructure-financing facility.

The Bank's role in developing capital markets has depended on the needs and capabilities of its borrowers. In the weaker economies and in the transition economies, the Bank has focused primarily on the provision of basic financial services and the creation of sound banking intermediaries. For many borrowers, the Bank has focused on developmental lending through financial intermediaries—if their health was assured. For sophisticated borrowers, including many larger borrowers such as Argentina and Mexico, the Bank has been active in providing assistance to promote capital markets. The Bank's resources have also helped strengthen the capacity of governments to promote acceptance and liquidity for securities backed by creditworthy issuers, which might otherwise be unmarketable as a result of concerns about broad economic policy and performance.

Better dissemination of knowledge. One of FPD's main responsibilities is to enhance the Bank's role in the realms of knowledge, policy advice, and dissemination of best practices in the area of financial and private sector devel-opment. The Bank's work in these areas undergirds its financial role. With its repository of research, knowledge, and information about development—and with its unique global reach—the Bank is increasingly becoming a knowledge-based institution. The global economy is increasingly driven by knowledge—by ideas, relationships, and innovations. And value added and comparative advantage now come as much from these factors as from raw materials, labor, or capital.

As countries move up the development ladder, their ability to compete and integrate into world markets moves beyond knowing *what* to do to knowing *how* to do it. The Bank is thus doing more as a collector and disseminator of best practices and innovations for meeting the broad array of requirements to compete in world markets.

FPD has actively disseminated knowledge about best practices through conferences, seminars, and training programs, often held in collaboration with the IFC. In fiscal 1994, FPD held sixty seminars and training sessions, providing more than 1,800 person-days of training to Bank staff (largely on private sector development) and 2,000 person-days to external participants (largely on financial sector development, industry, and energy). The Bank's six regional vice presidencies, the IFC, and MIGA also organized similar events, covering a broad array of topics.

In May 1994 an innovative Bank seminar on international experience in restructuring the coal industry drew government officials from a broad range of ministries in Russia, as well as industry experts. In addition, a June 1994 conference, "Development, Environment, and Mining: Enhancing the Contribution of the Mineral Industry to Sustainable Development"—cosponsored by various international organizations and attended by 300 government, industry, and NGO representatives two thirds of them from developing countries—covered issues related to mining activities and the preservation of the environment.

The Bank and the IFC have forged informal and formal ties with a range of trade groups, commercial enterprises, business-promotion agencies, multilateral organizations, and NGOs to bring new ideas to the Bank, build public support, and initiate joint programs.

The Bank has also begun holding industry-by-industry roundtables to create an environment for dialogue and problem solving. A series of workshops and roundtables on the private provision of power supply was conducted with producers, regulators, donors, government representatives, and developing country operators. These fora helped foster a broad dialogue, allowed the Bank to listen to experts from outside, and facilitated a consensus on the agenda for moving ahead. In the oil and gas sector, the Bank has sponsored workshops and conferences for investors and host countries to develop better understanding of gas trade and markets, and of opportunities for investment. It has also used these fora as a means of disseminating experience and best practices. In the same spirit, the Bank and the IFC worked with the government of Morocco and the private sector on developing options for attaining quickly a higher threshold of competitiveness. As a follow up to this work, the Moroccan government hosted a major seminar in early June 1994 with the private sector on ways to improve the business environment and compete in global markets.

Experimenting with Innovative Ideas. During the past year, the Bank intensified its *work on renewable energy alternatives*, working with countries, representatives from the energy industry, and NGOs. The objectives are to identify and prepare solar energy projects suitable for financing by the Global Environment Facility and other funding sources—and to encourage collaboration among countries in research and development and in demonstration projects.

The Bank has also been active in developing *new types of lending assistance* to support the increased role of the private sector in the provision of public services.

To support domestic bond markets, the Bank has designed catalytic operations that create a bridge between institutional investors (pension funds, insurance carriers, mutual funds) and the need for long-term funds for enterprises and infrastructure. This will enhance the sustainability of the financial system in borrowing countries and reduce the heavy reliance on foreign exchange.

A capital-market development project in Argentina broke new ground by finding effective ways of fostering the growth of local market institutions. The $500 million Capital Market Development Project, approved in March 1994, will help prime-rated commercial banks overcome longer-term funding constraints through a backstop facility that would ensure them a source of continued funding at predetermined financial costs.

In principle, the project could have been structured as a Bank guarantee or as a loan fully disbursed into an escrow account, rather than as a loan with disbursement contingent on market conditions. The form of the Bank's credit extension was not crucial. The product innovation lay in the creation of the facility and its associated fund—and its potential for helping local market institutions to grow. The project also says much about the Bank's willingness to change. It would disburse against financial assets rather than goods and services; it is supporting market development as its principal objective; and it is focusing not on Bank disbursements but on facilitating market flows and creating confidence.

There was also a Bank effort to expand financial intermediation lending by developing a new format, using the better intermediaries in countries, with as light a structure as possible. The $120 million Private Investment Credit Project for Tunisia, approved in December 1993, epitomizes the new approach. Under the old approach, the Bank would have insisted on an elaborate structure for apex operations and on close monitoring of all lending decisions. Now, most lending decisions are up to the intermediaries, whose own capital is at risk.

Small and medium-sized enterprises have an important role in creating jobs. But their special technical, marketing, and financial needs have proved difficult to meet in a cost-effective way. To move forward on this, the Bank has been working with four NGOs with strong track records in delivering credit schemes. The repayment rates of many of these schemes have been high (90 percent to 99 percent), but their transaction costs have also been high—primarily to cover their start-up costs and the technical assistance needs of their borrowers. The Bank has been helping these NGOs devise sustainable and replicable programs, obtain donor finance, and disseminate the results of their efforts. The Bank has also engaged governments in policy and institutional issues that affect small and medium-sized enterprises. In this capacity, it acts as a broker and partner to help NGOs extend the reach and effectiveness of their programs.

Section Four
World Bank Operations: Fiscal Year 1994

World Bank (IBRD and IDA combined) commitments to countries during fiscal year 1994 totaled $20,836 million, down $2,860 million from the previous year.

The decrease was accounted for principally by a sharp decrease in commitments from the IBRD—from $16,945 million in fiscal 1993 to $14,244 million. IDA commitments, at $6,592 million, were only marginally below fiscal year 1993's $6,751 million amount. One project, for $30 million, in the Occupied Territories was approved. It was funded by the $50 million Trust Fund for Gaza, which had been approved by the executive directors in the first half of fiscal 1994.

Shortfalls in the IBRD's lending program, as compared with the budget, which set indicative IBRD lending at between $17 billion and $19.5 billion, were particularly sharp in Latin America and the Caribbean, in the Middle East and North Africa (where the lending program in Algeria has suffered), and in South Asia, particularly in India. Increases occurred in East Asia and Pacific (up $219 million) and Africa (up $81 million).

The number of IBRD and IDA operations approved in fiscal 1994—228—was slightly lower than the previous year's 245. One hundred twenty-four IBRD operations were approved, as opposed to 122 in fiscal 1993. The lending-instrument "mix" in fiscal 1994 showed an increase in investment operations, which could not compensate, in volume terms, for the larger size of a typical adjustment loan.

The largest borrower of IBRD funds was China ($2,145 million for eight projects), followed by Mexico ($1,530 million for five projects), and Russia ($1,520 million for six projects). The three largest borrowers of IDA credits were China ($925 million for six projects), India ($835 million for six projects), and Bangladesh ($597 million for three projects).

The sector with the largest number of approved projects was agriculture (forty-six projects), followed by transportation (twenty-five projects) and "multisector," which includes support for reform programs and emergency imports (twenty-two projects).

Adjustment lending, at $2,425 million, accounted for 12 percent of the World Bank's fiscal 1994 portfolio ($510 million, or 4 percent, for the IBRD; $1,915 million, or 29 percent, for IDA). In fiscal 1993, adjustment lending amounted to slightly more than $4,000 million ($2,645 million for the IBRD and $1,363 million for IDA), or 17 percent of that year's portfolio. To a certain extent, the decline in adjustment lending has been purposeful, especially in Latin America, where the transition from adjustment to lending operations is well under way, and in the Middle East and North Africa region, where no further adjustment operations are currently being planned for Egypt, Morocco, and Tunisia.

In addition, the explosive increase, to $177 billion net, during 1993 of capital flows to developing countries eliminated, in some cases (India, for example), the balance-of-payments justification for adjustment lending.

The principal reason for the turnaround in private flows has been the economic policy reforms of developing countries, especially privatization, fiscal consolidation, greater openness to trade, reduction of commercial bank debt overhangs, domestic price liberalization, and market-oriented reform. To an unquantifiable extent, the World Bank has helped to foster the environment that has allowed these flows to increase through its support of policy reform.

It cannot be assumed, of course, that $177 billion in flows will continue to find its way to developing countries annually. Some of the money is volatile, and market perceptions, as well as relative returns, will change. One of the risk in the years ahead for the developing countries is the possibility of a substantial decline in these flows and the associated consequences.

Disbursements

The lower level of World Bank lending had its consequence for disbursements, as well, since a substantial part of the reduction in lending was caused by a decline in fast-disbursing adjustment assistance. Gross disbursements to countries by the Bank totaled $15,979 million in

Table 4-1. IBRD and IDA Foreign and Local Disbursements, by Source of Supply

(amounts in millions of US dollars)

Period	IBRD and IDA						
	Foreign[a]		Local		Net advance disbursements[b]		Total amount
	Amount	%	Amount	%	Amount	%	
Cumulative to							
June 30, 1989	85,673	58	58,218	39	3,761	3	147,652
Fiscal 1990	8,883	57	6,099	39	648	4	15,629
Fiscal 1991	8,877	57	6,606	42	184	1	15,667
Fiscal 1992	9,038	55	6,807	42	537	3	16,381
Fiscal 1993	9,813	56	7,887	45	−325	−2	17,375
Fiscal 1994	9,009	56	7,442	47	−473	−3	15,979
Cumulative to							
June 30, 1994	131,294	58	93,059	41	4,331	2	228,684

NOTE: Details may not add to totals because of rounding.

a. Amounts exclude debt reduction disbursements of $2,160 million in FY90, $313 million in FY91, $50 million in FY92, and $515 million in FY93 for IBRD.

b. Net advance disbursements are advances made to special accounts net of amounts recovered (amounts for which the Bank has applied evidence of expenditures to recovery of the outstanding advance).

Table 4-2. IBRD and IDA Foreign Disbursements, by Source of Supply

(amounts in millions of US dollars)

Period	IBRD					IDA				
	OECD		Non-OECD		Total Amount	OECD		Non-OECD		Total Amount
	Amount	%	Amount	%		Amount	%	Amount	%	
Cumulative to										
June 30, 1989	55,468	86	8,846	14	64,314	17,427	82	3,932	18	21,359
Fiscal 1990	5,290	79	1,388	21	6,678	1,491	68	714	32	2,205
Fiscal 1991	4,953	80	1,230	20	6,183	1,802	67	891	33	2,694
Fiscal 1992	5,067	76	1,634	24	6,701	1,515	65	822	35	2,337
Fiscal 1993	5,048	72	1,928	28	6,976	1,784	63	1,052	37	2,837
Fiscal 1994	3,966	73	1,491	27	5,457	2,175	61	1,378	39	3,553
Cumulative to										
June 30, 1994	79,793	83	16,517	17	96,310	26,194	75	8,791	25	34,984

NOTE: Disbursements for debt reduction and net advance disbursements are excluded. Details may not add to totals because of rounding. OECD amounts are based on current OECD membership, excluding Mexico, which became a member in May 1994.

fiscal 1994: $10,447 million by the IBRD and $5,532 million by IDA. In fiscal 1993, gross disbursements by the IBRD and IDA were $12,942 million and $4,947 million, respectively. (The IBRD amount in fiscal 1993 included extraordinary disbursements of $1 billion to Peru when it cleared its arrears.)

Disbursements, by source of supply. Projects financed by the World Bank require procurement from foreign and local sources to achieve project goals. Disbursements are made primarily to cover specific costs for foreign procurement and some local expenditures.

The procurement rules and procedures to be followed in the execution of each project depends on individual circumstances. Three considerations generally guide the Bank's requirements: the need for economy and effi- ciency in the execution of the project; the Bank's interest, as a cooperative institution, in giving all eligible bidders from developing countries and developed countries an opportunity to compete in providing goods and works financed by the Bank; and the Bank's interest, as a development institution, in encouraging the development of local contractors and manufacturers in borrowing countries. In most cases, international competitive bidding is the most effective method of procurement. The Bank prescribes conditions under which preferences may be given to domestic or regional manufacturers and, where appropriate, to domestic contractors. Through the end of fiscal 1994, 58 percent of IBRD and IDA disbursements covered goods and services provided directly by foreign suppliers located outside the

Table 4-3. IBRD and IDA Payments to Suppliers in Active Borrowing Countries for Foreign and Local Procurement in Fiscal 1994
(millions of US dollars)

Borrowing countries	Local procurement	Foreign procurement	Total amount	Percentage of total disbursements[a]
Albania	4	†	4	*
Algeria	46	3	49	0.31
Angola	2	†	2	*
Argentina	173	26	199	1.25
Bahamas, The	†	†	†	*
Bangladesh	128	6	134	0.84
Barbados	1	2	3	*
Belarus	—	†	†	*
Belize	3	—	3	*
Benin	7	2	9	0.05
Bhutan	1	†	1	*
Bolivia	31	1	32	0.20
Botswana	4	2	6	*
Brazil	378	151	529	3.31
Bulgaria	†	16	16	0.10
Burkina Faso	28	1	29	0.18
Burundi	14	†	14	0.09
Cameroon	19	3	22	0.14
Cape Verde	2	†	3	*
Central African Republic	6	†	6	*
Chad	10	*	10	0.06
Chile	78	12	90	0.56
China	1,104	273	1,378	8.62
Colombia	175	6	181	1.14
Comoros	2	*	2	*
Costa Rica	6	6	12	0.08
Côte d'Ivoire	20	41	61	0.38
Croatia	—	11	11	0.07
Cyprus	22	21	43	0.27
Czech Republic	—	27	27	0.17
Djibouti	1	1	2	*
Dominica	—	†	†	*
Dominican Republic	14	2	16	0.10
Ecuador	64	1	65	0.41
Egypt, Arab Republic of	54	6	60	0.37
El Salvador	22	1	23	0.15
Equatorial Guinea	1	5	6	*
Estonia	2	1	3	*
Ethiopia	16	8	24	0.15
Fiji	2	—	2	*
Gabon	4	1	5	*
Gambia, The	4	†	4	*
Ghana	42	3	45	0.28
Guatemala	2	2	3	*
Guinea	17	†	17	0.11
Guinea-Bissau	5	3	8	*
Guyana	3	1	4	*
Honduras	5	1	6	*
Hungary	74	61	135	0.84
India	1,206	133	1,339	8.38
Indonesia	840	36	877	5.49
Iran, Islamic Republic of	22	7	29	0.18
Jamaica	13	†	13	0.08
Jordan	32	3	35	0.22
Kazakhstan	†	†	†	*
Kenya	39	50	90	0.56
Korea, Republic of	165	343	508	3.18
Kyrgyz Republic	6	†	6	*
Lao People's Dem. Rep.	3	12	14	0.09
Latvia	—	2	2	*
Lebanon	3	6	9	0.06
Lesotho	3	†	3	*
Lithuania	6	2	8	0.05

Borrowing countries	Local procurements	Foreign procurements	Total amount	Percentage of total disbursements
Macedonia, FYR	3	†	3	*
Madagascar	25	1	26	0.16
Malawi	25	1	27	0.17
Malaysia	115	27	142	0.89
Maldives	1	—	1	*
Mali	21	†	21	0.13
Mauritania	8	7	15	0.09
Mauritius	2	1	4	*
Mexico	761	32	792	4.96
Moldova	7	†	7	*
Mongolia	†	†	†	*
Morocco	112	2	114	0.72
Mozambique	14	1	15	0.09
Myanmar	1	5	6	*
Nepal	18	2	20	0.12
Nicaragua	7	1	7	*
Niger	10	†	10	0.06
Nigeria	179	156	335	2.10
Oman	2	2	3	*
Pakistan	248	39	287	1.80
Papua New Guinea	16	†	16	0.10
Paraguay	5	3	8	0.05
Peru	†	9	9	0.06
Philippines	229	11	240	1.50
Poland	29	56	85	0.53
Romania	1	15	16	0.10
Russia	4	125	129	0.81
Rwanda	11	†	11	0.07
São Tomé and Principe	3	—	3	*
Senegal	25	11	35	0.22
Seychelles	†	—	†	*
Sierra Leone	3	—	3	*
Slovak Republic	—	2	2	*
Slovenia	6	21	27	0.17
Solomon Islands	1	1	2	*
Sri Lanka	50	9	59	0.37
St. Lucia	†	2	2	*
St. Vincent and the Grenadines	†	†	†	*
Sudan	7	1	9	0.05
Tanzania	25	4	29	0.18
Thailand	92	56	148	0.93
Togo	3	1	4	*
Tonga	†	—	†	*
Trinidad and Tobago	2	16	17	0.11
Tunisia	64	7	70	0.44
Uganda	30	1	30	0.19
Ukraine	—	30	30	0.19
Uruguay	23	11	34	0.22
Vanuatu	†	—	†	*
Venezuela	25	55	80	0.50
Western Samoa	4	—	4	*
Yemen, Republic of	21	1	22	0.13
Zaire	8	6	14	0.09
Zambia	12	5	18	0.11
Zimbabwe	11	24	35	0.22
Total	7,201	2,066	9,267	58

— Zero, † less than $0.5 million, * less than 0.05 percent.

NOTE: Disbursements for debt reduction and net advance disbursements are excluded. Details may not add to totals because of rounding.

a. Refers to the share of all IBRD and IDA payments for fiscal 1994 (excluding disbursements for debt reduction), which totaled $15,979 million.

Table 4-4. **IBRD and IDA Payments to Supplying Countries for Foreign Procurement**
(amounts in millions of US dollars)

Supplying country	IBRD cumulative to June 30, 1994		IBRD fiscal 1994		IDA cumulative to June 30, 1994		IDA fiscal 1994	
	Amount	%	Amount	%	Amount	%	Amount	%
Afghanistan	2	*	†	*	1	*	†	*
Albania	†	*	—	*	†	*	†	*
Algeria	25	*	1	*	11	*	2	0.06
Angola	9	*	†	*	†	*	†	*
Antigua and Barbuda	1	*	†	*	1	*	—	*
Argentina	749	0.78	15	0.28	92	0.26	11	0.31
Australia	1,023	1.06	92	1.69	389	1.11	47	1.31
Austria	1,249	1.30	117	2.14	214	0.61	25	0.72
Bahamas, The	79	0.08	†	*	8	*	†	*
Bahrain	66	0.07	2	*	125	0.36	8	0.21
Bangladesh	13	*	†	*	39	0.11	6	0.16
Barbados	11	*	2	*	4	*	†	*
Belarus	†	*	—	*	†	*	†	*
Belgium	1,435	1.49	45	0.82	929	2.65	70	1.96
Belize	1	*	—	*	6	*	—	*
Benin	3	*	—	*	13	*	2	0.05
Bhutan	†	*	—	*	1	*	†	*
Bolivia	24	*	1	*	3	*	†	*
Botswana	6	*	1	*	7	*	2	*
Brazil	1,680	1.74	87	1.59	310	0.89	64	1.81
Bulgaria	13	*	9	0.17	8	*	7	0.18
Burkina Faso	1	*	†	*	7	*	1	*
Burundi	1	*	—	*	10	*	†	*
Cambodia	1	*	—	*	†	*	—	*
Cameroon	5	*	†	*	20	0.06	3	0.07
Canada	2,203	2.29	115	2.11	646	1.85	69	1.95
Cape Verde	†	*	—	*	†	*	†	*
Central African Republic	2	*	—	*	1	*	—	*
Chad	1	*	—	*	1	*	—	*
Chile	357	0.37	9	0.17	30	0.09	3	0.08
China	1,190	1.24	108	1.88	875	2.50	171	4.80
Colombia	208	0.22	5	0.09	14	*	1	*
Comoros	†	*	—	*	—	*	—	*
Congo	6	*	1	*	8	*	1	*
Costa Rica	31	*	5	0.10	11	*	1	*
Côte d'Ivoire	35	*	†	*	186	0.53	41	1.16
Croatia	13	*	8	0.14	5	*	3	0.09
Cyprus	24	*	2	*	30	0.09	19	0.54
Czech Republic	34	*	25	0.45	3	*	3	0.07
Czechoslovakia[a]	25	*	—	*	3	*	—	*
Denmark	633	0.66	59	1.08	271	0.77	37	1.04
Djibouti	†	*	—	*	23	0.07	1	*
Dominica	3	*	†	*	1	*	—	*
Dominican Republic	6	*	†	*	7	*	2	0.06
Ecuador	113	0.12	1	*	1	*	†	*
Egypt, Arab Republic of	47	*	1	*	28	0.08	5	0.14
El Salvador	18	*	1	*	3	*	†	*
Equatorial Guinea	†	*	—	*	5	*	5	0.14
Estonia	1	*	†	*	1	*	1	*
Ethiopia	1	*	—	*	11	*	8	0.23

Supplying country	IBRD cumulative to June 30, 1994		IBRD fiscal 1994		IDA cumulative to June 30, 1994		IDA fiscal 1994	
	Amount	%	Amount	%	Amount	%	Amount	%
Fiji	†	*	—	*	1	*	—	*
Finland	399	0.41	36	0.66	115	0.33	14	0.41
France	6,773	7.03	400	7.34	3,529	10.09	386	10.86
Gabon	14	*	†	*	10	*	1	*
Gambia, The	3	*	—	*	†	*	†	*
Germany	10,893	11.31	568	10.42	3,190	9.12	197	5.55
Ghana	10	*	1	*	6	*	2	0.07
Greece	182	0.19	7	0.12	64	0.18	8	0.21
Grenada	1	*	—	*	4	*	—	*
Guatemala	17	*	†	*	12	*	1	*
Guinea	3	*	—	*	1	*	†	*
Guinea-Bissau	†	*	†	*	5	*	3	0.08
Guyana	9	*	†	*	1	*	1	*
Haiti	6	*	1	*	4	*	†	*
Honduras	12	*	1	*	2	*	†	*
Hungary	254	0.26	59	1.08	23	0.07	2	0.07
Iceland	8	*	†	*	1	*	†	*
India	327	0.34	28	0.52	624	1.78	105	2.95
Indonesia	145	0.15	10	0.18	71	0.20	27	0.75
Iran, Islamic Republic of	144	0.15	†	*	184	0.53	7	0.21
Iraq	459	0.48	†	*	30	0.08	—	*
Ireland	125	0.13	5	0.08	77	0.22	14	0.38
Israel	230	0.24	16	0.29	87	0.25	10	0.28
Italy	5,348	5.55	227	4.15	1,529	4.37	128	3.61
Jamaica	16	*	†	*	1	*	†	*
Japan	13,473	13.99	464	8.50	3,887	11.11	228	6.40
Jordan	49	0.05	†	*	129	0.37	3	0.09
Kazakhstan	—	*	—	*	†	*	†	*
Kenya	28	*	†	*	220	0.63	50	1.42
Kiribati	—	*	—	*	†	*	†	*
Korea, Republic of.............	1,341	1.39	287	5.27	604	1.73	56	1.57
Kuwait	252	0.26	29	0.54	205	0.58	42	1.18
Kyrgyz Republic	†	*	†	*	—	*	—	*
Lao People's Dem. Rep..........	12	*	12	0.21	†	*	—	*
Latvia	2	*	2	*	†	*	†	*
Lebanon	74	0.08	6	0.10	21	0.06	†	*
Lesotho	†	*	—	*	†	*	†	*
Liberia	26	*	—	*	21	0.06	2	0.06
Libya	92	0.10	†	*	7	*	—	*
Lithuania	2	*	2	*	†	*	†	*
Luxembourg	70	0.07	†	*	32	0.09	1	*
Macedonia, FYR	—	*	—	*	†	*	†	*
Madagascar	8	*	—	*	2	*	1	*
Malawi.......................	2	*	1	*	10	*	1	*
Malaysia	321	0.33	10	0.18	215	0.61	17	0.48
Maldives	1	*	—	*	†	*	—	*
Mali	†	*	—	*	5	*	†	*
Malta	20	*	20	0.36	†	*	—	*
Mauritania	8	*	—	*	14	*	7	0.19

(continued)

Table 4-4 (continued)

Supplying country	IBRD cumulative to June 30, 1994		IBRD fiscal 1994		IDA cumulative to June 30, 1994		IDA fiscal 1994	
	Amount	%	Amount	%	Amount	%	Amount	%
Mauritius	1	*	†	*	13	*	1	*
Mexico	493	0.51	29	0.53	94	0.27	3	0.07
Moldova	†	*	†	*	—	*	—	*
Mongolia	†	*	—	*	1	*	—	*
Morocco	160	0.17	1	*	48	0.14	1	*
Mozambique	4	*	—	*	7	*	1	*
Myanmar	23	*	2	*	15	*	3	0.09
Namibia	†	*	—	*	1	*	†	*
Nepal	1	*	—	*	3	*	2	0.05
Netherlands	1,844	1.91	120	2.20	886	2.53	107	3.01
New Zealand	150	0.16	9	0.17	89	0.25	5	0.13
Nicaragua	9	*	1	*	6	*	†	*
Niger	3	*	†	*	10	*	†	*
Nigeria	388	0.40	74	1.36	300	0.86	82	2.30
Norway	309	0.32	57	1.04	122	0.35	21	0.60
Oman	37	*	1	*	14	*	1	*
Pakistan	109	0.11	12	0.21	164	0.47	27	0.77
Panama	370	0.38	8	0.15	48	0.14	21	0.59
Papua New Guinea	3	*	—	*	†	*	†	*
Paraguay	112	0.12	†	*	7	*	3	0.09
Peru	124	0.13	7	0.14	16	*	2	*
Philippines	69	0.07	3	*	78	0.22	8	0.23
Poland	164	0.17	54	0.98	41	0.12	2	0.07
Portugal	53	0.05	6	0.10	212	0.61	29	0.81
Qatar	123	0.13	†	*	13	*	4	0.10
Romania	252	0.26	12	0.22	64	0.18	3	0.08
Russia	150	0.16	120	2.20	8	*	5	0.13
Rwanda	3	*	—	*	1	*	†	*
São Tomé and Principe	—	*	—	*	†	*	—	*
Saudi Arabia	557	0.58	98	1.79	216	0.62	9	0.24
Senegal	23	*	2	*	68	0.20	9	0.25
Seychelles	—	*	—	*	†	*	—	*
Sierra Leone	4	*	—	*	2	*	—	*
Singapore	909	0.94	73	1.34	621	1.78	64	1.80
Slovak Republic	2	*	2	*	1	*	†	*
Slovenia	28	*	20	0.37	†	*	†	*
Solomon Islands	1	*	1	*	1	*	1	*
Somalia	1	*	—	*	2	*	—	*
South Africa	385	0.40	38	0.70	664	1.90	154	4.34
Spain	1,075	1.12	65	1.18	228	0.65	34	0.95
Sri Lanka	21	*	8	0.15	16	*	1	*
St. Kitts and Nevis	†	*	—	*	1	*	—	*
St. Lucia	1	*	†	*	4	*	1	*
St. Vincent and the Grenadines	†	*	—	*	4	*	†	*
Sudan	5	*	†	*	12	*	1	*
Suriname	1	*	—	*	2	*	†	*
Swaziland	18	*	†	*	22	0.06	5	0.15
Sweden	1,520	1.58	63	1.16	396	1.13	35	0.99
Switzerland	4,051	4.21	194	3.55	942	2.69	54	1.52
Syrian Arab Republic	24	*	†	*	14	*	2	*

Supplying country	IBRD cumulative to June 30, 1994		IBRD fiscal 1994		IDA cumulative to June 30, 1994		IDA fiscal 1994	
	Amount	%	Amount	%	Amount	%	Amount	%
Tanzania	7	*	†	*	20	0.06	3	0.09
Thailand	141	0.15	4	0.07	318	0.91	53	1.48
Togo	29	*	1	*	21	0.06	†	*
Tonga	—	*	—	*	†	*	—	*
Trinidad and Tobago ..	19	*	1	*	18	0.05	15	0.41
Tunisia	88	0.09	4	0.07	32	0.09	3	0.08
Turkey	218	0.23	43	0.79	42	0.12	9	0.25
Turkmenistan	—	*	—	*	1	*	1	*
Uganda	3	*	†	*	4	*	1	*
Ukraine	29	*	28	0.51	2	*	2	0.05
United Arab Emirates .	536	0.56	2	*	333	0.95	23	0.64
United Kingdom[b]	7,380	7.66	523	9.59	4,797	13.71	438	12.34
United States	19,381	20.12	751	13.77	3,609	10.32	219	6.17
Uruguay	87	0.09	11	0.19	6	*	1	*
Uzbekistan	—	*	—	*	5	*	5	0.14
Vanuatu	5	*	—	*	†	*	—	*
Venezuela	465	0.48	18	0.33	167	0.48	37	1.05
Viet Nam	42	*	1	*	40	0.11	16	0.45
Western Samoa	2	*	—	*	†	*	—	*
Yemen, Republic of ...	†	*	†	*	207	0.59	†	*
Yugoslavia, SFR of[c] ...	854	0.89	5	0.10	169	0.48	4	0.12
Zaire	6	*	†	*	36	0.10	6	0.16
Zambia	29	*	1	*	107	0.30	5	0.13
Zimbabwe	34	*	†	*	85	0.24	24	0.67
~Other	867	0.90	86	1.57	182	0.52	52	1.47
Total	96,310	100	5,457	100	34,984	100	3,553	100

— Zero, † than $0.5 million, * less than 0.05 percent

NOTE: Disbursements for debt reduction and net advance disbursements are excluded. Details may not add to totals because of rounding.

a. Figures represent supply from the former Czechoslovakia prior to January 1, 1993.

b. United Kingdom includes Hong Kong.

c. Figures represent supply from SFR Yugoslavia in FY1994 for IBRD/IDA as follows: Bosnia-Herzegovina $4.2 million; Federal Republic of Yugoslavia (Serbia and Montenegro) $5.5 million.

borrowing country. While most foreign procurement comes from suppliers in developed member countries, suppliers from developing countries have increasingly been effective in winning contract awards. Through the end of fiscal 1989, 15 percent of foreign procurement was awarded to developing country suppliers; in fiscal 1994, developing country suppliers' share was 32 percent of total foreign disbursements.

Table 4-1 shows consolidated foreign and local disbursements for the IBRD and IDA through the end of fiscal 1989 and for each of the next five fiscal years to the end of fiscal 1994. Advance disbursements consist of payments made into special accounts of borrowers, from which funds are paid to specific

suppliers as expenditures are incurred. Because balances in these accounts cannot be attributed to any specific supplying country until expenditures have been reported to the Bank, these are shown as a separate category.

Table 4-2 provides details for foreign disbursements by OECD and non-OECD countries for the IBRD and IDA separately.

Table 4-3 shows disbursements made in fiscal 1994 by the IBRD and IDA for local and foreign procurement from all active borrowing countries and disbursements made for goods, works, and services procured from them by other Bank borrowers for projects funded by the Bank.

Table 4-4 shows the amounts disbursed from the IBRD and IDA separately for foreign pro-

Table 4-5. **IBRD and IDA Payments to Supplying Countries for Foreign Procurement, by Description of Goods, Fiscal 1994**
(amounts in millions of US dollars)

Supplying country	Equipment		Civil works		Consultants		All other goods		Total disbursements	
	Amount	%	Amount	%	Amount	%	Amount	%	Amount	%
Afghanistan	†	*	—	*	—	*	†	*	†	*
Albania	†	*	—	*	—	*	—	*	†	*
Algeria	3	*	—	*	—	*	—	*	3	*
Angola	†	*	—	*	—	*	—	*	†	*
Antigua and Barbuda	†	*	—	*	—	*	—	*	†	*
Argentina	20	0.27	5	0.90	1	0.10	1	0.22	26	0.29
Australia	117	1.59	1	0.26	20	2.59	1	0.29	139	1.54
Austria	134	1.82	1	0.14	6	0.82	2	0.47	142	1.58
Bahamas, The	†	*	†	*	—	*	—	*	†	*
Bahrain	5	0.07	1	0.21	†	*	3	0.94	9	0.10
Bangladesh	5	0.06	†	*	†	*	1	0.30	6	0.07
Barbados	†	*	2	0.31	†	*	†	*	2	*
Belarus	†	*	—	*	—	*	—	*	†	*
Belgium	89	1.22	5	0.90	13	1.73	7	2.05	115	1.27
Benin	†	*	2	0.28	†	*	—	*	2	*
Bhutan	†	*	†	*	—	*	—	*	†	*
Bolivia	1	*	—	*	†	*	—	*	1	*
Botswana	2	*	—	*	—	*	†	*	2	*
Brazil	139	1.90	8	1.4	3	0.36	1	0.39	151	1.68
Bulgaria	15	0.21	—	*	†	*	—	*	16	0.17
Burkina Faso	1	*	—	*	†	*	—	*	1	*
Burundi	†	*	—	*	†	*	†	*	†	*
Cameroon	3	*	†	*	†	*	—	*	3	*
Canada	106	1.44	6	1.02	68	8.82	5	1.52	184	2.05
Cape Verde	†	*	—	*	†	*	—	*	†	*
Central African Republic .	†	*	—	*	—	*	—	*	†	*
Chile	10	0.13	—	*	2	0.31	†	*	12	0.13
China	164	2.24	92	16.13	4	0.54	13	3.63	273	3.03
Colombia	4	0.05	1	0.18	1	0.07	1	0.26	6	0.07
Congo	2	*	—	*	†	*	—	*	2	*
Costa Rica	1	*	—	*	5	0.64	†	*	6	0.07
Côte d'Ivoire	27	0.37	12	2.17	1	0.17	†	0.06	41	0.46
Croatia	2	*	8	1.47	—	*	—	*	11	0.12
Cyprus	21	0.28	—	*	1	0.10	†	*	21	0.24
Czech Republic	27	0.37	—	*	†	*	†	0.12	27	0.30
Denmark	63	0.86	15	2.68	17	2.22	1	0.20	96	1.06
Djibouti	†	*	—	*	—	*	1	0.26	1	*
Dominica	†	*	—	*	—	*	—	*	†	*
Dominican Republic	2	*	—	*	†	*	—	*	2	*
Ecuador	1	*	—	*	†	*	—	*	1	*
Egypt, Arab Republic of .	3	*	2	0.36	1	0.08	†	0.05	6	0.06
El Salvador	1	*	—	*	—	*	—	*	1	*
Equatorial Guinea	5	0.07	—	*	—	*	—	*	5	0.05
Estonia	1	*	—	*	—	*	—	*	1	*
Ethiopia	8	0.11	—	*	†	0.05	†	*	8	0.09
Finland	47	0.65	—	*	2	0.28	1	0.30	50	0.56
France	628	8.58	66	11.46	85	11.13	7	2.02	786	8.72
Gabon	1	*	—	*	—	*	—	*	1	*
Gambia, The	—	*	†	*	†	*	†	*	†	*
Germany	657	8.97	45	7.88	44	5.74	20	5.68	766	8.50
Ghana	2	*	†	*	1	0.08	—	*	3	*

Supplying country	Equipment		Civil works		Consultants		All other goods		Total disbursements	
	Amount	%	Amount	%	Amount	%	Amount	%	Amount	%
Greece.................	11	0.15	3	0.53	†	*	†	*	14	0.16
Guatemala	2	*	—	*	†	*	—	*	2	*
Guinea	—	*	—	*	†	*	—	*	†	*
Guinea-Bissau	3	*	—	*	—	*	—	*	3	*
Guyana	†	*	1	0.15	—	*	—	*	1	*
Haiti	1	*	—	*	†	*	—	*	1	*
Honduras	1	*	—	*	†	*	—	*	1	*
Hungary	56	0.76	5	0.91	1	0.07	—	*	61	0.68
Iceland	—	*	—	*	†	*	—	*	†	*
India	103	1.41	10	1.81	6	0.83	13	3.78	133	1.48
Indonesia	29	0.40	—	*	†	*	7	1.93	36	0.40
Iran, Islamic Republic of .	7	0.10	—	*	—	*	—	*	7	0.08
Iraq	—	*	†	*	—	*	—	*	†	*
Ireland	8	0.11	†	0.08	9	1.13	1	0.32	18	0.20
Israel	21	0.28	—	*	5	0.62	†	0.13	26	0.29
Italy	259	3.53	81	14.09	8	1.03	8	2.20	355	3.94
Jamaica	—	*	—	*	†	*	†	*	†	*
Japan	632	8.63	25	4.42	18	2.30	17	4.73	691	7.67
Jordan	3	*	—	*	†	*	—	*	3	*
Kazakhstan	†	*	—	*	—	*	—	*	†	*
Kenya	15	0.21	†	*	5	0.65	30	8.56	50	0.56
Kiribati	†	*	—	*	—	*	—	*	†	*
Korea, Republic of	321	4.38	13	2.30	6	0.78	3	0.88	343	3.81
Kuwait	71	0.98	—	*	—	*	—	*	71	0.79
Kyrgyz Republic	†	*	—	*	—	*	—	*	†	*
Lao People's Dem. Rep...	12	0.16	—	*	†	*	—	*	12	0.13
Latvia	2	*	—	*	—	*	—	*	2	*
Lebanon	†	*	4	0.63	2	0.28	†	*	6	0.07
Lesotho	—	*	—	*	†	*	†	*	†	*
Liberia	1	*	1	0.19	—	*	—	*	2	*
Libya	†	*	—	*	—	*	—	*	†	*
Lithuania	2	*	—	*	—	*	—	*	2	*
Luxembourg	1	*	—	*	1	0.13	—	*	2	*
Macedonia, FYR	†	*	—	*	—	*	—	*	†	*
Madagascar	†	*	—	*	†	*	—	*	1	*
Malawi	1	*	—	*	†	*	†	0.11	1	*
Malaysia	23	0.32	1	0.18	†	*	2	0.56	27	0.30
Mali	—	*	†	*	†	*	—	*	†	*
Malta	20	0.27	—	*	—	*	—	*	20	0.22
Mauritania	7	0.09	—	*	—	*	—	*	7	0.08
Mauritius	†	*	—	*	†	0.06	†	0.09	1	*
Mexico	29	0.40	†	*	†	*	2	0.48	32	0.35
Moldova	†	*	—	*	—	*	—	*	†	*
Mongolia...............	†	*	—	*	—	*	—	*	†	*
Morocco	1	*	—	*	1	0.11	—	*	2	*
Mozambique	†	*	—	*	—	*	†	*	1	*
Myanmar	5	0.07	—	*	†	*	—	*	5	0.06
Namibia	†	*	—	*	—	*	†	*	†	*
Nepal	2	*	—	*	—	*	—	*	2	*

(continued)

Table 4-5 *(continued)*

Supplying country	Equipment Amount	%	Civil works Amount	%	Consultants Amount	%	All other goods Amount	%	Total disbursements Amount	%
Netherlands	186	2.54	10	1.80	27	3.46	5	1.38	227	2.52
New Zealand	9	0.12	1	0.25	4	0.48	†	*	14	0.16
Nicaragua	1	*	—	*	†	*	—	*	1	*
Niger..................	†	*	—	*	—	*	†	*	†	*
Nigeria	156	2.13	—	*	†	*	—	*	156	1.73
Norway	67	0.91	—	*	6	0.82	5	1.44	78	0.87
Oman	†	*	1	0.25	†	*	—	*	2	*
Pakistan	18	0.25	18	3.21	2	0.22	†	0.12	39	0.43
Panama	29	0.40	†	*	—	*	—	*	29	0.32
Papua New Guinea	†	*	—	*	—	*	—	*	†	*
Paraguay	2	*	1	0.26	†	*	—	*	3	*
Peru	7	0.10	—	*	†	*	2	0.49	9	0.10
Philippines	1	*	2	0.41	6	0.74	2	0.44	11	0.12
Poland	55	0.75	†	*	1	0.09	†	0.06	56	0.62
Portugal	16	0.22	1	0.11	15	2.01	2	0.71	34	0.38
Qatar	†	*	4	0.64	—	*	—	*	4	*
Romania	12	0.17	3	0.44	†	*	†	*	15	0.17
Russia	124	1.70	†	*	1	0.07	†	*	125	1.38
Rwanda	†	*	†	*	†	*	†	*	†	*
Saudi Arabia	104	1.42	1	0.13	—	*	2	0.53	106	1.18
Senegal	9	0.13	1	0.20	†	*	—	*	11	0.12
Singapore	119	1.62	4	0.78	7	0.93	7	1.95	137	1.52
Slovak Republic	2	*	—	*	—	*	†	*	2	*
Slovenia	18	0.24	2	0.43	†	*	†	0.10	21	0.23
Solomon Islands	1	*	—	*	—	*	†	*	1	*
South Africa	155	2.12	†	*	9	1.22	27	7.79	192	2.13
Spain	73	0.99	20	3.49	5	0.69	†	0.10	98	1.09
Sri Lanka	2	*	—	*	†	0.05	7	2.00	9	0.10
St. Lucia	†	*	1	0.24	—	*	†	*	2	*
St. Vincent and the Grenadines	—	*	†	*	†	*	—	*	†	*
Sudan	1	*	†	*	†	*	†	*	1	*
Suriname	—	*	—	*	†	*	—	*	†	*
Swaziland	5	0.06	—	*	†	*	1	0.25	6	0.06
Sweden	84	1.14	4	0.76	4	0.53	6	1.75	98	1.09
Switzerland	216	2.95	9	1.51	16	2.14	7	2.06	248	2.75
Syrian Arab Republic	2	*	—	*	†	*	†	*	2	*
Tanzania	3	*	†	*	†	*	1	0.25	4	*
Thailand	54	0.74	2	0.28	†	*	†	0.12	56	0.63
Togo	1	*	—	*	—	*	—	*	1	*
Trinidad and Tobago	15	0.21	†	*	†	*	†	*	16	0.17
Tunisia	6	0.08	—	*	†	0.06	†	*	7	0.07
Turkey	50	0.68	1	0.12	1	0.08	1	0.21	52	0.58
Turkmenistan	1	*	—	*	—	*	—	*	1	*
Uganda	†	*	†	*	†	*	†	*	1	*
Ukraine	29	0.39	—	*	—	*	1	0.32	30	0.33
United Arab Emirates	14	0.19	3	0.59	—	*	7	1.91	24	0.27
United Kingdom[a]	774	10.57	23	3.94	112	14.59	53	15.17	961	10.67
United States	775	10.59	28	4.82	149	19.43	19	5.45	971	10.77
Uruguay	11	0.16	—	*	—	*	—	*	11	0.13
Uzbekistan	5	0.07	—	*	—	*	—	*	5	0.06

Table 4-5 (continued)

Supplying country	Equipment Amount	Equipment %	Civil works Amount	Civil works %	Consultants Amount	Consultants %	All other goods Amount	All other goods %	Total disbursements Amount	Total disbursements %
Venezuela...............	55	0.76	—	*	†	*	—	*	55	0.62
Viet Nam	16	0.23	†	0.06	—	*	—	*	17	0.19
Yemen, Republic of......	†	*	†	0.08	—	*	†	*	1	*
Yugoslavia, SFR of[b]	1	*	9	1.50	—	*	—	*	10	0.11
Zaire	6	0.08	—	*	†	*	—	*	6	0.06
Zambia	4	0.06	†	*	†	*	†	0.13	5	0.06
Zimbabwe	21	0.29	—	*	1	0.08	2	0.57	24	0.26
~Other	35	0.48	1	0.24	60	7.76	41	11.86	138	1.53
Total	7,319	100	573	100	767	100	350	100	9,009	100

— Zero, † less than $0.5 million, * less than 0.05 percent.

NOTE: Disbursements for debt reduction and net advance disbursements are excluded. Details may not add to totals because of rounding.

a. United Kingdom includes Hong Kong.

b. Figures represent supply from SFR Yugoslavia in FY94 for IBRD/IDA as follows: Bosnia-Herzegovina $4.2 million; Federal Republic of Yugoslavia (Serbia and Montenegro) $5.5 million.

Table 4-6. IBRD and IDA Foreign Disbursements, by Description of Goods, for Investment Lending, Fiscal 1992–94

Item	1992 OECD	1992 Non-OECD	1992 Total	1993 OECD	1993 Non-OECD	1993 Total	1994 OECD	1994 Non-OECD	1994 Total
					millions of US dollars				
Investment lending									
Civil works	339	154	493	337	176	513	317	209	526
Consultants	577	72	649	612	105	717	615	125	740
Goods	2,665	456	3,121	2,888	597	3,485	2,816	865	3,681
All other	81	50	132	246	142	388	59	70	128
Total	3,662	732	4,394	4,083	1,020	5,103	3,807	1,268	5,075
					percent[a]				
Civil works	69	31	11	66	34	10	60	40	10
Consultants	89	11	15	85	15	14	83	17	15
Goods	85	15	71	83	17	68	77	23	73
All other	61	38	3	63	37	8	46	55	3
Total	83	17	100	80	20	100	75	25	100

NOTE: Disbursements for debt reduction and net advance disbursements are excluded. Disbursements for structural adjustment loans, sector adjustment loans, and hybrids (loans that support policy and institutional reforms in a specific sector by financing both a policy component disbursed against imports and an investment component) are also excluded. OECD amounts are based on current OECD membership, excluding Mexico, which became a member in May 1994.

All of the percentages are based on the dollar amounts shown under the total disbursements section. These percentages show both the breakdown between OECD and non-OECD countries for individual goods categories and the share of each goods category compared with total disbursements.

curement of goods and services from member countries in fiscal 1994 and cumulatively through fiscal 1994.

Table 4-5 shows the proportion of foreign disbursements from the IBRD and IDA for specific categories of goods and services provided by member countries in fiscal 1994.

Table 4-6 provides a summary listing of the amounts paid to OECD and non-OECD country suppliers in each fiscal year from 1992 to 1994 under investment projects. Amounts dis-

bursed are compared with respect to significant categories of goods procured from foreign suppliers. The extent to which OECD and non-OECD countries participated in supplying these major categories of goods in each of the past three fiscal years is also compared.

In all of these tables IBRD figures exclude disbursements for loans to the International Finance Corporation and "B" loans. IDA figures include Special Fund and Special Facility for sub-Saharan Africa credits. Disbursements for

Project Preparation Facility advances are excluded for both the IBRD and IDA. Minor adjustments have been made between the foreign and local disbursements for fiscal 1993 as reflected in Tables 4-1, 4-2, 4-4, and 4-6.

Technical Assistance

Technical assistance activities financed through IBRD loans and IDA credits continue to represent a significant segment of total Bank lending. A number of reasons underlie the increase in technical assistance activity in recent years.

• First, an increase in technical assistance for institutional development is an appropriate complementary response to efforts to deepen policy reform and retool the public sector for its new roles. It may also reflect the current phase of Bank assistance after key macro policy changes have been put in place.

• Second, there has been a shift in lending to human resources development and environmentally sustainable development and away from adjustment loans. Historically, these sectors have had the highest percentage of technical assistance components as a share of total lending—well above 10 percent.

• Third, there has been a general decline in grant funding for technical assistance from the United Nations Development Programme (UNDP) and bilateral donors, particularly to some of the Bank's major borrowers who are major recipients of technical assistance components.

Loan-financed technical assistance (freestanding and components) by the Bank in calendar year 1993 amounted to $2.2 billion. Of this amount, $1.9 billion, or 85 percent of the total, funded components of projects, while $300 million was accounted for by twenty-two freestanding technical assistance projects. Ten countries (led by Brazil, China, Indonesia, and Mexico) accounted for more than half of all technical assistance financed through Bank lending. These large technical assistance borrowers share common characteristics: They are long-standing, mature borrowers and have the capacity to work with the Bank in determining their technical assistance needs. In addition, because most receive inconsequential amounts of technical assistance grants from bilateral and multilateral donors, the technical assistance provided by the Bank is highly valued.

Key issues of technical assistance. With the drive toward open and competitive markets of hitherto centralized economies, a new set of issues is emerging. In many countries, downsizing the large bureaucracies that have been set up to manage state-led economic policies is

a major challenge. There is the need to restore efficiency and commitment within the civil service, which has been eroded over time by the politicization of career management and declining remuneration in real terms. This deterioration in public administration constitutes a major obstacle to launching needed policy reforms, restoring good governance, and improving the delivery of public services.

The Bank is paying increased attention to the strategic management of technical assistance for institutional development through the targeting of public sector management and institutional development issues in economic and sector work and country-strategy work. A by-product of this increased upstream effort is an enhanced policy dialogue with governments on systemic institutional issues and countrywide management of technical assistance. The result could be reform-based adjustment operations, freestanding technical assistance, and improved institutional development interventions in projects. Overall, although there has been some progress in this area and some best practices are emerging, more time is required to build up skills in macro-institutional analysis and to integrate public sector management issues into economic and sector work and the country dialogue. In a number of countries, these issues are highly sensitive and require time and persistence to build up borrower ownership and commitment at the highest levels.

Use of local consultants. The Bank encourages borrowers to employ local consultants either alone or in combination with foreign firms. To some extent, however, local consultants have been handicapped by a lack of marketing expertise. The Bank is currently financing the preparation of a "how-to" manual that deals with consultant operations and marketing. When finished, it will be the focus of discussion in one-week seminars in preselected borrowing member countries. The Bank will follow up the seminars by monitoring progress made by local firms and by facilitating their association with firms from industrialized countries.

In addition, during the past year, workshops were held at the Bank's headquarters for consultant associations from Africa, Asia, and Latin America to review ways and means to enhance participation of their member firms. The increased emphasis the Bank is giving to the issue of local consultant use is, in part, a response to feedback from borrowers that the development of greater institutional capability is essential to project success—and that this includes making more use, and improving the capabilities, of local consultants.

Institutional Development Fund (IDF). The IDF, which became effective on July 1, 1992, was designed to fill gaps in the Bank's set of instruments for financing technical assistance for institutional development work associated with policy reform, country economic management programs, poverty-reduction programs, public sector management, private sector development, and environment management.

The IDF provides a quick-response instrument for funding small, action-oriented proposals identified during (and closely linked to) the Bank's economic and sector work and policy dialogue in countries where institutional development is a significant country-assistance objective. There is a $500,000 ceiling on individual grants. All borrowing member countries of the Bank are eligible to apply.

The introduction of the IDF was partially driven by the expectation of a pent-up demand for a grant facility to address capacity-building requirements in many countries. This expectation has not yet fully materialized. Demand for IDF resources has been limited partly as a result of its newness and also because of the availability of resources from competing trust funds. In calendar year 1993, fifty-three grants were approved to forty-three countries for a total amount of $14.3 million. Some delays in implementation have occurred, inevitably caused by the introduction of a new program that required putting in place special procedures and familiarizing member governments and staff with the new grant facility.

Notwithstanding the IDF's modest start-up, the use of IDF funds has permitted the Bank to help initiate difficult institutional changes, such as reform of economic ministries in Albania, disseminate the experience of privatization in Poland, and enable timely work to begin on a privatization strategy for Belarus.

Project Preparation Facility (PPF). The PPF was established in 1975 when the executive directors authorized the Bank's president to approve project preparation advances to an aggregate amount of $5 million. At the time, it was expected that the typical tasks would cost in the range of $50,000–$150,000. This limit was subsequently raised in 1978 to $1 million and to $1.5 million in 1986.

During fiscal 1994, a new ceiling of $2 million per advance was established for all advances except those in connection with loans exceeding $200 million; for them, the ceiling was set at $3 million.

At the end of calendar year 1993, 138 PPF advances had been approved, involving a total commitment of $84 million. One hundred one advances, for an amount of $49.6 million, had been made on IDA terms, and thirty-seven advances, for an amount of $34.3 million, had been made on IBRD terms. Most of the advances have been made to sub-Saharan African countries.

The Bank and the UNDP. The Bank interacts with the UNDP through many programs and at many levels. During calendar year 1993, the Bank was the executing agency for 132 UNDP projects having a total value of $303 million. This reflects a decline from 1992, when the Bank was the executing agency for 175 projects with a total value of $348 million. This trend is expected to continue as the UNDP's total resources continue to decline and as the UNDP accelerates the shift from agency execution to national execution and from project to program financing. At present, the loss of funding by the UNDP has been more than adequately compensated for by funding from other sources, notably Japan's Policy and Human Resources Development Fund. In the long term, however, the decline of untied grant fund for technical assistance from the UNDP will be felt in many operations. The Bank and the UNDP are reviewing the implications of this trend.

At the same time, many borrowers, particularly in Latin America, are using the services of the UNDP to implement technical assistance financed by the Bank. This is done through two mechanisms: first, a cost-sharing arrangement under which proceeds from Bank loans are comingled with UNDP funds to create unified UNDP projects, executed either by the UNDP or by others; second, a management-service agreement—a form of contractual relationship between the Bank's borrower and the Office of Project Services of the UNDP for the implementation of Bank-financed technical assistance. This arrangement is particularly helpful in expediting implementation by taking advantage of the UNDP's "privileges and immunities" to process important transactions with minimum delay.

The Bank and the UNDP also collaborate in the field of aid coordination to ensure that technical assistance issues receive adequate attention at consultative group meetings chaired by the Bank and at roundtables chaired by the UNDP.

Cofinancing

The Cofinancing and Financial Advisory Services (CFS) vice presidency continued to play a catalytic role in facilitating the flow of financial resources to developing countries by undertaking various activities relating to cofinancing, project financing, and private sector development. These activities included providing operational support and technical assistance to the Bank's country departments, borrowing member countries, and cofinancing partners such as donor governments, official development aid agencies, export-credit agencies, and international financial markets.

In fiscal 1994, the volume of cofinancing anticipated in support of Bank-assisted operations was $8.8 billion, down from the $11.6 billion mobilized in fiscal 1993 (see Table 4-7). This reduction was directly related to the declines in IBRD and IDA lending commitments during the year, which fell short of fiscal 1993 amounts by $2,860 million.

The decline is also the result of economic slowdown in both donor and borrowing countries, which has contributed to a significant cut in aid and investment budgets on both the supply and the demand sides. The diminishing weight of quick-disbursing operations in the portfolio of Bank operations, as well as the slow pace of the project cycle arising from the increased attention to qualitative aspects of interventions, also played a role. Nonetheless, the decline in cofinancing is viewed with concern in view of the need for increased financial flows to developing countries.

The cofinancing figures, which represent planned cofinancing, not actual commitments by cofinanciers, are captured at the time of the presentation to the executive board of each IBRD and IDA operation.

About 51 percent of all Bank-assisted projects and programs were cofinanced in fiscal 1994, up from 49 percent in the previous year. Although official cofinancing declined to $6.3 billion from $8.1 billion in fiscal 1993, it still accounted for the largest source of anticipated cofinancing support, some 72 percent of the total. Export credit and private cofinancing fell from $1.2 billion to $591 million and $2.3 billion to $1.9 billion, respectively. The only notable exception to this trend was the support mobilized from the private sector in the East Asia and Pacific region, which reached $1.3 billion for the year, compared with $373 million during fiscal 1993. Investment loans received the largest share of cofinancing support, followed by structural adjustment loans and sector adjustment loans.

In fiscal 1994, official cofinancing provided by Japan's Overseas Economic Cooperation Fund and the Export-Import Bank of Japan continued to account for the largest percentage of bilateral support to Bank-assisted operations, reaching a total of $1,404 million equivalent for thirteen projects approved in fiscal 1994, or 48 percent of the aggregate amount of bilateral cofinancing. Other large bilateral cofinancing support came from Germany ($196 million equivalent), France ($84 million equivalent), Sweden ($78 million equivalent), the United Kingdom ($71 million equivalent), and the United States ($66 million). Total cofinancing currently expected from multilateral financial institutions amounted to $3.4 billion. The Inter-American Development Bank, with $1,021 million of planned cofinancing, continued to be the largest multilateral cofinancier, accounting for 30 percent of the total.

The power sector attracted the largest amount of cofinancing with an aggregate of $2,100 million (as opposed to $3,116 million in fiscal 1993). It was followed by transportation ($1,929 million, down from $2,107 million in the previous year); agriculture ($1,106 million); telecommunications ($519 million); and the multisector category of lending, which includes lending in support of reform programs and of reconstruction and rehabilitation programs ($437 million).

In fiscal 1994, three main activities were carried out in CFS to formulate a policy framework to facilitate cofinancing as a main business tool. They were (a) the undertaking of a Cofinancing Task Force study that focused on developing a coherent Bank policy on cofinancing and identifying other ways the Bank can play a catalytic role in facilitating capital flows to developing countries; (b) the launching of a special policy study on how to mainstream the use of guarantees to mobilize private capital in support of Bank operations, particularly for privatized energy and infrastructure investments; and (c) the establishment of Accelerated Cofinancing Facilities with the Export-Import Bank of Japan, under which cofinancing will be arranged using an accelerated and streamlined procedure.

In March 1994, the Cofinancing Task Force issued a report that addressed various cofinancing-related issues and concerns. The task force concluded that cofinancing has been, and will continue to be, an important activity for the Bank as an instrument for maintaining partnerships between the Bank and other donors to accomplish joint objectives and to mobilize significant development resources from official institutions, private sources, and export-credit agencies.

The Accelerated Cofinancing Facilities with the Export-Import Bank of Japan are designed to tap Japan's ever-increasing official development assistance in a more active and systematic manner. In the summer of 1993, the Japanese authorities announced their Funds for Development Initiative, consisting of a pledge totaling approximately $120 billion equivalent over the 1993–97 period. The Japanese authorities emphasized cofinancing with the Bank and other international development institutions as one of the initiative's operational priorities. The facilities would allow

Table 4-7. **World Bank Cofinancing Operations, by Region, Fiscal Years 1993–94**
(amounts in millions of US dollars)

Region and year	Projects cofinanced No.	Projects cofinanced Amount	Source of cofinancing[a] Official[b] No.	Source of cofinancing[a] Official[b] Amount	Source of cofinancing[a] Export credit No.	Source of cofinancing[a] Export credit Amount	Source of cofinancing[a] Private No.	Source of cofinancing[a] Private Amount	World Bank contribution IBRD	World Bank contribution IDA	Total project costs
Africa											
1993	41	1,198.6	41	1,185.1	1	10.0	2	3.5	27.0	1,588.9	3,288.3
1994	35	1,592.9	31	1,538.4	—	—	8	54.5	7.7	1,649.4	3,698.9
East Asia and Pacific											
1993	13	1,113.1	11	583.9	2	156.5	2	372.7	880.4	166.9	3,392.2
1994	14	1,948.0	9	515.2	1	92.0	7	1,340.8	1,898.5	634.9	7,261.8
South Asia											
1993	11	2,189.0	11	1,800.0	2	289.0	1	100.0	1,145.0	949.0	8,182.2
1994	9	1,584.1	9	1,258.7	1	300.0	1	25.4	474.0	948.7	8,875.7
Europe and Central Asia											
1993	18	1,433.5	18	1,433.5	—	—	—	—	2,041.0	100.4	4,351.7
1994	25	1,280.0	22	901.4	3	173.6	5	205.0	2,253.3	44.6	4,965.7
Latin America and the Caribbean											
1993	27	3,741.6	27	2,008.7	1	699.8	3	1,033.1	2,721.3	248.5	10,565.7
1994	25	1,582.7	22	1,447.5	1	1.9	5	133.3	1,739.5	264.5	5,615.1
Middle East and North Africa											
1993	10	1,919.9	8	1,077.4	1	47.8	3	794.7	1,239.0	—	6,132.0
1994	9	781.3	8	649.5	1	23.0	2	108.8	561.0	100.0	3,213.0
Total											
1993	120	11,595.6	116	8,088.5	7	1,203.1	11	2,304.0	8,053.7	3,053.7	35,912.0
1994	117	8,768.9	101	6,310.6	7	590.5	28	1,867.8	6,934.0	3,642.1	33,628.8

— Zero.

NOTE: The number of operations shown under different sources add up to a figure exceeding the total number of cofinanced projects because a number of projects were cofinanced from more than one source. Details may not add to totals because of rounding.

a. These statistics are compiled from the financing plans presented at the time of approval of the World Bank loans and credits by its board of executive directors. The amounts of official cofinancing are, in most cases, firm commitments by that stage; export credits and private cofinancing amounts, however, are generally only estimates since such cofinancing is actually arranged as required for project implementation and gets firmed up a year or two after board approval. The statistics of private cofinancing in these tables for any fiscal year do not necessarily reflect market placements in that year.

b. These figures include cofinancing with untied loans from the Export-Import Bank of Japan.

the Bank to mobilize cofinancing resources more easily and systematically in support of its priority operations. Similar cofinancing arrangements will be pursued with other donor countries.

The Special Program of Assistance (SPA) for sub-Saharan Africa constituted the most important aid coordination and cofinancing exercise promoted by the Africa region. The third phase of the program was launched in October 1993, covering the period 1994–96. By the time of the April 1994 meeting of SPA donors, $6.6 billion of quick-disbursing balance-of-payments assistance had already been pledged. In addition to mobilizing resources, the key SPA objective of improving the quality of donors' adjustment assistance was also advanced

during fiscal 1994. Of particular importance in this context was the adoption of guidelines for donor financing of civil service compensation, which will be followed in future interventions by donor member countries participating in the program. Considerable progress was also made in implementing previously approved SPA guidelines for simplifying and harmonizing donors' procedures for disbursing balance-of-payments support.

As in previous years, the donor community provided substantial support throughout the year to the Bank through trust funds and other external funding arrangements. Contrary to generally decreasing cofinancing trends, this type of support is growing. The Policy and Human Resources Development (PHRD) Fund, financed by Japan, continued to provide a broad range of support for various Bank-supported programs and projects in fiscal 1994. Fund grants totaling $141 million were approved for technical assistance for preparing 200 Bank-assisted projects in eighty-seven countries. Continuing support was also provided to the EDI and to finance scholarship grants. Among the special programs approved was a grant to support Russia's privatization and restructuring program. The first operational review of the PHRD Fund, completed during fiscal 1994, concluded that the fund was fully meeting the objectives for which it was established and that it had been particularly effective as a source of untied technical assistance for project preparation. The review also noted that the fund also helped the Bank expedite its work on private sector development.

The Consultant Trust Fund Program—which makes available consultancy services in support of the Bank's operational work in borrowing member countries—also continued to grow. Ten new trust funds were established in fiscal 1994, with grants totaling $29 million. The program, which is now supported by twenty-six donors, including four developing member countries, allocated $52 million in fiscal 1994, enabling the Bank to tap new sources of expertise and to undertake a wider range of analytical work in priority areas and issues, including the environment, poverty reduction, health and nutrition, and women in development.

Projects in the power, telecommunications, and transport sectors dominated CFS's project-finance activities in fiscal 1994, with substantial increases taking place in the use of expanded cofinancing operations (ECOs). The ECO program uses limited Bank guarantees against certain specified risks, such as sovereign risks, to encourage private financing, obtain or increase access to capital markets, and provide improved terms—especially longer maturities—for projects in developing countries. In March 1994, the executive board approved a $120 million ECO in the syndicated loan market for China's Yangzhou Power Project, while in May, proposals for a $100 million ECO to support commercial bond financing for part of the $1.3 billion Leyte-Luzon Geothermal Power Project in the Philippines and for an ECO guarantee of up to $50 million to help finance a telecommunications project in Jordan were approved. Other ECOs under active development include those for projects in Chad, China, Colombia, Lebanon, and Morocco. The CFS vice presidency is also engaged in structuring non-ECO project finance for power in Jamaica and the Dominican Re-

public, tourism in Egypt, and for a variety of projects in Pakistan, Sri Lanka, Tanzania, and elsewhere.

CFS continues to provide specialized advisory services to member countries on debt reduction under both the Debt-reduction Facility for IDA-only Countries and the "Brady" type of debt and debt-service reduction (DDSR) program. CFS, which administers the Debt-reduction Facility, provides extensive legal and reconciliation work prior to the structuring of complex debt-reduction operations. During the year, facility operations were completed in Uganda and Bolivia, while similar operations were under preparation in Albania, Ethiopia, Guinea, Mali, Mauritania, Nicaragua, São Tomé and Principe, Sierra Leone, Tanzania, and Zambia. Under CFS's monitoring of the DDSR program, extensive financial and sensitivity analyses are performed, and soundings are conducted to assess the receptivity of markets and creditors to proposed DDSR packages. DDSR operations under preparation include those for Bulgaria, the Dominican Republic, and Poland. A deal for Brazil was completed in April 1994.

CFS consolidated its position as a technical center for privatization and private sector development services. The primary focus continued to be on providing technical services to the Bank's six operational regions for the design and implementation of Bank privatization and private sector development operations. Specialized support was given to almost fifty projects covering all aspects of public enterprise reform, privatization programs, divestitures, and project financing. Increasing focus was given to private sector participation in infrastructure sectors such as telecommunications, transport, and water supply.[1]

Several technical assistance programs—in Argentina, Kazakhstan, Pakistan, Romania, and Ukraine, for example—were managed directly by CFS in support of privatization programs. Pilot projects were also implemented in areas such as small-scale privatization, retail sector privatization, trucking privatization, and the development of business programs in a number of the republics of the former Soviet Union. In Pakistan, a team was rapidly deployed to help reinvigorate Pakistan's privatization program, while in Romania an innovative assistance effort was mounted to help develop management contracts as one of the country's privatization strategies. This direct assistance to client governments was le-

---

[1] Details of the Bank's activities in private sector development during the year may be found beginning on page 50.

veraged by funds mobilized from bilateral donors.

Best practice and comparative studies were also undertaken to disseminate cross-country experience, and new instruments and approaches were designed to mobilize private finance for privatization and enterprise development. Six papers in the "CFS Discussion Papers" series were published, and three studies were launched, one assessing Eastern Europe's experience with medium-scale and large-scale trade sales, another comparing international postal reforms, and a third reviewing private sector support for the power sector in several developing countries.

Improving Portfolio Management, Accountability, and Openness

In fiscal year 1992, the Task Force on Portfolio Management, charged with examining the quality of the World Bank's project portfolio and making recommendations on what might be needed to reverse the decline in the proportion of successful projects over the past decade, was formed.

Its report, transmitted to the Bank's executive board in November 1992, found that although more than three quarters of Bank-assisted projects demonstrated good performance during implementation, there had been a decline in the performance of the portfolio. According to the report, worsening external and country environments contributed prominently to the performance decline. Certain aspects of Bank practice also contributed to portfolio-management problems or were not sufficiently effective in resolving them. The task force's fundamental conclusion was that the institution needed to modify some of its key institutional values that shape its approach to all facets of its lending operations.

Early in fiscal 1994, the executive directors endorsed a detailed plan of action designed to make the Bank more effective in pursuing its basic goal of reducing poverty in borrowing countries.

As the core of its action plan, the Bank introduced a country-by-country approach into the management of its lending operations. This was designed to allow it to take a strategic view of its $148 billion portfolio. To complement the changes it made in its own policies and practices, the Bank began collaborating with the authorities in borrowing countries to review the performance of the portfolio in each country and resolve systemic problems.[2]

The various initiatives set in motion to improve portfolio performance represented an important shift in the Bank's business practices—from what was perceived to be an excessive preoccupation with lending targets and volumes to a greater concern with the development results in the field of Bank-supported operations.

Since the executive directors' approval of the action plan in July 1993, significant progress has been made in various areas. They include, but are not limited to:

• Placing portfolio performance, or the management of operations under implementation, at the center of country-assistance strategies. Improved guidelines for the formulation of country-assistance strategies now mandate that the Bank's six operational regions account for portfolio performance in the design of their country-assistance strategies and business plans.

• Restructuring projects and country portfolios, and, as a measure of last resort, canceling problem projects.

• Improving the quality of projects at entry by ensuring country commitment to the project at the outset, fostering broad-based participation in project design, and monitoring stakeholder commitment throughout the life of the project.

• Simplifying and modifying the Bank's cofinancing practices so as to minimize project complexity that is often associated with cofinancing.

• Introducing more rigorous analysis of project risk and sensitivity during project preparation and throughout implementation through the issuance of new operational policy and Bank procedures statements, as well as the distribution of a handbook on risk and sensitivity analysis that provides more extensive guidance at the sectoral level.

• Increasing budgetary resources devoted to project supervision, including increasing the role of field offices in enhancing portfolio management.

• Enhancing the role of the Operations Evaluation Department (OED) and strengthening the application of evaluation results to the Bank's current operations.[3]

• Providing intensive training to borrowers on the Bank's procurement processes so as to speed up project implementation. For its part, the Bank is preparing standard bidding documents for some specialized areas of procurement, and a committee was formed to ensure Bankwide consistency on decisions for the award of large contracts.

---

[2] Details of the task force's report, as well as of the action plan endorsed by the Bank's executive directors, may be found on pages 60–64 of the World Bank *Annual Report* for fiscal 1993.

[3] For details, see page 154.

Box 4-1. Independent Inspection Panel Is Established

An independent Inspection Panel, which will receive and investigate complaints that the Bank has not followed its own policies and procedures with respect to the design, appraisal, and/or implementation of a development project that it supports, was established in fiscal 1994, and the appointment of its chairman and members announced in April 1994.

The panel complements the Bank's existing systems for quality control in project preparation and implementation. As such, it will help the executive board in its governance of the Bank and will not affect the president's accountability to the executive directors for the management of Bank operations. The panel is part of the Bank's policy of improving project implementation, accountability, and openness. The panel will be functionally independent and will report directly to the Bank's executive board.

The environment favoring the establishment of an independent inspection function in the Bank was fostered by the confluence of two events: the taking of office in September 1991 of a new World Bank president, who undertook to review the overall efficiency of Bank operations, and growing criticism of the Bank on the part of nongovernmental organizations, which reflected a broad concern by some of the Bank's larger shareholders that international organizations in general, and the Bank in particular, should be more open in their activities.

Since 1991, as well, some members of the Bank's executive board, in discussions on operations evaluation and on certain problematic projects, advocated the establishment of an inspection unit. This resulted in a proposal in February 1993 by four members of the Bank's executive board for the establishment of an inspection unit to evaluate ongoing projects. A management proposal was discussed by the executive board in July, together with the February proposal; at that time, broad agreement was reached on the need for an inspection function. Subsequent discussion, including discussion on a compromise proposal, led to the decision in September 1993 to establish the panel in its current form.

An investigation by the panel must be requested by a group of people adversely affected by a particular Bank project. After the Bank's executive directors have considered a request for inspection, the Bank will make publicly available the request for inspection, the panel's recommendations on the request, and the executive directors' decision on whether to proceed. The Bank will also make publicly available the panel's report on its investigation and the management's response to it. In addition, the panel's annual report to the executive board will be published by the Bank.

Inspection in the territory of a country will be undertaken with the consent of its government.

Panel members are appointed on the basis of their professional qualifications, as well as their developmental knowledge and experience. Members are nominated by the Bank's president and are appointed by the executive directors. The members, other than the chairman, will serve initially on a part-time basis.

Appointed for a five-year term was Ernst-Gunther Broder, who served as president of the European Investment Bank and as German governor of the European Bank for Reconstruction and Development. Mr. Broder will serve as the panel's first chairman.

Alvaro Umaña Quesada, who served as minister of natural resources for Costa Rica and has been a board member of several environmental and research institutes, was appointed for a four-year term.

Richard Etter Bissell, who served for several years with the United States Agency for International Development and who has taught and overseen research at several American universities and research institutes, was appointed for three years.

By the end of fiscal 1994, the inspectors had accepted their appointments, effective August 1. The panel is expected to open for business during the first week of September.

• Enhancing those staff skills required for good portfolio management. Some 122 new staff in the seven skills areas identified as being both critical to the process and in short supply—environment, financial sector development, population and human resources, private sector development, the social sciences of anthropology and sociology, procurement, and public sector management—were recruited during fiscal year 1994.

• Developing a new training curriculum that emphasizes portfolio management and related Bank and professional skills and introducing a new performance-evaluation system designed to recognize and reward portfolio-performance management skills.

• Establishing an independent inspection panel for the review of Bank-supported projects (see Box 4-1).

• Opening a Public Information Center, which makes available to the public previously restricted operational documents (see Box 4-2).

In July 1993, a commitment was made to undertake eighty-four actions during fiscal 1994 to enhance portfolio management. According to a report made available to the executive board at

Box 4-2. Public Access to Bank Information Expands

The public's access to the World Bank's operational information was significantly expanded in fiscal 1994 with the opening at the Bank's headquarters in Washington, D.C. of a Public Information Center that responds to requests from interested parties for a variety of documents, ranging from staff appraisal reports and environmental assessments to descriptions of individual projects under preparation.

Although the Bank's relationship of trust with its borrowers rests on the institution's ability to maintain the confidentiality of certain types of information, in recent years there has been a presumption in favor of disclosure, both outside and within the Bank, in the absence of a compelling reason not to disclose. It was that presumption that was expanded during the year.

Information available at the center and through the offices of the Bank in London, Paris, Tokyo, and through other field offices includes:

• A new project information document for all projects under preparation. The document provides substantially more information on projects—and at an earlier stage—than has hitherto been available. The availability of this information will allow interested parties to raise substantive questions and concerns at an early stage.

• Staff appraisal reports—once the project concerned has been approved by the executive board. The availability of these documents is expected to help increase participation during project implementation by those affected by the project.

• Country economic and sector work (CESW). Although many CESW reports were being published after government concurrence, there is now a presumption that all these reports will be made available to the public. The Bank will continue to consult with the governments concerned to insure that confidential information is protected.

• Environmental assessments. Public availability of environmental assessment reports and analyses—before project appraisal—was expanded to include, with the borrower's consent, assessment reports and analyses for all IBRD projects, thus unifying Bankwide policy on the issue. (Availability of environmental assessment reports of IDA projects was assured in July 1993.)

• Summaries of evaluation reports, prepared by the Bank's independent Operations Evaluation Department, are included in the expanded list of public documents.

• Legal opinions prepared for the executive board, access to which had been restricted under the rule of confidentiality of board proceedings, may now be made publicly available by decision of the board on a case-by-case basis.

Interested parties can use the Internet computer network to access project information documents and to view (and order) the titles of all Bank documents available on request, as well as the abstracts and entire text of selected documents. The project information documents and environmental data sheets are available worldwide free of charge. Documents on a country where there is a Bank field office are provided free of charge at that office. Residents of a country where there is no Bank field office may obtain documents on their own country free of charge through the Public Information Center in Washington, D.C. All other documents carry a standard charge of $15.

---

the end of the past fiscal year, almost all of those actions—most of them grouped within the areas as described above—had either been completed or were at an advanced stage of completion by June 30, 1994.

The report cautioned, however, that the steps taken over the past year were only the beginning of what will be a continual, evolutionary process and that specific goals of the program of actions will only be realized over time.

According to the report, the greatest challenges for the future include fully integrating effective and efficient participatory practices into the Bank's work, altering and simplifying Bank procedures in order to shift attention to obtaining more results in the field, and getting the organizational signals and incentives right in order to truly establish a "culture of implementation" in the institution.

During the past year, the Bank also ad-dressed other sensitive issues in its project work that were not specific to the recommendations of the task force on portfolio management. Following a comprehensive review of the Bank's resettlement practices, resettlement policies were further refined.[4] In addition, a report on the Bank's experience with governance issues was issued (see Box 4-3). These two studies provided a candid assessment of the issues and a framework for improvements in Bank strategies for dealing with them. Steps such as these are an integral part of the Bank's efforts to improve participation in project preparation and project management and in the overall way that the Bank does business.

The most visible impact thus far of these efforts, particularly project restructurings and closing or cancellation of loans for poorly performing projects, has been to prevent a slide in

---

[4] For details, see page 44.

Box 4-3. The World Bank's Experience with Governance

The Bank's interest in governance—defined by the Bank as the manner in which power is exercised in the management of a country's economic and social resources for development—derives from its concern for the sustainability of the programs and projects it helps to finance.

If sustainable development is to occur, a predictable and transparent framework of rules and institutions for the conduct of private and public business must exist. Governance of borrowing countries is relevant to the Bank's work because, in its absence, much of what the institution seeks to achieve through its lending is at risk.

A 1992 report to the executive directors on governance described some of the activities the Bank was supporting in the area of governance in the form of studies, technical assistance, and its lending operations. In the intervening two years, according to a follow-up report,[1] the Bank has moved rapidly and far to support borrowing countries in strengthening the governance underpinning of their development efforts, and it has been able to do so within the framework of the economic and social dimensions of governance permissible under the Bank's Articles of Agreement.

Much of the governance work in which the Bank is engaged comprises traditional public sector management categories such as civil service reform, public expenditure management, and public enterprise reform. This is a reflection that these categories are central to how power is exercised and that, in these areas, there is a substantial agenda for rehabilitation, modernization, and change. At the same time, the Bank has extended its governance activities to entirely new areas of support under the rubrics of accountability, rule of law, and transparency. While the Bank's activities in the new areas are expanding, the bulk of the Bank's governance work will continue to be public sector management.

Public sector management work, mainly technical in character, addresses the processes and machinery of public sector performance, not necessarily its causes. This suggests that the Bank's future governance agenda should be developed at two levels: first, through more determined attempts to foster local ownership of reform programs, and second, through encouragement of institutions of civil society so that they can grow and, in turn, seek greater accountability from governments in the economic sphere.

The new procedures that have been introduced to improve project preparation and portfolio management are likely to have a strong positive influence on the Bank's work on governance. Thus:

• increased emphasis will be placed on the systemic problems of project implementation, many of which are governance related, through the country-portfolio performance-review process;

• the Bank's new disclosure policy provides an excellent opportunity to make much more transparent to the outside world how the Bank approaches complex situations in borrowing countries.

In addition, the country-assistance strategy dialogue, one of the primary vehicles for reviewing the Bank's lending strategy in a given country, can provide a forum for frank evaluation of factors, including governance issues, that constrain the effectiveness of development assistance.

---

[1] World Bank. 1994. *Governance: The World Bank's Experience*. Washington, D.C.

---

overall portfolio performance.[5] Specifically, the latest annual report on portfolio performance—for fiscal year 1993—revealed that the overall health of the Bank's portfolio—based on overall status ratings—was relatively stable between fiscal years 1992 and 1993. Since peaking at over 20 percent in fiscal 1991, the percentage of problem projects has fallen to 18 percent in fiscal years 1992 and 1993.[6]

The report also found that the percentage of problem projects based on development-objectives ratings increased marginally, from 12 percent in fiscal 1992 to 13 percent in fiscal 1993. The slight increase did not necessarily reflect a real deterioration in development performance of the Bank's portfolio, however. Rather, it reflected efforts by the Bank's six operational regions, within the limitations of the current rating methodology, to base development-objective ratings on more realis-

tic expectations about the extent to which project-development objectives would be achieved. (See Box 4-4 for a discussion of the rating systems used to indicate project effectiveness.)

---

[5] By the end of fiscal 1993, the latest date for which data are available, restructuring of 104 projects had been completed or was under way, while restructuring of thirty-six others was being planned. Seventy-seven problem projects were closed or canceled in fiscal 1993 as compared with thirty-eight projects in fiscal year 1992. The project restructurings and closings/cancellations have had a positive effect on the age structure of problem projects, with the greatest improvement in the proportion of projects that had been rated as being problematic for two consecutive years. They have also helped to increase the disbursement ratio in the Bank's portfolio in most operational regions.

[6] Excluding countries that were in nonaccrual status and/or suffered serious civil conflict in fiscal 1993, the percentage of problem projects declined from more than 18 percent in fiscal 1991 to 16 percent in fiscal 1992 and 15 percent in fiscal 1993.

Box 4-4. Increasing the Reliability of Rating Project Effectiveness

Projects are rated on a four-point scale to determine the extent to which project-development objectives (DOs) are expected to be met and to determine their overall status (OS). Projects are rated on a four-point scale, with a 1 representing the best rating and a 4 the worst. A DO rating of 1, for instance, means that all project development objectives are expected to be substantially achieved, while a 4 rating means that major objectives will probably not be achieved, and the project appears to be no longer justified. An OS rating of 1 means no significant problems, while a 4 rating indicates the existence of major problems that are not being adequately addressed.

Although DO ratings are supposed to be reflected in the OS ratings, a recent analysis of the divergence between *Annual Report on Portfolio Performance (ARPP)* and project completion report/performance audit report ratings for a sample of more than 1,000 projects completed in the 1980s concluded that OS ratings seemed to be dominated by short-term concerns about implementation, while DO ratings reflected longer-term optimism that objectives would be achieved once implementation problems were resolved. Neither rating, therefore, was judged as being reliable in measuring the development effectiveness of projects in the sample. As a result, Bank staff were required, for the purposes of the most recent *ARPP*, to pay greater attention to the quality of DO ratings. In addition, any significant gap in assessments based on OS and DO was to be explained.

The greater attention of staff to the DO ratings in the *Annual Report on Portfolio Performance* for fiscal 1993 helped to improve the reliability of those ratings. However, key to further and substantial improvement in their reliability are the precise definition of the expected development results for each project and better means for gauging progress toward these results during the loan disbursement or implementation period.

In principle, progress should be assessed using the same cost/benefit or cost-effectiveness criteria that are applied at project appraisal or at completion. If costs were not a constraint, this would involve repeating periodically during project implementation the original cost/benefit or cost-effectiveness analysis done at appraisal with revised or updated data or estimates. As a practical and less costly alternative, however, the portfolio management task force recommended that progress toward expected development results be monitored based on the evolution of a limited number of variables ("performance indicators") that have been identified in the risk/sensitivity analysis at appraisal as critical to achieving the expected project development results. This requires substantial improvements in risk/sensitivity analysis and performance-indicator monitoring.

As part of the action plan to improve portfolio management, work is proceeding on developing guidance to staff on risk/sensitivity analysis and performance indicators. Based on this work, revision of the project-rating methodology and project-performance rating system was initiated in June 1994. The major revision entails, among other things, the adoption of a dual rating system that would give separate overall ratings to the implementation status of a project and to its development effectiveness (thus, DO ratings would no longer be subsumed as part of the OS ratings); greater attention to risks in the new DO ratings; greater use of performance indicators to measure development effectiveness; and the adoption of guidelines for *ex-post* evaluation of development results of completed projects and for the evaluation of development results of ongoing projects. Full implementation of these improvements will realistically take a few years given the sharp departure from current practices that is entailed and the large number of projects in the Bank's portfolio.

Beyond the immediate effects of portfolio clean-up, however, a definitive turnaround in overall performance in the next few years is not assured. Against the ongoing efforts to improve the management of portfolio performance must be reckoned the implementation risks inherent in the ambitious and complex development agenda of the Bank and its borrowers. The risks associated with Bank lending to borrowers that are at an early and difficult stage of transition to a market economy, or of economic reform and adjustment, are also significant. As experience shows, country economic and institutional factors have ultimately a considerable effect in determining the development outcome of projects.

A sandy lane beneath poplar trees is the main roadway for conveying goods to market in this part of Chinese Turkestan.

Section Five
1994 Regional Perspectives

Africa

The year 1993, on the whole, was a difficult one for the countries of the Africa region, as gross domestic product (GDP), excluding South Africa, grew by just 1.4 percent. Although this represents an improvement over 1992, it is nevertheless disappointing, considering the region's high rate of population growth and the level needed for development. As in previous years, the countries implementing major reforms, and therefore benefiting from the Special Program of Assistance (SPA), saw their aggregate output increase by 2.1 percent, or more than the average for the region.[1] The sixteen core (or steady) reformers did still

better, as their GDP rose by 2.8 percent; the countries comprising the CFA Zone, however, saw their economies contract for a third consecutive year.[2] A positive development in 1993

---

[1] The SPA for low-income, debt-distressed sub-Saharan African countries provides quick-disbursing balance-of-payments assistance to twenty-nine eligible countries (as of the end of June 1994) in support of reform programs developed in conjunction with the Bank and the International Monetary Fund (IMF).
[2] The countries are Benin, Burkina Faso, Cameroon, Central African Republic, Chad, Comoros, Congo, Côte d'Ivoire, Gabon, Mali, Mauritania, Niger, Senegal, and Togo.

Table 5-1. **Africa: 1992 Population and Per Capita GNP of Countries that Borrowed during Fiscal Years 1992–94**

Country	Population[a] (millions)	Per capita GNP[b] (US dollars)	Country	Population[a] (millions)	Per capita GNP[b] (US dollars)
Angola[c]	9.7	—	Madagascar	12.4	230
Benin	5.0	410	Malawi	9.1	210
Burkina Faso	9.5	300	Mali	9.0	310
Burundi	5.8	210	Mauritania	2.1	530
Cameroon	12.2	820	Mauritius	1.1	2,700
Cape Verde	0.4	850	Mozambique	16.5	60
Central African Republic	3.2	410	Niger	8.2	280
Chad	6.0	220	Nigeria	101.9	320
Comoros	0.5	510	Rwanda	7.3	250
Congo	2.4	1,030	São Tomé and Principe	0.1	360
Côte d'Ivoire	12.9	670	Senegal	7.8	780
Equatorial Guinea	0.4	330	Seychelles	0.1	5,460
Ethiopia	54.8	110	Sierra Leone	4.4	170
Gabon	1.2	4,450	Sudan[d]	26.5	—
Gambia, The	1.0	370	Tanzania	25.9	110
Ghana	15.8	450	Togo	3.9	390
Guinea	6.1	510	Uganda	17.5	170
Guinea-Bissau	1.0	220	Zaire[d]	39.8	—
Kenya	25.7	310	Zambia[d]	8.3	—
Lesotho	1.9	590	Zimbabwe	10.4	570

NOTE: The 1992 estimates of GNP per capita presented above are from the "World Development Indicators" section of *World Development Report 1994*.
— Not available.
a. Estimates for mid 1992.
b. *World Bank Atlas* methodology, 1990–92 base period.
c. Estimated as lower-middle-income ($676–$2,695).
d. Estimated as low-income ($675 or less).

was that, on average, the low-income countries performed better than the middle-income ones, although neither group recorded an increase in per capita terms.

Some of the highest growth rates were achieved by those countries, such as Lesotho, Malawi, Mozambique, and Zambia that were recovering from the severe drought of 1991–92. The rather quick recovery of these and other countries from the effects of the drought is testimony to the relative resilience of their economies and to the effectiveness of collaboration among their public administrations, donors, and nongovernmental organizations (NGOs). The improvement in weather conditions was not generalized, however. Drought persisted in some areas, posing a serious threat in parts of Ethiopia and Kenya, and the countries of the western Sahel experienced poor rainfall. In addition, in these and other countries growth was held back by political transition, a high debt burden (despite debt forgiveness and reschedulings), a deterioration in the terms of trade, and weak policy implementation.

The political transition sweeping the continent has resulted in increasing multiparty democracies; whereas there were just six democracies a few years ago, the number had reached twenty-nine by the end of June 1994. The transition, however, has not been easy, without cost, or uniformly smooth. Where transition governments are in place, power sharing has proven difficult to achieve, and opposing groups still vie for power in many places. On the economic front, the transition has sometimes disrupted production and commerce, affected the mobilization and allocation of resources, and diverted attention away from needed policy reforms. Yet the transition continues nearly everywhere.

There were sharp contrasts on the African scene in 1993/94. The installation of democratically elected governments in Malawi and South Africa stand in sharp contrast to the mass killings in Rwanda. There were a variety of outcomes in the economic sphere, too, due to the contradictory forces at play not just across countries, but within them and even

Table 5-2. **Lending to Borrowers in Africa, by Sector, 1985–94**
(millions of US dollars; fiscal years)

Sector	Annual average, 1985–89	1990	1991	1992	1993	1994
Agriculture	533.9	997.4	504.9	707.4	318.3	152.6
Energy						
Oil and gas	20.6	—	300.0	48.5	2.4	186.2
Power	113.9	230.0	155.0	86.0	356.0	90.0
Environment	—	—	—	—	—	2.6
Human Resources						
Education	122.8	350.7	265.9	402.9	417.4	325.5
Population, health, and nutrition	75.7	232.7	432.8	100.3	131.2	161.6
Social sector	—	—	—	—	—	—
Industry and Finance						
Industry	124.6	180.1	11.0	200.0	83.5	29.6
Finance	241.3	193.6	138.8	619.9	252.3	400.1
Infrastructure and Urban Development						
Telecommunications	50.0	225.0	12.8	—	89.1	—
Transportation	339.4	543.6	309.5	242.8	483.0	515.0
Urban development	177.2	360.4	98.3	233.8	61.2	111.4
Water supply and sewerage	102.9	257.2	256.0	297.4	67.2	74.1
Mining and Other Extractive	31.5	—	21.0	6.0	—	—
Multisector	504.0	285.6	861.0	895.0	434.2	711.0
Public Sector Management	81.0	76.6	27.2	133.6	121.5	48.2
Tourism	—	—	—	—	—	—
Total	2,519.0	3,932.9	3,394.2	3,973.6	2,817.3	2,807.9
Of which: IBRD	909.3	1,147.0	662.9	738.4	47.0	127.7
IDA	1,609.7	2,785.9	2,731.3	3,235.2	2,770.3	2,680.0
Number of operations	80	86	77	77	75	60

NOTE: Details may not add to totals because of rounding.
— Zero.

Tanzanian women fishing in the Rufiji river delta. The Bank is preparing long-term projections on Africa's coastal fishing.

within sectors. Some countries (such as The Gambia, Sierra Leone, and Zimbabwe), where the implementation of reform programs is on track, nonetheless experienced low GDP growth rates due to the deterioration of their terms of trade, weather conditions, the lingering effects of the 1991–92 drought, or the disruptions caused by rebel activity and political transition. In contrast, other countries (such as Equatorial Guinea and Sudan, for example), where reform programs were lacking or off-track, registered growth of 6 percent to 7 percent, helped by oil exports or favorable agricultural conditions. In yet other countries, results were uneven, with agricultural growth coinciding with a decline in industrial production and services, or a decline in overall exports accompanied nevertheless by an expansion of nontraditional exports. Contrasts also marked the implementation of policies. While the countries of the CFA Zone as a group failed to take the necessary measures to restore their competitiveness in 1993, many of them implemented significant structural reforms in the fiscal, financial, trade, and other areas. In several of the good performers, the improvements that took place were still inadequate, however; savings rates, for example, remained too low to support rapid, sustained growth, and social conditions continued unsatisfactory.

Despite this panoply of variations, the events of the past twelve months have some common elements that provide encouraging signs for the future. Despite delays and costs in terms of lives and physical assets, the democratization process is moving ahead. Despite economic and political hardships, reform programs have survived in most countries and have even been strengthened in some. Several countries improved their performance in the course of the past year, and the members of the CFA Zone have taken an historic, bold step to improve their competitiveness. While much remains to be done, more countries are embarked on reform programs and face better prospects than compared with a year ago.

Varying Policies, Varying Performance

Another common thread of Africa's experience, despite the contrasts noted, is that African countries that have sustained adjustment policies generally have performed better than those countries that have not. This observation, made in a recently released staff study that covered the adjustment experience in sub-Saharan Africa from 1981 through 1991 (see Box 5–1), is complemented by comparing the more recent experience of a country where policy reform has been seriously interrupted (Nigeria) with a country that strayed from, but

---

Box 5-1. Implementation of Economic Reform: Overview and Seven Case Studies

The encouraging news from sub-Saharan Africa is that countries that have persisted in implementing economic reforms have begun to see payoffs. A recent World Bank report[1] has traced the effects of policy reforms during 1981–91 in a group of twenty-nine countries. Of this group, the six with the greatest success in eliminating macroeconomic imbalances enjoyed the strongest resurgence in economic performance, experiencing a median increase of almost 2 percentage points in the growth rate of GDP per person. The increase in their industrial and export growth rates was even more striking. Agricultural growth also accelerated in the countries that taxed their farmers less. By contrast, countries that did not improve their policies saw median incomes decline by 2 percent a year.

Seven case studies completed by the Africa Regional Office of the World Bank—from Burundi, Côte d'Ivoire, Ghana, Kenya, Nigeria, Senegal, and Tanzania—reinforce this finding, while explaining in greater detail the interaction between initial conditions, external developments, and social and political choices in implementing economic reforms.[2] The primacy of sound macroeconomic policies and stability for sustaining economic development, responding effectively to domestic and external shocks, and sending credible signals to the private sector are clearly shown in the case studies.

Broadly speaking, the economic reform programs in all seven countries addressed the problems of high budgetary and balance-of-payments deficits, distortions in markets for goods and services and factors of production, suppressed private sectors, and inefficient public services.

Policy adjustments were undertaken to establish market-determined exchange rates; improve revenue mobilization, while reallocating or reducing government expenditures, especially investment; liberalize domestic prices (especially in agriculture), trade and tariff regimes, and agricultural marketing; introduce nondistortionary interest rates and strengthen financial sector regulation; enhance the efficiency of public enterprises and labor markets; and improve the coverage and quality of social services.

The case studies highlight several factors that could explain the diverse economic outcomes in the region. The ability to persist with the fundamentals—macroeconomic stability, price and market liberalization, and adequate social sector allocations—separates the successes from the failures. Ghana, Kenya, and Tanzania are examples where a fairly good track record in these areas was beginning to be established by the late 1980s. However, even where there is some progress on the fundamentals, the lack of action on other fronts—notably the financial sector and public enterprise and civil service reform—has proven costly. Most policy reversals have been caused by the inability to move forward in a coordinated manner in the core reform areas or the inability or unwillingness to maintain the initial momentum of such reforms.

---

[1] World Bank. 1994. *Adjustment in Africa: Reforms, Results, and the Road Ahead.* New York: Oxford University Press.
[2] Husain, Ishrat, and Rashid Faruqee, eds. 1994. *Adjustment in Africa: Lessons from Country Case Studies.* World Bank, Washington, D.C.

---

reembarked on, policy reform (Kenya) and with one that has remained steadily on the reform path (Uganda).

Nigeria went through a tumultuous period in both 1992 and 1993. The planned democratic transition was protracted and, in the end, did not establish civilian rule. The process generated considerable uncertainty, economic disruptions, and social unrest. Budgetary control deteriorated, leading to fiscal deficits, which exceeded 10 percent of GDP. Inflation rose to 40 percent in 1992 and 58 percent in 1993. The official exchange rate was pegged below market rates, with the spread reaching 100 percent by late 1993. The external balance deteriorated significantly, with reserves dwindling and arrears to external creditors rising to more than $6 billion, or one fifth of outstanding debt. Meanwhile, the economy grew by only 4.1 percent in 1992 and 1.9 percent in 1993, compared with an average 5 percent in the preceding six years. The economic policies announced in the

1994 budget abolished free transactions in the foreign exchange and credit markets, thereby removing the remaining core pillars of the structural adjustment program adopted in 1986.

In 1990–92, Kenya witnessed a sharp decline in all major macroeconomic performance indicators. However, in early 1993, the Kenya authorities signalled an interest in restarting the reform process, and, as a result, the conditions for strong medium-term growth in Kenya have improved significantly. Implementation of stabilization policies and more effective enforcement of financial sector regulations have sharply reduced runaway inflation (falling to an annual rate of around 15 percent during the last quarter of 1993 after peaking at around 100 percent during the second quarter). Important steps towards structural reform, particularly in the area of external trade, have begun to gradually restore domestic and international confidence in the government's commitment to reform. With the elimination of all but a short list of import licenses and the introduction of a unified and stabilized market-determined exchange rate (the Kenya shilling becoming fully convertible in May 1994), the stage has been set for the private, and especially the export, sector to lead the recovery. By the end of 1993, monetary control had been tightened, discipline had been reintroduced in the financial sector, the maize market had been fully liberalized, and foreign-exchange reserves had recovered to comfortable levels. These improvements facilitated the approval by the International Monetary Fund (IMF) of a one-year Enhanced Structural Adjustment Facility arrangement during the fourth quarter of 1993, as well as the successful rescheduling of external arrears with the Paris Club in January 1994.

Uganda has gone quite far in creating a free enterprise economy. At the same time, the government has stabilized the economy through tight fiscal and monetary programs. Inflation was reduced to around 4 percent in 1993, down from 45 percent in 1992 and 240 percent in 1987, the year in which the present adjustment program was initiated. Uganda has in place a program of comprehensive structural reforms covering the civil service, public enterprises, and major financial institutions, and is undertaking a large reduction in military forces to release resources for priority spending programs. These reforms have had a positive effect on the economy: Real GDP growth is estimated to have reached 6 percent in 1993, enabling per capita consumption to rise by about 2.5 percent. The lowered inflation has contributed to a stable exchange rate and renewed confidence in the country's currency. In addition, the downward slide in coffee production, the country's main export, has been halted. There are also signs that nontraditional exports are growing rapidly; that the public's willingness to hold financial assets in the form of savings and time deposits, which have increased fourfold in the past two years, is increasing; that the inflow of private capital has been substantial; and that investment, including rehabilitation and reconstruction work on properties of returning entrepreneurs, is on the rise. All of these gains, together with the increased focus of government spending on basic social services, are expected to have a positive impact on poverty reduction.

Improved Competitiveness

The countries of the CFA Zone have faced major economic, financial, and social difficulties since 1986. These difficulties were caused by a downward deflationary spiral of production, incomes, and expenditures that cut average real per capita income by 40 percent, reduced the capacity of governments to provide basic social services, increased the incidence of poverty, and undermined the Zone's financial institutions. The spiral, in turn, was caused by a massive loss of competitiveness that resulted from a combination of the inflated cost structure existing in the mid 1980s and the major external shocks suffered since then. The prices of the Zone's major exports (coffee, cocoa, cotton, phosphate, uranium, and oil) dropped sharply in the second half of the 1980s, causing its terms of trade to fall by 40 percent between 1985 and 1992. The Zone's real effective exchange rate (REER) appreciated by 39 percent over the same period. That movement was the result of the depreciation, since 1985, of the United States dollar and the large depreciation achieved by many competing developing countries of their own REERs through nominal devaluations in the context of economic reforms. The internal adjustment programs and structural reforms pursued by various CFA countries in the period 1986–93 were able neither to correct this massive loss of competitiveness nor halt the ongoing downward spiral.

Recession and financial crisis in the CFA Zone continued throughout 1993. Moreover, as it became increasingly clear that internal adjustment programs were not working, external financing for them dried up. For 1993 as a whole, per capita real income declined by 4.5 percent, exports fell by 3.9 percent in volume, and investment further contracted to 13.8 percent of GDP.

Against this backdrop, in early January 1994 the heads of state of the CFA countries met in Dakar to discuss ways to end the economic crisis. The meeting resulted in the historic decision to change the parity of the CFA franc from 50 per French franc, a level at which it had been fixed in 1948, to 100 per French franc.[3] At the Dakar meeting, another important, although less publicized, step was taken: the signing of a treaty transforming the West African Monetary Union into a full economic union. A common approach to the implementation of economic reforms that were needed to accompany the parity change was also discussed.

The decisions made at the Dakar meeting have provided a unique opportunity to restart the stalled structural adjustment process in the fourteen countries, restore growth, and reduce poverty. Indeed, since January, nearly all countries have adopted reform programs that

---

[3] The parity of Comoros' currency was changed to 75 per French franc.

are being supported by the World Bank and the IMF. All postdevaluation programs give priority to restraining inflation to ensure that the nominal parity change actually leads to a substantial depreciation of the real exchange rate. Hence, public sector wage increases have generally been limited to 10 percent to 15 percent to prevent a wage-price spiral. To allow some time for urban wage earners to adjust to the higher cost of imported items, increases in the prices of selected imported goods (petroleum products, rice, sugar, edible oils, medicines, and school books, for instance) are being curtailed through temporary tax reductions and direct subsidies. Fiscal reform—reduction of deficits to sustainable levels, tax reform, and restructuring of expenditures—also figures prominently as an objective of the reform programs. Priority, however, has been given to protecting vulnerable groups and relaunching poverty-reduction programs by increasing public expenditures on basic education and health services, developing and implementing social funds targeted at the poorest groups, and expanding labor-intensive public works programs.

Regional Cooperation Efforts

The recent events in the CFA Zone and the new challenges facing South Africa and its neighbors call for strengthened regional cooperation. Various actions have already been taken in this direction, and others are under consideration. In the CFA Zone, the member countries of the new West African Economic and Monetary Union (UEMOA) and the Central African Monetary Union have decided to form economic—as well as monetary—links. In Western Africa, the signing of the treaty for the new union by the six member states was accompanied by further efforts to render budgetary policies coherent, harmonize tariffs and indirect taxes, and develop a regional financial market. In Central Africa, the six member states of the Central African Customs and Economic Union have taken advantage of their increased competitiveness to accelerate the implementation of a new common external tariff. Nontariff barriers have been removed, and rates have been lowered.

These efforts are being supported by the Bank, together with the IMF, the European Union, and other interested donors.

At the level of the entire CFA Zone, progress was made during the fiscal year in the areas of social-security provision and collection of statistics. With a view to providing a positive environment for private sector-led growth, a treaty has been signed that will put into place a common framework for business law.

The World Bank, together with the IMF, the European Commission for the European Union, and the African Development Bank, is cosponsoring an initiative to facilitate private investment, trade, and payments in Eastern and Southern Africa and in the Indian Ocean countries—the cross-border initiative (CBI).

The CBI is based on a new integration concept that promotes mobility of factors, goods, and services across national boundaries among participating countries while minimizing chances for diversion of trade and investment. It involves voluntary participation by countries that are ready to accelerate the reform effort, and is based on the principle of reciprocity among the participating countries. The proposed reform measures are in the areas of trade liberalization, liberalization of the exchange system, deregulation of cross-border investment, strengthening of financial intermediation, and the movement of goods and persons among the participating countries. The reform agenda supported under the CBI has been developed through a two-year process of discussion by public and private sector representatives of the participating countries, as well as consultations with regional institutions.

The CBI was endorsed by thirteen countries at a meeting in Kampala, Uganda, in August 1993. To date, nine countries (Kenya, Malawi, Mauritius, Namibia, Rwanda, Swaziland, Uganda, Zambia, and Zimbabwe) have confirmed their intention to participate and have established mechanisms to prepare country-specific proposals for implementing the CBI-supported reform agenda.

In addition, the heads of state of Kenya, Tanzania, and Uganda (the members of the former East African Community) recently met in Arusha, Tanzania, to reaffirm their commitment to strengthened cooperation. There is a consensus that this cooperation should be based on practical improvements in investment incentives and tax regimes, and streamlined border formalities.

The Bank's Assistance Strategy

The priorities for the Bank in Africa are poverty reduction through environmentally sustainable development; human resources development—not just through lending but also by defining frameworks for effective interventions by governments and donors, as in a recent staff study on health in Africa (see Box 5-2); providing an exceptional response, already in progress, to the situation and events in the CFA Zone; working with major partners to fulfill the objectives and the priorities of the SPA; and "getting results in the field" through the improved quality of projects and their

Box 5-2. Toward Better Health in Africa

Health issues are assuming an increasingly important place in the Bank's assistance strategy in Africa. Reflecting this trend, a major sector study was completed in 1993 in close cooperation with the World Health Organisation, the United Nations Children's Fund, and other partners. The study, *Better Health In Africa*, aimed at building consensus on future health strategies in Africa among the many stakeholders.[1] It found that while dramatic improvements had taken place since independence, most African countries lagged well behind other developing countries in health status. At fifty-one years in 1991, life expectancy at birth in Africa is eleven years less than in the low-income countries as a group, and Africa's infant mortality rate, at over 100 deaths per 1,000 live births, is about one third higher on average than for the universe of low-income countries. New health problems, such as AIDS, and new strains of well-known diseases such as malaria, threaten the important health gains made in Africa over the past generation.

The report discussed "best practices" for health improvement by African governments and their external partners in three areas. First, as did *World Development Report 1993—Investing in Health*, the report emphasized the importance of strengthening the capacity of households and communities to recognize and respond to health problems. This requires health and development strategies that increase the access of the poor to income and opportunity, pay special attention to female education and literacy, provide for community monitoring and management of health services, and furnish information to the public and health-care providers on health conditions and services. Second, the report called for reform of African health-care systems, and especially for making a basic package of cost-effective health services available to Africans near where they live and work through health centers and first-referral hospitals. Third, the report underscored the need for more efficient allocation and management of public financial and human resources devoted to health improvement, and for their progressive reallocation away from less cost-effective interventions (largely provided through tertiary facilities) to a basic package. It found substantial room for increases in technical efficiency.[2]

The report concluded that substantial health improvement in Africa is feasible, despite the severe financial constraints facing most African countries. The will to reform and to provide a limited package of quality, low-cost, and highly cost-effective health services to the vast majority of the population is central to success. The study found that higher-income and middle-income African countries, in due course, should be able to finance a basic package of health services for their people from public and nongovernmental resources, without substantial external support. However, the low-income countries are likely to need donor assistance in support of health for an extended period. These countries now spend about $8 per capita annually on health from all sources—public, nongovernmental, and external—compared with the indicative estimate for the basic package in the study of about $13. The transition from the current to the indicative level of spending will have to be implemented flexibly, on a country-by-country basis, with provisions put in place for interim targets to be met along the way.

---

[1] World Bank. 1994. *Better Health in Africa*. Washington, D.C.

[2] For example, poor drug selection, procurement, distribution, and prescription practices are responsible, together with other factors, for an effective consumption of only about $12 on drugs for every $100 in public spending on pharmaceuticals in many African countries.

---

implementation, especially through strong capacity-building efforts.

Poverty reduction through environmentally sustainable development. The need and urgency to reduce poverty in the region is evident; however, progress has been limited in Africa as a whole, despite success in some countries. Achieving a high rate of economic growth, combined with a pattern of growth favoring increases in incomes in the poorest sections of society, is central to the Bank's poverty-reduction strategy. The Bank's two-pronged strategy, as elaborated in *World Development Report 1990*, acts as a guide to the institution's economic and sector work, as well as to its lending operations.

Fighting land degradation and desertification have been key objectives of the Bank in its environmental program for the region. This program has been addressed primarily through the elaboration and implementation of national environmental action plans (NEAPs) and through the Bank's lending program. NEAPs—which provide a basis for the Bank's dialogue with borrowers on environmental issues, describe a country's major environmental problems and concerns, and formulate actions to address whatever problems are identified—have systematically paid attention to arresting land degradation through better natural resource management. The Bank's regional portfolio includes more than $500 million in environmental projects, some of which can be directly linked to the NEAP process. The Bank has also been involved in the preparation of a new international convention on desertification that is cur-

Table 5-3. **World Bank Commitments, Disbursements, and Net Transfers in Africa, 1990–94**
(millions of US dollars; fiscal years)

Item	Nigeria start 1994	1994	1990–94	Côte d'Ivoire start 1994	1994	1990–94	Sudan start 1994	1994	1990–94	Total region start 1994	1994	1990–94
Undisbursed commitments	2,461			423			181			13,118		
Commitments		—	1,954		376	1,365		—	98		2,808	16,953
Gross disbursements		353	1,646		306	1,073		48	378		3,195	14,002
Repayments		348	1,402		183	769		3	49		1,116	4,678
Net disbursements		5	243		123	304		45	329		2,079	9,324
Interest and charges		270	1,325		149	767		4	36		868	4,221
Net transfer		−265	−1,082		−26	−463		41	293		1,211	5,103

NOTE: Disbursements from the IDA Special Fund are included. The countries shown in the table are those with the largest amounts of public or publicly guaranteed long-term debt. Details may not add to totals because of rounding.
— Zero.

rently being negotiated and is prepared to be a partner in its implementation when it enters into effect.

Assistance to CFA countries. Since the parity change and as of June 30, 1994, IDA has provided approximately $1 billion in quick-disbursing credits and adjustment operations to the CFA countries. For the short term, the Bank-supported postdevaluation programs include, in addition to steps to limit the price increases of essential goods, (a) a draw-down of reserve stocks and additional imports of essential foodstuffs to counter speculative commercial practices, (b) increased budgetary appropriations for education and health, and (c) steps to assure adequate supplies of essential drugs in public health facilities and of low-cost generic drugs in private pharmacies. For the longer term, expenditures on labor-intensive civil works programs, rural infrastructure, education, and health will be increased, as will special programs (nutrition in particular) that target the poorest groups and that will be implemented by NGOs and community associations.

SPA—phase three. The third phase of the Special Program of Assistance (SPA-3), launched by the program's donors in October 1993, will cover the three calendar years 1994–96. Since the CFA Zone countries instituted a parity change in their currency and launched comprehensive economic reforms, two additional countries, Comoros and Côte d'Ivoire, have met SPA eligibility requirements, bringing the total of eligible countries to twenty-nine. The estimated requirements of donor adjustment assistance for these countries is $12 billion over the three-year period. The SPA donors have met twice since the parity change to discuss financing requirements. Total donor

pledges have increased, and some disbursements will be accelerated in response to these needs. In addition to mobilizing additional resources, SPA donors have stressed the need to pursue greater selectivity in allocating resources to ensure that countries with strong reform programs are adequately funded and that scarce resources are used efficiently. As of June 30, 1994, the donor community had pledged $6.6 billion in quick-disbursing balance-of-payments assistance, and further efforts are continuing to close the remaining gap.

The priorities and objectives of SPA-3 are achieving higher growth rates and alleviating poverty; supplementing policy-reform programs with more investment in human resources and infrastructure; raising the level of domestic savings and private investment; placing greater emphasis on ensuring that the benefits of growth are directed at reducing poverty; and strengthening local economic management and institutional capacity. The SPA's primary objective continues to be to assist countries to strengthen their policy-reform programs and structural reform efforts. However, to accelerate growth, reduce poverty, and realize the full benefits of policy reforms, the efficiency of public investment financing by donors, which still accounts for about 80 percent of total donor financing, must be improved substantially. Discussion is continuing on sectorwide approaches to donor financing aimed at improving aid coordination and effectiveness. The SPA's role would be to serve as a catalyst to encourage donor support for such integrated sector programs, to monitor outcomes, and promote the harmonization of donor procedures. Mobilization of resources and coordination of specific sector-investment programs will continue at the country level through mechanisms such as consultative groups, roundtables, and country-based local aid-coordination groups.

Project quality and implementation. Despite the difficulties faced by the region, portfolio performance was relatively stable in 1993. Differences among countries were caused, in part, by variation in macroeconomic performance. Overall, adjusting countries had a better record of project performance than the nonadjusting ones, and operations in the particularly difficult areas of agriculture and adjustment lending improved their implementation records. The most serious general constraints to effective implementation are uncertain borrower ownership and limited local capacity. To increase ownership, the Bank is making a concerted effort to involve stakeholders (governments, beneficiaries, the private sector) in project preparation and implementation. The use of participatory approaches—beneficiary assessments, participatory rural assessments, and participatory workshops—is steadily increasing. In many cases, stakeholders participate not just in project design and preparation but also in economic and sector work (ESW). Several actions are under way to improve project quality at entry such as preparation of "letters of sector policy," avoiding unnecessary complexity in project design (through participatory approaches to project preparation and greater involvement by resident missions in the process, for example), testing new or complex approaches in small pilot operations, and identifying project-monitoring indicators that reflect both output and impact. In fiscal 1993, the most recent year for which numbers are available,

the amount of loan cancellations expected to result from completed or planned restructurings of problem projects totaled about $500 million.

The need for capacity building in Africa cuts across all sectors, and, in all cases the need is urgent and acute. The challenge involves both making greater use of existing local capacity and helping to build such capacity where it does not exist. The Bank's approach recognizes that capacity-building issues need to be addressed at an early stage in the project cycle and that the effort cannot succeed without improving the performance and productivity of the civil service. This concern has led the Bank to appoint a Capacity Building Committee to make recommendations on the most effective ways to advance toward this goal. The committee's recommendations (which highlight "best practices" to follow and cover a broad spectrum, from ESW and lending to the role of resident missions) have been approved and are being carried out.

Capacity building—as well as dialogue with the intended beneficiaries of development—continued to be the focus of the Bank's work in South Africa during the past year. In that country, the Bank's informal work has dealt with the entire political spectrum, including nongovernmental organizations, the private sector, teachers, and trade unions. Dozens of South Africans have been trained in economics, and relationships have been built up with many of the country's economic and political actors. In April 1994, the Bank opened up a resident mission, following a request from the multiparty South African transitional council.

East Asia and Pacific

Strong economic growth across almost all countries dominated the development picture in the East Asia and Pacific region in calendar year 1993. In addition to its remarkable poverty reduction in recent years, East Asia and Pacific again led all regions—developing and developed—in posting a 9.2 percent growth rate, up slightly from 8.7 percent in 1992. Export growth continued to be substantial, registering an increase similar to 1992's 13.6 percent. China, the world's largest developing economy, recorded 13.4 percent growth in gross domestic product (GDP), despite concerns during 1993 about overheating the economy. China also continued to implement fiscal,

monetary, and basic market reforms (see Box 5-3). Indonesia—the region's second-largest economy—maintained a steady 6.6 percent growth rate, with significant increases in industrial production and exports; a large debt burden and environmental issues loomed as challenges to the quality and sustainability of its growth. Other countries with real rates of growth in GDP in excess of 5 percent included the Republic of Korea, the Lao People's Democratic Republic (Lao PDR), Malaysia, Thailand, and Viet Nam. A recent study concluded that if economic growth had been randomly distributed among countries, there would have been one chance in 10,000 that it would be so concentrated in a single region (see Box 5-4).

A remarkable feature of the region's economic performance in the past year was the relative evenness of steady high growth rates. The Philippines was the only major country in which the regional average lagged significantly, but recent events (successful completion of the stand-by arrangement with the IMF, completion of a Brady-type of debt agreement, reforms that encourage greater domestic and foreign competition, and efforts to increase the level and efficiency of public investment in infrastructure) gave reason for cautious optimism that better economic times may be ahead.

The small Pacific island economies witnessed a mixed performance in 1993. Fiji, the largest of these, recorded a real GDP growth rate of only 1.7 percent, compared with 3.1 percent in the previous year, as a result of the effects of a severe cyclone that struck in January 1993. The Solomon Islands also recorded a sharp drop in GDP growth to about 2.5 percent—as compared with 8.2 percent in 1992—reflecting a slowdown in logging activity and a decline in fishing. Signs of recovery were seen elsewhere, however: Recovering from the effects of two major cyclones, the Western Samoan economy grew by about 5 percent; Vanuatu also saw a slight upturn during the year.

Economic growth in some of the islands benefited from a pick-up in tourism following the recovery from recessionary conditions in major source markets. The Pacific island economies also continued to benefit from substantial

Table 5-4. **East Asia and Pacific: 1992 Population and Per Capita GNP of Countries that Borrowed during Fiscal Years 1992–94**

Country	Population[a] (millions)	Per capita GNP[b] (US dollars)
Cambodia[c]	9.1	—
China	1,162.2	470
Fiji	0.8	2,010
Indonesia	184.3	670
Korea, Republic of	43.7	6,790
Lao People's Democratic Republic	4.4	250
Malaysia	18.6	2,790
Maldives	0.2	500
Mongolia[d]	2.3	—
Papua New Guinea	4.1	950
Philippines	64.3	770
Solomon Islands	0.3	710
Thailand	58.0	1,840
Viet Nam[c]	69.3	—
Western Samoa	0.2	940

NOTE: The 1992 estimates of GNP per capita presented above are from the "World Development Indicators" section of *World Development Report 1994*.

— Not available.

a. Estimates for mid 1992.

b. *World Bank Atlas* methodology, 1990–92 base period.

c. Estimated as low income ($675 or less).

d. Estimated as lower-middle income ($676–$2,695).

Box 5-3. China: Continuing Reform and Development

During the past year, China's economy, in many ways, experienced the enviable difficulties that arise from significant economic success and bold market reforms. In fiscal 1994, China's tax revenues increased, as did deposits of individuals in the banking system. The nominal exchange rate remained stable after a substantial devaluation resulting from the unification of the official and swap market rates in January. Export growth was healthy, foreign direct investment continued to flow into the country in large volume, and foreign exchange reserves were steady.

The struggle to contain inflation, however, points to structural difficulties in the economy that can no longer be ignored. Ongoing price reforms and relatively large state-owned enterprise (SOE) deficits are the main causes of inflationary pressure in China.

Despite the sense of volatility as the economy continued its strong growth, most recent indicators have shown a welcome improvement and, in some areas, evidence of stabilization. In particu-lar, fixed asset investment and industrial output grew at a more reasonable pace than in the first half of the fiscal year, and month-on-month inflation appeared to be subsiding. Tighter credit—one of the most effective monetary instruments available to the central government—caused increased difficulty for SOEs, especially in the northeast of the country and the interior. Growth in output of SOEs was low, even negative, in the northeast and southwest in the second half of the fiscal year, raising the possibility of urban tension as the adjustment to the market progresses.

A Bank report recommends additional measures in key areas to address structural weaknesses in the fiscal and financial system. Provided this overall reform plan is properly implemented, China appears likely to be able to achieve high and sustainable economic growth without the benefits being dissipated in high inflation. In the coming years, however, the risk of accelerating inflation remains high as such reforms are enacted.

Box 5-4. The East Asian Miracle

A major work in fiscal 1994 was the publication of "The East Asian Miracle: Economic Growth and Public Policy," the product of a World Bank research team.[1] The report stimulated widespread debate on the components of economic policy that underpinned the spectacular performance of the high-performing East Asian countries. Significantly, the report found that there was little that could be described as "miraculous" about the economic performance, even though the chances of such a concentration of growth, assuming it were randomly distributed worldwide, were just one in 10,000. "Fundamentally sound development policy was a major ingredient in achieving rapid growth," the report observed. But—and it was this finding that aroused the most active debate—the book also noted that government intervention had played a role. How much of a role was not easy to discern, the researchers concluded.

Previous Bank studies had described these policy interventions—suppressing interest rates or promoting favored industries, for example—as always harmful to growth. The study said that "export push," a combination of sound fundamentals and selective interventions, had been crucial to East Asia's success. "Of the many interventions tried in East Asia, those associated with export push hold the most promise for other developing economies," the study concluded. Even so, it added, developing countries hoping to follow in the footsteps of East Asia should limit policy interventions and focus instead on the fundamentals.

The fundamentals that East Asian economies focused on included:
- Managing monetary and fiscal policy to ensure low inflation and a competitive exchange rate;
- Concentrating public investment in education on primary and secondary levels of schooling;
- Fostering effective and secure financial systems to encourage savings and investment;
- Limiting protection so that domestic prices are close to international prices; and
- Supporting agriculture by assisting the adoption of "green revolution" technologies, investing in rural infrastructure, and limiting taxation on agricultural goods.

A summary of the book is available in English, French, Japanese, and Spanish.

---

[1] World Bank. 1993. *The East Asian Miracle: Economic Growth and Public Policy*. A World Bank Policy Research Report. New York: Oxford University Press.

resource flows and remittances. The combination of external resource availability, openness to trade, and generally sound fiscal and monetary management has ensured relative exchange-rate stability and control over inflation. Emerging fiscal deficits in some island economies need to be reduced to ensure macroeconomic stability, however.

The Pacific islands continue to face a unique set of development challenges: They are constrained by small domestic markets, a narrow resource and production base, and high unit costs of infrastructure; they are also heavily dependent on external trade and are vulnerable to external shocks and natural disasters. Despite an almost complete absence of absolute poverty, the islands are confronting acute environmental issues which, in some cases, will significantly affect their long-term economic outlook. Deforestation in the Solomon Islands, in particular, is an issue of major economic and environmental importance to the country. Papua New Guinea also faces important issues of deforestation and preservation of ecological diversity. It has recently enjoyed rapid growth fueled by rising mineral and new oil exports, but it must cope with problems of promoting growth in the rest of the economy.

Viet Nam rejoined the Bank's list of borrowers in fiscal year 1994 after a fifteen-year hiatus, and Cambodia became a first-time borrower (see Box 5-5). By the end of the year, IDA credits, totaling $324.5 million, had been made to Viet Nam for projects in the education, transportation, and agriculture sectors, while one emergency rehabilitation credit, for $62.7 million, was approved for Cambodia. Both countries are among the poorest in the world, with annual per capita incomes of about $200, but each, for different reasons, offered signs of hope for sustainable economic development.

While overall the region performed impressively, the picture was far from unblemished, and areas of concern highlighted in last year's *Annual Report* remained as obstacles to sustained development for most, if not all, countries of the region. In particular, serious environmental damage, associated with rapid urbanization, inadequate regulation and planning, and incorrect pricing of resources, continues to impose major costs. Land degradation and deforestation also remained as serious threats to sustained growth. Because the poor suffer disproportionately from the effects of environmental degradation, environmental issues

Table 5-5. **Lending to Borrowers in East Asia and Pacific, by Sector, 1985–94**
(millions of US dollars; fiscal years)

Sector	Annual average, 1985–89	1990	1991	1992	1993	1994
Agriculture	726.9	743.0	1,374.7	826.7	1,089.3	1,735.4
Energy						
Oil and gas	54.0	86.0	—	100.0	225.0	266.0
Power	533.0	813.0	275.0	1,745.9	760.0	1,048.5
Environment	—	—	—	—	50.0	306.5
Human Resources						
Education	272.0	434.4	592.0	474.1	478.9	346.6
Population, health, and nutrition	72.8	—	164.0	129.6	200.4	160.0
Social sector	—	—	—	—	—	9.7
Industry and Finance						
Industry	259.2	—	361.7	82.7	250.0	40.0
Finance	373.1	68.0	439.3	—	457.0	100.0
Infrastructure and Urban Development						
Telecommunications	7.0	391.7	—	375.0	134.0	250.0
Transportation	726.9	497.2	323.6	1,182.5	1,132.2	1,340.0
Urban development	249.7	86.2	543.1	168.0	110.0	349.0
Water supply and sewerage	77.5	349.0	177.8	275.0	310.0	—
Mining and Other Extractive	25.2	—	—	—	—	—
Multisector	298.0	250.0	250.0	70.0	200.0	82.7
Public Sector Management	6.1	—	62.0	17.0	173.0	—
Tourism	—	—	—	—	—	—
Total	3,681.4	3,718.5	4,563.2	5,446.5	5,569.8	6,034.4
Of which: IBRD	3,107.2	3,066.8	3,471.0	4,386.9	4,404.8	4,623.8
IDA	574.2	651.7	1,092.2	1,059.6	1,165.0	1,410.6
Number of operations	40	35	39	45	45	43

NOTE: Details may not add to totals because of rounding.
— Zero.

Box 5-5. Lending to Viet Nam Resumes; Is Initiated in Cambodia

After a fifteen-year hiatus, lending resumed to Viet Nam during fiscal 1994, when two credits totaling about $228 million were approved in October 1993. One credit, for $70 million, will support a primary education project, while the second, for $158.5 million, will support highway repair. A third credit, for $96 million, was approved in January 1994; it supports a program to provide more credit and back-up services to small farmers in Viet Nam. In addition to these three investments, the Bank has been providing technical assistance for the preparation of a public investment program and for improving capacity in core ministries. The assistance is expected to enable the Bank to identify further projects in priority areas such as infrastructure, agriculture, natural resource protection, and the social sectors.

The three credits were approved after a support group of donor countries assisted Viet Nam in clearing its arrears to the IMF in October 1993.

In advance of actual lending, the Bank had done a great deal of preparatory work. Analytical work had resumed in 1989, with the result that several economic and sector reports had been completed, and a solid basis for resumption of lending had been established.

An initial donors' group meeting for Viet Nam, sponsored by the Bank and the United Nations Development Programme, was held in Paris in November, and pledges of $1.8 billion in aid were given by multilateral and bilateral donors. It was agreed that, in the future, the World Bank would chair a consultative group meeting each year, as it does for other countries.

During the past year, the Bank extended its first-ever credit to Cambodia, which joined the institution in 1970. The $62.7 million credit was in support of an emergency rehabilitation project, designed to arrest the deterioration in basic services by financing priority imports.

In addition, a policy framework paper, prepared jointly by the government, the Bank, and the IMF, was agreed upon. The paper provides details of the country's medium-term adjustment and reform program. Over the next three years, the government intends to consolidate the initial restoration of macroeconomic stability, undertake a process of institutional strengthening supported by comprehensive technical assistance, substantially increase public investment in order to address rehabilitation and reconstruction needs, and initiate a process of wide-ranging structural reforms aimed at enhancing savings, investment, and growth over the longer term.

In view of the legacy of war and devastation and the recent political transition, restoring financial stability, strengthening the central institutions of macroeconomic management, and initiating investment for rehabilitation and reconstruction comprise the most immediate tasks. The donor community has pledged its support for Cambodia's recovery. In March 1994, at a meeting of the International Committee on the Reconstruction of Cambodia, donors renewed that support based on an economic report prepared by the Bank: *Cambodia, from Rehabilitation to Reconstruction*.

Against this background, the government has adopted a medium-term adjustment program for which it is seeking support from the IMF through a three-year arrangement under the Enhanced Structural Adjustment Facility and has begun preparations for a structural adjustment credit and a companion technical assistance project with the World Bank.

---

are a major concern for the countries in the region and the Bank.

Another serious problem that has been exposed and exacerbated by the region's high growth rates is the historical inadequacy of infrastructure investment relative to rapidly growing demand. Reflecting this, Bank lending emphasizes effective infrastructure development across the region, with lending for transportation, power, and irrigation again the largest component of the overall program. Because the region's infrastructure needs, however, are so large, the Bank alone cannot have more than a marginal effect. The private sector in the countries themselves and through foreign direct investment (FDI) will have to play an increasingly critical role in developing and modernizing East Asia's infrastructure base.

Despite recent gains, the countries of the region have an average income of about $600 a year, which is low among developing countries worldwide. About 80 percent of the population is emerging from socialism—more than in Central and Eastern Europe and the former Soviet Union—while the middle-income countries of Korea, Malaysia, and Thailand comprise just 5 percent of East Asia's people. The significance of this is that East Asia has sustained rapid growth and far-reaching social and economic reforms at relatively low income levels and when their economies were undergoing major internal reforms. This augurs well and suggests that further inroads may be made in reducing poverty and protecting the environment as the reform process advances, underpinned by larger regional flows of trade and investment.

Progress in Poverty Reduction

Among all regions, East Asia and Pacific stands out as the one that has made the most

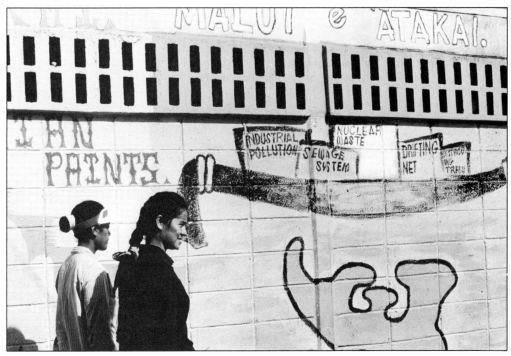

Consciousness about the environment has been raised in Tonga, as these murals attest to the vigor with which the inhabitants try to get the message across.

impressive gains in poverty reduction, as well as being the fastest growing. Living standards have quadrupled in a generation, and health and education indicators have posted significant gains. One striking feature of growth in East Asia has been its evenness; it is spread across most of the population and is not confined to a wealthy elite. Absolute poverty has fallen sharply in East Asia, from a third of the population in 1970 to a tenth in 1990, at a time when the overall population was growing.[4] In absolute numbers, East Asia's population living in absolute poverty numbered 400 million in 1970 and 180 million in 1990. Not only were 220 million people lifted above the absolute poverty mark, but over the same period, 425 million people were added to the population—also above the poverty level. The most impressive gains have been made in Indonesia, where the percentage share of absolute poverty has fallen from 60 to 15 of the total population over the period, and China, where it fell from 33 to 10 percent. But progress was impressive almost throughout the region, with Korea and Malaysia cutting their proportion of absolute poor from 23 and 18 percent, respectively, to about 5 percent in each country.

Though the gains have been outstanding, the task ahead is even more challenging. The remaining poor live in remote, barren areas and are the hardest to lift from poverty, even by sustained economic growth. For this reason, the Bank places special emphasis on targeted poverty strategies in its lending program. But there is reason for confidence: Governments in the region have shown themselves determined to invest in basic human needs, such as health care and education—steps that have proven central to an effective fight against poverty.

Obstacles to Sustained Growth

Despite its impressive performance, the region faces a number of obstacles to sustained growth; indeed, some are so formidable that, if unresolved, they could stop or even reverse the progress now being made. These obstacles include:

The environment. Developing countries of the East Asia and Pacific region have paid insufficient attention to protecting and restoring the environment as population growth, rapid urbanization, and the spread of industry have placed sizable demands on air, water, and forest resources. The consequences today are heavy, with unacceptably high pollution levels in air and water throughout much of the

---

[4] Absolute poverty is defined here as income insufficient to maintain a subsistence intake of 2,150 calories a day.

Table 5-6. **World Bank Commitments, Disbursements, and Net Transfers in East Asia and Pacific, 1990–94**
(millions of US dollars; fiscal years)

Item	China start 1994	China 1994	China 1990–94	Indonesia start 1994	Indonesia 1994	Indonesia 1990–94	Philippines start 1994	Philippines 1994	Philippines 1990–94	Total region start 1994	Total region 1994	Total region 1990–94
Undisbursed commitments	7,720			4,785			1,988			16,554		
Commitments		3,160	11,028		1,490	7,215		478	3,414		6,124	25,422
Gross disbursements		1,926	7,111		1,170	5,909		480	2,623		4,209	18,888
Repayments		282	984		833	3,332		343	1,580		2,669	11,308
Net disbursements		1,644	6,127		336	2,576		137	1,043		1,540	7,581
Interest and charges		365	1,379		882	4,038		346	1,570		2,043	9,577
Net transfer		1,279	4,748		−546	−1,462		−209	−527		−503	−1,996

NOTE: Disbursements from the IDA Special Fund are included. The countries shown in the table are those with the largest amounts of public or publicly guaranteed long-term debt. Details may not add to totals because of rounding.

region—particularly in major urban centers. Urgent steps are necessary to reverse this trend and to foster a more efficient and "environment friendly" growth in the years ahead. Addressing the region's environmental needs will cost an estimated $24 billion each year by the year 2000. The Bank has prepared environmental assessments for most countries in East Asia and is seeking to focus borrowers' attention on the long-term benefits of sound environmental policies. Environmental screening of projects, and full impact assessment and mitigation of many, is now standard Bank procedure. Reflecting this priority, the Bank emphasizes sustainable environmental practices in all its lending. In calendar year 1993—the most recent period for which complete figures are available—the Bank lent $3.6 billion dollars for projects in the region with specific environmental components. The Bank was also involved in broad-ranging policy analysis, through the publication of "Toward an Environmental Strategy for Asia,"[5] and with other initiatives including:

• the Asia Water Resources Initiative, advocating a comprehensive, river basin approach to water policy;

• the Asian biodiversity strategy, involving consultation with nongovernmental organizations and specific project preparation in the region in concert with the Global Environment Facility;

• the Metropolitan Environment Improvement Program, a coordinated approach to urban environmental management in cities such as Beijing, Jakarta, and Manila;

• Analytical work on deforestation in the vast area covered by Cambodia, the Lao PDR, and Viet Nam;

• "Rains Asia," a computer analysis of acid rains, from which national and regional policy on atmospheric emission can be drawn; and

• increased investment in environmental projects throughout the region.

Infrastructure bottlenecks. Rapid economic expansion has outstripped the capacity of existing infrastructure and has created serious impediments to further investment and rapid growth. Greater electricity-generation capacity, sufficient telecommunications facilities, better urban and intercity roads, and efficient ports are high on the list of East Asia's infrastructure needs. Bank estimates suggest that, in the 1980s, infrastructure investment in East Asia may have lagged necessary levels by much as 2 percent to 3 percent of GDP. To make up this shortfall, the region will need an estimated $1.5 trillion in infrastructure investment during the 1990s. Fifty-eight percent of Bank lending to East Asia in fiscal 1994 was for infrastructure, with most going to transportation ($1,340 million). Other infrastructure commitments included power generation ($1,049 million), irrigation ($491 million), urban development ($349 million) and telecommunications ($250 million). (See Table 5-5 for details.) The size of the investment shortfall demands that the private sector play an expanding role in infrastructure financing; in turn, governments of the region will need to establish the appropriate regulatory and legal frameworks to attract and secure such investment.

Financial sector reform. Increased flows of trade and FDI to East Asia are placing strains on existing financial structures, indicating the

---

[5] Brandon, C., and R. Ramankutty. 1993. "Toward an Environmental Strategy for Asia." World Bank Discussion Paper No. 224. Washington, D.C.

need for more flexible and responsive finance systems. The trend is already under way, but it needs to move more quickly and to incorporate building new or stronger banking systems and money markets. The Bank is working with its member countries, at a range of levels, to upgrade and liberalize finance markets and institutions.

State enterprise reform. Large, inefficient state enterprises obstruct and delay economic growth and the transition to a more efficient market economy. Progress is being made in this highly sensitive reform area across much of the region, particularly in China and Viet Nam. Malaysia is pursuing an ambitious privatization program. The Bank is encouraging borrowing countries to create a competitive environment for business growth and to take steps to expose state enterprises to the discipline of the market. At the same time, however, steps must be taken to provide alternative employment, or some social safety net, for those displaced by such reforms.

Trade imbalances. East Asia is currently running substantial trade surpluses with other trading partners, which is neither desirable nor sustainable. Although regional levels of protection are currently relatively high, reductions in tariff levels (on a nondiscriminatory basis), now under way, are projected to increase penetration of foreign products and lower surpluses while boosting the region's growth and welfare. With the region expected to provide about half the incremental growth in world trade to the year 2000, this is a priority reform area. The Bank is advocating that East Asia become a more active participant in global trade discussions, reflecting the region's rise as a major importer and exporter.

Institution building and strengthening. The need for expanding competent management across most areas of development is emerging as a major issue in East Asia. Whether in pollution monitoring and control, design and implementation of monetary and fiscal policies, or traffic-management planning and regulation, effective institutions are essential. The Bank is assisting countries in a range of fields to establish or strengthen such institutions.

Bank Activities in the Region

Past lending. The World Bank has been actively involved in lending and policy guidance in the region since it made its first loans to Thailand (for railways, ports, and irrigation) in 1950. Japan was also an early borrower and now stands as a monument to successful economic development worldwide. Cumulative Bank lending to the region is more than $70 billion, with lending to agriculture and rural development ($16.3 billion), transportation ($13.2 billion), and power ($11.8 billion) the major categories.

Fiscal year 1994. Today, the Bank deals with twenty countries in East Asia and Pacific, lending $6 billion in fiscal year 1994. China ($3.1 billion), Indonesia ($1.5 billion), and the Philippines ($478 million) were the biggest regional borrowers. Roughly $1.4 billion of the lending program was in the form of IDA credits. After a fifteen-year hiatus, lending resumed to Viet Nam; in Cambodia, the Bank extended its first-ever credit during the past year.

The Bank's mandate in all its borrowing member countries is to support broad-based economic development and the reduction of poverty. Lending, economic and sector work, and associated technical assistance is aimed at realizing this goal. Central to the Bank's overall approach, however, is the reduction of poverty. In fiscal 1994, twelve projects, valued at $1,035 million had specific poverty reduction components and were included in the program of targeted interventions; that amount was up $391 million from last year's total (eight projects worth $644 million). During the year, one poverty assessment was completed, bringing to six the cumulative total for the region.

Supervision—Next Steps

The Bank, in accordance with the recommendations of the 1992 report of the Task Force on Portfolio Management, is undertaking more regular supervision of all projects to monitor the quality and effectiveness of implementation. In addition, reviews are conducted annually or biennially of country project performance generally. Management of projects has become computerized, and field offices are now taking a more active role in supervising projects. The region expects to supervise some 300 projects a year over the next three years.

Though portfolio performance is strong, extra attention is needed because newer and less experienced member countries—in terms of economic and institutional strength—make up a growing share of the portfolio. The complexity of projects also is increasing, with some having many components (flood control, power generation, irrigation, and complete resettlement packages, for example), and some applying to several provinces in a single country.

South Asia

South Asia is a region full of contrasts. On the one hand, its economic potential is considerable. During the 1980s, the rate of economic growth in the region was 5.2 percent a year, compared with 3.9 percent among all low-income countries (excluding India and China). Its growth was exceeded—albeit significantly so—only by that in East Asia and Pacific. Progress in reducing fertility led to annual growth, in per capita terms, of nearly 3 percent during a period often referred to as the "lost decade" in many other regions of the world.

On the other hand, South Asia is also characterized by widespread poverty and unacceptably low standards of living for many of its people. While accounting for a fifth of the world's population, South Asia is also home to nearly half the world's poor (estimated at 390 million persons).[6] Regional per capita income currently averages $310, and, with the notable exception of Sri Lanka and several states in India, social indicators are poor. Life expectancy is lower than in any other region except Africa; of every ten children born, at least one is expected to die before the age of one. Problems of poor health and high rates of malnutrition are compounded by low levels of literacy—as of 1990, only 45 percent and 31

percent of South Asian men and women, respectively, were literate—and low school enrollments and high drop-outs. Nearly half of the region's children do not complete primary school.

The Challenges of Development

The Gulf crisis of 1990–91, coupled with political upheavals in the former Soviet Union (which sharply diminished traditional export markets), exposed major weaknesses in the development path that countries of the region took in the 1980s. This was demonstrated for India in 1991, when, as a result of the Gulf crisis-induced oil-price shock, a severe balance-of-payments crisis ensued, and gold reserves had to be pledged to avoid a disruption in debt servicing. Pakistan has thus far avoided the same sort of crisis, but its reserve position needs strengthening, and the government has been slow to bring chronic fiscal deficits under control. Other countries remain heavily dependent on concessional funding and are thus vulnerable to external shocks from an environment in which aggregate aid is unlikely to expand and competition for scarce funds is becoming increasingly strong.

While rates of growth in the 1980s were high, they were not sustainable. Progress at reducing poverty was most rapid in the early 1980s, but the pace moderated in the latter part of the decade, in large part the result of the worldwide slowdown in economic growth. The fundamental challenge facing South Asia today is how to continue the high economic performance of the previous decade with concomitant rapid and sustained reductions in poverty and improvements in social indicators. A sustainable growth path for the 1990s must be based on small fiscal deficits, a sustainable balance-of-payments outlook, and improved environmental quality. Countries of the region—be they small, island economies like the Maldives or semi-industrial giants like India—face three

Table 5-7. **South Asia: 1992 Population and Per Capita GNP of Countries that Borrowed during Fiscal Years 1992–94**

Country	Population[a] (millions)	Per capita GNP[b] (US dollars)
Bangladesh	114.4	220
Bhutan	1.5	180
India	883.6	310
Nepal	19.9	170
Pakistan	119.3	420
Sri Lanka	17.4	540

NOTE: The 1992 estimates of GNP per capita presented above are from the "World Development Indicators" section of *World Development Report 1994.*
a. Estimates for mid 1992.
b. *World Bank Atlas* methodology, 1990–92 base period.

[6] As estimated from Chen, Shaohua, Guarav Datt, and Martin Ravallion, "Is Poverty Increasing in the Developing World?" (Policy Research Working Paper number 1146, June 1993).

major challenges in ensuring continued progress through the 1990s:

First, to deepen economic reforms in order to attain high growth and greater economic resilience;

Second, to broaden and further accelerate efforts to reduce poverty and improve living conditions—as East Asia has shown can be done; and

Third, to better manage the environment to ensure sustainable development.

Deepening Reforms

Two themes have characterized until recently the development approach of most South Asian economies: a strong economic role for the state and relatively inward-looking development strategies. The broad consensus in development thinking—borne by the successes and failures of past decades—is that countries do better, both in generating growth and reducing poverty, with more market-friendly policies and outward-looking strategies. While there is general agreement in South Asia about the direction of needed reforms, the

pace has been uneven, typically reflecting broader political economy issues and electoral cycles. Recent progress is most evident in fiscal developments and tax reforms, external policies, and financial reforms.

In the public sector, the primary focus is on structural reforms to underpin medium-term fiscal adjustment, particularly tax reform and expenditure reduction and restructuring. In the area of tax reform, India has made significant progress in removing several tax-induced distortions. Measures set out in the fiscal year 1995 budget continue tax-reform progress by broadening the tax base and reducing the dispersion of tax rates. Excise taxes were streamlined, with many being shifted from specific to *ad valorem* rates. Taxes on corporate income, as well as on capital gains, were also reduced. Progress continued in Nepal, Pakistan, and Sri Lanka towards moving to a full-fledged value-added tax, and Pakistan made important progress in broadening the tax base by introducing an agricultural income and wealth tax.

On the fiscal side, Pakistan's political transition in 1993 contributed to a deterioration in

Table 5-8. **Lending to Borrowers in South Asia, by Sector, 1985–94**
(millions of US dollars; fiscal years)

Sector	Annual average, 1985–89	1990	1991	1992	1993	1994
Agriculture	943.9	668.0	773.0	346.1	480.7	387.8
Energy						
Oil and gas	287.2	—	735.2	330.0	—	—
Power	982.0	1,012.3	200.0	730.0	960.0	230.0
Environment	—	—	—	—	—	14.7
Human Resources						
Education	133.1	580.8	307.1	145.6	339.0	220.0
Population, health, and nutrition	65.6	192.5	388.5	377.5	827.0	233.1
Social sector	—	—	—	—	—	—
Industry and Finance						
Industry	202.0	300.0	528.0	—	—	250.3
Finance	344.8	375.0	123.5	28.4	65.8	—
Infrastructure and Urban Development						
Telecommunications	93.4	—	57.0	55.0	—	—
Transportation	310.9	191.5	178.9	306.0	120.0	491.3
Urban development	248.1	—	—	—	—	246.0
Water supply and sewerage	97.4	89.9	306.6	—	208.2	—
Mining and Other Extractive	117.6	—	—	—	12.0	—
Multisector	107.9	94.4	7.0	655.2	403.5	—
Public Sector Management	—	—	—	25.0	—	296.8
Tourism	—	—	—	—	—	—
Total	3,939.3	3,504.4	3,604.8	2,998.8	3,416.2	2,370.0
Of which: IBRD	2,465.4	1,725.5	1,540.1	1,348.0	1,145.0	474.0
IDA	1,473.8	1,778.9	2,064.7	1,650.8	2,271.2	1,896.0
Number of operations	32	26	30	24	26	19

NOTE: Details may not add to totals because of rounding.
— Zero.

A Nepalese woman sorts recently threshed grain in a remote village where mechanized labor has yet to make inroads.

the fiscal deficit, which rose to a record high 9.5 percent of gross domestic product (GDP).[7] The caretaker government moved rapidly to strengthen the fiscal position, control monetary expansion, and reduce the balance-of-payments deficit. The rupee was devalued, and measures were enacted to contain spending and increase revenue. Fiscal adjustment has continued under Pakistan's new government, leading to a notable reduction in the fiscal deficit in the second half of 1993. Fiscal stability continued in Bangladesh. Although buoyant revenues helped increase public savings from 2 percent to 2.4 percent of GDP, the expected increase in public investment lagged as a result of continuing delays in project implementation. In Sri Lanka, a reduction in current expenditures led to positive public savings for the first time in many years. In India, however, fiscal slippage occurred: The central government deficit widened from 5.6 percent of GDP in 1992 to more than 7 percent in 1993. Forty percent of the increment in the deficit can be attributed to shortfalls on the revenue side, while 60 percent was the result of an overshooting of spending targets.

Progress was slow in the area of privatization and public enterprise reform. While the privatization of small and medium-scale enterprises continued briskly in Sri Lanka, Pakistan's political transition slowed the process. In April 1994, however, the government announced that it intended to privatize fifty-one industries by the end of the calendar year. Over the past year, Nepal either privatized or liquidated seven (out of fifty-one) enterprises earmarked for divestiture.

Developing a leaner and more efficient public sector is only one part of the reform agenda. A dynamic private sector has an important complementary role to play to ensure sustained, high-quality growth. While notable advances have been made in recent years, much still remains to be done to improve the environment for private sector development in the region. In addition to continued public enterprise reform and privatization, infrastructure must be expanded and measures undertaken to improve the overall business environment through deregulation, further reductions in trade barriers, exchange-rate reforms, and financial sector development and integration—all key enabling factors necessary for private sector development.

Countries of the region continued to pursue more outward-looking strategies through trade liberalization and exchange-rate reforms. In

---

[7] The fiscal years of the region's countries vary widely. Year-specific numbers in this section, therefore, correspond roughly, unless otherwise indicated, to calendar years.

Nepal, for example, steps are under way to liberalize trade and industrial policies, unify the
exchange rate, and attain full convertibility on
the current account. In Pakistan, the government is implementing a comprehensive three-
year program of tariff reduction and trade-
policy liberalization that includes the reduction
of maximum tariffs from 92 percent to 35 percent by mid 1997. India's current budget includes additional measures to reduce peak
tariffs and lower tariff rates on imports of capital and intermediate goods. In Sri Lanka, the
government has implemented measures to
achieve current account convertibility, the forward foreign exchange market was further liberalized, and steps were taken to lower tariff
and nontariff barriers and eliminate many export and import-licensing requirements.

A recent development that underlines the
confidence of international investors in South
Asia's growth potential is the surge in capital
flows, particularly for Sri Lanka and India. In
1993, foreign direct investment (FDI) and portfolio investment in Sri Lanka were equivalent
to 2.4 percent of GDP ($248 million), while in
India, these flows reached $4.9 billion, or
nearly 2 percent of GDP. The majority of flows
in India consisted of portfolio investment,
while in Sri Lanka FDI accounted for the larger
share. Increased private capital flows represent a response by international investors to
the increasing credibility of reforms in these
countries. For the countries, these flows represent a major opportunity to increase investment performance and hence to raise growth
rates. However, making effective use of private capital flows is contingent on a continued
momentum in domestic policy reforms—both
macroeconomic and microeconomic. Without
such reforms, there would be increased risks of
rising consumption, higher inflation, and/or declining export growth, all of which could cause
reversals in capital flows.

Advancing the Agenda for Poverty Reduction

Reducing poverty and improving living conditions are central development objectives for
countries throughout South Asia. It is now uni-
versally recognized that high and sustained
economic growth is necessary for reducing levels of poverty. South Asia's growth record was
good over the past decade, and there is con-
vincing evidence that these high growth rates
were reflected in rising per capita consumption
across the income-distribution scale and falling
levels of poverty. For example, between the
mid 1970s and the end of the 1980s, poverty
levels in India fell from roughly 55 percent of
the population to 39 percent. In Pakistan, the

incidence of poverty fell from one third of the
population in the early 1980s to about a quarter
in 1991. However, country averages mask dramatic interregional differences. In India, the
populous states of Bihar and Orissa have poverty rates of nearly 55 percent, compared with
27 percent for Andhra Pradesh and 13 percent
for Punjab. Similarly, in Pakistan, 23 percent of
those who live in the northern part of Punjab
province fall below the poverty line, while
37 percent of people in the southern part are
poor.

Further progress in reducing poverty depends crucially on the success of ongoing reforms. At the same time, efforts are under way
to encourage greater use of labor, the poor's
most abundant asset. Given that the vast majority of the poor in South Asia live in rural
areas and depend on agriculture for their live-
lihood, particular emphasis is being given to
policies designed to expand output in agriculture and increase employment and earnings in
the rural off-farm sector. Efforts are also under
way to improve the enabling environment for
growth in rural areas—for example, through
accelerated investments in rural infrastructure
and reform of rural credit institutions.

Clearly, however, growth alone is not sufficient. Indeed, for many South Asian countries,
the economic growth performance of the 1980s
did not translate into commensurate improvements in social indicators. Better access to
services—particularly basic education, health,
nutrition, and family planning—and more effective safety net programs are essential. As an
element of ongoing reform programs, most
countries in the region have taken steps to re-
orient the pattern of public expenditures to address better the needs of the poor. The
prominent place of women among the beneficiaries of these initiatives reflects a growing
and welcome commitment to improving economic opportunities and living conditions for
women. For example, Pakistan is moving
ahead firmly in implementing its social action
program (SAP), which is the government's
principal vehicle for expanding coverage, quality, and effectiveness of basic services, with a
particular focus on women and children.
Progress over the past year included higher
budgetary allocations to SAP sectors (such as
basic education, health, family planning, and
rural water supply), reduction of many regulatory bottlenecks, and the initiation of institutional reforms to strengthen implementation of
the program. India has also made substantial
progress. A new, national primary school development program has been launched that
gives highest priority to districts with low rates
of female literacy, and central government

Table 5-9. **World Bank Commitments, Disbursements, and Net Transfers in South Asia, 1990–94**
(millions of US dollars; fiscal years)

Item	India start 1994	India 1994	India 1990–94	Pakistan start 1994	Pakistan 1994	Pakistan 1990–94	Bangladesh start 1994	Bangladesh 1994	Bangladesh 1990–94	Total region start 1994	Total region 1994	Total region 1990–94
Undisbursed commitments	10,374			2,793			1,523			15,891		
Commitments		929	9,788		742	3,238		597	2,021		2,370	16,134
Gross disbursements		1,716	9,793		540	2,812		360	1,722		2,768	15,284
Repayments		963	3,570		194	685		33	110		1,211	4,448
Net disbursements		753	6,223		345	2,127		327	1,612		1,558	10,836
Interest and charges		838	3,833		215	875		40	174		1,114	4,980
Net transfer		−85	2,390		130	1,252		287	1,438		444	5,856

NOTE: Disbursements from the IDA Special Fund are included. The countries shown in the table are those with the largest amounts of public or publicly guaranteed long-term debt. Details may not add to totals because of rounding.

funding has been increased for endemic disease-control programs. In Sri Lanka, steps have been taken to improve the targeting of income-transfer and social safety net programs.

The role of local governments is expanding, and a more hospitable environment in which nongovernmental organizations (NGOs) can operate in the region is being created. Bangladesh is in the midst of implementing a new local government structure, with the objective of increasing grassroots participation in the design and implementation of programs to develop human resources and local infrastructure. District elections have been held; sub-district development coordinating committees established; and the entire local government structure is expected to be in place by mid 1994. Governments' attitudes towards NGOs have become far more positive over the past several years, and the region is host to some of the world's best-known NGO initiatives, such as Bangladesh's Grameen Bank, the Bangladesh Rural Advancement Committee, India's Self-Employed Women's Association, the Aga Khan Rural Support Project (AKRSP) in Pakistan, and Sri Lanka's Sarvodaya, as well as a wide range of lesser-known but equally impressive NGO efforts. These diverse programs have great potential for helping to reduce poverty and improve living conditions in the region. Some governments have begun to replicate elements of NGO programs: For example, the government of Pakistan has recently initiated a National Rural Support Program (modeled after the AKRSP), which is designed to promote community-level self-sufficiency and reduce poverty.

Ensuring Environmental Sustainability

South Asia's current development strategies hold forth the promise of sustained, rapid, and poverty-reducing economic growth. This growth, superimposed on a rapidly growing and urbanizing population, inevitably will put more pressure on air, water, and land resources. Problems are already apparent in terms of increased levels of air and water pollution, contamination by toxic wastes, soil erosion, land degradation, and deforestation. In addition, the environment is adversely affected in many countries by the presence of incentive regimes that encourage intensive use of high-polluting energy, inefficient use of surface water and groundwater, underinvestment in sanitation and waste management, and inadequate protection of soils and forests.

Protecting the natural resources of the region is a complex and long-term process. Governments face difficult policy dilemmas as they search for ways to accelerate growth and ensure environmental sustainability. Some progress has been made in recent years in addressing these issues. National environmental action plans (NEAPs) were completed and openly debated in Sri Lanka in 1991, and in India, Nepal, and Pakistan in 1993. These documents, together with follow-up workshops in each country, provide a base for prioritizing donor assistance. Parallel to the NEAP process, explicit steps have been taken to strengthen environmental management. For example, new ordinances have been passed in Pakistan that mandate higher environmental quality standards, decentralized responsibility for pollution control, and an expansion of the staff of national and provincial-level environmental institutions. In India, new national policies have been adopted to combat industrial pollution through both increased regulations and some fiscal incentives. In addition, in 1994 the government strengthened regulations governing environmental assessments, requiring, among other things, broad consultation and public participation. Many Indian states have adopted participatory approaches that utilize economic incentives to protect forests and preserve biodiversity.

The Bank's Strategy for the Region

The direction of the Bank's lending program in fiscal 1994 and the underlying economic and sector work were guided by the challenges facing countries in South Asia—the need to promote sustained growth, reduce poverty, and improve living conditions. In line with these objectives, a key focus of the economic and sector work program was on the role of fiscal reforms and reforms in the agriculture, infrastructure, and human resources sectors in promoting sustainable growth and reducing poverty. Analysis of factors that encourage private sector development was also central to the work program, and efforts were made to improve dissemination of findings both within the region and more broadly outside.

The South Asia loan portfolio includes 242 projects and commitments totaling $26.6 billion as of June 30, 1994. The portfolio consists primarily of investment loans. The principal change has been in sectoral composition, as the share in lending for agriculture has gradually dropped while the share accounted for by the human resources sectors has increased (from an average 5 percent in the period fiscal 1985–89 to 19 percent in fiscal 1994).

Bank lending during the past year totaled $2,370 million, a decrease of $1,046 million over fiscal 1993. The decrease can be attributed to two factors; first, both the Bank and governments are exercising greater care during the project cycle in order to achieve higher quality-at-entry for new projects, particularly in complex sectors dealing with sensitive issues (such as resettlement and the environment); second, a buildup of reserves and an improved balance-of-payments situation in several countries has made adjustment borrowing less necessary, at

least for the present. The past year's lending program had a strong focus on the poor. Five operations (accounting for $741.8 million, or 31 percent of new lending) are included in the program of targeted interventions (PTI), while one adjustment operation (accounting for $250 million) had a poverty focus.

During the past year, the region focused on three types of portfolio-implementation issues in an attempt to strengthen performance and improve the quality of the Bank's lending portfolio. First, by giving priority to reducing project complexity and ensuring readiness for implementation, the quality of new projects entering the portfolio has been upgraded. Second, actions were taken to strengthen portfolio-management practices to deal expeditiously with problem projects and reduce project gestation time. Problem projects are reviewed on a quarterly basis to ascertain the extent of progress in implementing remedial measures and to recommend and/or endorse restructuring as required. Gestation time is being reduced by focusing on accelerating project start-up, undertaking mid term reviews of projects to provide for early diagnosis and corrective actions, and working to ensure that projects close on time. Third, systemic implementation issues are being tackled through the identification and adoption of measures to improve deficiencies in project funding, procurement, and project management. Country-implementation reviews, sectoral supervision strategies, and vigorous resident-mission support were the principal vehicles for addressing these problems.

Efforts to strengthen performance and improve quality of the portfolio have been successful: Year-to-year average portfolio performance indicators indicate progress in the timely start-up of new operations, in decreasing the number and proportion of problem projects, and in increasing disbursements on investment operations as a percentage of the fiscal year's opening undisbursed balance.

Europe and Central Asia

The process of transition from centrally planned economic systems to market economies has presented difficult challenges for the countries of the Europe and Central Asia region. The economic challenges are complicated by the concurrent political and social transfor-

Table 5-10. **Europe and Central Asia: 1992 Population and Per Capita GNP of Countries that Borrowed during Fiscal Years 1992–94**

Country	Population[a] (millions)	Per capita GNP[b] (US dollars)
Albania[c]	3.4	—
Armenia[d]	3.7	780
Belarus[d]	10.3	2,930
Bulgaria	8.5	1,330
Croatia[c]	4.8	—
Cyprus	0.7	9,820
Czech Republic	10.3	2,450
Estonia[d]	1.6	2,760
Hungary	10.3	2,970
Kazakhstan[d]	17.0	1,680
Kyrgyz Republic[d]	4.5	820
Latvia[d]	2.6	1,930
Lithuania[d]	3.8	1,310
Macedonia, FYR[c]	2.2	—
Moldova[d]	4.4	1,300
Poland	38.4	1,910
Romania	22.7	1,130
Russian Federation[d]	149.0	2,510
Slovak Republic	5.3	1,930
Slovenia	2.0	6,540
Turkey	58.5	1,980
Ukraine[d]	52.1	1,820
Uzbekistan[d]	21.5	850

NOTE: The 1992 estimates of GNP per capita presented above are from the "World Development Indicators" section of *World Development Report 1994.*

— Not available.

a. Estimates for mid 1992.

b. *World Bank Atlas* methodology, 1990–92 base period.

c. Estimated as lower-middle income ($676–$2,695).

d. Estimates for the former Soviet Union are subject to more than the usual range of uncertainty and should be regarded as very preliminary.

mation, as well as by the legal and institutional reforms taking place in all of these countries. Successfully addressing these challenges will be critical for completing the transition.

In general, the external environment was adverse during fiscal 1994. Many countries of Central and Eastern Europe, whose economies have been in transition for several years, were attempting to rebound in the face of continued economic slowdown by their major trading partners in Western Europe. Such slowdown contributed in part to a dampening of export expansion for countries such as Bulgaria, Hungary, Poland, and Romania.

The states of the former Soviet Union (FSU) continued to face problems stemming from dissolution of the union, including the breakdown of the trade-and-payments system. Trade within the republics of the FSU contracted further during the year. Importers of energy from the FSU faced further terms-of-trade deterioration as energy prices from Russia and elsewhere moved closer to world levels. Terms of trade deteriorated by more than 20 percent in 1993 in Belarus, the Kyrgyz Republic, and Moldova.

Country experiences have become increasingly differentiated. On the one hand, some economies have stabilized and are on the way to a restoration of growth. In 1993, for instance, Poland registered a second consecutive year of expansion, the economy surged in Albania, and output stabilized in Estonia, the Czech Republic, and Romania.

On the other hand, some countries have yet to make progress towards sustained stabilization. Since the beginning of 1994, inflation has been reduced in the Russian Federation, largely as a result of tighter credit in the latter part of 1993 that was associated with a build-up in arrears of government wage and other payments. However, maintaining this reduction will require further progress on structural reforms, such as lower fiscal deficits consistent with the new role of the state and further liberalization of the incentive regime and improved allocation of credit, in particular.

In several countries, the transition process is being eased by flows of private capital investment and technology from abroad: Hungary received more than $1 billion in foreign direct investment (FDI) during 1993; the Czech Republic and Poland were also major recipients; and FDI more than doubled in 1993 compared with 1992 in Kazakhstan, Estonia, Latvia, Lithuania, and the Slovak Republic.

Acceleration of private sector activity appears to have been a key component of any turnaround in growth in most countries. Today, more people work in the private sector than in the public enterprise sector in the Czech Republic, Hungary, and Poland.

Most countries are experiencing rising unemployment associated with the downsizing of public sector enterprises. In Central and Eastern Europe, open unemployment continued to increase in 1993. In the republics of the FSU, open unemployment has emerged more slowly. However, "hidden unemployment" in the form of short hours or unpaid leave at the enterprise level is growing. In Ukraine, for example, it was estimated at 9 percent during 1993. Although registered unemployment remains at under 2 percent of the labor force in Russia, the real level of unemployment is substantially higher. In many countries, employment and wages in declining industries are being maintained only through significant credits from the banking system.

The introduction of individual currencies, which began in fiscal years 1992 and 1993, accelerated—in Armenia, Azerbaijan, Georgia, Kazakhstan, Moldova, Turkmenistan, and Uzbekistan, for example. Exchange-rate regimes vary across countries, ranging from a fixed exchange rate based on a currency board with full reserve backing in Estonia and Lithuania, to floating regimes in Kazakhstan, the Kyrgyz Republic, and Latvia.

In Turkey, the many improvements in economic policies and performance during the 1980s have been undermined by a steady deterioration in public finances in recent years and deterioration of the external position in 1993, culminating in a severe currency crisis in January 1994. In April, the government unveiled an adjustment program focusing on stabiliza-

Table 5-11. **Lending to Borrowers in Europe and Central Asia, by Sector, 1985–94**
(millions of US dollars; fiscal years)

Sector	Annual average, 1985–89	1990	1991	1992	1993	1994
Agriculture	281.4	263.0	100.0	155.0	525.4	582.9
Energy						
Oil and gas	56.0	—	520.0	246.0	703.0	856.1
Power	238.0	250.0	600.0	270.0	—	—
Environment	—	18.0	—	—	—	—
Human Resources						
Education	52.8	90.2	250.0	—	67.0	59.6
Population, health, and nutrition	15.0	—	—	280.0	91.0	—
Social sector	—	—	—	—	—	10.9
Industry and Finance						
Industry	289.4	—	100.0	60.0	—	375.0
Finance	210.5	326.0	710.0	—	55.0	280.0
Infrastructure and Urban Development						
Telecommunications	14.0	—	270.0	—	30.0	153.0
Transportation	200.0	445.0	300.0	—	378.0	352.0
Urban development	30.8	—	—	200.0	285.0	171.0
Water supply and sewerage	92.4	198.0	—	32.0	129.5	109.6
Mining and Other Extractive	—	—	—	—	—	—
Multisector	—	600.0	1,017.0	691.1	1,245.0	566.3
Public Sector Management	—	—	—	209.2	335.0	210.0
Tourism	—	—	—	—	—	—
Total	1,480.4	2,190.2	3,867.0	2,143.3	3,843.9	3,726.4
Of which: IBRD	1,480.4	2,190.2	3,867.0	2,102.2	3,739.5	3,533.3
IDA	—	—	—	41.1	104.4	193.1
Number of operations	12	14	19	14	30	42

NOTE: Details may not add to totals because of rounding.
— Zero.

Still struggling in the aftermath of the 1988 earthquake, many Armenians have been forced to live in "container communities" of dwellings built from fuel tanks and railway boxcars. A $28 million IDA credit, approved in fiscal 1994, will provide shelter for 2,000 families.

tion and key structural reforms, particularly privatization and the containment of current government expenditures and transfers.

Privatization, Enterprise and Financial Sector Reform

In general, privatization continued to accelerate during the past year, with small-scale privatization continuing to take the lead. Small-scale privatization is essentially complete in the Czech and Slovak Republics, Hungary, and Poland. Substantial progress has been made in Albania, the Baltic states, the Kyrgyz Republic, Romania, and Russia (see Box 5-6). However, the process is only in its inception in countries such as Belarus, Ukraine, and Uzbekistan. Mass privatization programs gained momentum: The first wave of voucher privatizations was completed in the Czech Republic and Slovakia, and a second was begun in the Czech Republic. Russia has used a combination of voucher privatization and management/employee buyouts on a very large scale: More than 8,000 medium-scale and large enterprises—including about a third of all state-owned industrial enterprises—were privatized in 1993, and two thirds of all small service enterprises were privatized by the end of 1993. Investment funds participating in the voucher auctions exceeded 400 in the Czech Republic and Slovakia, 600 in Russia, and 300 in Lithua-

nia; and mass privatization programs were adopted in Kazakhstan, Poland, Moldova, and Slovenia.

Privatization of the largest state-owned enterprises, however, has not advanced nearly as quickly. In Russia, only a few have been privatized. In spite of a vigorous marketing effort aimed at strategic investors, Estonia was able to sell fewer than fifty large enterprises in 1993, although negotiations are well-advanced for some fifty others. Sale to managers and workers has been successful in a number of countries when prices were favorable or installment sales were permitted.

Concurrent with progress on privatization, reform of banking systems has continued, and efforts are under way to strengthen accounting and payments systems. In some countries, the number of commercial banks has expanded rapidly, to over 2,000 in Russia in 1993, for example. Other banking sectors have experienced consolidation. For example, in Estonia, the total number of banks has decreased by half since independence. Privatization of the banking sector was initiated in Latvia, Lithuania, and Poland. In the first wave of voucher privatizations in the Czech Republic and in Slovakia, the biggest commercial banks were partially privatized.

A range of approaches has been put in place to address the legacy of nonperforming loans in

Box 5-6. Privatization Progress in the Russian Federation

Progress in privatization has been the centerpiece of the government's achievements in structural reform of the economy. The Russian privatization program has privatized a larger number of enterprises than any other program in the world. As of March 1994, more than 60 percent of the industrial workforce was employed in privatized enterprises. More than 12,000 enterprises were privatized via voucher auction by June 1994 when voucher privatization was brought to a close. This will still leave several thousand large and medium enterprises to be privatized through either cash auctions, investment tenders, or other special arrangements.

Small-scale privatization has also kept pace, though with significant regional variation; currently more than 70 percent of all small-scale retail, catering, and service enterprises have been privatized.

Many state and collective farms have been technically privatized, though they remain under collective leadership, and most have not been significantly restructured. Privatization has accelerated, however, with the recent removal of restrictions on buying and selling of agricultural land. Under a pilot program in the Nizhny Novgorod region currently being promoted by the International Finance Corporation, the private sector investment arm of the World Bank, members of collectives can elect to divide their farms and then bid on parcels of land to work individually or in partnership with other owners. By June 30, 1994, some six collective farms in the region had been sold under the program. In March 1994, the government committed itself to expanding the program beyond Nizhny Novgorod, and the IFC is now moving to help the country implement the expanded program.

Housing privatization began late in 1992, with more than 1 million units in Moscow and more than 25 percent of eligible units nationwide having been privatized to date; most have been given to occupants under a nationwide framework of providing housing on a giveaway basis.

---

the portfolios of commercial banks—a legacy that has undermined the dual objectives of restructuring existing enterprises and providing adequate credit to emerging enterprises. A decentralized approach, relying heavily on bank leadership in restructuring, has been put into place in Poland; it is being complemented by a special support mechanism for handling large or locally sensitive loss-makers. In Hungary, more emphasis has been placed on strengthening and enforcing bankruptcy laws. Elsewhere—in Albania, the Kyrgyz Republic, and Romania, for example—more centralized approaches have been introduced, in which a subset of problematic enterprises has been isolated from the rest of the banking system.

The Bank's Strategic Objectives

The Bank's operations have rapidly evolved to respond to the diverse needs of its borrowing countries. The former Yugoslav Republic (FYR) of Macedonia fulfilled requirements pursuant to resolutions of the Bank's executive board providing for succession to membership of the Socialist Federal Republic of Yugoslavia and became a member of the Bank; a financial workout program was developed under the leadership of the Netherlands that cleared that country's arrears to the institution ; and an economic recovery loan to the country was approved in February 1994. Lending operations were also initiated in Belarus, Croatia, Kazakhstan, Slovenia, and Uzbekistan, as well as in the newly formed Czech Republic and Slovakia.

The speed and comprehensiveness with which borrowers have embarked on a reform program vary greatly, as do the initial conditions facing their economies. As a result, the Bank's assistance is tailored to match individual country circumstances. However, some features of the adjustment effort have been common across countries. The start of transition has usually taken place in the midst of strong output declines. At this stage, the Bank has quickly provided balance-of-payments support to help redress such declines. These have been the so-called "rehabilitation" loans. During fiscal year 1994, such rehabilitation operations were approved for Belarus, Kazakhstan, and Moldova; similarly, an economic recovery loan was approved for Slovakia and FYR Macedonia. These operations are complemented by institution-building and technical assistance operations essential for the early development of institutions needed in the development of markets.

The Bank also has helped finance selected critical infrastructure-maintenance investments to avoid deterioration of key infrastructure. In Kazakhstan, a project was approved to restore public transport services, and in Estonia and Russia, programs of highway rehabilitation are being supported. In some cases, output collapse has been compounded by natural disasters to which the Bank has responded, including a drought-recovery loan for Moldova in fiscal year 1993 and an earthquake-rehabilitation credit for Armenia in fiscal year 1994.

Table 5-12. **World Bank Commitments, Disbursements, and Net Transfers in Europe and Central Asia, 1990–94**
(millions of US dollars; fiscal years)

Item	Russia start 1994	Russia 1994	Russia 1990–94	Poland start 1994	Poland 1994	Poland 1990–94	Turkey start 1994	Turkey 1994	Turkey 1990–94	Total region start 1994	Total region 1994	Total region 1990–94
Undisbursed commitments	457			2,610			3,176			9,478		
Commitments		1,520	2,890		146	3,657		100	2,219		3,726	15,971
Gross disbursements		284	587		307	1,204		386	2,084		1,980	7,666
Repayments		—	—		—	—		753	3,414		1,149	6,183
Net disbursements		284	587		307	1,204		−367	−1,330		831	1,483
Interest and charges		25	26		73	146		422	2,395		817	4,113
Net transfer		259	561		234	1,058		−789	−3,725		14	−2,630

NOTE: Disbursements from the IDA Special Fund are included. The countries shown in the table are those with the largest amounts of public or publicly guaranteed long-term debt. Details may not add to totals because of rounding.
— Zero.

Support for privatization and financial sector development. A major focus of Bank support is the privatization and restructuring of public enterprises and complementary financial sector reform and development. Technical assistance is being provided early in the process throughout the region, particularly in the former Soviet Union. In Kazakhstan, a comprehensive program was developed with close Bank collaboration, with implementation being supported under a technical assistance loan approved in fiscal year 1994.

Bank operations were also approved during the past year to strengthen financial infrastructure in Belarus, Kazakhstan, and Uzbekistan. For example, support has been provided for the modernization of the interbank payments system, essential for improving the trade and payments situation. Twinning arrangements are being financed to strengthen commercial and savings banks—their success in Poland has contributed to the ability of the commercial banks to clean up their portfolios. After some progress is made, Bank support has been expanded into sector adjustment lending to deepen sectoral reforms in this area. The Bank approved an enterprise and financial sector adjustment operation for Slovenia to further development of the private sector. After initial balance-of-payments support to the Kyrgyz Republic in fiscal 1993, an adjustment operation is now focusing on privatization, reducing the financial burden stemming from large loss-making enterprises, and enhancing the environment for private sector development. Under certain circumstances, the Bank has also provided some financial intermediation lending. The Russia Enterprise Support Project supports initiation of term lending to private enterprises from a core of commercial banks,

while another project is providing for institutional strengthening and systems modernization for those banks. The Bank has also approved an onlending facility in Romania to finance export and industrial investments by the private sector.

Public enterprise reforms, including privatization, are also important for the long-run reduction of public sector deficits and improved efficiency in Turkey. Here, the fiscal year 1994 lending program supported a build up in institutional capacity for accelerated preparation and implementation of the government's privatization agenda; this support included a safety net program that will alleviate the impact of state-owned enterprise downsizing and divestiture on displaced workers and their families.

Infrastructure, energy, and environment. In countries where structural transformation is well advanced and the public finance situation is stable, sectoral lending has intensified to alleviate constraints to the growth of the private sector. Fiscal 1994 evidenced active support to the oil and gas, telecommunications, and transportation sectors.

During the past year the Bank continued work begun in 1992 at the request of the major industrialized countries (the G-7) to develop energy strategies in certain countries of the region with high-risk, Soviet-designed nuclear reactors. This effort has been carried out in close collaboration with the European Bank for Reconstruction and Development, the European Investment Bank, the International Energy Agency, the G-7, and the countries themselves. Regional strategies and country-specific studies—Lithuania and Ukraine this past fiscal year—are being developed to lay out an integrated approach to power sector development and nuclear safety. The Bank is playing its part in support of the necessary policy reforms and the financing of conventional power investments, while working in a coordinated manner with other financing sources for nuclear safety and nuclear power.

National environmental actions plans (NEAPs) were completed in fiscal year 1994 for Belarus and Ukraine—adding to the eight completed earlier—and work began on NEAPs for the Kyrgyz Republic and Moldova. Based on these strategies, Bank assistance can be coordinated with other financing sources to provide financing for conventional power investments while supporting policy reforms critical for cost-effective energy conservation and public safety. The second oil rehabilitation project in Russia includes a component to prevent negative environmental effects from the project and to begin remedial actions to address past damage. In Bulgaria, the Water Companies Restructuring and Modernization Project is financing investments in wastewater treatment that will reduce river pollution as well as contribute to the clean-up of the Danube river and the Black sea. In most of the former socialist countries, actions to establish clear rules on environmental liability have been included in operations supporting privatization. Four Central and Eastern European countries have received assistance from the Global Environment Facility for biodiversity conservation, mainly to improve transboundary protected areas, and good early progress on implementation was made during the fiscal year.

Poverty and social sectors. To promote employment opportunities and reduce or prevent poverty, recovery of output and job creation are essential. The Bank's programs, including support for enterprise restructuring, private sector development, and deregulation of prices and marketing channels, are critical in this regard. At the same time, however, social protection must be provided for those unable to take advantage of these opportunities. Improved targeting and rationalization of social services remain crucial. To facilitate targeting of social benefits to the neediest and the development of policies aimed at poverty reduction, the Bank is supporting collection of household survey data and careful in-depth analysis. In fiscal year 1994, a poverty assessment was carried out for Poland, and poverty-assessment work was initiated in several countries, including Russia. During fiscal 1994, an operation to improve the social safety net was approved for

Albania. In fiscal year 1994, a Women in Development Fund was established in the Bank's Europe and Central Asia regional office to support work in new areas of inquiry on gender and transition.

The Bank also is supporting the rationalization of social sector expenditures and prevention of the deterioration in key social services. Work on the health sector in Russia was carried out during the year, laying the groundwork for the development of lending operations. Education projects were approved for Albania and Romania.

Focus on Portfolio Quality

The institutional and economic flux characterizing countries in transition calls for a sharp focus on portfolio quality and effective implementation. Among new member countries, implementation is complicated by the lack of familiarity with Bank procedures. Procurement and disbursement, in particular, present difficulties. The Bank is helping to develop efficient counterpart units and is establishing project accounts and audit procedures. Thus, in Moldova, procurement and disbursements have been accelerated for two projects approved in fiscal 1993. It is also continuing to prepare and translate standardized bidding documents, adapted to local conditions, to promote the reform of public procurement regulations through technical assistance or Institutional Development Fund grants, and to hold procurement and disbursement seminars.

The Bank is also quickly incorporating lessons learned into project design. Efforts are being made to keep project design simple and limit project components. Given the unprecedented situation facing many borrowers in the region, the Bank puts a premium on its ability to be flexible and adaptable. Institutional development is an imperative, and almost all projects have significant institutional development components.

Field offices are playing an increasing role in effective project implementation, in addition to facilitating policy dialogue. Two new resident missions were established during the past year—in Belarus and Kazakhstan—bringing the total in the region to fourteen. The number of field-office staff has grown as well, and higher-level staff—including those who are locally recruited—are increasingly involved in implementation assistance to the borrower, including procurement administration.

Latin America and the Caribbean

The Latin America and the Caribbean pan-
orama in 1993 shows large disparities in growth
rates across countries, a definite downward
trend in inflation in most countries, continued
capital inflows, significant expansion of regional trade, and a growing perception that investment in social and economic infrastructure
must be increased.

During 1991–93, the region grew, on average,
by 3.2 percent annually, almost double the av-

***Table 5-13*. Latin America and the
Caribbean: 1992 Population and Per
Capita GNP of Countries that Borrowed
during Fiscal Years 1992–94**

Country	Population[a] (millions)	Per capita GNP[b] (US dollars)
Argentina	33.1	6,050
Barbados	0.3	6,540
Belize	0.2	2,220
Bolivia	7.5	680
Brazil	153.9	2,770
Chile	13.6	2,730
Colombia	33.4	1,330
Costa Rica	3.2	1,960
Ecuador	11.0	1,070
El Salvador	5.4	1,170
Guatemala	9.7	980
Guyana	0.8	330
Haiti[c]	6.7	—
Honduras	5.4	580
Jamaica	2.4	1,340
Mexico	85.0	3,470
Nicaragua	3.9	340
Panama	2.5	2,420
Paraguay	4.5	1,380
Peru	22.4	950
Trinidad and Tobago	1.3	3,940
Uruguay	3.1	3,340
Venezuela	20.2	2,910

NOTE: The 1992 estimates of GNP per capita presented
above are from the "World Development Indicators" section of *World Development Report 1994*.
a. Estimates for mid 1992.
b. *World Bank Atlas* methodology, 1990–92 base period.
c. Estimated as low-income ($675 or less).

erage growth that took place during the post-
debt crisis years. Average growth of 3.5 percent in 1993 compares favorably with the 2.8
percent achieved in 1992.

The region's growth figures are greatly influenced by Brazil's performance. If Brazil were
excluded, the region's growth record worsened
in 1993 with respect to the average of the previous two years, dropping from about 5 percent
to 2.8 percent. The fall was due mainly to the
poor performance of Mexico and Venezuela.
Some Central American countries, however,
continued to show strong growth: Panama (7
percent), Costa Rica (5.6 percent), and El Salvador (5 percent). In South America, Argentina, Chile, and Colombia also experienced
growth of more than 5 percent.

Until 1993, the Caribbean countries had experienced a decade marked by high rates of
growth (6 percent on average). During 1993,
however, growth slowed in some countries
(particularly in Jamaica) and was elusive in
others—in Haiti, Suriname, and Trinidad and
Tobago, for example. Only Guyana continued
to record a high growth rate—7 percent, following 8 percent in 1992 and 6 percent in 1991.
The Dominican Republic was not able to continue at the fast pace of the previous year (7.5
percent), falling to 3.5 percent.

The sluggishness of growth in the Caribbean
means that the efforts to improve competitiveness were not sufficient to cope with the rapidly changing external scenario. The key
challenges are to find ways to offset the decline
in official flows and the erosion of preferential
trading arrangements, particularly for bananas
and sugar.

The slowdown in the rate of growth in many
Latin American countries appears to be mainly
cyclical. It is partly the result of the recession
in the industrialized world, which reduced demand for the region's exports. The 4.5 percent
fall in the region's term of trade during 1993
reinforced the effect of this recession. In addition, some countries that recently adopted reforms are still adjusting to a new set of widely
different relative prices. Adjustment takes
time, and the costs of resource realignment
must be borne before benefits are reaped.

As a result of wide world interest rate differentials, capital continued to flow into the region, thereby blunting some of the recessionary tendencies.[8] Spurred by a record number of bond issues and large new flows of foreign direct investment, net transfers to the region were positive for the third year in a row. Argentina, Brazil, and Mexico were the leaders in bond issuances (totaling more than $15 billion among the three), while the privatization of Argentina's state oil company was expected to generate some $3 billion of additional equity investment flows.

Inflation continued to decrease in most countries. Excluding Brazil, the region's (weighted) inflation rate dropped from 76 percent in 1991 to 23 percent in 1992 and to 15 percent in 1993. The reduction in the rate of inflation in many countries is the result of structural-adjustment programs that have emphasized strong fiscal and monetary measures coupled with market liberalization. The success that most Caribbean countries experienced in reducing infla-

tion during 1992 was maintained in 1993. The fiscal accounts improved substantially in a number of countries, particularly in Grenada and Jamaica.

Despite relatively high per capita income levels in most countries, poverty and income distribution continue to be major problems. About 32 percent of the region's population lives in poverty, and the lower 20 percent of the population on the income scale receives only 4 percent of total gross domestic product (GDP). The level of poverty is particularly acute among indigenous groups. Poverty in these groups is in excess of 70 percent in Peru and Bolivia, and more than 80 percent in Mexico and Guatemala—rates significantly higher than

---

[8] While many countries have benefited from increased flows of private capital, those same flows have put serious upward pressures on the exchange rate in country after country. How to handle the inflow of capital without reducing competitiveness through exchange-rate appreciation is a major challenge.

Table 5-14. **Lending to Borrowers in Latin America and the Caribbean, by Sector, 1985–94**
(millions of US dollars; fiscal years)

Sector	Annual average, 1985–89	1990	1991	1992	1993	1994
Agriculture	1,031.8	855.7	941.5	1,569.6	390.0	446.9
Energy						
Oil and gas	127.9	—	260.0	110.1	44.9	—
Power	647.1	897.5	—	11.0	372.0	—
Environment	—	—	—	—	16.3	418.0
Human Resources						
Education	103.8	—	595.3	786.1	588.7	1,083.3
Population, health, and nutrition	62.8	389.2	337.3	47.5	374.0	331.0
Social sector	5.6	—	—	—	—	130.0
Industry and Finance						
Industry	293.4	77.5	—	—	—	—
Finance	982.6	471.1	844.5	877.0	125.0	604.5
Infrastructure and Urban Development						
Telecommunications	9.0	22.0	—	—	—	—
Transportation	417.4	1,029.0	218.0	564.2	1,697.5	595.0
Urban development	316.5	457.7	260.0	490.0	170.0	402.0
Water supply and sewerage	190.0	—	485.0	250.0	439.0	521.5
Mining and Other Extractive	11.4	—	200.0	—	250.0	14.0
Multisector	631.2	1,378.0	422.3	593.8	1,318.1	62.2
Public Sector Management	114.9	387.0	672.8	362.2	383.0	118.3
Tourism	—	—	—	—	—	20.0
Total	4,945.4	5,964.7	5,236.7	5,661.5	6,168.5	4,746.7
Of which: IBRD	4,840.8	5,726.7	5,067.2	5,256.5	5,851.8	4,434.5
IDA	104.7	238.0	169.5	405.0	316.7	312.2
Number of operations	44	41	44	45	50	48

NOTE: Details may not add to totals because of rounding.
— Zero.

In Peru, female laborers work on a water-diversion scheme, lining a canal that will carry water from the Andes to their village. Such projects are village-based and tend to involve participation from women.

those of the nonindigenous populations. An important correlate of poverty among indigenous groups is a lack of education, which is substantially below that of the general population.

The Bank's commitment to development and to poverty reduction go hand in hand. In general, trends in income inequality appear to have been significantly influenced by trends in per capita income; thus, the higher the growth in income per capita, the lower the inequality. In Latin America, as elsewhere, the Bank's efforts to reduce poverty follow a two-pronged approach: promotion of broad-based economic growth and the targeting of assistance to poor and vulnerable groups.

The Americas: Trade and Integration

One of the most significant economic features of the late 1980s and early 1990s has been the dramatic increment in intraregional trade. This was due, first, to trade liberalization and second, to regional/bilateral trade agreements—MERCOSUR (Argentina, Brazil, Paraguay, and Uruguay), CARICOM (the Caribbean Common Market) with Colombia and Venezuela, and other initiatives. These initiatives are likely to be replicated through the North American Free Trade Agreement (NAFTA), as well as through additional bilateral agreements. Chile has signed bilateral agreements with Ar-

gentina, Bolivia, Mexico, and Venezuela, while Mexico has signed agreements with Costa Rica and Venezuela-Colombia. Guatemala and El Salvador have entered into a regional free-trade agreement, which will also involve Honduras. Bolivia, Colombia, Ecuador, Peru, and Venezuela have signed a multilateral trade agreement. Trade has been opened up in most CARICOM countries (with the exception of Antigua and Barbuda, and Belize), the first stage of a common external tariff has been implemented, and nontariff trade barriers continue to be reduced. Representatives of twenty-two countries and several dependent territories in the Caribbean basin have concluded the first round of talks aimed at creating a new regional trading bloc.

The NAFTA is one of the world's most comprehensive free-trade pacts (short of being a common market) among regional partners. Some provisions took place on January 1, 1994, the day the agreement went into effect, and others will be implemented over a period of five, ten, and fifteen years. Special features include: the opening up of service sectors, particularly in finance, land transportation, and telecommunications; the immediate conversion of key agricultural restrictions into tariff-rate surcharges (which will be phased out in no more than fifteen years); the dismantling of traditionally high barriers by the United States and Canada on imported textiles and apparel; the introduction of innovative dispute-settlement procedures; and the establishment of a mechanism to address cross-border environmental issues. The NAFTA's long-term effect on Mexico will have major secondary effects on poverty reduction, the environment, human resources, and rural/urban development.

The most notable increment in intraregional trade has occurred in the MERCOSUR countries. From 1987 to 1993, the share of intramember trade increased from about 22 percent to almost 40 percent in Argentina; 13 percent to 23 percent in Brazil; and from about 30 percent to some 48 percent in Uruguay. MERCOSUR has also changed the trade patterns of its partners. In 1990, for instance, the Brazilian government ceased providing incentives to its wheat producers, thus giving a boost to imports of cheaper Argentinian wheat; it is expected that Argentina will eventually fill about 70 percent of Brazil's wheat-import needs. Argentina's substantial exports to Brazil during 1993 helped reduce its bilateral trade deficit from $1.7 billion to $600 million.

Trade between Argentina and Chile has also increased significantly, from about $600 million in 1990 to about $1 billion in 1993. Further economic integration will be boosted by the construction of new transAndean oil and gas pipelines. Moreover, since 1991, Chile has become one of the biggest investors in Argentina, with total investment of about $2.7 billion.

Although the increasing share of intraregional trade might have involved some diversion of trade from the rest of the world, for many countries there was also significant trade creation: During the period 1987–93, Argentina expanded the value of its trade to GDP from 13 percent to 20 percent, Chile from 56 percent to 73 percent, Colombia from 37 percent to 44 percent, Costa Rica from 64 percent to 92 percent, Mexico from 25 percent to 39 percent, and the Caribbean countries from 67 percent to 78 percent. This aggregate expansion of trade decelerated in 1992, however, and came to a halt in 1993, as the ratio of exports to GDP remained roughly the same for most countries. Only seven countries increased (slightly) their exports during the year.

Overall trade expansion was stalled by two events. The world demand for regional exports was weakened by recession in the industrial countries, and the exchange rate in many countries of the region appreciated as a result of large capital inflows, thereby reducing the international competitiveness of the region's exports. These inflows are currently financing

increased domestic expenditures and will pose important challenges if they slow down.[9] This slowdown process will require significant relative price adjustments that may be difficult to engineer in countries with fixed or quasi-fixed nominal exchange rates. The possibility exists that a reduction in capital inflows might be answered by increased trade protection, thereby negating the effects of the recent opening up of international trade, which has been the backbone of the region's reform effort.

The key to the enhancement of the region's competitive edge is increased productivity. This requires further trade liberalization, further deregulation of domestic markets (in particular, labor markets), and improvements in the supervision of the deregulation process. Deeper trade liberalization would increase productivity as economies shift their resources to areas of comparative advantage, and the region absorbs state-of-the-art technology. Further domestic market deregulation would also make economies more efficient and, consequently, more competitive. In Peru, for example, it is estimated that labor productivity in the manufacturing sector has increased by about 21 percent since the beginning of the 1990 reform program, which has emphasized both trade liberalization and domestic market deregulation.

Stabilization and Reform in Brazil

Brazil's economy represents about 40 percent of the region's GDP. During the past few years, the economy has experienced large macroeconomic imbalances and several attempts at "shock" stabilization, among them the 1985 "Cruzado Plan" and the 1990 Collor Plan, neither of which reduced long-term inflation.

Despite high rates of inflation in 1993, Brazil's economy experienced a substantial recovery, improving from a 0.9 percent decline in output in 1992 to a positive 4.9 percent rate of growth. At the same time, however, the inflation rate increased dramatically. Despite a significant increase in taxes collected, which changed the operational deficit into a 0.7 percent surplus, inflation jumped from about 400 percent in 1992 to 2,752 percent in 1993, and, by December 1993, it was running at an annual rate of about 5,000 percent. Yet another stabilization program was launched in March 1994. With this effort, Brazil has taken the first steps

---

[9] Most of these inflows have been received by the five largest Latin American economies—mostly in fixed-income securities. From a modest bond issuance of about $400 million in 1989, the market soared to about $23 billion in 1993. The stock markets in the area also boomed during 1993 due to their small capitalization base and increased investor confidence.

Table 5-15. **World Bank Commitments, Disbursements, and Net Transfers in Latin America and the Caribbean, 1990–94**
(millions of US dollars; fiscal years)

Item	Brazil			Mexico			Argentina			Total region		
	start 1994	1994	1990–94	start 1994	1994	1990–94	start 1994	1994	1990–94	start 1994	1994	1990–94
Undisbursed commitments	4,789			3,712			1,607			16,183		
Commitments		1,137	5,277		1,530	8,663		609	3,621		4,747	27,779
Gross disbursements		437	3,399		997	8,663		392	2,789		2,769	22,307
Repayments		1,292	6,139		1,007	4,588		441	1,691		4,489	19,714
Net disbursements		−855	−2,740		−10	4,075		−49	1,097		−1,720	2,593
Interest and charges		544	3,177		907	4,157		276	1,090		2,657	13,711
Net transfer		−1,399	−5,917		−917	−82		−325	7		−4,377	−11,118

NOTE: Disbursements from the IDA Special Fund are included. The countries shown in the table are those with the largest amounts of public or publicly guaranteed long-term debt. Details may not add to totals because of rounding.

in a long-term program that is designed to resolve its fiscal problems and introduce monetary discipline. A return to high and sustainable growth will require that substantial progress be made in the near future on the stabilization front.

Brazil has made major headway in trade reform. In June 1993, it completed a multiyear trade-reform program that reduced average tariffs to 14 percent in the context of a trade-liberalization program. Exports reached $38.7 billion (compared with $36.1 billion in 1992), and manufactured exports grew from $20.6 billion to $23.8 billion. Overall, its trade surplus in 1993 was $13 billion. The capital account continued to show large inflows and, by the end of 1993, reserves exceeded $32 billion (up $8 billion from the year before). Brazil's trade sector has ample room to grow; the total value of trade to GDP was only 15 percent in 1993.

The Road Ahead

The region's challenges are to reduce poverty and increase the well-being of its people through environmentally sustainable development. In this context, outward-oriented growth, integrated with the world economy, is crucial. It is also important to sustain fiscal reform and increase domestic savings. In this endeavor, a carefully planned and executed reform of the social security system in many countries of the region could be critical (see Box 5-7). Success will depend on increasing efficiency through more rapid growth in productivity. An integrated approach to increased productivity requires action in several areas:

• Domestic markets need to be more deregulated at all levels.

• Labor markets need to be deregulated and high payroll taxes reduced. These taxes increase costs, reduce net wages, and promote the informal economy.

• As regional growth is led by growth in the private sector, actions to sustain that sector's development should continue, and the enabling environment necessary for private sector growth nurtured.

• Public sector activities should be reoriented to maximize their efficiency; priority should be given to investment in infrastructure, which, in many cases, has lagged as a result of spending cuts mandated by stabilization programs.

• Investment in health and education is crucial for labor productivity. The cost-effectiveness of governments' health and education expenditures must be assessed. Many countries still provide blanket higher-education subsidies to students through reduced or free tuition; by doing so, income disparities are widened, and resources are spent inefficiently.[10]

• Public sector decentralization has to be carefully implemented because local governments are often weaker in their administrative capacities than central governments.

• The judicial system, which has become a constraint on productivity, must be simplified and strengthened, and archaic and cumbersome procedures eliminated.

The Bank's Strategic Objectives

The Bank has made considerable progress in the planned transition in lending from adjustment to long-term issues—human resources development, environmentally sustainable development, and private-sector development. A

---

[10] The bottom 40 percent of the population in the region receives only 13 percent of total higher-education subsidies.

Box 5-7. Pension Reform in Latin America

During the debt and fiscal crisis of the 1980s, Latin America's pension schemes became seriously underfunded. By the end of the decade, falling pensions (in real terms), large social-security deficits, and depleted reserves had irreparably damaged the credibility of traditional pension schemes. As the countries of the region entered the 1980s, the movement to privatize pensions gained momentum, encouraged by the apparent success in Chile.

In 1981, Chile introduced a fully funded social-security system with individual accounts. It was a mandatory, defined-contribution system to which workers contributed for old age, survivor, and disability benefits. The funds collected from workers were (and are) managed by thirteen private firms that operate under tight supervision with strict investment limitations. A committee selects the stocks in which the thirteen firms can invest. The government guarantees workers a minimum return of the lesser of (a) the average return on all funds less 2 percent or (b) half the average return on all funds. Workers are free to switch their accumulated funds between the firms, thereby creating intense competition among them. Upon retirement, accumulated funds can be taken in a phased withdrawal and/or may be used to purchase indexed annuities.

If other governments are not exactly beating the door down in their haste to move toward a social-security system, Chilean style, it's because of the fiscal implications involved. In Chile, the transition to the new system meant that the public system lost many contributors (and, therefore, much revenue); at the same time, however, it remained liable for pension payments to retirees and retirees-to-be during the transition. A deficit of the public social-security system on the scale of the Chilean reform would likely intensify fiscal pressures, thereby making a balanced budget that much more difficult to achieve. Other issues that countries have to address include equitable treatment of different generations of workers, potential problems that could arise from implementing a Chilean-style system in the absence of well-

developed financial markets, and the need for a strong regulatory and supervisory system. In countries with fiscal problems a combination of a pay-as-you-go system that provides a minimum base with a complementary fully funded private system might be warranted.

Nonetheless, the move toward the privatization of social-security systems has begun in several countries. It is furthest along in Argentina and Peru. In 1992, both governments proposed changes that effectively privatized a large share of the pension sector. Peru's new pension law went into effect in June 1993, while Argentina's was signed into law in October 1993.

Not unexpectedly, the new social-security schemes in the three countries have a number of common features. Argentina and Peru have set up schemes for the management of social-security funds that are very similar to the one in Chile; in fact, they largely adopted the Chilean regulatory structure.

But the newest schemes also differ from Chile's in certain important ways as a result of the countries' differing political climates and institutions. For example, the political power of unions and pensioners has led Argentina to maintain a large public "pillar." Thus, all eligible workers receive a flat benefit equal to 30 percent of average covered wages from the first pillar in addition to their pension from the second pillar. And, in contrast to their counterparts in Chile and Argentina, the privately managed investment firms in Peru operate in limited domestic capital markets, which provide few investment options. In addition, the absence in Peru of reliable records has forced officials to accept the "sworn statements" of workers to establish their past contributions.

The future of pension systems is currently a matter of debate in Bolivia, Brazil, Costa Rica, Mexico, Uruguay, and Venezuela. While the outcomes will vary, general weaknesses in social-security arrangements in Latin America make it likely that, given the chance, increasing numbers of workers in this region will trade in public promises for private accounts.

comparison of the actual fiscal 1991–93 lending program with the proposed program for fiscal 1994–96 shows a decline in lending for adjustment and debt reduction from 24 percent to 3 percent, an increase in lending for human resources/poverty reduction from 23 percent to 33 percent, and an increase in environment and forestry commitments from 7 percent to 13 percent.

The focus on human resources and poverty issues reflects the region's historically highly stratified social structure and skewed distribution of income. The situation cannot be reversed quickly, but improvements can be made

through economic stabilization supported by targeted safety nets, stronger social sector institutions, long-term investments in health and education, the elimination of hidden subsidies for the rich (such as free higher education) and hidden taxes on the poor (such as inflation and trade barriers). During the past year, the Bank approved social sector and/or social investment fund projects in Ecuador and Peru (for $30 million and $100 million, respectively), both broadly patterned on programs begun earlier in Bolivia, El Salvador, and Mexico.

Much of the Bank's investment lending and technical assistance in the environmental area is oriented towards improving the environmental management capacity of governments (both national and subnational). This focus on institutional strengthening is taking place within a context of widespread privatization, decentralization, and governmental "downsizing" in many countries. The Bank is working with member governments to ensure that adequate capacity exists for carrying out those environmental functions (particularly legal, regulatory, and planning) that remain the responsibility of governments. At the same time, many projects are promoting the increased use of the private sector (including nongovernmental organizations) for the in-the-field implementation of environmental activities such as delivery of urban services, protected area management, and environmental monitoring.

The Bank has been in the forefront of promoting private-sector development. Private sector assessments, which aim at determining the most important factors hampering the business environment, were completed for several countries of the region during the year. Implicit in this work is the idea that governments have a comparative advantage in certain areas— providing price stability, an efficient legal system, secure property rights, security, education and health services, and infrastructure; the private sector, however, has the advantage in the production of goods and services.

Portfolio Performance and Trends

There was further improvement in the region's portfolio performance during the past year. Good overall economic performance and years of economic reform in many countries have had a positive effect on portfolio performance. The correlation between economic reform and good project implementation is strong; in addition, the convergence of thinking between the Bank and its borrowers on economic issues has made it easier to resolve outstanding problems. Implementation of some projects has been slowed, however, by (among other reasons) shortages of counterpart funds resulting from austerity drives. This problem is typical of countries that are in the early stages of adjustment. Other projects, however, have benefited as governments, such as those in Jamaica and Mexico, have concentrated resources on priority projects. Some countries have established or reinforced mechanisms for monitoring project implementation.

The Bank's emphasis on quality at entry and borrower commitment and ownership has been the key to the improved quality of its portfolio. Furthermore, importance has been placed on effective supervision of the portfolio of ongoing projects. The quality at entry concept includes not only the traditional standards of project quality but also borrower ownership and commitment to a project and to design-for-implementation. Borrower commitment and ownership is developed upstream with the involvement of borrowers and other stakeholders in sector work that eventually leads to sector strategies and identification and preparation of projects.

Middle East and North Africa

In calendar year 1993, the Middle East and North Africa region experienced a continued decline in growth rates and marked variability in performance among countries. Real gross domestic product (GDP) growth in 1993 for the eight countries in which the Bank was most active[11] was about 1.5 percent, compared with 4.3 percent in 1992 (see Table 5-17). Rates of GDP growth ranged from −1.7 percent in Algeria to 7 percent in Lebanon.

In the Maghreb, Algeria remains in recession as a result of a further decline in petroleum prices, a heavy debt burden, and drought-related declines in agricultural production. Morocco is coming out of two years of drought, during which GDP declined by a cumulative 4 percent. The underlying macroeconomic indicators remain favorable for long-term growth, however, and the outlook for 1994 is good because of improved rainfall. Tunisia's GDP grew at about 2.5 percent.

Table 5-17. **Real GDP Growth Rates, 1991–93, Selected Economies**

Country	1991	1992	1993
Algeria	0.2	2.3	−1.7
Egypt	2.1	0.3	0.5
Iran	10.5	6.4	3.0
Jordan	1.0	11.0	6.0
Lebanon	38.2	4.5	7.0
Morocco	6.2	−4.0	0.0
Occupied Territories	−4.0	23.6	−10.1
Tunisia	3.8	8.0	2.6
Yemen	0.0	0.1	0.3
Region[a]	6.3	4.3	1.5

a. Weighted by GDP; does not include Lebanon and Yemen.

Table 5-16. **Middle East and North Africa: 1992 Population and Per Capita GNP of Countries that Borrowed during Fiscal Years 1992–94**

Country	Population[a] (millions)	Per capita GNP[b] (US dollars)
Algeria	26.3	1,840
Egypt	54.7	640
Iran, Islamic Republic of	59.6	2,200
Jordan[c]	3.9	1,120
Lebanon[d]	3.8	—
Morocco	26.2	1,030
Tunisia	8.4	1,720
Yemen[e]	13.0	—

NOTE: The 1992 estimates of GNP per capita presented above are from the "World Development Indicators" section of *World Development Report 1994*.

— Not available.

a. Estimates for mid 1992.

b. *World Bank Atlas* methodology, 1990–92 base period.

c. Estimates refer to East Bank only.

d. Estimated as lower-middle-income ($676–$2,695).

e. Estimated as low-income ($675 or less).

In Iran, real growth slowed from 5.8 percent in 1992 to 3 percent. Two factors, in particular, contributed to the slowdown. First, an oil-price decline reduced export earnings by 15 percent. Second, arrears on short-term trade credits reduced Iran's access to new credit and contributed to a sharp decline in imports and growth.

Egypt continued to pursue its ambitious program of stabilization and structural reform. Growth of output remained below 1 percent in fiscal 1993, with only agriculture and construction showing signs of recovery; overall growth is expected to increase gradually to reach 4.3 percent in fiscal 1996.[12] Elsewhere in the Mashreq, Jordan's high rate of growth in 1992 carried over into 1993; GDP growth exceeded 6 percent. But, in contrast to 1992, when growth was largely concentrated in construction and domestic services, 1993 saw a more broadly based pattern of growth. In addition to construction, nonmineral exports, trade services, transportation, and tourism all recorded gains. Lebanon's reconstruction, supported by large private capital inflows, resulted in robust (7 percent) growth.

Economic reforms remain high on the agenda of most countries. Governments in

---

[11] Algeria, Egypt, Iran, Jordan, Lebanon, Morocco, Tunisia, and Yemen.

[12] Egypt's fiscal year runs from July 1 to June 30.

Egypt, Iran, and Jordan continued to implement stabilization policies effectively. Morocco and Tunisia have moved from stabilization to longer-term macroeconomic management and structural reform. Algeria is implementing a stabilization program that is being supported by a one-year, $1 billion standby arrangement with the International Monetary Fund. Virtually all economies reduced their fiscal deficits, most notably in Egypt, where the deficit fell from 22 percent of GDP in fiscal 1991 to about 4.7 percent in fiscal 1993. Inflation was kept in check throughout the region; balance-of-payment deficits were reduced, and (with the exception of Iran) large movements in exchange rates were avoided. There were also encouraging signs that private sector activity is picking up—especially in Jordan, Lebanon, Morocco, and Tunisia. Increasing foreign direct investment (FDI) is playing an important role in this resurgence. FDI in 1992 almost doubled 1991's total due to an improved investment climate and was expected to reach $2 billion in 1993.

The historic signing of the peace accord between Israel and the Palestine Liberation Organization was the most significant political event in the region during the past fiscal year. The Bank has been a central player in providing technical assistance and aid coordination in support of the peace process (see Box 5-8).

Beyond the immediate impact of the accord on the Occupied Territories, the peace process—should it widen beyond its current scope—would have a number of important implications for future economic development in the region:

• Greater stability would likely increase trade flows, especially for Egypt, Jordan, Lebanon, and the Syrian Arab Republic. Stability will also favor inflows of private capital and private investments.

• The reduction in geopolitical tensions could allow governments to shift public resources away from military expenditures and place greater emphasis on sustainable economic growth, especially human resources development.

• The scope for regional economic cooperation could increase, especially in the areas of water management, the environment, and infrastructure.

Key Development Challenges

The ability of the region to realize the economic benefits of the evolving peace process will depend fundamentally on its capacity to meet three key development challenges: (a) restoring sustained growth; (b) developing human resources; and (c) managing scarce natural resources, especially water.

Restoring sustained growth. Following relatively good economic performance in the 1960s and 1970s, the 1980s and the first years of the current decade have been host to economic crisis, which has led to a drop in per capita incomes in most countries of the region. The crisis has been characterized by a deteriorating external economic environment, particularly the sharp drop in international oil prices, decreasing efficiency in the use of capital, low levels of private investment, and poor export performance. In many countries, GDP growth remains below the rate of population growth. This, in turn, is reflected in high and increasing rates of unemployment, which range from 15 percent in Tunisia and Morocco to 27 percent in Yemen. The consequences of past population growth will continue to be felt through large increases in the labor force. Levels of poverty are also related to growth and employment, a more equitable distribution of the benefits of economic growth, and targeted social safety net interventions. Countries, on the one hand, such as Morocco, which have achieved relatively high, sustained rates of growth, have also been able to reduce the number of poor (from an estimated 5.7 million people in 1985 to about 3.4 million in 1991). In Jordan, on the other hand, where economic growth has not been as sustained, the number of poor has not decreased.

To prevent further increases in unemployment and poverty, the region's economy must grow at about 5 percent per year and be accompanied by labor-intensive methods of production, including the promotion of small and medium-sized enterprises. Growth of that magnitude could be realized if rates of investment were to increase to around 25 percent of GDP (compared with an average of 20 percent now) and if the incremental capital-output ratio (ICOR) could be reduced to five from its current level of ten through increased productivity and labor-intensive production. A private sector-oriented growth strategy offers the best prospects of realizing increases in investment and improvements in the ICOR. Traditionally, countries of the region have relied more than other low-income and middle-income countries on public investment. Although the level of private investment nearly doubled between 1970 and 1990, it is still less than 10 percent of GDP (rates are well above the 15 percent mark in the high-performing countries of the East Asia and Pacific region). Moreover, the declining efficiency of investment is largely associated with the implementation of a public sector-led strategy. In most countries of the region, large but inefficient parastatal enterprises continue to dominate the economy.

Box 5-8. The World Bank and the Occupied Territories

The economies of the West Bank and Gaza (the Occupied Territories) are in a state of crisis, and a new course will have to be charted to ensure renewed growth and job-creation in the economic environment likely to be faced in the 1990s. Sustainable growth prospects are contingent on developing central institutions, rehabilitating and expanding infrastructure, attracting private investments, and building a financial sector. In addition, the new Palestinian self-governing authority must also develop a reformed legal system, enforce property rights, and collect taxes. The World Bank became involved in the Occupied Territories in early 1993, when it was invited by the European Community, the chair of the Economic Working Group, and other participants to prepare a series of reports on regional development with a special emphasis on the Occupied Territories. *Developing the Occupied Territories, an Investment in Peace*[1] was completed by the time of the historic handshake between Palestine Liberation Organization Chairman Yasir Arafat and Israeli Prime Minister Yitzhak Rabin, and it provided the basis for a meeting in October 1993 in Washington, D.C. of the donor community, at which $2.1 billion was pledged to rebuild the Occupied Territories. In that same month, the Bank approved the establishment of two trust funds aimed at providing urgent assistance to the West Bank and Gaza.

A $50 million trust fund, drawn from the IBRD's fiscal 1992 surplus and administered by IDA, is aimed at supporting an emergency reha-

bilitation program for Gaza. A separate $35 million trust fund aims to provide technical assistance and to finance feasibility studies in the Occupied Territories.

In the wake of the October meeting, the Bank has moved ahead on three fronts: donor coordination, institution building, and program development.

Donor coordination. Following the October donors' meeting, a consultative group meeting was convened in December to discuss and agree on the proposed emergency assistance to the Occupied Territories. When it became apparent that a significant proportion of assistance would have to be allocated to urgent recurrent expenditures of a start-up or transitional nature, the Bank was asked to prepare the groundwork for a second meeting of the group in January 1994. The meeting proved to be an unprecedented success in that substantial pledges were made for financing recurrent transitional and start-up expenditures— types of expenditures not normally funded by the donor community. Donors were also given the opportunity to contribute to a newly created Holst Peace Fund (named after the late Norwegian Minister of Foreign Affairs, Johan Holst), which would be administered by the Bank. The fund, which is short term in nature (disbursements are to be completed by around the end of calendar 1994), will finance items such as consumable health and education supplies and salaries of key Palestinian staff.

Institutional building. The Palestinian Eco-

Because the discrepancy between domestic levels of savings and investments is still large, external capital flows remain vital to the region. In Egypt, for example, investments equal about 18 percent of GDP, whereas savings amount to a mere 7 percent. Overall, savings for the region average about 18 percent of GDP, while investment is about 22 percent. If governments were to shift to a private sector-led growth strategy, an increasing share of external flows would be directed to the private sector. The potential exists in the region to increase private capital flows—not only through FDI and larger levels of workers' remittances but also through the reflow of assets held abroad. Improvements in macroeconomic management and in the investment climate, as well as progress in privatization, will play central roles in this process.

Developing human resources. In spite of impressive gains made in social indicators during the 1980s, many countries still lag behind other middle-income countries on all the basic indicators of educational achievement and health.

Even in well-performing countries such as Tunisia and Morocco, the adult illiteracy rate is more than 10 percentage points higher than the average for all middle-income countries. The average infant mortality rate for the region is around 60 per 1,000 live births, compared with 38 for all middle-income countries. The average population growth for countries of the Middle East and North Africa is among the highest in the world: During the 1980s, the average annual rate of 3.2 percent was actually higher than in the 1970s. Further improvements in social indicators are key to the region's long-term development prospects. To achieve these improvements, additional efforts will be needed to expand and improve the quality of basic services. In most cases this would justify substantially increased budgetary allocations. There is also room to improve the internal efficiency of public social services, mobilize private financing, and encourage the private provision of social services.

Managing natural resources. Natural resource management is another pressing re-

nomic Council for Development and Reconstruction (PECDAR), organized by the Palestine Liberation Organization with the support of the donor community and the Bank, has been designated as the agency in charge of aid coordination and public investment programming during the peace process. To help support PEDCAR and the emerging Palestinian institutions, a wide-ranging program of technical assistance (about $40 million over three years) was tabled at the December meeting of the consultative group. This program, which consists of some 100 activities, is being coordinated in the context of the $35 million technical assistance trust fund, which has drawn cofinancing commitments from nine donors, with the prospects of additional cofinancing from five other donors.

Program development. The Bank's report on developing the Occupied Territories recommended that a major investment program in Gaza and the West Bank be initiated over the next five years. Following agreement in May 1994 on the implementation of the Declaration of Principles between the Palestinians and the Israelis, the Bank released a report outlining a three-year $1.2 billion program to assist the Palestinians in the transition to autonomous rule.[2]

The goal of the program is to rebuild the infrastructure of the Occupied Territories in order to stimulate economic growth by attracting private investment opportunities from expatriate Palestinians, international investors, and Arab states. The $1.2 billion is the initial installment of the

$2.1 billion pledged over five years at the October 1993 conference (the pledges subsequently increased to $2.4 billion).

The first tangible result of the program was the approval in May 1994 of a $30 million Trust Fund for Gaza credit on IDA terms in support of an Emergency Rehabilitation Project, which has attracted $98 million in firm cofinancing commitments from the Arab Fund for Economic and Social Development ($30 million), the Saudi Fund for Development ($30 million), Denmark ($20 million), the Kuwait Fund for Arab Economic Development ($10 million), and Switzerland ($8 million). The project is financing the rehabilitation, reconstruction, and/or improvement of priority infrastructural services in the education, power, water supply and sewerage, and roads sectors. Technical assistance to help strengthen the capacities of municipalities in Gaza and the West Bank, to support the operations and development of PEDCAR and to ensure that the project is efficiently and effectively implemented, will also be provided. Project implementation is being supported by Bank staff through intensive field work in the Occupied Territories and from Washington.

---

[1] World Bank. 1993. *Developing the Occupied Territories: An Investment in Peace.* Six volumes. Washington, D.C.

[2] World Bank. 1994. *Emergency Assistance Program for the Occupied Territories.* Washington, D.C.

gional issue, especially in the case of water. With a few exceptions, the region is moving toward a water crisis. Rainy seasons are short, and agriculture is heavily dependent on irrigation. Rapid population growth and urbanization have pushed demand for water to the point where withdrawals are exceeding replenishments. Few untapped sources of fresh water remain, and countries are increasingly mining groundwater aquifers. By the year 2000, withdrawals in most countries will exceed total freshwater potential. Competing demands from agriculture, industries, and municipalities dictate the need for appropriate demand-management policies—especially in the area of water pricing. But demand management alone cannot meet the full water requirements of burgeoning populations. Technological innovation and modern on-farm technologies, which, in several countries, have succeeded in halving water use while doubling yields, should complement demand-management policies. Alternative sources of water need to be explored, including desalination, wastewater treatment

and reuse, and water imports. These are much more expensive than traditional sources, and research efforts designed to reduce costs, such as the desalination program recently embarked upon in Oman, need to be stongly suppported. Moreover, because many rivers and some important underground aquifers cross national boundaries, agreements at the national and transnational level will increasingly be required.

The Bank's Strategy for the Region

The World Bank's strategy for the Middle East and North Africa region emphasizes sustained commitment to operations and analytical work to promote employment-led growth, foster human resources development, and improve natural resource management. Increasing attention was devoted in fiscal 1994 to the important interrelationships among economic growth, human resources development, and poverty. While the thrust of the Bank's assistance strategies is aimed at the needs and constraints of individual economies, efforts to promote regional cooperation in areas such as environmental protection and water-resource management are becoming increasingly important.

Stabilization and structural reform also remain high on the Bank's agenda for the region. In Morocco and Tunisia—which are well advanced in stabilizing their economies and are continuing to undertake structural reforms—the Bank's focus has shifted from stabilization to long-term development. Agricultural sector loans to the two countries that were approved during the past year are emblematic of this shift. Jordan and Egypt are also steadily proceeding on the path of reform. In Egypt, reform is being advanced by the Bank's support for the second phase of the government's Economic Reform and Structural Adjustment Program, which provides the framework for continued economic reform, even though it is not associated with a specific lending operation. In Jordan, an $80 million energy-sector loan, approved in fiscal 1994, aims at addressing supply-side constraints to growth.

Improvements in the structure of incentives, the regulatory framework, and protection of property rights are needed in many countries of the region to provide the private sector with the environment required for increased levels of job-creating investment. During the past year, the Bank addressed private sector development in a variety of ways. In Tunisia, for instance, financial sector reforms were supported through a private investment project that uses a number of financial institutions to provide long-term credit at market terms to a broad range of private investors. Private sector assessments, which analyze the structure of, and constraints to, the private sector in given countries and which lay out concrete steps that can be taken to advance private sector development, were carried out for Egypt, Morocco, and Tunisia. The Morocco assessment was the centerpiece of a high-level seminar at which the private and public sectors produced an agenda of recommended actions to promote private sector development. Together with the govern-

Table 5-18. **Lending to Borrowers in Middle East and North Africa, by Sector, 1985–94**
(millions of US dollars; fiscal years)

Sector	Annual average, 1985–89	1990	1991	1992	1993	1994
Agriculture	374.6	129.0	13.2	299.2	463.0	601.7
Energy						
Oil and gas	3.5	—	84.0	160.0	—	80.0
Power	104.8	15.5	114.0	220.0	165.0	—
Environment	—	—	—	—	—	6.0
Human Resources						
Education	122.2	30.5	241.4	75.0	115.2	33.0
Population, health, and nutrition	11.9	119.0	245.0	26.8	188.0	—
Social sector	—	—	—	—	—	—
Industry and Finance						
Industry	18.8	99.5	365.0	—	—	—
Finance	106.6	196.0	235.0	—	—	120.0
Infrastructure and Urban Development						
Telecommunications	36.8	—	—	—	100.0	20.0
Transportation	113.4	79.0	162.0	—	35.0	—
Urban development	32.5	105.5	250.0	110.0	684.0	—
Water supply and sewerage	167.1	12.0	—	57.0	—	270.0
Mining and Other Extractive	11.6	25.0	—	—	—	—
Multisector	118.0	450.0	310.0	525.0	—	—
Public Sector Management	5.5	130.0	—	9.0	—	19.9
Tourism	—	—	—	—	130.0	—
Total	1,227.3	1,391.0	2,019.6	1,482.0	1,880.2	1,150.6
Of which: IBRD	1,180.8	1,323.5	1,784.0	1,324.0	1,756.4	1,050.6
IDA	46.7	67.5	235.6	158.0	123.8	100.0
Number of operations	21	20	20	17	19	16

NOTE: Details may not add to totals because of rounding.
— Zero.

Table 5-19. **World Bank Commitments, Disbursements, and Net Transfers in Middle East and North Africa, 1990–94**
(millions of US dollars; fiscal years)

Item	Egypt start 1994	Egypt 1994	Egypt 1990–94	Algeria start 1994	Algeria 1994	Algeria 1990–94	Morocco start 1994	Morocco 1994	Morocco 1990–94	Total region start 1994	Total region 1994	Total region 1990–94
Undisbursed commitments	1,134			1,474			1,579			6,218		
Commitments		121	1,290		140	1,484		412	2,395		1,151	7,924
Gross disbursements		183	767		198	1,353		311	1,894		1,057	5,921
Repayments		199	977		189	806		292	1,230		964	4,343
Net disbursements		−16	−210		9	547		19	664		92	1,578
Interest and charges		120	657		114	498		264	1,212		730	3,321
Net transfer		−136	−867		−105	49		−245	−548		−638	−1,743

NOTE: Disbursements from the IDA Special Fund are included. The countries shown in the table are those with the largest amounts of public or publicly guaranteed long-term debt. Details may not add to totals because of rounding.

ment and the private sector, the Bank is developing an operation to support this agenda.

Human resources development also features prominently in the Bank's operations and sector work. Strategies are molded to the specific needs of individual countries. For example, basic educational services are being supported through an education project approved during the year in Yemen. The Bank's analytical work is also focusing increasingly on the human resources sectors. In Morocco, for example, issues in education were addressed through a literacy and schooling study and through a review of the costs and financing of the education sector, and a nutrition strategy was developed to deal with pertinent health issues. In Tunisia, an analysis of the issues facing post-basic education and training was prepared on the basis of field work and subsequent analysis carried out by national teams. This joint approach is expected to result in strong country ownership of the study's conclusions.

Environmental issues are being addressed at both the country and regional levels. At the country level, environmental studies and strategies have been completed for Algeria, Egypt, Iran, and Yemen. Specific operations, such as water-supply projects in Algeria and Morocco, dealt directly with pressing water problems. The Morocco Environment Technical Assistance Project was the Bank's first stand-alone lending operation in the region to focus primarily on environment planning and management. In Egypt, three projects related to the country's national environmental action plan, which was jointly prepared and endorsed by ten external donors, are currently in the Bank's lending program. At the regional level, cooperative action continued in the context of the Mediterranean Environmental Technical Assistance Program (METAP), which is jointly sponsored by the European Commission of the European Union, the European Investment Bank, the United Nations Development Programme, and the World Bank. Under the first phase of this program, more than twenty transnational and country-specific projects have been prepared in the areas of water-resource management, hazardous waste management, marine oil and chemical-pollution prevention and control, and coastal zone management. The program has also helped to create important networks of concerned national institutions.

Poverty was the focus of both analytical work and operations. Three poverty assessments, which provide the basis for a collaborative approach to poverty reduction by country officials and the Bank, illustrate the extent to which economic growth has a noticeable effect on poverty reduction. These assessments, for Egypt, Jordan, and Morocco, are also providing the analytical basis for improving public spending in the social sectors and putting in place more effective social safety nets. The poverty assessment for Egypt served as the basis for ongoing reforms in health, human resources development, as well as for improvements in the social safety net and in the pension scheme. The deficiencies in social indicators highlighted by the poverty assessment for Morocco are being addressed in a series of social priorities projects currently under preparation. Targeted poverty-reduction interventions are critical components in the Northwest Mountainous Areas Development Project in Tunisia, as well as in the National Rural Finance Project in Morocco, which also has a component designed to funnel credit to women.

In infrastructure, Bank lending continues to focus on removing key constraints and creating an enabling environment for private sector participation. The Telecommunications Project in

Young workers in Egypt lay drainage pipes in a waterlogged field near their village.

Jordan, for example, supports the creation of a new sector policy and telecommunications law in addition to providing for service improvements. Supported by an expanded cofinancing operation, the Bank is helping the Jordan Telecommunications Corporation in raising private funds to commercialize, corporatize, and subsequently privatize its operations.

From Strategy to Implementation

Implementation of the Bank's operational strategy has emphasized the ability to respond quickly to changing economic and political circumstances. Total staff resources in fiscal 1994 increased modestly above the levels of the previous two fiscal years to accommodate the new challenges of work on the Occupied Territories. Within the total, however, a marked redeployment of staff has taken place to improve portfolio implementation, and significant reallocations continued to be made across countries in light of evolving circumstances. Thus, reductions in programs in some countries of the region allowed additional resources to be committed to the work on the Occupied Territories. The Bank has reacted quickly and flexibly to emerging needs: Assistance to the Occupied Territories was characterized by both flexibility and innovation; in Lebanon, the focus of the Bank's assistance strategy was on reconstruction, while the Emergency Desert Locust Control Project in Algeria provided a quick response (it was appraised in October 1993 and approved in early December) to the challenge of incipient natural disaster.

Efforts continued to improve portfolio management and project quality by:

• Linking the lending program, project design, and portfolio performance explicitly through the conduct of thorough country portfolio-performance reviews (CPPRs) and reflecting the outcome of those reviews in country-assistance strategies;

• Undertaking additional initiatives to improve project quality at entry by involving the technical department and relevant central vice-presidential units in project design and by explicitly linking project content to well-articulated sectoral strategies;

• Increasing high-level managerial review of portfolio performance and recognizing excellence in portfolio management;

• Simplifying business processes to improve accountability and encourage initiative; and

• Increasing supervision efforts. In the case of Egypt, for example, where supervision work is increasingly being delegated to the Bank's resident mission, the direct supervision input per project increased from 14.6 staffweeks in fiscal 1992 to 16.2 staffweeks in fiscal 1993.

CPPRs have now been carried out for all major borrowing countries and are on an annual cycle. These efforts to link portfolio performance and country strategy are already having an effect on the volume, structure, and design of lending programs in the region. For example, the country-assistance strategy for Egypt was revised during the year to reflect major changes in project identification and development processes resulting from agreements with the government reached during the country-portfolio review.

Summaries of Projects Approved for IBRD, IDA, and Trust Fund for Gaza Assistance in Fiscal 1994

Acronyms and Abbreviations Used in This Section

ACBF—Africa Capacity Building
  Foundation
ADF—African Development Fund
AfDB—African Development Bank
AGCD—Administration Générale de la
  Coopération Belge
AFESD—Arab Fund for Economic and
  Social Development
AsDB—Asian Development Bank
BADEA—Arab Bank for Economic
  Development in Africa
BITS—Swedish Agency for International
  Technical and Economic Cooperation
BOAD—Banque Ouest-Africaine de
  Développement
CDB—Caribbean Development Bank
CFD—Caisse française de
  développement
CIDA—Canadian International
  Development Agency
DANIDA—Danish International
  Development Agency
EBRD—European Bank for
  Reconstruction and Development
EU—European Union
ECO—Expanded cofinancing operation
EDF—European Development Fund
EIB—European Investment Bank
FAC—Fonds d'aide et de coopération
FINNIDA—Finnish International
  Development Agency
GEF—Global Environment Facility
IBRD—International Bank for
  Reconstruction and Development
  (World Bank)

IDA—International Development
  Association
IDB—Inter-American Development Bank
IFAD—International Fund for Agricultural
  Development
IMF—International Monetary Fund
IsDB—Islamic Development Bank
JExIm—Export-Import Bank of Japan
JICA—Japan International Cooperation
  Agency
KFAED—Kuwait Fund for Arab
  Economic Development
NDF—Nordic Development Fund
NORAD—Norwegian Agency for
  Development Cooperation
ODA—Overseas Development
  Administration
OECF—Overseas Economic Cooperation
  Fund
OPEC—Organization of the Petroleum
  Exporting Countries
PHARE—Pologne-Hongrie: aide à la
  réconstruction économique
SDC—Directorate for Development
  Cooperation and Humanitarian Aid
  (Switzerland)
SFD—Saudi Fund for Development
SIDA—Swedish International
  Development Authority
UNDP—United Nations Development
  Programme
UNICEF—United Nations Children's Fund
USAID—United States Agency for
  International Development
WFP—World Food Programme

Agriculture

ALGERIA: IBRD—$30 million. Attempts to thwart a locust plague, forecast for late 1993 and early 1994, will be made through truck-and-airplane applications of pesticides, and the country's existing locust surveillance and monitoring systems will be upgraded, thus facilitating planning and implementation of future control programs in situations of both plague and recession. Total cost: $51.2 million.

BELARUS: IBRD—$41.9 million. Forestry resource management will be improved and medium-term strategic resource management plans developed; the decline in timber harvest will be reduced through the import of spare parts; and the establishment of private sector harvesting, transport, and other services to the sector promoted. Technical assistance is included. Total cost: $54.7 million.

NOTE: Data used in this section have been compiled from documentation provided at the time of project approval. Projects marked by an asterisk (*) are included in the Program of Targeted Interventions, and those marked with a pound sign (#) are poverty-focused adjustment operations. Projects marked by a dagger (†) included the participation of primary stakeholders.

†*BENIN: IDA—$9.7 million. The government will be assisted in alleviating poverty and improving food security and nutrition standards for vulnerable groups in about twenty areas of the country through a project that helps finance community-development initiatives, income-generating activities, micro-infrastructure, nutrition activities, and institution-building assistance. Cofinancing is expected from DANIDA ($4.9 million) and the WFP ($700,000). Total cost: $19.1 million.

†BHUTAN: IDA—$5.4 million. The government's efforts to develop and implement an approach for sustainable protection, management, and use of its forest resources will be supported through a project that will help finance a comprehensive program of activities for forest-resource development in eastern Bhutan, with maximum participation of forest users. Cofinancing ($2.7 million) is being provided by the SDC. Total cost: $8.9 million.

BULGARIA: IBRD—$50 million. Access of the private sector to medium-term and long-term credit for investments in primary agriculture and agribusiness will be improved through provision of foreign exchange resources to participating financial intermediaries. Total cost: $63.4 million.

CHINA: IBRD—$460 million. Through the construction of the 154-meter high Xiaolangdi rockfill dam and a power station with an installed capacity of 1,800 mW, flood protection will be provided for 103 million people in the North China plain, sediment accretion in the lower reaches of the Yellow river will be controlled for some twenty years, hydropower will be generated, irrigation water supplied for about 2 million hectares, and a stable water supply furnished for downstream cities and industries. Total cost: $2,294.7 million.

†CHINA: IDA—$205 million. The living standards of more than a half million farm families living in the Songliao plain area of Liaoning and Jilin provinces are expected to increase as a result of a project that will expand irrigation and drainage facilities, develop marginal lands for orchards, develop aquaculture infrastructure, and invest in agroprocessing facilities. Total cost: $382.3 million.

†CHINA: IDA—$200 million. The productivity of forest resources, the efficiency of resource use, and the institutional capacity for sustainable management in the three major types of forest land in the country—plantations, watershed-protection forests, and nature reserves—will be enhanced. Cofinancing ($18.4 million) is expected from the GEF. Total cost: $356 million.

†CHINA: IDA—$150 million. The per capita incomes of some 67,000 households living in resource-constrained remote upland areas of Zhejiang, Fujian, and Jiangxi provinces are expected to triple as a result of a second project supporting the integrated development of paddy, upland, and forest areas. Total cost: $296.4 million.

†*CHINA: IDA—$150 million. Agricultural production will increase on more than 15,000 square kilometers of land in the Loess plateau watershed and incomes raised for the more than 1 million people in the project area by creating sustainable crop production on high-yielding level farmland and replacing areas devoted to crops on erodible slope lands with plantings to a range of trees, shrubs, and grasses for land stabilization and the production of fuel, timber, and fodder. Total cost: $248.7 million.

†CHINA: IDA—$110 million. One hundred fifty-four thousand people directly affected by the construction of the Xiaolangdi dam will be resettled and their livelihoods both restored and improved through the reconstruction of villages and towns, development of agricultural land, relocation of small industries and commercial enterprises, and the establishment of new county, township, and village industries. In addition, income opportunities for about 300,000 people in the host areas receiving the resettlers will be expanded. Total cost: $571.3 million.

†*COLOMBIA: IBRD—$39 million. The first phase of a long-term Natural Resource Management Program—designed to develop policies and mechanisms to help arrest the degradation of natural renewable resources—will be implemented in the Choco region, which has a 90 percent African-Colombian and indigenous population and a high incidence of poverty. The project will thereby generate the policy, institutional, and technical base for future forest management and land-titling investments in the Choco region. Total cost: $65.3 million.

†COTE D'IVOIRE: IDA—$21.8 million. The first phase of a five-year program designed to support, through improved research and extension, the generation, dissemination, and adoption of environmentally sound

technology required to sustain productivity gains in agriculture, will be supported. Institution-building assistance is included. Cofinancing is anticipated from the CFD ($5 million), the AfDB ($2.3 million), IFAD ($1.9 million), the UNDP ($700,000), and the AGCD ($500,000). Total cost: $44.6 million.

COTE D'IVOIRE: IDA—$2.2 million. Through the rehabilitation and development of rural savings and loan cooperatives, rural dwellers will be provided with much needed deposit-safekeeping services and access to short and medium-term financing for productive and social expenses, thereby improving rural incomes and living conditions and reducing poverty. Institution-building assistance is included. Cofinancing is expected from the CFD ($6.5 million), CIDA ($3.5 million), and the FAC ($2 million). Total cost: $15.8 million.

*ECUADOR: IBRD—$20 million. The government will be assisted in undertaking the process of modernization of the irrigation subsector through the provision of technical assistance (public institutional strengthening and reform, private sector development, and preparation of a public sector irrigation-investment plan). In addition, poor farmers will be helped through pilot irrigation projects. Total cost: $25.5 million.

†EGYPT: IBRD—$54 million; IDA—$67 million. An agriculture-modernization project will be supported through provision of financing and advisory services to farmers and rural entrepreneurs, development of competition in the rural financial market, and the launching of pilot efforts in administrative reform and institutional development. Total cost: $268.8 million.

†*GHANA: IDA—$21.5 million. Through the financing of investments for the benefit of rural communities (small water schemes, rural markets, market-access roads, storage and food-processing facilities) and provision of technical assistance by the local private sector, agricultural production is expected to increase, agricultural marketing made more efficient, rural associations strengthened, and vulnerable groups helped through increased income and food security. Total cost: $25.4 million.

GHANA: IDA—$5.7 million. Funds from IDA reflows will be provided to supplement the agriculture-sector adjustment credit, approved in fiscal 1992 in the amount of $80 million.

GUYANA: IDA—$15 million. By financing a limited capital-investment program, current levels of sugar production at the Guyana Sugar Corporation (GUYSUCO) will be ensured and the operation of the country's sugar industry stabilized; at the same time, technical assistance will be provided to help GUYSUCO restructure itself and prepare for eventual privatization. Cofinancing is expected from the CDB ($3 million) and suppliers' credits ($1.9 million). Total cost: $40.5 million.

#†HONDURAS: IDA—$60 million. The government's medium-term Agricultural Sector Modernization and Development Program, designed to improve land use, lay the basis for a sustainable management of the country's rich forest resources, eliminate distortions that affect smallholder farmers, and help improve sector planning and coordination, will be supported. Cofinancing, in the amount of $50 million, is anticipated from the IDB.

HONDURAS: IDA—$27.9 million. Funds from IDA reflows will be provided to supplement the agriculture-sector adjustment credit, approved in fiscal 1994 in the amount of $60 million (see above).

†*INDIA: IDA—$258 million. Through support for the water-resource development program of Haryana state, agricultural productivity will be enhanced and environmental sustainability assured; civil works will also generate employment and increase incomes for the landless poor and marginal farm families. Total cost: $483.4 million.

†*INDIA: IDA—$77.4 million. About 700,000 households of fringe forest dwellers and small farmers, including about 150,000 tribal households, are expected to benefit directly from a project designed to improve management and protection of nearly 400,000 hectares of land in Andhra Pradesh state and directly or indirectly increase the production of wood, nontimber forest products, and animal products. In addition, forest-sector policies will be streamlined and strengthened so as to reverse the process of forest degradation. Total cost: $89.1 million.

†INDIA: IDA—$47 million. The capacity of national and state institutions to plan and undertake priority forestry research programs, to improve the system of forestry education in research and academic institutions, and to improve the extension of research findings will be strengthened. Total cost: $56.4 million.

†INDONESIA: IBRD—$165.7 million. More than a million farm families are expected to benefit from a project that has been designed to create the framework for integrated water-resources management, increase rice production on Java, and protect existing irrigation infrastructure from deterioration while relieving the government of responsibility for a large number of small irrigation schemes. Total cost: $304 million.

†*INDONESIA: IBRD—$65 million. About 32,000 poor farm families are to benefit from a project that will further develop twenty reclaimed swampland schemes in Sumatera and Kalimantan. Technical assistance and training are included. Total cost: $106 million.

INDONESIA: IBRD—$55 million. The risk of dam failures will be reduced through the establishment of dam-safety institutions, the provision of basic safety facilities at existing dams where such facilities are lacking, and the implementation of remedial works at dams with safety deficiencies. Total cost: $97.4 million.

†*LAO PEOPLE'S DEMOCRATIC REPUBLIC: IDA—$8.7 million. The government will be helped in implementing a new resource-management system, which concentrates on poor forest dwellers, in order to better achieve the sustainable management and conservation of the country's forest resources. Cofinancing is anticipated from FINNIDA ($5.6 million) and the GEF ($5 million). Total cost: $20.3 million.

LATVIA: IBRD—$25 million. Private agricultural development will be supported by providing initial investment credits to new private farmers and for the expansion and technological upgrading of private agroindustries and forest-based industries. Technical assistance is included. Cofinancing, totaling $4.9 million, is expected from the PHARE and BITS. Total cost: $45.1 million.

†*LEBANON: IBRD—$57.2 million. Some 34,000 farm families are expected to benefit from a project that seeks to increase agricultural production and agriculture-based income and employment in previously neglected poor rural areas through the rehabilitation and adequate operation and maintenance of surface-irrigation infrastructure. In addition, basic public support services will be provided. Total cost: $70.5 million.

†*MALAYSIA: IBRD—$70 million. The productivity and incomes of about 150,000 rubber smallholders—the country's largest poverty group—will increase through a project that will help finance the second phase of a rubber-replanting scheme. Institution-building assistance is included. Total cost: $253.2 million.

MALI: IDA—$20 million. Finance will be provided to help implement the first six-year phase of the Institut d'Economie Rurale's strategic plan for national agricultural research, whose principal objective is to ensure that adequate technology will become available to farmers as a means to increase agricultural growth and to reverse the decline in the productive capacity of the natural resource base. Cofinancing is expected from USAID ($23.3 million), the Netherlands ($13.8 million), France ($3.4 million), the UNDP ($250,000), and Switzerland ($234,000). Total cost: $111.7 million.

†MAURITANIA: IDA—$18.2 million. The first five-year time slice of a long-term national program to upgrade the provision of agricultural services nationwide, focusing on strengthening the linkages among extension, research, and agricultural training, will be supported. Total cost: $19.8 million.

†MEXICO: IBRD—$200 million. Some 42,000 farmers residing in fourteen irrigation districts, whose management responsibility was transferred from the National Water Commission to water-user organizations, will be assisted in completing the transfer process. In addition, minor irrigation-network and on-farm improvements will be financed. Total cost: $568.8 million.

MOROCCO: IBRD—$121 million. Selected investments in the budget of the Ministry of Agriculture will be financed, and reforms designed to improve the efficiency of investments or operations in the sector will be supported. Cofinancing ($113 million) is being provided by, among others, France, Germany, the EU, the AfDB, and IFAD. Total cost: $993 million.

*MOROCCO: IBRD—$100 million. Finance will be provided to support the continued financing of the core activities of the National Agricultural Credit Bank as well as its diversification into a more universal bank, still geared to rural finance (and thereby the poorer population), but with a broader portfolio and resource base. Institution-building measures are included. Cofinancing is expected from the OECF ($95 million), the EIB ($60 million), the AFESD ($60 million), Germany ($34 million), and the CFD ($30 million). Total cost: $1,150 million.

†MOROCCO: IBRD—$25 million. Agricultural production on about 200,000 farms is expected to increase as a result of a project that will provide for technology transfer to farmers in irrigated as well as adjacent rainfed areas, support services, and promotion of farmer organizations. Technical assistance is included. Total cost: $34.7 million.

†NICARAGUA: IDA—$44 million. Some 50,000 small and medium-scale farmers are to benefit from a project that seeks to "jump-start" the agricultural sector by introducing a new demand-driven approach to technology generation and transfer and by supporting the required technological and institutional framework for defining and ensuring property rights to land. Cofinancing ($4.5 million) is expected from the SDC. Total cost: $57.8 million.

POLAND: IBRD—$146 million. The government's program designed to improve forest-management practices will be supported, thereby ensuring the protection and expansion of the country's forest ecological capital, providing for social benefits, and accommodating sustainable forestry. Cofinancing ($15 million) has been secured from the EIB, while $26.9 million is being sought from bilateral agencies. Total cost: $335.4 million.

†RUSSIA: IBRD—$240 million. Critical agricultural support services—focusing on the enabling policy environment for private sector participation in seed and market development, a nationwide market-information system, and farmer information and advisory services—will be created and strengthened. Total cost: $325 million.

RUSSIA: IBRD—$80 million. The implementation of the government's land-reform program will be assisted through the creation and strengthening of infrastructure and institutional capacity for land registration. Total cost: $115 million.

RWANDA: IDA—$15 million. Through development and implementation of a program of institutional reforms, the quality, relevance, and accountability of priority agricultural research programs will be improved. Cofinancing, totaling $11.5 million, is expected from Canada, France, Germany, Switzerland, the EU, and IFAD. Total cost: $36.5 million.

TANZANIA: IDA—$24.5 million. The functions of the Ministry of Agriculture will be rationalized and strengthened, its institutional capacity to formulate and

implement policies built up, and its capacity to produce reliable information on crop and livestock production and productivity, as well as on marketing and trade, will be strengthened, rationalized, and expanded. Total cost: $27.2 million.

†TUNISIA: IBRD—$120 million. Priority investments—in water mobilization and use efficiency, natural resource conservation, animal health and production, and land consolidation—linked to policy reforms through a government-prepared development action plan will be supported. Institution-building assistance is included. Total cost: $211 million.

†*TUNISIA: IBRD—$27.5 million. Living conditions of the population of the impoverished mountainous northwest region will be improved by promoting measures to increase farm productivity and off-farm income-supporting activities, implementing watershed and rangeland management measures, and providing basic infrastructure and social services. Institution-building assistance to the executing agency and village committees is included. Total cost: $50.7 million.

†UGANDA: IDA—$14 million. The government's strategy to revive cotton production and exports through increased competition in cotton processing and marketing and improved supporting services will be assisted. Cofinancing ($12.5 million) is anticipated from IFAD. Total cost: $31.4 million.

†URUGUAY: IBRD—$41 million. A soil and water-management strategy—focused on rehabilitation and development of irrigation/drainage schemes and related service infrastructure, improvements in the efficiency of surface and groundwater use, establishment of a well-balanced operation and maintenance and capital cost-recovery policy, and support for water and soil management and conservation—will be developed and implemented. Technical assistance is included. Total cost: $74 million.

†*VIET NAM: IDA—$96 million. The incomes of some 50,000 smallholder farm families are expected to increase through provision of supervised credit, extension, and plant-protection services supported by research. In addition, the first steps toward encouraging smallholder rubber development will be taken by rehabilitating existing state-owned estates, which will form the nucleus of the program. Technical assistance is included. Total cost: $106.7 million.

Education

ALBANIA: IDA—$9.6 million. Damaged and dilapidated primary school facilities will be rehabilitated, and the capacity of the Ministry of Education to stimulate efficient use of fiscal resources and assure quality of learning outcomes strengthened. Total cost: $11.3 million.

*BARBADOS: IBRD—$7.8 million. The country's human-capital base will be solidified and the unemployed and less able students helped by strengthening the quality and efficiency of basic education; improving the effectiveness, efficiency, and responsiveness of technical and vocational education; and by reinforcing employment services and labor-market information. Total cost: $15.6 million.

†*BENIN: IDA—$18.1 million. A third education project seeks to increase the access to primary schools, with a specific emphasis on girls' participation at both the primary and secondary levels; improve the quality and internal efficiency of primary and secondary education; and strengthen sector institutional capacity. Total cost: $22.9 million.

*BRAZIL: IBRD—$206.6 million. The quality of schooling for approximately 3 million children a year in the first four grades of state and municipal primary schools in five northeastern states will be improved, thus contributing to reducing grade repetition, raising student achievement, and increasing attainment. Total cost: $366.9 million.

†*BRAZIL: IBRD—$150 million. The quality of schooling for approximately 3 million primary school children in Minas Gerais state will be improved through a project that will support policy improvements, finance educational inputs, and increase teachers' access to training opportunities. Total cost: $302 million.

†*BRAZIL: IBRD—$96 million. Educational attainment in the state of Paraná, as defined by increases in student learning and graduation from primary school, will be improved through the delivery of a package of essential educational inputs to primary schools and improvements in educational management. Total cost: $198.4 million.

†*COLOMBIA: IBRD—$90 million. Implementation of the government's higher education strategy, which centers on cofinancing educational investments with the departments and municipalities and supporting the municipalization of education by building local capacity for

planning, cofinancing, and project execution, will be supported. In addition, access to secondary education by the poor will be increased through implementation of a voucher program. Total cost: $150 million.

COTE D'IVOIRE: IDA—$100 million. Supplementary funds will be provided to help finance the Human Resources Development Program, approved in fiscal 1992. (An amount equivalent to $100 million on an IBRD loan that was approved to help finance the same program has been canceled.)

COTE D'IVOIRE: IDA—$85 million. Funds from IDA reflows will be provided to help supplement the Human Resources Development Program, approved in fiscal 1992 in the amount of $150 million.

†*COTE D'IVOIRE: IDA—$17 million. By supporting governmental efforts in three areas—training, retraining, and apprenticeship; training outreach support; and labor-market monitoring and analysis—and by emphasizing the informal sector and women's enterprises, labor productivity and employability will be enhanced, thereby improving the country's economic competitiveness. Total cost: $19.5 million.

INDONESIA: IBRD—$58.9 million. The quality of graduate education will be improved through the improved planning and management of graduate education and university research and support for selected competitive grant and fellowship programs. Total cost: $97.6 million.

INDONESIA: IBRD—$27.7 million. Innovative industrial skills-training schemes within private enterprises will be developed and implemented in three provinces (West Java, East Java, and North Sumatera) for possible replication elsewhere, and a special training program for unemployed university graduates in those provinces, as well as in South Sulawesi and Bali, will be supported. Institution-building assistance to the Ministry of Manpower is included. Total cost: $39.7 million.

KENYA: IDA—$42.2 million. Funds from IDA reflows will be provided to supplement the education-sector adjustment credit, approved in fiscal 1992 in the amount of $100 million.

†*KENYA: IDA—$21.8 million. The potential for employment creation in the informal sector will be increased through a project that seeks to diversify and improve public and private sector training capacity, stimulate information exchange and

innovation in product development, and develop a new partnership between the public and private sector guaranteeing the full participation of informal sector entrepreneurs and workers in training and technology policy. Total cost: $24.2 million.

KOREA, REPUBLIC OF: IBRD—$190 million. Policy improvements in science and technology education will be implemented, and educational quality in selected private universities and junior technical colleges upgraded through the provision of specialized laboratory and workshop equipment. Total cost: $324.8 million.

†*MEXICO: IBRD—$412 million. Primary school students' academic achievement levels will be improved and high repetition and dropout rates reduced in ten of the country's poorest states through the training of teachers and school administrators, provision of classroom-tested educational materials, and the strengthening of the institutional capacity of the education system. Total cost: $616.7 million.

NEPAL: IDA—$20 million. The first phase of Tribhuvan University's ongoing reform process will be supported by helping finance the implementation of a package of policy changes, including the initiation of systemic changes in the university's administrative, financial, and management processes. Total cost: $23.1 million.

†*NIGER: IDA—$41.4 million. Sector reforms, designed to promote more cost-effective use of public education resources, will be supported, and the access to and quality of primary education will be improved through constructing or rehabilitating classrooms, developing and implementing a program to accelerate girls' education, improving the quality of primary school teachers' training programs, provision of textbooks, and support for a micronutrients program. Cofinancing is expected from Germany ($10.2 million) and Norway ($4.8 million). Total cost: $76 million.

†*PAKISTAN: IDA—$200 million. The country's broad-based Social Action Program, designed to expand and improve primary education, primary health care, family-planning services, and rural water-supply and sanitation investments, will be supported. Cofinancing is anticipated from the AsDB ($100 million) and the Netherlands ($13 million), while other contributions are being explored. Total cost: $4,020 million.

ROMANIA: IBRD—$50 million. The quality of basic and secondary education will be improved by strengthening curriculum and teacher training, assessment and examinations, and textbook quality. In addition, measures to increase efficiency in the management of public resources for education will be developed and introduced. Total cost: $73.5 million.

†*URUGUAY: IBRD—$31.5 million. The quality, equity, and efficiency of the primary education system will be improved. In addition, the quality of preschool education will be enhanced, as well as expanded into areas with unsatisfied basic needs. Institution-building measures are included. Total cost: $45 million.

†*VENEZUELA: IBRD—$89.4 million. The government will be assisted in raising the level of student achievement, reducing the incidence of repetition and dropout, and increasing graduation rates of basic education through improvements in the quality of education and administrative efficiency, particularly in rural and poor urban areas. Total cost: $178.9 million.

*VIET NAM: IDA—$70 million. The Bank's first project in the country since 1978 seeks to improve the quality and relevance of primary education (especially in rural areas and for ethnic minorities), rehabilitate existing infrastructure, extend access through the construction of a limited number of new classrooms, and strengthen the management of primary education at the school, district, provincial, and national levels. Total cost: $78 million.

†YEMEN: IDA—$33 million. Secondary students' learning achievements will be enhanced through reduction of classroom overcrowding, provision of science equipment, and improved teacher performance; female access to secondary education will be increased through provision of school places for 5,000 girls, incentive programs to recruit female headmasters, and specialized home-based learning programs; and two-year post-secondary programs, oriented toward labor-market needs, will be established. Cofinancing is expected from the OPEC Fund for International Development ($8 million). Total cost: $49.7 million.

Environment

CHINA: IBRD—$160 million. An investment program of environmentally oriented capital works and related institutional strengthening—designed to provide safe drinking water while improving water quality in the Huangpu river—will be financed. Total cost: $456.6 million.

THE GAMBIA: IDA—$2.6 million. Technical assistance will be provided to the National Environment Agency and other relevant agencies to build up the capacity to develop and guide an effective system for environmental planning and management and to ensure that environmental concerns are fully integrated and reflected in the country's social and economic development process. Cofinancing ($1.3 million) is expected from Germany. Total cost: $4.5 million.

†*INDONESIA: IBRD—$56.5 million. Through provision of institutional strengthening measures designed to improve the guidelines and policies of the national "regreening and reforestation" (r&r) program, the introduction of improved farming systems in a priority watershed in West Java, and investment support for the national r&r program, the living standards of poor, upland farmers will be raised, the productive potential of their resource base restored, watershed environmental quality enhanced, and downstream watershed resources protected. Total cost: $487.8 million.

KOREA, REPUBLIC OF: IBRD—$90 million. The ability of selected national research institutes to identify and adequately address environmental issues and to undertake environmental research and development activities will be strengthened. Institution-building assistance to the Ministry of Environment is included. Total cost: $156 million.

†MEXICO: $368 million. About fifteen subprojects in five or six cities bordering on the United States in the areas of water treatment and sanitation, solid waste management, and air quality and urban transport will be financed so as to improve environmental quality. Institutional strengthening measures are included. Total cost: $762 million.

MOROCCO: IBRD—$6 million. The government will be assisted in strengthening its institutional and regulatory framework for managing environmental protection. Total cost: $10.8 million.

†PAKISTAN: IDA—$14.7 million. The first phase of a long-term program to improve Balochistan's environmental protection and natural resource management will be supported through institutional

strengthening and investments in natural resource-rehabilitation subprojects. Total cost: $17.8 million.

†*PARAGUAY: IBRD—$50 million. This first-phase initiative to alter radically the use of natural resources in agriculture, particularly by small-scale farmers—from extensive expansion to growth through intensification, with emphasis on sustainable resource management and environmental protection—will be supported. Total cost: $79.1 million.

Financial Sector

ARGENTINA: IBRD—$500 million. Capital-market development will be accelerated through the introduction and consolidation of the necessary capital-markets infrastructure, which, along with developing indigenous skills, can produce a sustainable and orderly national market.

ARGENTINA: IBRD—$8.5 million. Technical assistance will be provided to help facilitate the implementation of the IBRD-assisted capital-market development project (see above) by supporting the creation of new institutions and the strengthening of others and by ensuring the development of more effective capital-market regulations. Total cost: $10.2 million.

CARIBBEAN DEVELOPMENT BANK: IBRD—$20 million; IDA—$11 million. Funds will be onlent by the CDB to IBRD and IDA-eligible Commonwealth Caribbean countries to finance the types of projects the World Bank would finance. Total cost: $68 million.

COLOMBIA: IBRD—$30 million. Wide-ranging improvements in the management of public finances, from revenue generation to the evaluation of public policies, will be made, thereby increasing public revenues, reestablishing public confidence in government and public administration, and contributing to an overall institutional environment conducive to private-sector initiatives and development. Total cost: $58 million.

COTE D'IVOIRE: IDA—$100 million. Supplementary funds will be provided to help finance the Financial Sector Adjustment Program, approved in fiscal 1992. (An amount equivalent to $100 million on an IBRD loan that was approved to help finance the same program has been canceled.)

COTE D'IVOIRE: IDA—$50 million. Supplementary funds will be provided to help finance the Competitiveness and

Regulatory Reform Adjustment Program, approved in fiscal 1992. (An amount equivalent to $50 million on an IBRD loan that was approved to help finance the same program has been canceled.)

KOREA, REPUBLIC OF: IBRD—$100 million. The government's liberalization program in the financial sector—designed to accelerate deregulation of domestic financial markets and increase competition and efficiency of financial intermediation—will be supported by a project that will channel long-term credits to private manufacturing enterprises through three participating financial intermediaries. Training and technical assistance are included. Total cost: $250 million.

#MOZAMBIQUE: IDA—$200 million. The government's economic and social rehabilitation program, whose objectives are to support macroeconomic stabilization through the strengthening of key elements of fiscal and monetary policy while supporting an interlinked program of enterprise and financial sector reform and continuing income transfers to poor households, will be supported.

MOZAMBIQUE: IDA—$9 million. By providing training (a) in key areas of central bank activity, (b) to meet the immediate training needs of commercial bank staff, and (c) to strengthen legal financial capacities, the ability to implement the government's policy and institutional reforms will be enhanced. Institution-building assistance to the banking system is included. Cofinancing ($1 million) is anticipated from the SDC. Total cost: $10.5 million.

†RUSSIA: IBRD—$200 million. A financial institutions development project has been designed to improve the quality of banking services, promote banking stability, and contribute to a more efficient allocation of bank credit by building up the capacity of a core group of thirty to forty private commercial banks. Cofinancing is expected from the EBRD ($99 million), the EU ($36 million), Japan ($18.6 million), and USAID ($3.4 million). Total cost: $389.4 million.

†RWANDA: IDA—$12 million. A line of credit will be made available to finance productive private sector investments, and a fund will be set up to finance technical assistance designed to improve the technical and managerial capacity of private sector firms. Institutional strengthening, designed to ensure proper implementation of reform measures, is included. Cofinancing ($1 million) is

expected from Belgium. Total cost: $19.3 million.

#SLOVENIA: IBRD—$80 million. The country's efforts to implement effective reform of its enterprise and financial sectors will be supported by a project that seeks to facilitate enterprise privatization and restructuring, accelerate the development of a strong and supportive financial sector, and support more effective labor-market policies and a social safety net for the poor. Technical assistance is included.

TUNISIA: IBRD—$120 million. Financially sound banks and financial leasing companies will be provided access to term resources at market rates to finance viable private investments during the current transitional period of emerging long-term capital markets.

UGANDA: IDA—$1.1 million. Funds from IDA reflows will be provided to supplement the financial sector adjustment credit, approved in fiscal 1993 in the amount of $100 million.

URUGUAY: IBRD—$35 million. A line of credit will be extended to participating financial intermediaries to finance private investment, associated permanent working capital, and leasing operations (excluding purchase of land and housing) of viable enterprises that have revenues predominantly in United States dollars. Technical assistance is included. Cofinancing ($90 million) is being provided by the IDB.

ZAMBIA: IDA—$18 million. Standards of accounting, public sector procurement, and legal services will be improved by strengthening key institutions involved in these three activities through improvements in their human and material resources. Total cost: $19.6 million.

ZAMBIA: IDA—$10 million. Supplemental funds will be provided to help finance the second Privatization and Industrial Reform Credit, approved in June 1993 in the amount of $100 million.

Industry

BANGLADESH: IDA—$247 million. Implementation of a program of reforms designed to restructure the jute-manufacturing industry will be supported.

BANGLADESH: IDA—$3.3 million. Funds from IDA reflows will be provided to supplement the jute sector-adjustment credit, approved in fiscal 1994 (see above).

*COMOROS: IDA—$5.1 million. The nascent private sector will be provided with the means and incentives to engage in productive investments through provision of finance and technical support to small-scale entrepreneurs engaged in labor-intensive and/or service activities; implementation of improvements in commercial and labor law, as well as legal and judicial procedures; and a strengthening of investment incentives. Total cost: $7.7 million.

MAURITIUS: IBRD—$7.7 million. Export competitiveness, and thereby prospects for sustainable rapid growth, will be enhanced by facilitating private sector access to know-how for improved productivity, quality, design, and response times, as well as diversification of export production. Total cost: $13.3 million.

PHILIPPINES: IBRD—$40 million. The program to attract private investors to the Subic Bay Freeport—until November 1992 it was the Subic Bay Naval Base—will be supported through provision of infrastructure improvements; maintenance of the freeport's asset base, including protection of the environment; and strengthening the capacity of the freeport's managing authority. Total cost: $54.1 million.

ROMANIA: IBRD—$175 million. Funds will be onlent to private enterprises for investments aimed at improving international competitiveness and/or to expand exports. In addition, partial to full coverage of preshipment finance needs for imported inputs will be provided. Technical assistance is included. Total cost: $334 million.

RUSSIA: IBRD—$200 million. Term finance for capital investments and permanent working capital will be made available to commercial banks for onlending to new private and newly privatized enterprises. Cofinancing ($100 million) is expected from the EBRD.

ZAMBIA: IDA—$16.8 million. Funds from IDA reflows will be provided to supplement the privatization and industrial reform credit, approved in fiscal 1992 in the amount of $200 million.

Mining/Other Extractive

ECUADOR: IBRD—$14 million. Implementation of the government's new mining sector policy and strategy, designed to attract private mining investment, will be assisted by financing (a) mapping and mining-information and cadastral systems to support increased, yet environmentally sound, mineral production and (b) measures to arrest and mitigate mining-related environmental degradation, including the upgrading of small-miner technology and management practices. Cofinancing, totaling $8.1 million, is expected from Sweden and the United Kingdom. Total cost: $24 million.

Multisector

BELARUS: IBRD—$120 million. The government's reform program, designed to promote competition, support the development of the private sector, and provide a financially sustainable and incentive-compatible social safety net in order to protect vulnerable groups during the transition, will be supported.

BELARUS: IBRD—$8.3 million. The government will be assisted in strengthening the institutional basis for economic reform through provision of technical assistance in four functional areas: resource mobilization and economic management, enterprise reform, banking sector reform, and social-sector reform. Total cost: $18 million.

BOLIVIA: IDA—$9.4 million. Funds from IDA reflows will be provided to supplement the structural-adjustment credit, approved in fiscal 1992 in the amount of $40 million.

#†BURKINA FASO: IDA—$25 million. The government's reform efforts following the devaluation of the CFA franc in January 1994 will be supported.

CAMBODIA: IDA—$62.7 million. Critical imports to enable key sectors of the economy to continue to operate will be financed. Cofinancing ($2.3 million) is expected from SIDA. Total cost: $73.1 million.

#CAMEROON: IDA—$75 million. The government's economic recovery program will be supported by this credit, which will finance the imports needed for economic recovery and growth following the recent devaluation of the CFA franc, while instituting short-term safety net measures to protect the poor.

CAMEROON: IDA—$51 million. Funds from IDA reflows will be provided to supplement the structural-adjustment credit, approved in fiscal 1994, in the amount of $50 million (see below).

CAMEROON: IDA—$50 million. The government's revised stabilization and adjustment program will be supported. (Concurrently, the third tranche of a $150 million IBRD loan in support of the government's structural-adjustment program was canceled.)

#CHAD: IDA—$20 million. The government's post-devaluation reform program, designed to restore order to public finances and lay the basis for growth and the alleviation of poverty, while instituting measures to protect the most vulnerable groups, will be supported.

CONGO: IDA—$100 million. The government's reform program, designed to improve public sector efficiency, strengthen the country's production capacity, develop human resources, and reduce poverty, will be supported.

#EL SALVADOR: IBRD—$50 million. The government's structural-adjustment program, designed to lay the analytical framework for public sector modernization; consolidate and deepen reforms supported by a previous structural-adjustment operation; implement a comprehensive poverty-alleviation plan; and strengthen public expenditures, the civil service, and environmental management, will be supported.

ETHIOPIA: IDA—$470,000. Funds from IDA reflows will be provided to supplement the structural-adjustment credit, approved in fiscal 1993, in the amount of $250 million.

#GABON: IBRD—$30 million. Emergency support will be provided to the government's program of economic recovery that was conceived in the wake of the devaluation of the CFA franc. Public expenditure reallocations towards basic social service areas, as well as policies to eliminate distortions faced by the poor, are included.

GUYANA: IDA—$2.8 million. Funds from IDA reflows will be provided to supplement the second structural-adjustment credit, approved in fiscal 1990 in the amount of $74.6 million.

KAZAKHSTAN: IBRD—$180 million. The government's reform program will be supported by provision of finance for (a) expansion of the country's foreign-exchange auction market, which provides hard currency to enterprises wishing to finance imports through normal commercial practices and (b) essential imports required for the continued operation of essential public services and a recovery in critical productive sectors.

KAZAKHSTAN: IBRD—$38 million. Critically needed technical assistance will be provided to help develop and implement key components of the government's reform program, assuring the prompt and concerted development of the essential components of a market economy. Total cost: $39.5 million.

#MACEDONIA, FORMER YUGOSLAV REPUBLIC OF: IBRD—$40 million; IDA—$40 million. Key structural reforms, designed to enable the government to achieve sustainable stabilization and restore growth, while protecting vulnerable groups through social safety net reforms, will be supported.

MALAWI: IDA—$4.3 million. Funds from IDA reflows will be provided to supplement the entrepreneurship-development and drought-recovery project, approved in fiscal 1992 in the amount of $120 million.

#MALI: IDA—$25 million. The country's post-devaluation reform program, whose main objectives are private sector-led growth and the reduction of poverty, will be supported.

MOLDOVA: IBRD—$60 million. Imports of essential production inputs and health-care supplies will be financed, foreign exchange will be provided to support the access of enterprises to the foreign-exchange market, and the social safety net system will be strengthened. Technical assistance is included.

MONGOLIA: IDA—$20 million. Imports and technical assistance urgently needed to maintain and develop coal and copper mining production and the transport sector will be financed. Total cost: $25.4 million.

#NIGER: IDA—$25 million. The country's post-devaluation reform program will be supported, in particular measures aimed at minimizing the negative short-term social impact of the devaluation.

OCCUPIED TERRITORIES: Trust Fund for Gaza—$30 million. Priority infrastructural services in the education, power, water and sewerage, and roads sectors in Gaza will be financed. In addition, technical assistance to help prepare and support implementation of investment activities, provide support for the development of much of the policy framework required to ensure the sustainability of the investment program, and lay the institutional basis for interim self-government will be provided. Cofinancing, which will support components in both Gaza and the West Bank, has been pledged by the AFESD ($30 million), the SFD ($30 million), the KFAED ($10 million), Denmark ($20 million), and the SDC ($8 million).

#SENEGAL: IDA—$25 million. The country's post-devaluation reform program will be supported, in particular measures aimed at minimizing the negative short-term social impact of the devaluation.

#SIERRA LEONE: IDA—$50 million. Government reforms in the areas of trade and exchange-rate policies, fiscal management, the civil service, the public enterprise sector, and delivery of social services to the poor will be extended and deepened.

SIERRA LEONE: IDA—$190,000. Funds from IDA reflows will be provided to supplement the structural-adjustment credit, approved in fiscal 1994 in the amount of $50 million (see above).

#SLOVAK REPUBLIC: IBRD—$80 million. The government's ongoing reform program—its central objective is the restoration of growth—will be supported by financing many of the one-time costs associated with restructuring and the breakup of the Czech and Slovak Federal Republic, including social sector reforms and funding of a social safety net for vulnerable groups.

#UGANDA: IDA—$80 million. The government's economic recovery program, designed to bring about rapid and sustained improvements in living standards through policy changes, which include increased public expenditure allocation toward basic social services, will be supported through a second structural-adjustment loan.

#ZAMBIA: IDA—$150 million. Implementation of the next phase of the country's structural-adjustment program will be supported through balance-of-payments financing and support for efforts to (a) restore macroeconomic stability, (b) generate a supply response through the removal of bottlenecks to exports and agricultural expansion, and (c) remove structural obstacles to the delivery of social services.

Oil and Gas

†CHINA: IBRD—$255 million. Implementation of the upstream oil and gas-sector restructuring will be supported, and the levels and structure of gas pricing will be rationalized. In addition, gas field development, stimulation, and rehabilitation in Sichuan province will be financed. Institution-building assistance is included. Cofinancing ($10 million) is being provided by the GEF. Total cost: $945.2 million.

ESTONIA: IBRD—$38.4 million. Rehabilitation and improvements in district heating systems will be undertaken in three of the country's five largest cities (Tallin, Tartu, and Parnu), thereby reducing fuel costs and import requirements and improving environmental conditions in affected areas. Capacity-building assistance is included. Cofinancing will be provided by the BITS ($10 million) and the EIB ($4.4 million), while another $3.8 million is being sought. Total cost: $64.5 million.

†ETHIOPIA: IDA—$74.3 million. By increasing the availability of fuel from the Calub natural gas deposit in the country's southeast region, Ethiopia's unbalanced structure of energy supply will be partially righted and the supply of petroleum products needed in the modern sectors of the economy increased. Road rehabilitation, technical assistance, and a poverty-alleviation component—aimed at supporting income diversification among poor urban fuelwood carriers—is included. Cofinancing is expected from the AfDB ($27 million) and has been confirmed by the Netherlands ($4 million). Total cost: $130.8 million.

HUNGARY: IBRD—$100 million. The next investment (construction of a gas-fired combined-cycle cogeneration unit) in the national least-cost power generation-investment program, designed to improve energy efficiency and environmental conditions at one of the country's most important power stations and reduce dependence on fuel imports, will be supported. Institution-building assistance and training are included. Total cost: $242.5 million.

JORDAN: IBRD—$80 million. The financial viability of the power subsector will be restored so as to ensure that it can operate on a commercial basis and finance its investment needs. In addition, the energy sector will be restructured in such a way as to establish an enabling environment for sustainable sector growth and development. Cofinancing ($80 million) is expected from Japan.

KAZAKHSTAN: IBRD—$15.7 million. Technical assistance will be provided to help the government strengthen the capacity of key petroleum subsector agencies to attract foreign investments, promote the efficiency and long-term financial viability of the petroleum industry, and formulate sound investment and organizational strategies for the integration of domestic primary petroleum production, processing, transport, and distribution. Total cost: $19.6 million.

LITHUANIA: IBRD—$26.4 million. Two thermal power plants will be rehabilitated, and the safety, reliability, and flexibility of the electricity-transmission system improved. Capacity-building assistance is included. Total cost: $32.9 million.

MADAGASCAR: IDA—$51.9 million. Governmental reforms in the petroleum sector, which have introduced a competitive environment and the involvement of the private sector, will be supported, and basic infrastructure investments required to increase operational efficiency and attract private operators and investors will be financed. Institution-building measures are included. Total cost: $79.2 million.

MOZAMBIQUE: IDA—$30 million. All predevelopment work necessary to enable the government and the private sector to make a firm decision to develop the Pande gas field to enable gas to be exported (mainly to South Africa) and used domestically will be undertaken. Interest in cofinancing ($3 million) has been expressed by Norway. Total cost: $48.7 million.

PAPUA NEW GUINEA: IBRD—$11 million. A second project in support of the country's petroleum sector will help strengthen the government's capability in policy formulation, safety regulation, evaluation of development proposals, and monitoring of ongoing sector-development programs, thereby enhancing the attractiveness of the sector to international investors. Total cost: $12.2 million.

ROMANIA: IBRD—$175.6 million. The government's petroleum-sector restructuring strategy, designed to promote private sector investments, strengthen institutional capabilities, and establish a suitable regulatory framework to facilitate the development of an efficient and commercially oriented petroleum sector, will be supported. Cofinancing is expected from the EIB ($51.2 million) and the EU's PHARE program ($2 million). Total cost: $345.6 million.

RUSSIA: IBRD—$500 million. A second oil-rehabilitation project seeks to slow the rate of oil-production decline in Western Siberia; transfer international technical, environmental, and managerial practice to the operation of oil fields in Western Siberia; and promote a more efficient and environmentally sustainable use of the country's petroleum resources. Total cost: $678 million.

ZAMBIA: IDA—$30 million. The Tazama pipeline from Dar es Salaam (Tanzania) to Ndola (Zambia) will be rehabilitated, and the oil-products depot at Ndola

modernized. Institutional strengthening and technical assistance, designed to support the petroleum industry's efforts to become more competitive and cost effective, are included. Cofinancing ($15 million) is expected from the EIB. Total cost: $48 million.

Population, Health, and Nutrition

†*ARGENTINA: IBRD—$100 million. An estimated 500,000 poor mothers and young children are expected to benefit directly from a project that seeks to expand and subsequently maintain coverage of good-quality basic health care, nutrition, and child-development services for the poor. Total cost: $160 million.

BRAZIL: IBRD—$160 million. It is expected that, based on a conservative model of behavioral change, human immunodeficiency virus (HIV) infections will be reduced by 300,000 cases as a result of a project designed to reduced the incidence and transmission of HIV/AIDS and sexually transmitted diseases. Institutional strengthening measures are included. Total cost: $250 million.

†*BURKINA FASO: IDA—$29.2 million. The government's efforts to improve significantly the quality, coverage, and utilization of basic health services; enhance the nutritional status of the population; and develop a national capacity for achieving sustainable control of endemic parasitic diseases will be supported. Cofinancing is anticipated from Germany ($4.1 million) and UNICEF ($3.6 million). Total cost: $38.9 million.

†*BURKINA FASO: IDA—$26.3 million. The government will be assisted in making family-planning services more accessible, particularly in rural areas, while at the same time stimulating the demand for contraceptive services. In addition, the spread of HIV infections will be slowed by promoting behavioral change and treating sexually transmitted diseases. Cofinancing is expected from Denmark and Norway ($3 million each). Total cost: $34.5 million.

†*CHAD: IDA—$18.5 million. Some 750,000 people, mostly women and children, stand to benefit directly from a project designed to increase the efficiency of the health system with the result that the access to and quality of health, nutrition, and family planning services will be increased and improved. Technical assistance is included. Cofinancing is anticipated from UNICEF ($2.3 million) and the UNDP ($1.3 million). Total cost: $25.7 million.

*CHINA: IDA—$110 million. Through the training (and retraining) of health workers and by improving their working conditions, the quality of service performed by rural health workers will be improved, thereby contributing to better health among the rural population in six provinces. Total cost: $186 million.

†*COMOROS: IDA—$13 million. The development of human resources will be strengthened by increasing the efficiency and effectiveness of basic health services through the establishment of efficient regional health administrations, a social development fund for the poor, and other supportive services. In addition, complementary community-development initiatives will be promoted to develop grassroots participation in small-scale productive activities. Total cost: $16 million.

*COSTA RICA: IBRD—$22 million. The government's effort to implement critical policy, institutional, and operational reforms that aim at improving the efficiency, effectiveness, and quality of the delivery of health-care services by the Costa Rican Social Security System— especially to the poorer population—and at improving quality control and surveillance in the health sector, will be supported. Total cost: $32 million.

†*GUINEA: IDA—$24.6 million. The coverage of low-cost health, nutrition, and family-planning services will be expanded, thereby helping improve the health status of the population—in particular, the most vulnerable groups. Institution-building assistance is included. Total cost: $27.3 million.

†*INDIA: IDA—$117.8 million. The quality of cataract surgery will be upgraded, the coverage of the National Program for the Control of Blindness will be expanded to underprivileged areas (with special attention to women, tribal, and other isolated groups), cataract prevalence reduced by more than 50 percent, and blindness incidence cut by more than 30 percent in the states of Maharashtra, Rajasthan, Uttar Pradesh, Andhra Pradesh, Madhya Pradesh, Orissa, and Tamil Nadu. Total cost: $135.7 million.

†*INDIA: IDA—$88.6 million. The family-welfare programs in the states of Assam, Rajasthan, and Karnataka will be strengthened and improved, and the current levels of fertility and maternal and childhood mortality lowered through targeting poor areas and tribal and migratory communities. Total cost: $103.8 million.

*MALAYSIA: IBRD—$50 million. Selected high-priority needs for health-sector development, including building and equipping health-care centers in three poor rural areas, strengthening prevention programs to meet emerging environmental and occupation concerns, improving equitable access to primary health care, introduction of appropriate new health technologies, and institutional strengthening, will be addressed. Total cost: $101.3 million.

NEPAL: IDA—$26.7 million. Key components of the government's family-planning/maternal and child health program will be financed, thereby providing support to efforts to increase contraceptive prevalence, decrease the total fertility rate, reduce maternal and child morbidity and mortality, and raise life expectancy. Total cost: $39 million.

*NICARAGUA: IDA—$15 million. Reforms in the health sector, which focus on decentralization of services, enhancement of primary care, strengthening the supply and distribution of drugs, rehabilitation of facilities, and greater cost recovery at the secondary level, will be supported. Cofinancing is anticipated from Norway ($3 million). Total cost: $20.1 million.

†*PERU: IBRD—$34 million. The health and nutritional status of residents (poor women and children in particular) living in three poor regions of the country, as well as one of Lima's poorest districts, is expected to improve through extending access and improving the quality of maternal and child health and nutrition services and through promotion of better health and nutrition practices. Total cost: $44.5 million.

†*UGANDA: IDA—$50 million. Attempts will be made to (a) prevent further sexual transmission of the HIV through promotion of safer sexual behavior, increased condom availability and usage, and provision of care and treatment of sexually transmitted diseases; and (b) mitigate the personal impact of the AIDS epidemic through the financing of drugs, protective supplies, and health-care services. Institution-building assistance is included. Cofinancing is anticipated from Germany ($6.8 million), SIDA ($5 million), and the ODA ($4.2 million). Total cost: $73.4 million.

Power

†CHINA: IBRD—$350 million. Through the construction of a coal-fired thermal power

plant, the erection of new transmission lines, and the reinforcement of the existing power-transmission network, the critically needed power-generation capability of Jiangsu province and the East China power grid as a whole will be greatly increased. Technical assistance and training are included. Cofinancing ($120 million) is being provided through an ECO involving the commercial bank market and the Japanese insurance-company market. Total cost: $1,081.4 million.

†INDONESIA: IBRD—$260.5 million. Efforts to increase private sector participation in electricity generation and to restructure the state electricity company (PLN) and establish it as a commercial entity will be supported. In addition, environmentally sustainable expansion of PLN's electricity-generation and transmission capacity will be financed. Cofinancing ($23.7 million) is anticipated from Austria and Australia and from export credits ($92 million). Total cost: $688.9 million.

PAKISTAN: IBRD—$230 million. The investment program of the Water and Power Development Authority (WAPDA) will be supported, and the stage will be set for a gradual and orderly privatization of the power sector in general and WAPDA in particular. Total cost: $4,470 million.

†PHILIPPINES: IBRD—$227 million. The rapidly increasing demand for power in Luzon will be met through the development of a geothermal energy field in the Eastern Visayas that will expand power plant capacity from 200 mW to 640 mW and the construction of related transmission systems that will interconnect most of the country. Institution-strengthening measures are included. Cofinancing is expected from the JExIm ($170 million), the BITS ($39 million), the GEF ($30 million), and an ECO to support commercial financing of $100 million for the project's high-voltage AC/DC converter stations. Total cost: $1,333.6 million.

†PHILIPPINES: IBRD—$211 million. The rapidly increasing demand for power in Cebu and the Visayas region will be met through the use of indigenous and environmentally superior geothermal energy. Institution-building assistance is included. Total cost: $458.9 million.

ZIMBABWE: IBRD—$90 million. The performance and reliability of the Hwange coal-fired power station, the country's largest generating station, will be increased, thereby minimizing the severity of the power shortage—caused by the recent drought—and facilitating economic recovery. Technical assistance and training are included. Total cost: $200.3 million.

Public-sector Management

BENIN: IDA—$5.2 million. Economic management capacity in the country will be improved through support to the management of a national training center, technical assistance to the Ministry of Planning and Ministry of Finance, and provision of studies and short-term expertise in support of adjustment implementation. Cofinancing is expected from DANIDA ($4 million) and the ACBF ($2 million). Total cost: $12 million.

CAPE VERDE: IDA—$8.1 million. The government's broad effort to transform and modernize key institutions, the laws supporting them, and the personnel staffing them will be supported by a project that seeks to modernize the civil service, build local capacity, strengthen economic management capacity, reform and modernize the justice system, and spur public procurement reforms. Total cost: $8.9 million.

EL SALVADOR: IBRD—$2.5 million. The country's adjustment process will be deepened through the provision of technical and financial support to the institutions in charge of the economic reform program. Cofinancing is expected from USAID, the UNDP, and the IDB. Total cost: $6.3 million.

HUNGARY: IBRD—$29 million. Through a program of institutional development, development and implementation of a new information-technology system, and training in the development and use of applications systems, the country's tax administration will be strengthened, thereby maximizing tax revenues in a sustainable way. Total cost: $55.6 million.

JAMAICA: IBRD—$35 million. Through the design of measures to improve the country's export-support systems and financial sector support for investment and trade finance, the investment and export-development process will be accelerated during the last major phase of trade liberalization in Jamaica, and constraints to local long-term sources of funds will be addressed. Total cost: $52 million.

JAMAICA: IBRD—$13.2 million. A tax-administration reform project seeks to raise revenues without increasing tax rates through a broadening of the tax base, improving the efficiency and effectiveness of the tax administration, and encouragement of improved voluntary compliance. Total cost: $42 million.

KYRGYZ REPUBLIC: IDA—$60 million. Implementation of enterprise privatization and restructuring will be accelerated, and efforts to stimulate private sector development, improve enterprise governance and efficiency, and advance banking sector reforms supported.

LEBANON: IBRD—$19.9 million. Government efforts to enhance revenues and strengthen fiscal management will be supported through a project whose main focus is on (a) filling the immediate gaps in key personnel, skills, equipment, and physical resources; (b) assisting in improving systems, procedures, and data bases; and (c) providing advice on future policy reforms. Cofinancing is expected from the UNDP ($1 million) and the IMF ($660,000). Total cost: $23.6 million.

LESOTHO: IDA—$11 million. Technical assistance will be supplied in support of the government's privatization and private sector development efforts. Total cost: $12.4 million.

MALAWI: IDA—$22.6 million. Specific systemic management issues that now constitute bottlenecks to efficiency and effectiveness in the civil service will be addressed through the provision of technical assistance and training. Total cost: $25.6 million.

MAURITANIA: IDA—$1.3 million. Funds from IDA reflows will be provided to supplement the public enterprise-sector adjustment credit, approved in fiscal 1990 in the amount of $40 million.

NICARAGUA: IDA—$60 million. The government's structural-adjustment program, which aims to carry out a major reform of the state, increase the efficiency of financial intermediation, and improve conditions for private sector development, will be supported.

NICARAGUA: IDA—$7.6 million. Funds from IDA reflows will be provided to supplement the second economic recovery credit, approved in fiscal 1994 (see above).

#PAKISTAN: IBRD—$150 million; IDA—$100 million. The government's reform program, which aims at building a sound and sustainable macroeconomic framework, privatization of certain public enterprises, a restructuring of the composition of public expenditures, continuation of a program of trade reform, and reallocation of public expenditures in favor of social services, will be supported.

PAKISTAN: IDA—$46.8 million. Physical investments that deal with some of the most urgent environmental and infrastructure problems in Karachi and three interior cities in Sindh province will be financed. Institution-building measures, as well as the preparation of engineering studies for future investments, are included. Total cost: $58.6 million.

†TURKEY: IBRD—$100 million. The development of the country's dynamic private sector will be furthered through the provision of assistance for an accelerated privatization process. Measures will also be financed to alleviate the impact of state-owned enterprise downsizing and divestiture on displaced workers and their families. Total cost: $129 million.

UZBEKISTAN: IBRD—$21 million. Institution-building and technical assistance activities in the areas of privatization and public enterprise reform, the legal and regulatory framework, the financial sector, social safety net/employment, and the energy and telecommunications sectors will be financed. Cofinancing is anticipated from the EU ($2.6 million) and Japan ($1 million). Total cost: $25 million.

Social Sector

*ALBANIA: IDA—$5.5 million. The government will be assisted in reforming its systems of social protection of the vulnerable, while, at the same time, configuring them in ways that make them compatible with a market-oriented economy. Total cost: $6.2 million.

*ALBANIA: IDA—$5.4 million. The government's labor market-development program, designed to meet the needs of the unemployed and facilitate their return to employment, will be supported through the provision of technical assistance, fellowships and training, and training materials and equipment. Total cost: $6 million.

†*ECUADOR: IBRD—$30 million. Substantial immediate and longer-term benefits will be generated for the poor through more than 2,700 subprojects expected to be financed by the Emergency Social Investment Fund (FISE) that will provide basic social and physical infrastructure, social services, and training. Cofinancing is expected from the IDB ($30 million), USAID ($4.5 million), Spain ($800,000), the UNDP ($100,000), and UNICEF ($100,000), while another $20.7 million is being sought. Total cost: $120 million.

†*LAO PEOPLE'S DEMOCRATIC REPUBLIC: IDA—$9.7 million. About 50,000 poor people living in Luang Namtha, one of the country's poorest provinces, will benefit from a rural infrastructure project that will provide improved access to markets and schools, as well as better water quality and sanitation services. Technical assistance and training are included. Total cost: $10.2 million.

†*PERU: IBRD—$100 million. Community-based projects in the areas of social assistance, social and economic infrastructure, and credits to small-scale farmers and entrepreneurs—all managed by the National Fund for Social Compensation and Development (FONCODES)—will be supported, thus helping to sustain the government's poverty-reduction efforts and mitigate the social costs of adjustment. Cofinancing is expected from the IDB ($100 million) and others ($53 million), including Germany. Total cost: $495 million.

Telecommunications

CHINA: IBRD—$250 million. Reforms, designed to develop a modern, commercial telecommunications sector that will evolve increasingly toward allocation of resources on the basis of competitive market forces, will be supported. In addition, some investments in modern technology for fiber-optic long distance links and local digital switching in three provinces will be financed. Cofinancing ($1.3 million) is expected from the BITS. Total cost: $623 million.

CZECH REPUBLIC: IBRD—$80 million. International and national long distance telephone networks will be expanded and strengthened so as to relieve congested services and provide modern telecom services to businesses. Institution-building assistance is included. Cofinancing is expected from the EBRD and the EIB ($80 million each) and in the form of export credits. Total cost: $891.5 million.

JORDAN: IBRD—$20 million. The capacity of the country's telecommunications system will almost be doubled (to as many as 570,000 lines), and support provided to the government in formulating and implementing reforms leading to sector development and the private provision of services. Cofinancing is anticipated from the EIB ($30 million), the JExIm ($23 million), the ODA ($6 million), the BITS ($4 million), and commercial sources ($50

million), which will be mobilized with the support of the Bank's ECO guarantee. Total cost: $223 million.

KYRGYZ REPUBLIC: IDA—$18 million. The government will be assisted in making priority replacement/expansion investments in telecommunications in such as way as to best facilitate the country's economic growth and improve service quality. Institution-building assistance is included. Cofinancing is expected from the EBRD ($8 million). Total cost: $31 million.

SLOVAK REPUBLIC: IBRD—$55 million. International and national long distance telephone networks will be expanded and strengthened so as to relieve congested services and provide modern telecom services to businesses. Institution-building assistance is included. Cofinancing is expected from the EIB ($55.3 million), the EBRD ($55 million), and export credits ($66.2 million). Total cost: $462.3 million.

Tourism

*BELIZE: IBRD—$20 million. The first phase of a seven-year infrastructure-development program for Belize City—representing a minimal critical mass of activities in the street network (including traffic management and control), drainage system (including canals and creeks), and coastal protection works, which will significantly benefit the poorer population—will be financed. Total cost: $28 million.

Transportation

†BANGLADESH: IDA—$200 million. The east and west parts of the country, separated by the Jamuna river, will be connected for the first time by the construction of a 4.8-kilometer-long bridge, thereby stimulating economic growth by facilitating interregional, cross-river transport of passengers, freight, and transmission of electricity more economically and efficiently. Cofinancing is anticipated from the AsDB and the OECF ($200 million each). Total cost: $696 million.

†BANGLADESH: IDA—$146.8 million. The total cost of road transport on the country's most travelled roads will be reduced by improving the road network through more effective planning, design, and construction (including reconstruction) of road investments and more effective programming and implementation of road maintenance. Cofinancing ($8.8 million) is expected from the ODA. Total cost: $252.2 million.

BRAZIL: IBRD—$220 million. Road-program management in the states of Maranhão, Piauí, and Tocantins will be strengthened—with a view to avoiding further deterioration of the important public assets that the paved road networks represent—through more efficient allocation of resources to maintenance and their effective management. Total cost: $602.8 million.

†CHINA: IBRD—$380 million. Transport congestion will be relieved and the integration of interregional commerce improved through the construction of 340 kilometers of the national trunk highway system in the principal north-south corridor. In addition, fourteen provincial highways interconnecting with the national highway will be upgraded. Technical assistance and training are included. Total cost: $894.7 million.

†CHINA: IBRD—$150 million. A second Shanghai Metropolitan Transport Project will help finance construction of about twenty-two kilometers of a four-lane expressway around the city, implementation of traffic-management and traffic-safety measures, and investments in public transport. Technical assistance is included. Total cost: $657.1 million.

CHINA: IBRD—$140 million. The continued development of road infrastructure in Fujian province will be supported, and an action plan for the strengthening of the provincial road-construction industry developed. Technical assistance and training are included. Total cost: $528.8 million.

ESTONIA: IBRD—$12 million. A two-year program of urgently needed highway-maintenance work will be financed, thereby avoiding costly rehabilitation or reconstruction at a later date. In addition, the efficiency of the country's road-maintenance operations will be improved. Cofinancing, totaling $2 million, is expected from Denmark, Finland, and Sweden. Total cost: $25 million.

INDIA: IBRD—$94 million. An enabling environment for container transport will be established, and the capacity and efficiency of long-haul transport of high-value general cargo increased. Cofinancing ($4 million) is expected from the Netherlands. Total cost: $151 million.

†INDONESIA: IBRD—$350 million. Problems caused by the rapid growth in road traffic will be eased and road-transport system costs reduced by improving the service quality of national and provincial roads and by expanding the capacity of the road network. Institutional strengthening measures are included. Total cost: $680.5 million.

INDONESIA: IBRD—$101.5 million. Access to commercial markets for the agriculture-dependent rural population will be improved by enhancing the capacity of government agencies that manage the development of rural-district roads and by improving the quality and capacity of the road network in selected rural districts. Total cost: $206.8 million.

KAZAKHSTAN: IBRD—$40 million. Public transport service in the country's three main cities will be restored to adequate levels of service quality, and key improvements in urban public transport-sector policies and institutions will be implemented. Technical assistance and training are included. Cofinancing ($600,000) is expected from the EU. Total cost: $42.4 million.

LAO PEOPLE'S DEMOCRATIC REPUBLIC: IDA—$30 million. The efficiency of the country's road network will be increased through specific road improvements and through strengthening of institutional capabilities to plan, manage, and maintain the national highway network. Total cost: $33.7 million.

MADAGASCAR: IDA—$13.1 million. Facilities damaged by two cyclones in early 1994, including several major roads that represent lifelines to the poorer regions, will be rebuilt, and measures to minimize potential damage from future cyclones will be strengthened. Total cost: $28.8 million.

†MALI: IDA—$65 million. The government will be supported in its efforts to strengthen transport-sector management and performance, restructure transport-sector parastatals, modify the regulatory and institutional framework to promote increased private sector involvement in the provision of services and the execution of works, and rehabilitate and maintain a priority network of transport infrastructure. Cofinancing is expected from the IsDB ($53.6 million), the EDF ($50 million), Germany ($19.8 million), France ($17.9 million), the ADF ($14.3 million), BOAD ($10.7 million), Canada ($7.1 million), and the OPEC Fund for International Development (amount to be determined). Total cost: $305.7 million.

MONGOLIA: IDA—$30 million. Key constraints in the transport sector will be addressed, in particular, by reversing the decline of the quality and quantity of transport services in railways, urban transport, trucking, and roads. Institution-building assistance is included. Total cost: $36.7 million.

†*MOZAMBIQUE: IDA—$188 million. Road transport will be improved, selected past road investments protected, and employment opportunities for the rural poor created through civil works programs to rehabilitate priority roads and eliminate the huge backlog of periodic maintenance. Capacity-building assistance is included. Cofinancing is anticipated from the EU ($97.9 million), the AfDB ($83.4 million), USAID ($25 million), the CFD/South Africa ($17 million), BADEA ($14.9 million), the KFAED ($14 million), and Germany ($9 million). Total cost: $814.6 million.

†NEPAL: IDA—$50.5 million. Through a program of road maintenance and rehabilitation, vehicle-operating costs and delays associated with a deteriorated road system will be reduced, and much-needed rural employment will be generated. Institutional strengthening assistance is included. Cofinancing is expected from the ODA ($12.4 million), the SDC ($2.8 million), and the UNDP ($1 million). Total cost: $81.1 million.

PANAMA: IBRD—$60 million. Transport efficiency will be improved and transport costs reduced throughout the country as a result of a roads-rehabilitation project that will finance a four-year time-slice of the government's publicly financed road program. Cofinancing ($180 million) is being provided by the IDB. Total cost: $406 million.

†PARAGUAY: IBRD—$65 million. Almost 200 kilometers of roads will be either improved or rehabilitated, and, through provision of institution-building assistance, the capacity of the Ministry of Public Works and Communications to deliver a good-quality, well-managed road network will be improved. Total cost: $90 million.

PERU: IBRD—$150 million. The rehabilitation of 725 kilometers of main highways, as well as of railway facilities, will be supported, and new initiatives in the areas of road maintenance, traffic safety, and nonmotorized transport will be undertaken. In addition, the process of railway privatization will be accelerated. Cofinancing is anticipated from Germany ($38 million) and the OPEC Fund for International Development ($5 million). Total cost: $242 million.

RUSSIA: IBRD—$300 million. About 1,500 kilometers of priority federal roads will be rehabilitated, maintenance and road-safety improvements will be carried out on about 9,500 kilometers of federal roads and 500 kilometers of regional roads, and the commercialization and privatization of the road-construction industry will be promoted. Technical assistance, training, and studies are included. Cofinancing ($5 million) is expected from the United States Federal Highway Administration. Total cost: $340 million.

SENEGAL: IDA—$3.7 million. Funds from IDA reflows will be provided to supplement the transport-sector adjustment credit, approved in fiscal 1991 in the amount of $65 million.

†TANZANIA: IDA—$170.2 million. Support will be provided for policy and institutional reforms to improve transport-sector administration, organization, and management; upgrading, rehabilitation, and backlog periodic maintenance of high-priority roads; measures to rehabilitate and improve rural transport infrastructure; and minimum civil aviation investments to ensure safety and continued service. Cofinancing is anticipated from the EU ($178.1 million), the AfDB ($108.9 million), NORAD ($41.7 million), the OPEC Fund for International Development ($38.3 million), the OECF ($19.8 million), the KFAED ($14.9 million), FINNIDA ($5.4 million), and the SDC ($5.1 million). Total cost: $650.3 million.

UGANDA: IDA—$75 million. The government's economic recovery program will be supported by improving the basic road infrastructure and by ensuring that it, along with the rail/ferry infrastructure, will be well maintained and efficiently managed. Cofinancing ($4.6 million) is anticipated from the NDF. Total cost: $99 million.

†VENEZUELA: IBRD—$100 million. By improving and strengthening national and local institutions engaged in the planning, financing, design, and operation of urban transport systems, the quality and efficiency of urban transport in Venezuelan cities will be improved. Total cost: $200 million.

†VIET NAM: IDA—$158.5 million. Two critical segments (totaling 430 kilometers) of the country's main highway will be rehabilitated, ferry operations improved at two Mekong delta crossings, and highway-maintenance capacity strengthened through the provision of technical assistance and equipment. Total cost: $176 million.

Urban Development

ALBANIA: IDA—$15 million. To help develop critical first steps in developing a market-based housing sector, the completion of construction of 4,500 apartments—originally intended as public rental units but which will now be sold to individual households under mortgage and condominium arrangements—will be financed. Cofinancing ($1.5 million) is expected from bilateral agencies, USAID in particular. Total cost: $40 million.

†*ARMENIA: IDA—$28 million. Funds will be provided to help finance reconstruction of housing, infrastructure, and factory shells in the area destroyed by the 1988 earthquake; a plan for the further reconstruction of the earthquake zone will be developed; and reform of housing-sector policies designed to promote the transition to a market-oriented economy will be supported. Vulnerable groups will be given priority in the allocation of apartments. Cofinancing ($400,000) is being provided by Japan. Total cost: $46 million.

†BOLIVIA: IDA—$42 million. The government's efforts to strengthen municipal management and improve the delivery of urban services will be supported through a project that aims at enhancing the capabilities of municipalities, local utilities, and service enterprises; strengthening financial intermediation in the sector; and encouraging the financing of municipal infrastructure in unserviced peri-urban areas. Total cost: $58 million.

†BRAZIL: IBRD—$150 million. Municipal financial management in Minas Gerais state will be strengthened through technical assistance and training, while environmental management will be improved through the development of a coherent state strategy for local provision of water and sewerage services, investment in priority basic sanitation infrastructure, and technical assistance and training. Total cost: $333.1 million.

†*CHAD: IDA—$17.4 million. Existing infrastructure will be protected from further decay through a maintenance and rehabilitation program, and additional urgently needed social infrastructure, identified and maintained by the beneficiaries, will be developed. In addition, labor-intensive public service schemes will generate employment opportunities, and training and technical support will be provided to small and medium-sized enterprises and beneficiaries. Cofinancing ($2 million) is being sought from the OPEC Fund for International Development and the EDF. Total cost: $20.4 million.

CHILE: IBRD—$10 million. Reforms that will increase the resources and responsibilities being transferred to municipalities and regions will be supported through a pilot project that seeks to increase the institutional and technical capacity of municipal governments to assume greater responsibilities and to improve the national government's capacity to accomplish its main macroeconomic goals at the municipal level. Total cost: $20 million.

CROATIA: IBRD—$128 million. Some of the conditions necessary for restoring productivity following war-related destruction will be reestablished through reconstruction of basic infrastructure, the replacement of vital agricultural assets, and by removing a major constraint to the resumption of normal tourism levels. In addition, a return of displaced households to their communities will be made possible through the reconstruction of housing and provision of supporting infrastructure. Total cost: $205.3 million.

†*THE GAMBIA: IDA—$11 million. Unemployment will be reduced by creating temporary jobs for unskilled workers in the public works and construction sectors, thereby maintaining infrastructure assets that might disappear for lack of maintenance due to financial constraints. Local capacity building, furnished through provision of training and technical support for small and medium-sized firms, is included. Cofinancing, in the amount of $2 million, is being explored with DANIDA, the EDF, the JICA, the UNDP, and USAID. Total cost: $14.5 million.

GHANA: IDA—$38.5 million. Infrastructure and services—roads, drainage, sanitation, garbage collection and disposal, bus parks, and public markets—will be improved in eleven secondary cities, thus improving living conditions for their more than 500,000 residents. Institutional strengthening of the eleven local governments involved is included, thereby furthering the government's decentralization efforts. Cofinancing ($8.3 million) is expected from Germany. Total cost: $55.5 million.

†INDIA: IDA—$246 million. The government of Maharashtra's rehabilitation program for the victims of the September 1993 earthquake, which killed an estimated 8,000 people and destroyed or damaged more than 130,000 homes, will be

supported. Cofinancing is expected from the United Kingdom (£10 million) and the AsDB ($600,000). Total cost: $328 million.

†*INDONESIA: IBRD—$175 million. Services and the quality of life for about 600,000 of Surabaya's inhabitants— especially those living in the poorer areas— will improve through a project that will provide water-supply, sanitation, and drainage improvements; and construction of access roads and paths. The implementation of a land-management program and provision of technical assistance is included. Cofinancing ($174.8 million) is anticipated from the OECF. Total cost: $617.6 million.

†*INDONESIA: IBRD—$174 million. The inhabitants of Semarang and Surakarta, and disproportionately the poorer inhabitants, will benefit directly from improvements to the quality, reliability, and accessibility of urban infrastructure services. In addition, technical assistance will be provided for implementation support and a strengthening of institutional capacity. Total cost: $320.8 million.

†MADAGASCAR: IDA—$18.3 million. A tested model for the efficient contracting-out of infrastructure maintenance will be created for, and implemented in, Antananarivo, resulting in the rehabilitation of about 300 kilometers of essential urban roads and creating about 70,000 manmonths of jobs. In addition, domestic small and medium-sized construction and engineering enterprises will be developed. Cofinancing ($200,000) is anticipated from the FAC. Total cost: $20.1 million.

†MEXICO: IBRD—$200 million. Solid waste services will be improved for an estimated 11 million people in the twenty-three cities that are expected to participate on a first-come, first-served basis. Institution-strengthening measures—at the federal and local government levels and for operating agencies—are included. Total cost: $415.5 million.

†*TOGO: IDA—$26.2 million. Implementation of the government's emerging urban development policy will be supported through the execution of priority urban works through labor-intensive schemes that focus on poor areas, the promotion of small contractors in the construction sector, and the active participation of local residents, community groups, and NGOs in neighborhood environmental improvement activities. Capacity-building assistance is included. Total cost: $29 million.

Water Supply and Sewerage

ALBANIA: IDA—$11.6 million. Water shortages and associated health risks to the population in the district of Durres will be eliminated, and a strong local institutional framework for the provision of water supply and sewerage services established, thereby ensuring that the improvements will be sustainable. Total cost: $19.5 million.

ALGERIA: IBRD—$110 million. Water-supply systems in ten cities and twenty-four sewage-treatment plants located throughout the country will be rehabilitated. In addition, the institutional arrangements in the urban water sector will be rationalized with a view to achieving full cost recovery by autonomous, self-financing utilities. Total cost: $170 million.

†*BENIN: IDA—$9.8 million. Rural water-supply and sanitation facilities will be built in smaller and poorer communities, hygiene education provided to communities interested in improving their water supply and sanitation facilities, and capacity building provided to all actors in the sector who will need to acquire new skills in promoting, planning, constructing, managing, and monitoring rural water supply and sanitation facilities. Cofinancing ($4 million) is anticipated from Denmark. Total cost: $15 million.

†*BRAZIL: IBRD—$154 million. The quality of life for about 1.2 million urban inhabitants of Espírito Santo state (and especially for some of the poorest inhabitants) will be improved, the incidence of waterborne disease reduced, and the quality of water for human consumption and recreational uses improved through a project that will help finance the state water company's 1994–99 investment program. Institution-building assistance is included. Total cost: $308 million.

BULGARIA: IBRD—$98 million. The autonomy and commercial orientation of the country's twenty-nine regional water and sewerage companies will be increased, and their management made more accountable to local authorities. In addition, selected water and sewerage facilities will be rehabilitated and upgraded. Total cost: $131 million.

†*GHANA: IDA—$22 million. Basic water and sanitation infrastructure will be provided to communities, schools, and health clinics, while health and the environment will be enhanced through the improvement of drinking-water quality,

personal hygiene, and excreta disposal. Institution building—with a focus on poverty reduction and women's participation—is included. Cofinancing ($1.7 million) is expected from Canada. Total cost: $27 million.

GUYANA: IDA—$17.5 million. The quality and reliability of potable water in selected regions of the country will be improved through the upgrading of water-supply facilities, and the efficiency of water-sector institutions will be enhanced through establishment of procedures and methods for ensuring proper system operations and maintenance. Cofinancing is anticipated from the CDB ($6.5 million) and the ODA ($6 million). Total cost: $33 million.

MEXICO: IBRD—$350 million. A second water supply and sanitation sector project is expected to benefit 10 million people directly by helping control cholera and reducing significantly other gastrointestinal diseases. Technical assistance to strengthen federal agencies, as well as local water utilities, is included. Total cost: $770 million.

*MOROCCO: IBRD—$160 million. Urban water-supply systems operated by six of the country's sixteen municipally owned water-distribution facilities (*régies*) will either be rehabilitated or expanded, thus providing access to safe water for some 9.6 million people. Rural water-supply facilities will also be rehabilitated and expanded, especially in poor areas of the country, directly benefiting 3 million people. Institution-building assistance is included. Cofinancing, totaling $84 million, is expected from the OECF and the AfDB. Total cost: $353.6 million.

†*UGANDA: IDA—$42.3 million. By extending the rehabilitation and expansion of water supply and sanitation facilities in eleven small (and two larger) towns, health conditions will be improved, poverty reduced, the lot of women improved, and environmental degradation reduced. Total cost: $48 million.

Table 5-20. **Projects Approved for IBRD and IDA Assistance in Fiscal Year 1994, by Region and Country**
(amounts in millions of US dollars)

Region and country	IBRD loans		IDA credits		Total	
	Number	Amount	Number	Amount	Number	Amount
Africa						
Benin...........................	—	—	4	42.8	4	42.8
Burkina Faso	—	—	3	80.5	3	80.5
Cameroon	—	—	2	176.0	2	176.0
Cape Verde	—	—	1	8.1	1	8.1
Chad	—	—	3	55.9	3	55.9
Comoros	—	—	2	18.1	2	18.1
Congo	—	—	1	100.0	1	100.0
Côte d'Ivoire	—	—	3	376.0	3	376.0
Ethiopia.........................	—	—	1	74.8	1	74.8
Gabon	1	30.0	—	—	1	30.0
Gambia, The	—	—	2	13.6	2	13.6
Ghana	—	—	3	87.7	3	87.7
Guinea..........................	—	—	1	24.6	1	24.6
Kenya	—	—	1	64.0	1	64.0
Lesotho.........................	—	—	1	11.0	1	11.0
Madagascar	—	—	3	83.3	3	83.3
Malawi..........................	—	—	1	26.9	1	26.9
Mali	—	—	3	110.0	3	110.0
Mauritania	—	—	1	19.5	1	19.5
Mauritius........................	1	7.7	—	—	1	7.7
Mozambique.....................	—	—	4	427.0	4	427.0
Niger	—	—	2	66.4	2	66.4
Rwanda	—	—	2	27.0	2	27.0
Senegal	—	—	1	28.7	1	28.7
Sierra Leone	—	—	1	50.2	1	50.2
Tanzania	—	—	2	194.7	2	194.7
Togo............................	—	—	1	26.2	1	26.2
Uganda	—	—	5	262.4	5	262.4
Zambia	—	—	3	224.8	3	224.8
Zimbabwe.......................	1	90.0	—	—	1	90.0
Total	3	127.7	57	2,680.2	60	2,807.9
East Asia and Pacific						
Cambodia	—	—	1	62.7	1	62.7
China...........................	8	2,145.0	6	925.0	14	3,070.0
Indonesia	11	1,489.8	—	—	11	1,489.8
Korea, Republic of	3	380.0	—	—	3	380.0
Lao People's Democratic Republic..	—	—	3	48.4	3	48.4
Malaysia	2	120.0	—	—	2	120.0
Mongolia........................	—	—	2	50.0	2	50.0
Papua New Guinea................	1	11.0	—	—	1	11.0
Philippines	3	478.0	—	—	3	478.0
Viet Nam	—	—	3	324.5	3	324.5
Total	28	4,623.8	15	1,410.6	43	6,034.4
South Asia						
Bangladesh......................	—	—	3	597.1	3	597.1
Bhutan..........................	—	—	1	5.4	1	5.4
India...........................	1	94.0	6	834.8	7	928.8
Nepal...........................	—	—	3	97.2	3	97.2
Pakistan.........................	2	380.0	3	361.5	5	741.5
Total	3	474.0	16	1,896.0	19	2,370.0

Region and country	IBRD loans		IDA credits		Total	
	Number	Amount	Number	Amount	Number	Amount
Europe and Central Asia						
Albania	—	—	5	47.1	5	47.1
Armenia	—	—	1	28.0	1	28.0
Belarus	3	170.2	—	—	3	170.2
Bulgaria.	2	148.0	—	—	2	148.0
Croatia.	1	128.0	—	—	1	128.0
Czech Republic	1	80.0	—	—	1	80.0
Estonia	2	50.4	—	—	2	50.4
Hungary	2	129.0	—	—	2	129.0
Kazakhstan.	4	273.7	—	—	4	273.7
Kyrgyz Republic	—	—	2	78.0	2	78.0
Latvia	1	25.0	—	—	1	25.0
Lithuania.	1	26.4	—	—	1	26.4
Macedonia, FYR of	1	40.0	—	40.0	1	80.0
Moldova	1	60.0	—	—	1	60.0
Poland	1	146.0	—	—	1	146.0
Romania	3	400.6	—	—	3	400.6
Russia	6	1,520.0	—	—	6	1,520.0
Slovak Republic	2	135.0	—	—	2	135.0
Slovenia	1	80.0	—	—	1	80.0
Turkey.	1	100.0	—	—	1	100.0
Uzbekistan	1	21.0	—	—	1	21.0
Total	34	3,533.3	8	193.1	42	3,726.4
Latin America and the Caribbean						
Argentina	3	608.5	—	—	3	608.5
Barbados.	1	7.8	—	—	1	7.8
Belize.	1	20.0	—	—	1	20.0
Bolivia.	—	—	1	51.4	1	51.4
Brazil.	7	1,136.6	—	—	7	1,136.6
Caribbean region	1	20.0	—	11.0	1	31.0
Chile	1	10.0	—	—	1	10.0
Colombia.	3	159.0	—	—	3	159.0
Costa Rica	1	22.0	—	—	1	22.0
Ecuador.	3	64.0	—	—	3	64.0
El Salvador.	2	52.5	—	—	2	52.5
Guyana	—	—	2	35.3	2	35.3
Honduras	—	—	1	87.9	1	87.9
Jamaica	2	48.2	—	—	2	48.2
Mexico	5	1,530.0	—	—	5	1,530.0
Nicaragua	—	—	3	126.6	3	126.6
Panama	1	60.0	—	—	1	60.0
Paraguay	2	115.0	—	—	2	115.0
Peru	3	284.0	—	—	3	284.0
Uruguay	3	107.5	—	—	3	107.5
Venezuela.	2	189.4	—	—	2	189.4
Total	41	4,434.5	7	312.2	48	4,746.7

(continued)

Table 5-20 *(continued)*

Region and country	IBRD loans		IDA credits		Total	
	Number	Amount	Number	Amount	Number	Amount
Middle East and North Africa						
Algeria............................	2	140.0	—	—	2	140.0
Egypt.............................	1	54.0	—	67.0	1	121.0
Jordan	2	100.0	—	—	2	100.0
Lebanon	2	77.1	—	—	2	77.1
Morocco	5	412.0	—	—	5	412.0
Tunisia...........................	3	267.5	—	—	3	267.5
Yemen............................	—	—	1	33.0	1	33.0
Total	15	1,050.6	1	100.0	16	1,150.6
Grand total.....................	124	14,243.9	104	6,592.1	228	20,836.0

— Zero.

NOTE: Supplements are included in the amount but are not counted as separate lending operations. Joint IBRD/IDA operations are counted only once, as IBRD operations.

Table 5-21. Trends in Lending, IBRD and IDA, Fiscal Years 1992–94
(amounts in millions of US dollars; fiscal years)

Sector	1992			1993			1994		
	IBRD	IDA	Total	IBRD	IDA	Total	IBRD	IDA	Total
	millions of US dollars								
Agriculture	2,525.7	1,378.3	3,904.0	1,918.8	1,347.9	3,266.7	2,233.3	1,674.0	3,907.3
Education	1,299.6	584.1	1,883.7	968.0	1,038.2	2,006.2	1,409.9	658.1	2,068.0
Energy									
Oil, gas, and coal	879.0	115.6	994.6	939.8	35.5	975.3	1,202.1	186.2	1,388.3
Power	2,824.9	238.0	3,062.9	2,093.0	520.0	2,613.0	1,368.5	—	1,368.5
Environment	—	—	—	11.5	54.8	66.3	730.5	17.3	747.8
Financial sector	1,102.0	423.3	1,525.3	637.0	318.1	955.1	1,093.5	411.1	1,504.6
Industry	142.7	200.0	342.7	250.0	83.5	333.5	422.7	272.2	694.9
Mining and other extractive	—	6.0	6.0	250.0	12.0	262.0	14.0	—	14.0
Multisector	1,970.0	1,460.1	3,430.1	2,980.0	620.8	3,600.8	606.3	815.9	1,422.2
Population, health, and nutrition	307.0	654.7	961.7	706.8	1,104.8	1,811.6	366.0	519.7	885.7
Public sector management	583.4	172.6	756.0	765.0	247.5	1,012.5	370.6	322.6	693.2
Social sector	—	—	—	—	—	—	130.0	20.6	150.6
Telecommunications	375.0	55.0	430.0	264.0	89.1	353.1	405.0	18.0	423.0
Tourism	—	—	—	130.0	—	130.0	20.0	—	20.0
Transportation	1,744.7	550.8	2,295.5	3,133.1	712.6	3,845.7	2,162.5	1,130.8	3,293.3
Urban development	868.0	333.8	1,201.8	1,139.0	171.2	1,310.2	837.0	442.4	1,279.4
Water supply and sewerage	534.0	377.4	911.4	758.5	395.4	1,153.9	872.0	103.2	975.2
Total	15,156.0	6,549.7	21,705.7	16,944.5	6,751.4	23,695.9	14,243.9	6,592.1	20,836.0
	percentage distribution								
Agriculture	16.7	21.0	18.0	11.3	20.0	13.8	15.7	25.4	18.8
Education	8.6	8.9	8.7	5.7	15.4	8.5	10.5	10.0	10.0
Energy									
Oil, gas, and coal	5.8	1.8	4.6	5.5	0.5	4.1	8.4	2.8	6.7
Power	18.6	3.6	14.1	12.4	7.7	11.0	9.6	—	6.6
Environment	—	—	—	0.1	0.8	0.3	4.5	0.3	3.6
Financial sector	7.3	6.5	7.0	3.8	4.7	4.0	7.7	6.2	7.2
Industry	0.9	3.1	1.6	1.5	1.2	1.4	3.0	4.1	3.3
Mining and other extractive	—	0.1	—	1.5	0.2	1.1	0.1	—	0.1
Multisector	13.0	22.3	15.8	17.6	9.2	15.2	4.3	12.4	6.8
Population, health, and nutrition	2.0	10.0	4.4	4.2	16.4	7.6	2.6	7.9	4.3
Public sector management	3.8	2.6	3.5	4.5	3.7	4.3	2.6	4.9	3.3
Social sector	—	—	—	—	—	—	0.9	0.3	0.7
Telecommunications	2.5	0.8	2.0	1.6	1.3	1.5	2.8	0.3	2.0
Tourism	—	—	—	0.8	—	0.5	0.1	—	0.1
Transportation	11.5	8.4	10.6	18.5	10.6	16.2	15.2	17.2	15.8
Urban development	5.7	5.1	5.5	6.7	2.5	5.5	5.9	6.7	6.1
Water supply and sewerage	3.5	5.8	4.2	4.5	5.9	4.9	6.1	1.6	4.7
Total	100.0	100.0	100.0	100.0	100.0	100.0	100.0	100.0	100.0

— Zero.

Table 5-22. **Projects Approved for IBRD and IDA Assistance in Fiscal Year 1994, by Sector**
(millions of US dollars)

Sector[a]	IBRD	IDA	Total
Agriculture			
Algeria..	30.0	—	30.0
Belarus..	41.9	—	41.9
Benin...	—	9.7	9.7
Bhutan..	—	5.4	5.4
Bulgaria	50.0	—	50.0
China...	—	150.0	150.0
China...	—	200.0	200.0
China...	460.0	—	460.0
China...	—	205.0	205.0
China...	—	150.0	150.0
China...	—	110.0	110.0
Colombia..	39.0	—	39.0
Côte d'Ivoire	—	21.8	21.8
Côte d'Ivoire	—	2.2	2.2
Ecuador...	20.0	—	20.0
Egypt	54.0	67.0	121.0
Ghana	—	21.5	21.5
Ghana	—	5.7	5.7 [b]
Guyana	—	15.0	15.0
Honduras..	—	60.0	60.0
Honduras..	—	27.9	27.9 [b]
India	—	258.0	258.0
India	—	77.4	77.4
India	—	47.0	47.0
Indonesia	65.0	—	65.0
Indonesia	165.7	—	165.7
Indonesia..	55.0	—	55.0
Lao People's Democratic Republic	—	8.7	8.7
Latvia...	25.0	—	25.0
Lebanon	57.2	—	57.2
Malaysia	70.0	—	70.0
Mali..	—	20.0	20.0
Mauritania...	—	18.2	18.2
Mexico..	200.0	—	200.0
Morocco	100.0	—	100.0
Morocco	121.0	—	121.0
Morocco	25.0	—	25.0
Nicaragua	—	44.0	44.0
Poland	146.0	—	146.0
Russia	240.0	—	240.0
Russia	80.0	—	80.0
Rwanda	—	15.0	15.0
Tanzania	—	24.5	24.5
Tunisia	120.0	—	120.0
Tunisia..	27.5	—	27.5

Sector[a]	IBRD	IDA	Total
Agriculture *(continued)*			
Uganda	—	14.0	14.0
Uruguay	41.0	—	41.0
Viet Nam	—	96.0	96.0
Total	2,233.3	1,674.0	3,907.3
Education			
Albania	—	9.6	9.6
Barbados	7.8	—	7.8
Benin	—	18.1	18.1
Brazil	206.6	—	206.6
Brazil	150.0	—	150.0
Brazil	96.0	—	96.0
Colombia	90.0	—	90.0
Côte d'Ivoire	—	17.0	17.0
Côte d'Ivoire	—	100.0	100.0 [b]
Côte d'Ivoire	—	85.0	85.0 [b]
Indonesia	27.7	—	27.7
Indonesia	58.9	—	58.9
Kenya	—	21.8	21.8
Kenya	—	42.2	42.2 [b]
Korea, Republic of	190.0	—	190.0
Mexico	412.0	—	412.0
Nepal	—	20.0	20.0
Niger	—	41.4	41.4
Pakistan	—	200.0	200.0
Romania	50.0	—	50.0
Uruguay	31.5	—	31.5
Venezuela	89.4	—	89.4
Viet Nam	—	70.0	70.0
Yemen	—	33.0	33.0
Total	1,409.9	658.1	2,068.0
Energy			
Oil, gas, and coal			
China	255.0	—	255.0
Estonia	38.4	—	38.4
Ethiopia	—	74.3	74.3
Hungary	100.0	—	100.0
Jordan	80.0	—	80.0
Kazakhstan	15.7	—	15.7
Lithuania	26.4	—	26.4
Madagascar	—	51.9	51.9
Mozambique	—	30.0	30.0
Papua New Guinea	11.0	—	11.0
Romania	175.6	—	175.6
Russia	500.0	—	500.0
Zambia	—	30.0	30.0
Total	1,202.1	186.2	1,388.3

(continued)

Table 5-22   *(continued)*

Sector[a]	IBRD	IDA	Total
Energy *(continued)*			
Power			
China....................................	350.0	—	350.0
Indonesia...............................	260.5	—	260.5
Pakistan................................	230.0	—	230.0
Philippines.............................	211.0	—	211.0
Philippines.............................	227.0	—	227.0
Zimbabwe..............................	90.0	—	90.0
Total................................	1,368.5	—	1,368.5
Environment			
China....................................	160.0	—	160.0
Gambia, The...........................	—	2.6	2.6
Indonesia...............................	56.5	—	56.5
Korea, Republic of......................	90.0	—	90.0
Mexico.................................	368.0	—	368.0
Morocco................................	6.0	—	6.0
Pakistan................................	—	14.7	14.7
Paraguay................................	50.0	—	50.0
Total................................	730.5	17.3	747.8
Financial sector			
Argentina...............................	500.0	—	500.0
Argentina...............................	8.5	—	8.5
Caribbean Region.......................	20.0	11.0	31.0
Colombia...............................	30.0	—	30.0
Côte d'Ivoire...........................	—	50.0	50.0 [b]
Côte d'Ivoire...........................	—	100.0	100.0 [b]
Korea, Republic of......................	100.0	—	100.0
Mozambique............................	—	200.0	200.0
Mozambique............................	—	9.0	9.0
Russia..................................	200.0	—	200.0
Rwanda.................................	—	12.0	12.0
Slovenia................................	80.0	—	80.0
Tunisia.................................	120.0	—	120.0
Uganda.................................	—	1.1	1.1 [b]
Uruguay................................	35.0	—	35.0
Zambia.................................	—	18.0	18.0
Zambia.................................	—	10.0	10.0 [b]
Total................................	1,093.5	411.1	1,504.6
Industry			
Bangladesh.............................	—	247.0	247.0
Bangladesh.............................	—	3.3	3.3 [b]
Comoros................................	—	5.1	5.1
Mauritius...............................	7.7	—	7.7
Philippines.............................	40.0	—	40.0
Romania................................	175.0	—	175.0
Russia..................................	200.0	—	200.0
Zambia.................................	—	16.8	16.8 [b]
Total................................	422.7	272.2	694.9
Mining and other extractive			
Ecuador................................	14.0	—	14.0
Total................................	14.0	—	14.0

Sector[a]	IBRD	IDA	Total
Multisector			
Belarus	8.3	—	8.3
Belarus	120.0	—	120.0
Bolivia	—	9.4	9.4 [b]
Burkina Faso	—	25.0	25.0
Cambodia	—	62.7	62.7
Cameroon	—	75.0	75.0
Cameroon	—	50.0	50.0
Cameroon	—	51.0	51.0 [b]
Chad	—	20.0	20.0
Congo	—	100.0	100.0
El Salvador	50.0	—	50.0
Ethiopia	—	0.5	0.5 [b]
Gabon	30.0	—	30.0
Guyana	—	2.8	2.8 [b]
Kazakhstan	38.0	—	38.0
Kazakhstan	180.0	—	180.0
Macedonia, FYR of	40.0	40.0	80.0
Malawi	—	4.3	4.3 [b]
Mali	—	25.0	25.0
Moldova	60.0	—	60.0
Mongolia	—	20.0	20.0
Niger	—	25.0	25.0
Senegal	—	25.0	25.0
Sierra Leone	—	50.0	50.0
Sierra Leone	—	0.2	0.2 [b]
Slovak Republic	80.0	—	80.0
Uganda	—	80.0	80.0
Zambia	—	150.0	150.0
Total	606.3	815.9	1,422.2
Population, Health, and Nutrition			
Argentina	100.0	—	100.0
Brazil	160.0	—	160.0
Burkina Faso	—	29.2	29.2
Burkina Faso	—	26.3	26.3
Chad	—	18.5	18.5
China	—	110.0	110.0
Comoros	—	13.0	13.0
Costa Rica	22.0	—	22.0
Guinea	—	24.6	24.6
India	—	117.8	117.8
India	—	88.6	88.6
Malaysia	50.0	—	50.0
Nepal	—	26.7	26.7
Nicaragua	—	15.0	15.0
Peru	34.0	—	34.0
Uganda	—	50.0	50.0
Total	366.0	519.7	885.7

(continued)

Table 5-22   *(continued)*

Sector[a]	IBRD	IDA	Total
Public-sector Management			
Benin......................................	—	5.2	5.2
Cape Verde	—	8.1	8.1
El Salvador	2.5	—	2.5
Hungary	29.0	—	29.0
Jamaica...................................	35.0	—	35.0
Jamaica...................................	13.2	—	13.2
Kyrghz Republic..........................	—	60.0	60.0
Lebanon	19.9	—	19.9
Lesotho...................................	—	11.0	11.0
Malawi	—	22.6	22.6
Mauritania	—	1.3	1.3 [b]
Nicaragua.................................	—	60.0	60.0
Nicaragua.................................	—	7.6	7.6 [b]
Pakistan	—	46.8	46.8
Pakistan	150.0	100.0	250.0
Turkey....................................	100.0	—	100.0
Uzbekistan...............................	21.0	—	21.0
Total	370.6	322.6	693.2
Social Sector			
Albania	—	5.4	5.4
Albania	—	5.5	5.5
Ecuador	30.0	—	30.0
Lao People's Democratic Republic...........	—	9.7	9.7
Peru......................................	100.0	—	100.0
Total	130.0	20.6	150.6
Telecommunications			
China.....................................	250.0	—	250.0
Czech Republic...........................	80.0	—	80.0
Jordan	20.0	—	20.0
Kyrghz Republic..........................	—	18.0	18.0
Slovak Republic	55.0	—	55.0
Total	405.0	18.0	423.0
Tourism			
Belize	20.0	—	20.0
Total	20.0	—	20.0
Transportation			
Bangladesh................................	—	146.8	146.8
Bangladesh................................	—	200.0	200.0
Brazil....................................	220.0	—	220.0
China.....................................	380.0	—	380.0
China.....................................	150.0	—	150.0
China.....................................	140.0	—	140.0
Estonia	12.0	—	12.0
India	94.0	—	94.0
Indonesia	350.0	—	350.0
Indonesia	101.5	—	101.5
Kazakhstan	40.0	—	40.0
Lao People's Democratic Republic...........	—	30.0	30.0
Madagascar	—	13.1	13.1

Sector[a]	IBRD	IDA	Total
Transportation (*continued*)			
Mali	—	65.0	65.0
Mongolia................................	—	30.0	30.0
Mozambique	—	188.0	188.0
Nepal...................................	—	50.5	50.5
Panama	60.0	—	60.0
Paraguay...............................	65.0	—	65.0
Peru....................................	150.0	—	150.0
Russia	300.0	—	300.0
Senegal	—	3.7	3.7 [b]
Tanzania...............................	—	170.2	170.2
Uganda	—	75.0	75.0
Venezuela..............................	100.0	—	100.0
Viet Nam	—	158.5	158.5
Total	2,162.5	1,130.8	3,293.3
Urban Development			
Albania	—	15.0	15.0
Armenia	—	28.0	28.0
Bolivia.................................	—	42.0	42.0
Brazil..................................	150.0	—	150.0
Chad	—	17.4	17.4
Chile	10.0	—	10.0
Croatia	128.0	—	128.0
Gambia, The	—	11.0	11.0
Ghana	—	38.5	38.5
India	—	246.0	246.0
Indonesia	174.0	—	174.0
Indonesia	175.0	—	175.0
Madagascar	—	18.3	18.3
Mexico	200.0	—	200.0
Togo	—	26.2	26.2
Total	837.0	442.4	1,279.4
Water Supply and Sewerage			
Albania	—	11.6	11.6
Algeria.................................	110.0	—	110.0
Benin...................................	—	9.8	9.8
Brazil..................................	154.0	—	154.0
Bulgaria................................	98.0	—	98.0
Ghana	—	22.0	22.0
Guyana	—	17.5	17.5
Mexico	350.0	—	350.0
Morocco	160.0	—	160.0
Uganda	—	42.3	42.3
Total	872.0	103.2	975.2
Grand total............................	14,243.9	6,592.1	20,836.0

— Zero.

NOTE: For additional details, see Appendixes 6 and 7.

a. Many projects include activity in more than one sector or subsector.

b. Supplementary financing to a previous loan, not counted as a separate operation.

Section Six
Other World Bank Group
Services and Activities

Operations Evaluation

Operations evaluation in the Bank provides a systematic, comprehensive, and independent assessment of Bank operations and activities. Its principal goals are to account for the outcome of Bank-supported projects and programs and to use the lessons from that experience to improve the design and conduct of future operations.

The director general, operations evaluation, has overall responsibility for evaluation. He reports directly to the Bank's executive board, with an administrative link to the president, and is supported by the Operations Evaluation Department (OED). The constitutional independence of evaluation in the Bank encourages evaluation staff to report candidly and allows them access to all relevant information and to select any topic for analysis.

The Joint Audit Committee of the executive board oversees the work of the OED. In fiscal 1994 the findings and recommendations of the committee were reviewed by the full board, as were the fiscal 1993 annual report of the director general, the annual review of evaluation results for 1992, and the evaluation work program for fiscal 1995.

Evaluation work program. The year's work in evaluation saw the realization of initiatives taken in response to the recommendations, made in 1993, of the Task Force on Portfolio Management. The task force recommended that the Bank strengthen its independent evaluation work—and the application of evaluation results to the Bank's current operations and policy development—as part of efforts to improve the performance and developmental impact of the Bank's lending operations.

The Bank's evaluation work program includes completion reports by operational staff; performance audit reports and impact evaluation reports on individual operations by the OED; and evaluation studies by the OED, including country and sector lending studies and reviews of Bank policies and processes.

Completion reports are prepared by the Bank's operational staff on all lending operations at the time the Bank completes disburse-ments. Staff of borrower agencies contribute to these reports. The reports allow the Bank's staff to discern and internalize the lessons of experience specific to the country and sector in which they work. The OED reviews all completion reports to assess their quality, record data, and facilitate the transfer of experience to new operations. The reports are sent to the board with an evaluative note from the director general.

Performance audits validate and augment the information provided in completion reports and examine topics of special interest so as to provide inputs for the OED's evaluation-studies program. The OED structures its audit work program (with regard to choice of projects, topics to be analyzed, and analytical approaches to be used) to provide inputs for comparative studies, as well as to meet requirements for accountability.

In fiscal 1994 the OED audited 80 percent of adjustment lending operations and at least 40 percent of the Bank's investment operations. The OED reviewed 266 completion reports in fiscal 1994 and audited 122 of them, of which ninety-nine were for investment projects and twenty-three for adjustment operations. The cumulative total of Bank operations subjected to *ex-post* evaluation reached 3,590 at the end of the fiscal year.

In its *impact evaluation* work, the OED, assisted by agencies in borrower countries, takes a second look at projects five to eight years after the close of disbursements. These reports focus on evaluating project impact, including intended and unintended effects. They are a powerful tool for assessing social and environmental impacts and economic worth, and offer valuable insights into what makes development sustainable. In fiscal 1994 seven impact evaluations were issued on projects in agriculture, treecrops, transmigration, and petrochemicals.

Evaluation studies are designed to examine particular programs, policies, or issues in a context broader than individual lending operations. The OED designs its studies program to investigate issues revealed by its audit work and to respond to current concerns of the Bank's board, management, and staff. In fiscal 1994, the OED sent eleven studies to the board.

Country-assistance reviews, introduced in fiscal 1994, assess the suitability of the Bank's assistance strategy in particular countries and the effectiveness of the instruments chosen. A review of Bank-Mexico relations was completed and work began on country-assistance reviews for Argentina, the Caribbean states, and Ghana. These reviews are geared to assessments of lending and nonlending services, and they offer lessons and recommendations for the Bank's regional staff to feed into country-portfolio performance reviews and the design of country-assistance strategies.

Process reviews examine how well the Bank applies its policies and assess the efficiency and effectiveness of business practices in reaching their intended development goals. In fiscal 1994 the OED issued a study of monitoring and evaluation in Bank-supported projects.

Sector reviews feed into the Bank's reviews of its sector-lending policies. Often these studies compare experience across countries; others are in-depth reviews of particular sectors in individual countries. Sector studies issued in fiscal 1994 covered urban development, agricultural extension, telecommunications, rural electrification in Asia, transport corridors in Africa, transmigration in Indonesia, gender issues in the Bank's lending, and industrial reorientation in East Africa. Topics of ongoing studies include the social impact of adjustment programs, irrigation, experience in lending for education, industrial restructuring, electric power in Africa, and the Bank's assistance for public sector management.

Dissemination and feedback. For some years the Bank's operational guidelines have required staff to seek out evaluation findings and apply them in new operations. To reinforce the actions the Bank is taking to strengthen portfolio management and the quality of new operations, the OED collaborated in fiscal 1994 with the Bank's central vice presidencies on the design of better methods for appraising projects and rating their progress. These efforts included:

• The introduction of selective dissemination of lessons learned in connection with proposals for new lending operations.

• Evaluation by the OED of the processes the Bank uses to review the progress of the portfolio under implementation. The OED recommended a revision of the rating system that the Bank uses for gauging the performance of projects in progress (see Box 4-4 on page 77); it is now collaborating with the Operations Policy Department to produce more reliable indicators of projects' expected development impact.

• The introduction of a "policy ledger," recording the responses of Bank management to the recommendations of OED studies, for reference by Bank staff.

In fiscal 1994 OED published *Human Resource Development in Sub-Saharan Africa*; *Evaluation Results for 1992*, including analyses of the Bank's assistance in agriculture and in institutional development; and a booklet, *Assessing Development Effectiveness: Evaluation in the World Bank and International Finance Corporation*. With the United Nations Development Programme and the United Nations Environment Programme, it published *The Global Environment Facility: Independent Evaluation of the Pilot Phase*.

Recognizing the need to take a more active role in disseminating lessons of experience to practitioners outside the Bank, the OED expanded the distribution of its "Précis" series and began a new series, "Lessons & Practices."

Twenty OED "Précis" were published. This series highlights findings and recommendations from evaluation studies and audits; it is issued in English, French, and Spanish.

Three issues of "Lessons & Practices" were published, covering railways, area development, and adjustment lending. This series synthesizes lessons and recommendations arising from the Bank's development experience.

The OED presented the results of its audits and studies at seminars within and outside the Bank, including some organized by borrower countries.

Support for evaluation in borrower countries. A growing number of the Bank's borrowing members have asked for help in establishing or strengthening evaluation agencies. Changing views on the role of the state, together with increasing scarcity of resources, are focusing attention on the effectiveness, efficiency, and accountability of public institutions as well as of public policies and programs.

OED support begins after a country makes a commitment to develop the evaluation function. During fiscal 1994 the OED attended to requests for advice on evaluation capacity development from Argentina, Brazil, China, Colombia, Indonesia, and Sri Lanka. Activities included designing diagnostic studies on evaluation capacity; organizing training and workshops; organizing the participation of country staff in OED's evaluation missions; and promoting borrower participation in the Bank's evaluation processes.

In response to a recommendation of the portfolio management task force, another task force made recommendations to the Bank's board of executive directors and management on future policy for assisting borrower countries to develop evaluation capacity in the public sector.

Other activities. OED participated as an observer in meetings of the OECD's DAC (Development Assistance Committee) Expert Group. Evaluation staff participated in training activities and attended workshops and seminars with evaluators from other international organizations and donor countries. They continued to participate as "resource persons" in seminars of the Economic Development Institute.

Internal Auditing

The Internal Auditing Department (IAD) acts as an independent appraiser that reviews and evaluates Bank operations and activities. It is headed by an auditor general who reports functionally to the president of the Bank and, since December 1991, administratively to the vice president and controller.

In response to requests from Bank management during the year, the IAD conducted a number of special reviews, including those of the $30 million technical assistance program to the Union of Soviet Socialist Republics (established in August 1991), the Africa Capacity Building Facility, the main complex rehabilitation project, and a number of field offices. These reviews were in addition to the regular work program, which, while covering all aspects of the Bank's administration, continued to emphasize the Bank's operations and focus on traditional topics such as the procurement of goods, works, and services; the disbursement process; and evaluation of procedures used to ensure proper accountability of borrowers during project implementation.

Staff from IAD also provided technical assistance as part of an implementation mission to Russia by carrying out an evaluation of developments in auditing and locally established audit firms.

A Bankwide review of time-recording systems currently in use was completed, and new, comprehensive audits were undertaken on loan processing in the East Asia and Pacific and Africa regions. A Bankwide review of internal controls was also initiated. The department's work program of regular audits of the Bank's financial and accounting systems and procedures was closely coordinated with reviews undertaken by the Bank's external auditors to avoid duplication of effort and maximize the audit coverage.

The Bank relies on information technology to support its business functions. In recognition of this reliance, the department conducted a series of technical audits addressing management, security, and control issues pertaining to the three principal computing environments in the Bank. The IAD also undertook computer-application reviews and system-development audits focusing on the efficiency, effectiveness, and control of critical applications. In order to position itself for an expanded program of audits in this increasingly important information-resource management area, the IAD added a significant contingent of staff with relevant experience.

In order to satisfy the professional standards of internal auditing, an external Quality Assurance Review of the department's policies and procedures was also commissioned during the past fiscal year.

Economic Development Institute

In fiscal 1994, a five-year strategic plan for the Economic Development Institute (EDI), designed to respond to the needs, challenges, and possibilities of the times, was developed. A key component of the plan, the mission statement, stresses the institute's commitment to investing in people and ideas as the most powerful means of development—a concept that distinguishes EDI's role from that of the operational arm of the World Bank, which invests much of its resources in physical infrastructure. At the same time, however, the plan is committed to undertake activities that center on the Bank's objectives of reducing poverty and promoting sustainable and equitable development.

Training. During the past year, the EDI conducted 140 training activities (see Table 6-1). A notable expansion in activities took place in the Europe and Central Asia region, where some fifty activities were carried out, an increase of seven over the previous year. Despite the high demand for EDI's assistance in that region, the institute nevertheless also increased the size of its program in Africa. The training program in Africa included an effort to increase the effectiveness of educational reforms through a seminar that brought together twenty-three education experts from The Gambia, Malawi,

Table 6-1. **Regional Distribution of EDI Training Programs in Fiscal Year 1994**

Region	Activities
Africa	41
Asia	22
Europe and Central Asia	50
Latin America and the Caribbean	12
Middle East and North Africa	11
Global	4
Total	140

Nigeria, Tanzania, and Zambia with Bank staff responsible for education projects in those countries. The seminar was felt to have been highly successful in creating a forum for the open exchange of ideas between the Bank and its borrowers, thereby helping to reshape both the governments' perspectives as well as the Bank's lending operations in those countries.

Although the total number of activities conducted remained about the same as in the previous year, the number of participants trained increased from 4,469 to 4,900.

The increase in the number of participants reflects a change in the "mix" of activities: fewer small seminars for senior officials and more courses in economic and sector management and "training of trainers"—courses that usually have a larger number of participants.

Program in the former Soviet Union (FSU). In response to the growing demand for assistance in the republics of the FSU, the EDI worked closely with local universities—the Tashkent State University of Economics, the Kazakh State Academy of Management, and the Economics State University of Kiev, for example—in designing seminars, recruiting trainers, and preparing teaching materials in local languages. The enterprise-management program in the FSU is a good example of a training-of-trainers program in which EDI first trains local trainers and then uses the local trainers to train practitioners. During fiscal 1994, 2,200 participants were directly or indirectly trained in this highly successful program.

Training materials and publications. EDI prepares most of its own training materials in the form of manuals, books, case studies, and collections of analytical papers and distributes them through its courses and seminars and, on request, to partner training institutions and senior officials and policymakers worldwide. The content of these materials often derives from World Bank experience, including country and sector studies, research reports, case studies of Bank projects, and Operations Evaluation Department findings. In fiscal 1994, EDI published eighty titles for use in its courses and seminars.

While most of EDI's materials are published in English, a certain number are issued in other languages, as well. In addition to five Russian titles published during the year, materials were also translated into French, Spanish, Chinese, and Arabic.

Scholarship and fellowship programs. The World Bank Graduate Scholarship Program, funded by the government of Japan, saw a class of twenty-five students graduate with a master's degree in Economic Policy Management from Columbia University. In all, the core program of the program, which supports students at universities of their choice worldwide, awarded ninety-four scholarships in fiscal 1994.

Changes were made in the Robert S. McNamara Fellowships Program that, beginning in fiscal 1995, would enable it to become a program of developing country research, with smaller fellowships and larger numbers of fellows. Through fiscal 1994, research had to be conducted outside a fellow's home country.

Initiatives undertaken. In adjusting to changes in its environment, the EDI introduced several initiatives to its core program:

• A program for the Occupied Territories was launched. The program, which began in June 1994, emphasizes efficient management of external assistance through training in topics such as project assessment, project management and procurement, restructuring of the regulatory framework in the housing sector, and development of policies that support economic development.

• In response to the 1993 report of the Task Force on Portfolio Management, the EDI began a program in portfolio management that is being supported by a series of training manuals and case studies that, in particular, deals with the economic analysis of projects, procurement, and project management. Initial implementation of this work began in fiscal 1994 in the FSU; the program is slated to be extended into China, Viet Nam, and the Occupied Territories.

• The EDI's program on environmentally sustainable development was expanded to include training to improve policies and practices in the involuntary resettlement of persons displaced by the effects of development projects. This expanded program was carried out during the year in China, India, and Turkey. In addition, a new program in environmental analysis and valuation to help governments deal with industrial pollution was designed in collaboration with the Foundation for Advanced Studies in International Development (Tokyo). This program, funded by the government of Japan, includes techniques for assessing, prioritizing, and managing environmental problems in the transitional economies of Central and Eastern Europe.

• Many of the EDI's teaching materials now include computer-based components and multimedia techniques. In addition to publishing a large number of its training materials on CD-ROM, the EDI has begun to use teleconferencing to bring together developing country officials and Bank staff. For example, as part of a seminar held in Cameroon in early 1994, journalists from French-speaking Africa were briefed by senior managers from the World Bank on important concepts that underlie economic reform. The United States Information Agency's Worldnet not only linked the journalists (in Yaoundé) with Bank officials (in Washington) but also broadcast the teleconference throughout Africa.

Joint Vienna Institute. The Joint Vienna Institute, which was established in collaboration with four other agencies—the International Monetary Fund, the Bank for International Settlements, the European Bank for Reconstruction and Development, and the Organisation for Economic Co-operation and Development—continues to conduct and host courses in market economics for officials from transitional economies. In its first year—September 1992 through August 1993—the institute organized forty-four seminars, totaling 108 training weeks, and involving more than 1,150 officials and managers from about thirty economies in transition. In fiscal 1994, the institute, which had been functioning under interim and informal arrangements, was established as an international organization under a board of directors composed of representatives of the sponsoring organizations.

EDI's Moscow office. The great demand for courses in the Europe and Central Asia region led the EDI to establish its first overseas office, in Moscow. The office is currently staffed by fifteen locally recruited trainers who coordinate and conduct training activities in the FSU (including those related to the Joint Vienna Institute) in collaboration with EDI's Washington-based staff.

Research at the World Bank

The Bank's contribution to a more comprehensive understanding of the processes of growth and development relies to a great extent on the research it conducts. That research is intended to provide information to enhance policy making of government officials who face rapidly changing domestic and global circumstances. It also answers questions that arise in designing and adapting the Bank's lending program to the needs of its members.

The major objectives of the Bank's current programs are poverty reduction and human resources development, enhancement of the role of women in development, private sector development, environmentally sustainable development, and economic management. Bank research is focused on those areas where critical policy questions remain unanswered.

Poverty reduction and human resources development. Poverty and human resources issues continue to dominate the Bank's research agenda, with a focus on the links between pol-icy and poverty reduction. One ongoing project is studying the effect of price liberalization on the rural poor in China; another is exploring how macroeconomic and sectoral policies affected consumption in India during 1951–90. Analysis of a panel data set constructed from rural household surveys in China is expected to lead to better understanding of the ways families rise out of poverty in rural China, and research on improving the productivity of women will examine the sustainability of three credit programs for the rural poor in Bangladesh.

Analysis of issues relating to economic growth and poverty reduction has been confounded by the scarcity of data and reliable measures that are comparable across countries. A cross-country data base for 1981–91, using uniform poverty measures and purchasing power parities, presents a disturbing picture: Nearly one out of three people in the world lives in poverty, and the number of poor has been growing commensurate with increases in the population.

Research on economic success and concomitant reduction in poverty in several Asian countries has prominently cited education as a critical factor in that success. A study conducted during fiscal 1994 analyzed the role of secondary education in raising labor productivity and in facilitating economic transition from agriculture to more capital-intensive services in newly industrializing Asian developing economies. Further study is now under way on ways to improve educational systems in developing countries. A major interagency project concluded during the year found that government subsidies for basic education yield important benefits and that public expenditures on higher education in poorer countries undermine equity and efficiency. Evidence on educational achievement and the cost-effectiveness of schooling inputs, analyzed in a fiscal 1994 study, has yielded recommendations for actions to improve educational outcomes. When families are willing to invest in the health and education of their members, the quality and availability of local social services critically influence the outcomes of their investments; Bank research completed during the year indicates the relative payoffs to different service programs and strategies across many countries and years.

An interagency study of contraceptive use suggests that policies to limit population growth must be tailored to a country's socioeconomic development. Three countries in different stages of the fertility transition demonstrated wide variations in response to different variables such as income, education, and access to contraceptive services.

Improvement of health programs is the objective of a study that is measuring the effect of higher user fees on the use of primary health services in Indonesia. Another is resurveying health and education indicators and facilities in Morocco to provide the basis for analyzing a crucial set of issues in the area of government expenditures on social services. Using an unusual longitudinal data set for Africa, one project is trying to identify the link between health and labor productivity.

Research on the impact of unions and policy interventions in the labor market on short-term adjustment and long-term economic performance will help to assess the appropriateness of the Bank's focus on product market reforms in the 1980s. It will also analyze the extent to which the private sector in developing countries has been able to circumvent government interventions in the labor market during the past two decades. A three-year study examined critical labor market policies and strategies to minimize the social costs of wage and labor reforms by improving the competitive operation of labor markets and increasing the efficiency of public and private spending on education and training. The goal was to identify "best practices" to improve labor market performances that have a bearing on the condition of the poor. The results of another labor market study, which will be published as a handbook on labor market policy, is designed to contribute to the policy dialogue between the Bank and member governments.

Environmentally sustainable development. The creation of the Environmentally Sustainable Development vice presidency has centralized resources for analysis of common and global environmental issues. Simultaneously, environmental research has been initiated in different units of the Bank to address local or regional environmental concerns. During fiscal 1994 the Bank investigated land use, conservation of biodiversity, and development in the Amazon floodplain; coastal zone management in the tropical areas of Latin America; and sustainable resettlement in areas of Western Africa from which people had migrated because of riverblindness infestation and to which they are now returning following the eradication of the black fly. Research of global significance includes analysis of the relationships among population growth, environmental degradation, and economic growth and a preliminary investigation into whether lumberwood plantations can help recover degraded pastureland and whether they can act as havens for the rehabilitation of indigenous species.

Private sector development. For many developing and transitional economies, private sector growth is constrained by high local transaction costs, uncompetitive currencies, and government interventions and restrictions that raise costs and limit opportunities to take advantage of otherwise competitive factor prices. In many countries the legacy of past problems is a moribund industrial sector for which bankruptcy and restructuring are the only answers; a research project developing recommendations for bankruptcy law is investigating what might be the most appropriate legal and regulatory framework.

In other cases, public sector infrastructure failures are so pervasive and costs so high that it is necessary to commercialize infrastructure services for the private sector to grow. The determinants of service contracting are being investigated to develop recommendations for commercialization of infrastructure. Transport systems are similarly overburdened and underfunded, and a set of performance indicators is being developed to help policymakers focus on priority areas for maintenance, upgrading, and investment.

Despite these problems, firms emerge and grow, and research is examining how they do. In Russia, determinants of private sector success are being analyzed; the study is also examining the potential usefulness of business service centers to provide information, credit, and advice to new entrepreneurs. The difficult process of commercialization and transfer of firms from the public to private sector in Poland has been relatively successful, and Bank research has uncovered lessons that other countries, both transitional and developing, can learn from that experience.

For many developing countries, the agricultural sector is the largest potential source of growth and development, and research is under way on a range of issues in agricultural development. In the former Soviet Union, land reform and farm restructuring is needed before farmers will respond to improved incentives, and a Bank project is investigating constraints to, and ways to enhance, that process. Alternative agricultural policies in Poland are being analyzed for their implications for other postsocialist countries, and a broader study is examining the transition of socialist agriculture in Europe and Asia.

Macroeconomic issues and economic management. Adjustment of fiscal and external balances, reduction of the role of government in production, and relieving constraints on the private sector have been the focus of economic reform in Africa for more than a decade. But growth continues to be elusive, and the reasons why are not readily apparent. A study of adjustment in twenty-nine African countries, completed in fiscal 1994, uncovered some answers: budget deficits and inflation remain high, and overvalued currencies make African products uncompetitive in international markets. The study found that those countries adopting reforms have grown; those only beginning the reform process still have a long way to go; and those not adopting reforms are experiencing alarming economic declines.

The catalyst for growth in many countries has been expansion of production for export. While the means and benefits of liberalizing trade policies have been well documented, drawn-out multilateral negotiations in the Uruguay Round of the General Agreement on Tariffs and Trade have generated renewed interest in groupings to promote regional trade. Research was conducted on regional arrangements and their advantages and costs relative to international agreements in order to advise developing country officials on the strategies that would be of greatest benefit.

Progress in the generation of government revenues continues to be highly variable across countries, and research on ways to mobilize resources for public services has been a staple of Bank research for years. The focus of public economics research shifted in fiscal 1994, however, toward public expenditures and fiscal decentralization. New projects are investigating expenditure equalization among provincial and local governments, are examining instruments for allocating expenditure responsibilities and revenues from central to local governments, and are studying the effects of fiscal decentralization on various measures of performance.

The Bank's sixth annual conference on development economics surveyed five topics: the transition in socialist economies; new institutional economics; economic geography—the dynamics of disparate regional development; pressures driving international migration; and labor markets under systemic change. The presentation of eleven papers on these topics was supplemented by a keynote speech on current development issues by the Bank's vice president, Development Economics and Chief Economist, and a roundtable discussion on employment and development (it was the initial forum on the theme of *World Development Report 1995*). The papers, with discussant comments, the keynote speech, and a summary of the roundtable discussion, will be published as *Proceedings of the World Bank Annual Conference on Development Economics, 1994*.

The Administrative Budget and Bank Administration

The Bank's administrative budget for fiscal 1994, as approved by the executive directors in fiscal 1993, was $1,388.7 million. Late in fiscal 1994, the directors approved an administrative budget for fiscal 1995 of $1,420.3 million, an increase of 2.4 percent in nominal terms (see Table 6-2).

The fiscal 1995 budget was designed to enable units to implement priority objectives with increased attention to project quality at entry and supervision. Special attention will be given to four key issues.

• Poverty reduction will be reflected in all components of country-assistance strategies involving greater staff intensity per operation.

• Portfolio-management activities will receive further emphasis to improve project implementation so as to enhance the developmental impact of Bank operations.

• Country dialogue on policy reform will be strengthened, and efforts to develop investment-lending opportunities increased, particularly in the newer members and in those moving out of adjustment lending.

• Collaboration with other multilateral and nongovernmental organizations and the private sector will be increased to make maximum use of the capacities of others.

World Bank regular and fixed-term staff on board at the end of fiscal year 1994 totaled 6,338, of whom 4,145 were higher-level staff from 123 nations. The number of staff increased 2.3 percent from the previous year; higher-level staff grew by 3.5 percent. Of the higher-level staff, 59 percent were from industrialized countries; the remaining 41 percent were from developing countries.

At the end of the year, 1,166 higher-level, long-term consultants (those with contracts with a duration of six months or more) were working for the Bank, an increase of 27.7 percent over fiscal year 1993, and 508 regular and fixed-term staff were in special positions.

Women employed as higher-level staff by the Bank increased from 28.4 percent of the total to 30.0 percent during fiscal 1994. The Bank recruited 257 new higher-level staff in fiscal 1994, of whom 32.7 percent were from developing countries and 39.3 percent were women. Forty-two of the Bank's recruits were selected through the Young Professionals Program; thirty were from developing countries, and eighteen were women. As an experiment, the Young Professionals Program hired ten technical specialists, rather than economists or financial specialists. The experiment proved to be a success, and the program will be expanded to hire more technical specialists and fewer economists and financial analysts in fiscal 1995. A special skills-mix recruitment strategy was set in motion to hire staff in seven skills areas greatly in need in the Bank. One hundred

Table 6-2. **World Bank Budget by Expense Category and Administrative Program, 1992–95**
(millions of US dollars; fiscal years)

Item	Actual			1995 program
	1992	1993	1994	
Expense category				
Staff costs	699.0	771.2	851.8	878.8
Consultants	89.2	104.8	113.7	128.2
Contractual services/representation	37.3	42.9	66.3	49.6
Operational travel	113.5	122.0	129.8	134.4
Overhead	176.1	209.1	231.6	215.0
Direct contributions to special grants program[a]	58.6	80.7	102.5	90.5
President's contingency[b]	n.a.	n.a.	n.a.	14.1
Reimbursements	(100.5)	(95.3)	(107.3)	(113.8)
Accrual for resettlement on termination	n.a.	n.a.	n.a.	23.0
Allocation for pending benefit initiatives[c]	n.a.	n.a.	n.a.	0.6
Total	1,074.0	1,235.6	1,388.4	1,420.3
Administrative program[d]				
Operational	496.3	582.0	612.2	630.7
Financial	87.0	92.4	98.5	102.1
Development and advisory	175.6	172.3	216.6	217.5
Administrative support	106.3	106.0	119.7	116.6
Corporate management and legal services	38.4	40.6	45.1	48.1
Total	903.6	993.3	1,092.1	1,115.0
Overhead/benefits[e]	154.0	193.8	210.3	223.0
President's contingency	n.a.	n.a.	n.a.	14.1
Reimbursements	(100.5)	(95.3)	(107.3)	(113.8)
Net administrative programs	957.0	1,091.7	1,195.0	1,238.3
Special programs[f]	65.7	88.8	110.2	98.4
Boards	40.1	43.1	46.5	53.9
Operations evaluation	11.2	12.0	13.8	14.6
Nondiscretionary items[g]	n.a.	n.a.	n.a.	14.6
Allocation for pending benefit initiatives[c]	n.a.	n.a.	22.9[i]	0.6
Total budget	1,074.0	1,235.6[h]	1,388.4	1,420.3[i]

NOTE: Details may not add to totals because of rounding.

n.a. Not applicable.

a. Includes Institutional Development Fund in fiscal 1993–95.

b. Allocations from president's contingency have been included in respective categories/programs for fiscal 1992–94.

c. Subject to executive board approval.

d. Fiscal 1992–93 figures differ from those in the fiscal 1993 *Annual Report* due to a change in the methodology of allocating benefits to different programs.

e. Centrally managed overhead and benefits.

f. Includes administrative expenses, and an additional $13 million for the Consultative Group for International Agricultural Research in fiscal 1994; the remaining $7 million will be paid in fiscal 1995.

g. Includes $7.1 million underfunding in the currency option of the Staff Retirement Plan (SRP), a net saving of $8.1 million under the Retired Staff Benefit Plan, a savings of $9.7 million due to SRP portfolio gains, and a $25.3 million provision for resettlement on termination due to accounting changes.

h. Excludes $20 million for Somalia relief.

i. Includes $25.3 million provision for resettlement, of which $22.9 million was ultimately paid from a budget underrun in fiscal 1994. The remaining $2.4 million is the fiscal 1995 increment.

twenty-two staff in those skills areas were hired, and the recruitment strategy will be continued in fiscal year 1995.

Improvement of skills is also being carried out through training that is offered in a wide range of new courses—environmental issues, health management, women in development, poverty, private sector development, and public sector management—to enhance technical and professional skills of staff. In response to the recommendations of the Task Force on Portfolio Management and the "next steps" action program, an integrated training curriculum on portfolio management and lending operations has been developed. The content addresses several major themes of portfolio management and lending operations developed from analyses of reports on portfolio management, business and institutional priorities, and staff training needs.

Occupancy of the Phase 1 building of the new main complex by Bank staff began in the first quarter of fiscal 1994. Work preparatory to the further demolition of buildings started in October 1993, demolition was completed in May 1994, and excavation and construction of the foundations for the Phase 2 building started in the same month. Completion of the Phase 2 building is scheduled for late fiscal 1996.

In December 1993, a new department, the Headquarters Construction Department, was formed to manage the main complex rebuilding project. It is managed and staffed by personnel experienced in construction.

The second Quadrennial Benefits Survey was conducted by the Bank and the International Monetary Fund in 1993. The survey revealed that the value of staff benefits (net of staff contributions) was at an intermediate position in relation to those of 109 comparator organizations in the United States, France, and Germany. European comparators were found to have more generous leave and subsidy provisions. The review concluded that the Bank's overall benefits envelope was reasonably related to those of comparators.

On January 1, 1994 the Bank adopted a worldwide business class travel policy. Since the Bank moved toward changes in its operational travel policy in 1993, the cost of airfares from headquarters has decreased by about 25 percent. The fiscal year also marked the first full year of operations of the dual-contractor arrangements for travel service and food services, contracted for through a competitive bidding process.

Results of the fifth Attitude Survey, made available in September, showed that despite improvements on some institutional indices, work group responses deteriorated in several respects. Staff indicated that they are generally satisfied with their work, pay, and benefits, identify with the institution's goals, and feel that their managers are doing good jobs; nonetheless, they feel ambivalent towards the institution itself. Dissatisfaction with career development, internal communications, and the personnel function were cited as contributing causes of ambivalence; stress is also greater now than in 1990. Managers were directed to work with their staff and to take action on local issues.

Problems encountered by staff (particularly expatriates or those who must travel frequently) in balancing the demands of work and their family obligations frequently contribute to stress. As a result, adjustments to policy and new programs complementing existing benefits were introduced. They include enhanced provisions for emergency and family leave, greater flexibility in working hours and schedules, counselling for family members on seeking employment in the Washington area, and assistance in identifying appropriate child and elder care arrangements. It is anticipated that these measures will improve the Bank's ability to attract the diversified and highly skilled staff required to carry out its mission.

Following a review by the Health Services Department into the possible causes and remedies of stress, a stress clinic was established. Bank Staff running the program provide individual stress-management consultations, distribute educational materials, hold monthly health-promotion talks on stress, and are currently developing a training course in stress management.

Standardized occupational streams were developed to assist staff and managers in achieving greater mobility across the institution. The streams, which cover more than 85 percent of all nonmanagerial jobs, clarify the requirements for entry and growth within various job families and are used for staffing and career counselling, as well as for job-grading and promotion decisions.

Substantial changes, designed to create a better, more balanced dialogue between supervisors and staff about performance effectiveness and skill development, were made in the Bank's performance-management process for headquarters-based staff. A key element is the use of job-family competencies to enhance the specificity and usefulness of performance feedback. The competencies are integrated into the annual performance review using streamlined forms and procedures that focus attention on dialogue rather than on text. The outcome is a joint staff/manager plan for increasing the staff member's effectiveness.

In January 1994 the Personnel and Administration vice presidency was reorganized and became the Management and Personnel Services vice presidency. The reorganization was designed to make the vice presidency, which is a service arm to the rest of the Bank, become more responsive to the needs of its clients, perform to a higher standard of service, and improve the effectiveness of the Bank's business processes, both within its own areas of responsibility and without, by helping other areas of the Bank improve business processes. A new department—Organization and Business Practices—was created by merging the Organization Planning Group and units of the Information Technology and Facilities Department. The new department will bring the power of information technology and systems to the design of new work processes and organization structures. Its primary responsibility is to improve existing business practices, processes, and procedures. At the same time, the facilities units of the Information Technology and Facilities Department were merged with the General Services Department.

The management team of the new vice presidency, in collaboration with its clients, established a set of business objectives and plans for fiscal years 1994 and 1995 that will lead to reduced costs and improved quality of services, with particular focus on the Organization and Business Practices, General Services, and the Personnel Management departments. The plans address the need to support the efforts of other vice presidencies to redesign their business processes and service delivery. Two vice presidencies—the East Asia and Pacific Region and Development Economics—have launched redesign efforts. One department in each vice presidency, with the support of Management and Personnel Services, has undertaken a comprehensive redesign of its core work processes. These redesign efforts were initiated because many of the work processes have become too cumbersome and costly and lack client participation. The redesign work will be completed in the fall of 1994, with implementation scheduled to take place in 1995. Once the redesign work is finished it will be evaluated and then expanded to other departments and regions.

Information technology initiatives currently being implemented on a Bankwide basis include centrally managed and supported technology service that allows voice, video, graphic, image, text, and numeric data to be shared easily throughout the institution and with external entities. Initiatives at early stages of development include a new desktop electronic mail service that is better integrated with standard software such as word processors and spreadsheets and an Electronic Document Management System that provides new capabilities of electronically capturing, storing, and managing information from the desktop. Accomplishments in the information-management field include the establishment of a new Field Office Information Services Unit; the development of policies, guidelines, and procedures for managing Bank records; and the conversion from microfiche to optical storage of internal Bank reports.

International Finance Corporation

The International Finance Corporation (IFC), a member of the World Bank Group, promotes private enterprise in its developing member countries. It does this by financing sound private sector projects, mobilizing debt and equity financing in the international markets for private companies, and providing technical assistance and advisory services to businesses and governments.

The growth of the IFC's operations in fiscal 1994 was strong. Financing approved for IFC's own account was $2.5 billion for 231 projects, compared with $2.1 billion for 185 projects in fiscal 1993. It was also a good year for the IFC's resource-mobilization activities. The corporation approved $1.8 billion in financing to be mobilized through loan syndications and the underwriting of securities issues and investment funds. Projects approved by the IFC had total investment costs of $15.8 billion; this means that other investors and lenders will provide a total of $5.43 for every dollar approved by the IFC.

The corporation approved projects in sixty-five countries, compared with fifty-four countries in fiscal 1993, as well as a number of projects with a regional or international scope. Approvals increased in most regions. IFC's approvals in Central Asia, the Middle East, and North Africa increased by 42 percent, to $383 million; in Asia, by 16 percent, to $605 million; in Latin America and the Caribbean, by 15 percent, to $815 million; and in Europe, by 6 percent, to $443 million. In sub-Saharan Africa, the number of projects approved increased from forty-five to fifty-seven, but the volume of financing decreased to $157 million, as more than half of the projects involved small and medium-sized enterprises.

The IFC was active in many sectors, including capital markets, power, telecommunications, agribusiness, tourism, manufacturing, oil and gas, mining, and petrochemicals, among others. Capital markets activities—for example, investments in banks and nonbank financial institutions and various funds, credit lines for intermediaries, and securities underwriting—accounted for 24 percent of the dollar volume approved. A new product launched by the IFC in fiscal 1994, the State Street Bank & Trust Company/IFC Emerging Markets Index Common Trust Fund, will invest in twenty-three stock markets covered by the IFC Investable Composite Index, a series launched in fiscal 1993.

The IFC approved a number of projects in sectors such as telecommunications, power, transport, and water supply, and made a $50 million investment in a global fund that will provide mezzanine financing for power projects throughout the developing world, as well as a $1 million investment in the fund management company.

New commitments signed during the year reached $1.8 billion, up from $1.4 billion in fiscal 1993. Disbursements were also up; they reached $1.5 billion, compared with $1.2 billion last year. The IFC's disbursed portfolio grew by 14 percent during the fiscal year, to reach $6.2 billion at June 30, 1994.

The Foreign Investment Advisory Service (FIAS), which is supervised by a committee consisting of representatives of the IFC, MIGA (until July 1, 1994), and the Bank, provides advice on matters related to foreign direct investment. In fiscal 1994, FIAS completed twenty-eight advisory assignments in twenty-five countries.

The IFC's financial performance was strong during the year, with record net income of $258 million, a return of 8.8 percent on IFC's net worth, which reached $3.2 billion at June 30, 1994. The IFC borrowed $1.5 billion in the international markets and $180 million from the IBRD and issued bonds in six currencies, including its first in the drachma market. The IFC's largest borrowing to date was a Eurodollar 500 million issue made in fiscal 1994.

In fiscal 1994 the IFC's board approved a revision of the corporation's leverage and capital-adequacy policies. Under the revised policies, the corporation would maintain at all times a level of capital (including paid-in capital, retained earnings, and general loss reserves) equal to at least 30 percent of risk-weighted assets and would borrow no more than four times the amount of its net worth (the total of subscribed capital and retained earnings). At June 30, 1994, IFC's capital adequacy stood at 43 percent, well above the policy minimum of 30 percent, while IFC's leverage stood at 1.7:1, well within the permitted maximum. Those ratios convey the strong level of the corporation's capital and reserves in relation to its risk exposures and borrowings and should permit the IFC, provided that profitability remains satisfactory, to maintain its current

growth rate of 12 percent to 13 percent annually in new investment approvals for the foreseeable future.

During the year the corporation's membership increased to 161 countries. The IFC welcomed five new members—Estonia, Kazakhstan, Latvia, Ukraine, and Uzbekistan.

Because of the growth of its operations and staff during the past decade, the corporation has outgrown its present office space, which is leased from the World Bank. After careful consideration, IFC management decided to buy a site near World Bank headquarters in downtown Washington, D.C. and construct new headquarters. The site was purchased in 1992, and excavation began in fiscal 1994. The IFC expects to move into its new headquarters in fiscal 1997.

Details of the IFC's fiscal year can be found in its *Annual Report*, published separately.

Multilateral Investment Guarantee Agency

The Multilateral Investment Guarantee Agency (MIGA) has as its mandate to increase the flow of productive investments to developing member countries by providing services that are client-oriented, cost-efficient, and complementary to those of other relevant public and private activities. It achieves this by (a) guaranteeing (or insuring) investments in developing countries made by private investors against specific noncommercial risks; and (b) advising and assisting these countries' efforts to attract and retain such investment.

During fiscal 1994, MIGA's board of directors reviewed and approved changes in the agency's operational regulations; reviewed the agency's operations during its first five years of activities; agreed to sever the relationship with the Bank Group's Foreign Investment Advisory Services (FIAS) as of July 1, 1994 so as to conserve the agency's resources and build up reserves; approved an increase in the risk-to-asset ratio to allow for further growth in the guarantees program; and concurred with the president's decision on thirty-six insurance projects conveyed to it.

The number of countries paying their capital subscription in full and becoming members of the agency increased from 107 to 121.

Guarantee program. In fiscal 1994, MIGA's guarantee program exceeded fiscal 1993 outputs in nearly every respect. Increases took place in the number of contracts executed (38 as compared with 27), income earned from premiums and commitment fees ($9.9 million as opposed to $5.8 million), and commitments of potential coverage ($140 million in contrast with $105 million).

The thirty-eight contracts issued in fiscal 1994 involved an associated total direct investment of some $1.3 billion and created 7,800 jobs directly in fourteen host countries—a fivefold increase in job creation over the previous fiscal year. In fiscal 1994, investments were assisted in Argentina, Brazil, Bulgaria, Cameroon, Chile, China, the Czech Republic, Hungary, Kazakhstan, Pakistan, Peru, Trinidad and Tobago, Uganda, and Uzbekistan.

Several milestones in the evolution of MIGA's guarantees program were reached in fiscal 1994. MIGA signed its 100th contract of guarantee; total contingent liabilities exceeded the $1 billion mark; the 1,500th preliminary application for coverage was received; and the agency was formally admitted as a member of the International Union of Credit and Investment Insurers (the Berne Union).

Technical assistance activities. MIGA furnishes a variety of technical assistance services to assist efforts to stimulate foreign direct investment in the developing world and the transitional economies (collectively referred to by MIGA as Category Two countries). Through the end of fiscal 1994, these services were furnished both directly and through the FIAS. Technical assistance is now focused primarily on investment promotion and information dissemination on investment opportunities in Category Two countries and the related capacity building of those countries' investment-promotion agencies.

During fiscal 1994, and in collaboration with other agencies, MIGA conducted two major multicountry promotional events and related activities—the first for the tourism sector of South America and the second for the mining sector of sub-Saharan Africa.

Other promotion activities carried out during the year included strategy workshops designed to help member countries in capacity building for marketing, workshops to strengthen investor services and linkages, and assistance in launching investment-promotion missions.

Reflecting MIGA's new emphasis to assist member countries in information dissemination on investment opportunities, work began on some major initiatives during fiscal year 1994. The most important was preparation for the launching of a global investment-promotion agency to be supported by a planned global electronic information exchange (IPAnet). The IPAnet will link official investment-promotion agencies, business associations, financial and other intermediaries, and ultimately, investors.

MIGA will provide the secretariat for the network, which will primarily enable members to meet and exchange information and experiences.

In compliance with its mandate, MIGA, directly or with FIAS, provided advice to a number of member countries on their foreign investment legislation. MIGA also actively promoted the conclusion of bilateral investment treaties among several members and encouraged the amiable settlement of a number of investment disputes.

Details of MIGA's activities in fiscal 1994 appear in the MIGA *Annual Report* for fiscal 1994, which is published separately.

International Centre for Settlement of Investment Disputes

The International Centre for Settlement of Investment Disputes (ICSID) is a separate international organization established under the Convention on the Settlement of Investment Disputes between States and Nationals of Other States (the Convention), which was opened for signature in 1965 and entered into force the following year.

ICSID seeks to encourage greater flows of international investment by providing facilities for the conciliation and arbitration of disputes between governments and foreign investors. In addition, ICSID undertakes advisory, research, and publications activities in the area of foreign investment law.

During the past fiscal year, ICSID's membership continued to grow with the ratification of the Convention by Peru, the Slovak Republic, Slovenia, and Zimbabwe. As of June 30, 1994, 113 countries had become members of ICSID; an additional seventeen countries had signed but not yet ratified the Convention.

During the same period, two new requests, one for arbitration and one for conciliation, were registered, and two awards were rendered. As of June 30, 1994, three cases were pending before the centre.

ICSID's publications include a semiannual law journal, "ICSID Review—Foreign Investment Law Journal," and multivolume collections of *Investment Laws of the World* and *Investment Treaties*. Two issues of the law journal and four releases of the investment laws and treaties collections were published in fiscal 1994.

Details of ICSID's activities during fiscal 1994 appear in its *Annual Report*, which is published separately.

Section Seven
World Bank Finances

The IBRD currently has 177 members. These members have subscribed about 1.41 million shares of the Bank's capital stock valued at $170 billion. The subscription price of the IBRD's shares is divided into a paid-in portion (currently 3 percent) and a larger callable portion. The former is payable to the IBRD at the time of subscription; the latter may be called only when required to meet IBRD obligations arising out of its borrowings or loan guarantees. The paid-in portion is divided in turn into a portion payable in gold or United States dollars and another payable in a member's own currency. The amount payable in a member's own currency is to be maintained in terms of its value against the standard value of the Bank's capital, which is expressed in United States dollars.

The IBRD's Articles of Agreement, as applied, require that the total amount outstanding of disbursed loans, participations in loans, and callable guarantees not exceed the total value of subscribed capital, reserves, and surplus. This defines the IBRD's statutory lending limit. The difference between that limit and the actual total of disbursed loans, participations, and callable guarantees is known as "headroom." Under current policy, the adequacy of the IBRD's capital is reviewed every three years, or more often if necessary.

Capital increases are the subject of negotiation and agreement among IBRD members. Two indicators are used to determine when and how large a capital increase may be required. One indicator is the amount of available headroom and the date by which it can reasonably be expected to be exhausted. Another is the "sustainable level of lending." This indicator is a useful planning tool since it identifies the level of lending that can be sustained indefinitely, under certain assumptions, without an increase in capital. The IBRD's current sustainable level of lending stands at about $27 billion, compared with a commitment level for fiscal 1994 of $14.2 billion.

The objective of the IBRD's financial policies is to provide the capacity to be an efficient intermediary of long-term funds borrowed from international capital markets to support development in the IBRD's borrowing countries. The maintenance of a strong AAA rating or its equivalent from the bond-rating services is critical to all shareholders, since it reflects the IBRD's outstanding financial strength and permits the institution to provide loans at lowest cost and to ensure continued access to capital markets.

The IBRD's AAA rating is underpinned by three factors: shareholder support for capital increases and access to their capital markets, the preferred-creditor status granted the IBRD by its borrowers, and the IBRD's prudent financial policies that keep risks well contained.

The IBRD accepts and manages the risk of lending to its developing member countries. That risk is assessed and managed at the country level and in aggregate. At the country level, the IBRD's lending levels are related explicitly to country creditworthiness and IBRD exposure. Creditworthiness is assessed in relation to a country's current and expected future ability to repay IBRD loans. At the aggregate level, the IBRD's overall country-portfolio risk is regularly reviewed by Bank staff, management, and the executive directors. The overall assessment of aggregate and country risk and their expected evolution are important factors in determining annual IBRD lending allocations and longer-term country-assistance strategies. They also help determine what levels of loan-loss provisions and reserves are required.

Market risks—currency, interest, and funding risk—are kept limited and are shared with borrowers.

Currency risk is limited by the IBRD's Articles of Agreement. The IBRD does not take currency risk on its borrowings; assets are held in the same currencies to match these liabilities. In addition, the IBRD's reserves and surplus are kept in the same currency composition as its outstanding loans. Interest risk is passed on to borrowers through the variable rate loans the IBRD makes. Funding risk (that is, the inability to gain access to sufficient funds to meet obligations at a particular time) is managed by borrowing medium term to long term and by carrying liquidity sufficient to meet 45 percent of the next three years' cash needs.

The lending rate on IBRD loans is based on the IBRD's own cost of borrowings. A spread of fifty basis points is added to this cost basis. This spread may be reduced by waivers that are annually decided by the executive directors in light of available net income.

The IBRD's net income is calculated net of expenses, which include loan-loss provisions. The IBRD's objective is to optimize, not maximize, net income so that reserves are adequate, while at the same time loan charges are kept low. Reserves are maintained to enable the IBRD to absorb potentially large but low-probability risks, such as a sizable unexpected increase in loan arrears, without resorting to a call on capital. A portion of net income is allocated annually in an amount sufficient to maintain the target level of reserves, currently set at a range of 13 percent to 14 percent of loans.

IBRD Financial Highlights

Financial highlights of the fiscal year ending June 30, 1994 included:
- disbursements to countries of $10.4 billion;
- borrowing the equivalent of $8.9 billion in twelve currencies, four after swaps; and
- net income of $1,051 million, well within the range that satisfies the IBRD's financial objectives.

In the first quarter of fiscal 1994, net income earned during fiscal 1993 was allocated as follows:
- $675 million to the general reserve, which, together with $1,090 million transferred from surplus to the general reserve, was intended to increase the IBRD's reserves-to-loan ratio at the end of fiscal 1994 to a minimum of 13 percent, excluding amounts allocated for prefunding of interest waivers;
- $215 million to the general reserve for prefunding of interest waivers to be granted in fiscal 1994;
- $100 million to the Debt-reduction Facility for IDA-only Countries; and
- $140 million to IDA.

Other funds transferred from surplus during the year included $325 million transferred to IDA and $50 million (from fiscal 1992 net income) to establish a trust fund for Gaza.

Financial Policies

Single-currency loans. During fiscal 1993, the IBRD began a $3 billion, two-year pilot program to offer eligible borrowers a choice of currencies as an alternative to the existing standard loan product, the targeted currency-pool loan. The IBRD offers single-currency loans in United States dollars, yen, deutsche mark, French francs, and pounds sterling, with an interest rate tied to six-month LIBOR in each loan currency (PIBOR in the case of French francs). By the end of fiscal 1994, a total of $1,715 million had been approved, involving nine loans to as many countries. Of that amount, $845 million was approved in fiscal 1994, involving five loans. All of these were United States dollar loans. At June 30, 1994, disbursements had begun on four single-currency loans. The IBRD will review the results of the pilot program during fiscal 1995.

Review of currency-pool targets. During fiscal 1994, the executive directors undertook an interim review of the target ratios for the composition of the currency pool that were established in January 1989. The objective of the 1989 policy was to achieve better predictability, balance, and understandability for borrowers by targeting the composition of their loan obligations within narrow tolerances. The executive directors affirmed that it is the intention of the IBRD to maintain at least 90 percent of the United States dollar equivalent value of the pool in targeted ratios of 1 United States dollar: 125 yen: 2 deutsche mark equivalent (comprised of deutsche mark, Swiss francs, and/or Netherlands guilders) until at least June 1996. At the end of the year, 97.7 percent of currency-pool loans were in the targeted currencies.

Accumulated provisions for loan losses. The level of loan-loss provisions is based on an assessment of the collectibility of loans in non-accrual status, together with an evaluation of collectibility risks in the remainder of the portfolio. For fiscal year 1994, loan-loss provisions were maintained at a level equal to 3 percent of total loans disbursed and outstanding plus the present value of guarantees for an amount equivalent to $3,324 million at the end of the fiscal year.

Loans

Disbursements. Gross disbursements by the IBRD to countries during fiscal 1994 were $10,447 million, down $2,495 million from fiscal 1993's total of $12,942 million. Net disbursements were negative, at -$731 million, down from $2,331 million in fiscal 1993. The decline in net disbursements is the result of the lower level of gross disbursements combined with a high level of prepayments, at $970 million, in fiscal 1994. Excluding prepayments, net disbursements declined $2,557 million to $239 million.

Lending rate. Under the IBRD's current semiannual variable lending-rate system, the interest rate was 7.43 percent for the first semester and 7.27 percent for the second semester of fiscal 1994. By comparison, the other variable lending rate—applicable to loans for which invitations to negotiate were sent before May 18, 1989, and not converted by borrowers to the new system—was 7.42 percent and 7.25 percent for the first and second semesters, respectively, of fiscal 1994. The difference between the rates is due to differences in allocations of borrowings to lending and/or to investments and to the weights applied to currency-specific costs.

The single-currency lending rates applicable in the second semester of 1994 (based on the IBRD's cost of six-month LIBOR-based funding in each loan currency (PIBOR in the case of French francs)) were 3.66 percent in United States dollars, 2.41 percent in yen, 5.91 percent in deutsche mark, 6.28 percent in French francs, and 5.72 percent in pounds sterling.

Interest waivers. During fiscal 1994, the IBRD waived twenty-five basis points of the semester interest rate on loans to all borrowers that had made all loan-service payments within thirty days of their due date. (Approximately 83 percent of the IBRD's total volume of outstanding loans is currently eligible for the interest-spread waiver.) This waiver was in addition to the continuation during the year of a waiver on part of the IBRD's commitment fee on undisbursed balances that resulted in a reduction of that fee from seventy-five to twenty-five basis points.

Loans in nonaccrual status. At the end of fiscal 1994, five member countries (Iraq, Liberia, Sudan, Syria, and Zaire), as well as two successor republics of the former Socialist Federal Republic of Yugoslavia (the Federal Republic of Yugoslavia (Serbia and Montenegro) and Bosnia-Herzegovina) were in nonaccrual status. Sudan and Zaire were new entrants to nonaccrual status in fiscal 1994, while the former Yugoslav Republic of Macedonia and Congo cleared all arrears on February 14, 1994 and on June 29, 1994, respectively. Moreover, Syria has been making periodic debt-service payments to the IBRD.

Liquid-assets Management

At the end of fiscal 1994, the IBRD's liquidity totaled $19 billion, or about 45 percent of anticipated net cash requirements over the next three fiscal years. At the end of fiscal 1993, liquidity amounted to $18.5 billion. The IBRD's primary objective in holding such liquidity is to ensure flexibility in its borrowings decisions should borrowing be adversely affected by temporary conditions in the capital markets.

The IBRD's liquid assets are invested exclusively in fixed-income markets and are actively traded. The attendant portfolio-management activities are fully supported by comprehensive risk-management and monitoring procedures covering both credit risk and interest-rate risk. Trading performance is measured daily against detailed benchmark portfolios.

Areas of continued enhancements in the management of the IBRD's liquid assets included the following areas: development of multiple trading approaches; integration of computer systems across trading, accounting, and control functions; and improvements in performance-measurement and risk-monitoring systems.

During fiscal 1994, the IBRD's financial return on its portfolio was 3.53 percent. The financial return on investments in fiscal 1993 was 6.07 percent. The portfolio continues to be managed in relation to a benchmark strategy of one-year duration. The low returns in fiscal 1994 reflect the combination of the absolute low level of short-term interest rates and capital losses due to the increase in rates since the middle of the year.

Borrowings and Liability Management

The objectives of the IBRD's borrowing and liability-management strategy are to ensure the long-term availability of funds to the IBRD for lending and liquidity and to minimize the costs of funds for the IBRD and its borrowers. The IBRD seeks to ensure the availability of funds by developing borrowing capacity in markets in advance of need and by diversifying its borrowings by currency, source, and maturity to provide maximum flexibility in funding. It also seeks to strengthen the continuing appeal of its securities by offering features that are tailored to satisfy investors' asset preferences and by positioning its securities advantageously in each capital market (for example, from a regulatory-tax and investment-classification perspective).

Within the framework of the currency composition of borrowings required to fund its lending products, the IBRD seeks to minimize the cost of borrowed funds by using, among other things, currency swaps to obtain cost savings compared with the cost of direct borrowings in target currencies; structured financings converted to conventional liabilities using over-the-counter financial derivatives; the use of short-term and variable rate instruments; and prepayments, market repurchases, and refinancings of higher-cost borrowings.

Medium-term and long-term (MLT) funding. During fiscal year 1994, the IBRD raised $8.9 billion through MLT borrowings in twelve currencies, including $7.8 billion of fixed rate borrowings and $1.1 billion of variable rate

Table 7-1. IBRD Borrowings, Fiscal Year 1994
(amounts in millions)

Type	Issue	Currency of issue		US-dollar equivalent[a]
Medium- and long-term public offerings				
Global	5.875% ten-year bonds, due 2003	DM	3,000	1,815.7
	4.5% seven-year bonds, due 2000	¥	225,000	2,114.3
	5.250% ten-year bonds, due 2003	US$	1,250	1,242.5
Eurobond market	5.5% three-year notes, due 1997	$A	100	67.4
	6.25% five-year bonds, due 1998	Can$	200	151.6
	6.25% five-year bonds, due 1998	Can$	150	111.9
	Ten-year structured notes, due 2004	DM	100	57.5
	9.45% ten-year notes, due 2003	Lit	300,000	192.7
	Five-year floating-rate notes, due 1998	Lit	150,000	96.2
	Seven-year structured notes, due 2001	¥	50,000	481.4
	Eight-year structured notes, due 2002	¥	2,000	19.3
	Three-year structured notes, due 1996	US$	100	100.0
	Two-year structured notes, due 1996	US$	100	101.0
	Seven-year structured notes, due 2001	Lit	200,000	126.7
Germany	Five-year structured notes, due 1999	DM	125	73.7
Greece	15.50% three-year notes, due 1997	Dr	15,000	61.4
Hong Kong	4.608% three-year bonds, due 1996	HK$	1,000	129.7
Japan	Zero-coupon bonds, due 1999	¥	100,000	832.2
Portugal	8.5% five-year bonds, due 1998	Esc	11,600	67.4
Spain	9.75% five-year bonds, due 1998	Ptas	10,000	75.0
United States	Four-year structured notes, due 1997	US$	25	25.0
	Two-year structured notes, due 1995	US$	10	10.0
	Two-year structured notes, due 1996	US$	10	10.0
Total medium- and long-term public offerings				7,962.6
Medium- and long-term placements with central banks and governments				
Germany	6.15% five-year note, due 1998	DM	250	145.3
	5.27% five-year note, due 1999	DM	250	143.1
International	4.00% two-year notes, due 1995	Sw F	189	132.8
Total medium- and long-term placements with central banks and governments				421.2
Medium- and long-term other placements				
Belgium	6.85% two-year loan, due 1995	BF	5,080	148.3
Switzerland	4.25% seven-year notes, due 2000	Sw F	300	200.8
	4.00% eight-year notes, due 2002	Sw F	250	174.7
Total medium- and long-term other placements				523.8
Total medium- and long-term borrowings, fiscal 1994				8,907.6
Short-term borrowings outstanding[b]				
Central bank facility[c]		US$	2,599	2,599.3
Discount notes		US$	560	560.0
Structured financings		US$	131	131.0
Structured financings		¥	2,000	20.2
Short-term borrowings outstanding as of June 30, 1994				3,310.5

a. Medium- and long-term borrowing amounts based on gross proceeds, expressed at exchange rates prevailing at the time of launch.
b. Maturing within one year.
c. These issues were placed with central banks, government agencies, and international organizations.

borrowings (see Table 7-1). After $1.1 billion of currency swaps and a notional par volume of $2.5 billion of interest-rate swaps, all of the year's borrowings, except for $193 million raised in United States dollars to fund single-currency loans and minor residuals in vehicle currencies, were fixed rate liabilities denominated in United States dollars, yen, deutsche mark, and Swiss francs. The average maturity of all this funding was 7.4 years, and the after-swap cost was 5.03 percent (see Table 7-2).

Noteworthy among the transactions in the IBRD's core currencies during the past year was the IBRD's first deutsche mark global

Table 7-2. IBRD Borrowings, after Swaps, Fiscal Year 1994
(amounts in millions of US dollars equivalent)

Item	Before swaps Amount	%	Maturity (years)	Currency swaps (amount)	After swaps Amount	%	Maturity (years)	Cost (%)
Medium- and long-term borrowings								
U.S. dollars	1,488.5	17	7.9	256.4	1,744.9	20	7.9	5.18
Japanese yen	3,447.2	39	6.6	—	3,447.2	39	6.6	4.26
Deutsche mark	2,235.3	25	8.5	811.4	3,046.7	34	8.5	5.91
Swiss francs	508.3	6	6.0	—	508.3	6	6.0	4.02
Others[a]	1,228.3	14	5.0	(1,067.9)	160.4	2	2.3	6.88
Total	8,907.6	100	7.4		8,907.6	100	7.4	5.03[b]
Short-term borrowings outstanding								
Central bank facility (U.S. dollars)	2,599.3	79	0.5					5.36
Discount notes (U.S. dollars)	560.0	17	0.4					3.60
Structured financings:								
U.S. dollars	131.0	4	0.3					3.14
Japanese yen	20.2	1	0.7					1.33
Total as of June 30, 1994[c]	3,310.5	100	0.6					4.95

— Zero.

NOTE: Details may not add to totals because of rounding.

a. Represents borrowings in Australian dollars, Belgian francs, Canadian dollars, Greek drachma, Hong Kong dollars, Italian lire, Portuguese escudos, and Spanish pesetas. After-swap figures include a Belgian franc borrowing for $148 million equivalent which was hedged into Netherlands guilders with an existing currency swap.

b. Excludes the cost of $193 million of single-currency loan funding, which was held at floating rates as of June 30, 1994.

c. Short-term borrowings outstanding on June 30, 1993 totaled $3,789 million.

Box 7-1. IDA's Ninth Replenishment Period (Fiscal 1991–93)

The three-year period of IDA's ninth replenishment (IDA-9)—July 1, 1990 to June 30, 1993— was marked by a difficult international economic environment characterized by a slowdown in the growth of world trade, recession in the industrialized world, a plunge in real prices for nonoil commodities, and a stagnation in flows of official development assistance.

Dramatic political changes also took place. The end of the Cold War saw new IDA borrowers, such as Albania, Belarus, and Mongolia, all bringing with them far-reaching agendas for transformation of their countries into market economies. Movement toward political democracy gave impetus to reform in several countries but distracted attention from reform programs in others. The economic impact of the 1991 Gulf War, although shorter and less severe than initially feared, called for (and subsequently received) a response from the association that could not have been anticipated at the replenishment's outset.

During the three-year period, the association provided funding to sixty countries. Lending commitments totaled SDR13.7 billion, an increase of 20 percent in nominal terms over the previous three-year period.[1]

African countries received 46 percent of total IDA-9 commitments, as did the countries of South Asia and East Asia together. Adjustment lending accounted for about 22 percent of total lending, while lending for education; population, health, and nutrition; and water supply and sanitation increased sharply, from 20 percent of the total in IDA-8 to 31 percent.

At the time of the agreement, reached on December 14, 1989, on a ninth replenishment of IDA's resources, donor-country negotiators (IDA deputies) identified three program areas deserving of the highest priority during the ninth replenishment period: poverty reduction, support for sound macroeconomic and sectoral policies, and the environment. The deputies also requested that IDA's executive directors review on an annual basis how well those priorities were being pursued. According to the final review of IDA's operations and policies during the IDA-9 period, a subject of discussion by the executive board in fiscal 1994, substantial progress was made in each program area.

New and refined instruments for directly reaching the poor—poverty assessments that analyze country poverty issues and focus the policy dialogue on poverty-reduction strategies; poverty-focused actions in adjustment lending; and poverty-targeted investment credits—were either initiated during the IDA-9 period or were in an early phase of implementation. By the end of the three-year period in question, formal poverty assessments had been completed for sixteen IDA countries, adjustment operations increasingly contained measures to mitigate poverty, and 40 percent of the association's investment commitments during the final two years of the replenishment period were targeted directly at the poor.

bond for DM3 billion. The IBRD raised $2.1 billion through structured financing transactions and vehicle-currency bond issues, including $61 million through the IBRD's first issue in Greek drachma.

During the past fiscal year, the IBRD called an aggregate volume of $1.0 billion of borrowings for prepayment, including borrowings in yen, deutsche mark, European Currency Units, Belgian francs, and Luxembourg francs. In addition, it redeemed $0.2 billion of United States dollar and yen borrowings through market repurchases.

At the end of the fiscal year, MLT borrowings outstanding amounted to $95.6 billion, or 97 percent of total debt outstanding. As of June 30, 1994, the average maturity of total MLT debt was 6.0 years, and its average cost, after swaps, was 6.72 percent.

Short-term funding. As of June 30, 1994, short-term borrowings outstanding were $3.3 billion, down $0.5 billion compared with the level of June 30, 1993. Short-term borrowings outstanding at June 30 comprised $2.6 billion from official sources through the IBRD's central bank facility and $0.7 billion from market borrowings in United States dollars and yen,

including $151 million raised through short-term structured financings. The cost of these borrowings was 4.95 percent compared with 3.58 percent at the end of fiscal 1993.

On June 30, 1994, short-term and variable rate funding aggregated $3.5 billion equivalent, representing about 3 percent of total outstanding debt.

Capital

On June 30, 1994, the total subscribed capital of the IBRD was $170.0 billion, or 92 percent of authorized capital of $184 billion. During fiscal year 1994, subscriptions to the $74.8 billion general capital increase (GCI), approved in April 1988, continued on schedule. Eighteen countries subscribed an aggregate $4.4 billion. A total of 555,328 GCI shares ($67 billion, or 84 percent of total allocations, including additional GCI shares allocated to new members that joined the IBRD after April 1988) have been subscribed. At the end of fiscal 1994, the permissible increase of net disbursements ("headroom") was $79.9 billion, or 42.2 percent of the IBRD's lending limit.

In 1988, the executive directors agreed to review the adequacy of the IBRD's capital every

---

More emphasis was placed on key groups and services. The role of women was given significantly greater recognition, and gender issues were incorporated more frequently into project design. About half of all IDA-supported projects during fiscal 1991–93 included components that addressed the specific needs of women. Greater efforts were also made to encourage the participation of beneficiaries in project design and implementation. Support for the provision of basic social services, including basic education, health, and family planning, increased substantially.

In the second program area—support for sound macroeconomic and sectoral policies—progress was made in most adjusting countries, notwithstanding the difficulties involved. Among some seventeen countries that continued to receive adjustment assistance in the IDA-9 period, reforms focused increasingly on rationalizing the public sector (by bringing government expenditures in line with available resources and capacities, streamlining the civil service, and restructuring public enterprises) and on enabling the private sector to respond to improved incentives. Nearly 120 credits during the IDA-9 period contained components aimed at improving the business climate, while a quarter of all investment lending supported infrastructural development. New reform programs were supported in an additional ten countries.

To help protect the environment, the foundation was laid during IDA-9 for comprehensive

support for environmentally sustainable development in all countries. National environmental action plans (NEAPs)—the most important tool for developing a country's environmental strategy— were completed by twenty-two IDA recipient governments and, by the end of the replenishment period, were well under way for almost all of the other active IDA borrowers. Once completed, the findings of a NEAP are factored into country priorities and the plans of IDA and other donors for projects, sector studies, and the policy dialogue.

IDA's policies in environmentally sensitive sectors, such as forestry and agriculture, energy, and water-resource management, were revamped to ensure that they promote environmental objectives in IDA's policy dialogue with governments and in the design of IDA's lending program. In addition, new environmental-assessment procedures were introduced to ensure that the views of people affected by the impact of projects on the environment would be taken into account. Greater emphasis was also placed on active participation at the national and community levels in both the preparation and implementation of environmental plans and programs.

---

[1] IDA gross disbursements during the period fiscal 1991–93 from the total universe of IDA credits—not just those approved during the IDA-9 period—totaled $14,261 million (of which $6,196 million was directed towards the Africa region and $5,008 million towards the countries of South Asia).

three years. In the second triennial review (June 1994), they agreed with the conclusions of a management report—that the IBRD's capital is expected to remain adequate to support the projected range of lending programs for the rest of the decade. They also agreed that the IBRD's current repayment options—first endorsed in March 1991—continue unchanged, thereby providing borrowing member countries greater flexibility in choosing repayment terms that best serve their particular country or project needs.

Reserves. On June 30, 1994, reserves amounted to $14.8 billion, and the reserves-to-loan ratio stood at 13.9 percent.

IDA Finances

In October 1993, the executive directors discussed a report on the use of resources during the IDA-9 period—fiscal years 1991–93—took note of it, and expressed their satisfaction with the use of resources during the period (see Box 7-1 for details).

IDA's commitment authority. On December 17, 1993, the tenth replenishment resolution (IDA-10) became effective. As of June 30, 1994, the association had received notifications of participation from Australia, Austria, Brazil, Canada, the Czech Republic, Denmark, Finland, France, Germany, Hungary, Iceland, Ireland, Japan, the Republic of Korea, Luxembourg, Mexico, the Netherlands, New Zealand, Norway, Poland, Saudi Arabia, South Africa, Sweden, Switzerland, Turkey, the United Kingdom, and the United States.

During the course of the year, the requests of Spain and Portugal to change their membership status in the association from Part II to Part I members were approved. In addition to technical differences between Part I and Part II memberships, Part I members are expected to make significant contributions to each IDA replenishment, commensurate with their economic standing.

The commitment period for IDA-10 began on July 1, 1993. As of June 30, 1994, available contributions to IDA-10 totaled SDR3,700 million. In addition, the executive directors approved advance commitment authority from future reflows amounting to SDR800 million annually for the period fiscal 1994–96 and further annual allocations in fiscal 1994 of SDR190 million for the "Fifth Dimension" program.[1] Other resources that were made available during the fiscal year included the transfer from the IBRD's surplus account totaling SDR333 million and additional resources amounting to SDR200 million as a result of a change in IDA's liquidity policy. The total available resources for the IDA-10 period during fiscal 1994 amounted, therefore, to SDR5,223 million.

Against these resources, the association made IDA-10 commitments of SDR4,734 million. Of this amount, 41 percent went to Africa, 21 percent to East Asia and the Pacific, 29 percent to South Asia, 3 percent to Europe and Central Asia, 2 percent to the Middle East and North Africa, and 5 percent to Latin America and the Caribbean. The fiscal 1994 lending program also reflected the approval of SDR450 million in additional lending to the countries of the CFA Zone.

IDA's commitment fee. For each fiscal year, the level of commitment fee is set by the executive directors based on an annual review of IDA's financial position. The commitment fee for fiscal 1995 was set at 0 percent for all IDA credits. IDA's commitment fee was 0 percent from fiscal 1989 through fiscal 1994.

---

[1] The "Fifth Dimension" program provides supplementary IDA resources to those IDA-only countries that have outstanding debt to the IBRD, are current in their debt-service payments to both the IBRD and IDA, and have in place IDA-supported adjustment operations. Such supplementary resources, therefore, take into account debt impact arising from IBRD interest payments.

Financial Statements of the International Bank for Reconstruction and Development

Balance Sheet

June 30, 1994 and June 30, 1993
Expressed in millions of U.S. dollars

	1994	1993
Assets		
DUE FROM BANKS		
Unrestricted currencies	$ 216	$ 68
Currencies subject to restrictions—Note A	544	571
	760	639
INVESTMENTS—Notes C and D		
Obligations of governments and other official entities	9,703	10,407
Time deposits and other obligations of banks and other financial institutions	11,622	9,392
	21,325	19,799
SECURITIES PURCHASED UNDER RESALE AGREEMENTS—Note C	577	567
NONNEGOTIABLE, NONINTEREST-BEARING DEMAND OBLIGATIONS ON ACCOUNT OF SUBSCRIBED CAPITAL (subject to restrictions—Note A)	1,507	1,547
AMOUNTS REQUIRED TO MAINTAIN VALUE OF CURRENCY HOLDINGS—Note A		
Amounts receivable	1,133	1,210
Amounts deferred	542	480
	1,675	1,690
OTHER RECEIVABLES		
Net receivables from currency swaps—Notes C and D	513	775
Receivables from investment securities sold	2,389	1,526
Accrued income on loans	2,294	2,248
Accrued interest on investments	106	123
	5,302	4,672
LOANS OUTSTANDING		
(see Summary Statement of Loans, Notes B and C)		
Total loans	164,300	158,879
Less loans approved but not yet effective	11,349	10,964
Less undisbursed balance of effective loans	43,660	43,464
	109,291	104,451
OTHER ASSETS		
Unamortized issuance costs of borrowings	494	501
Miscellaneous	1,245	1,135
	1,739	1,636
Total assets	$142,176	$135,001

	1994	1993
Liabilities		
BORROWINGS (see Summary Statement of Borrowings, Notes C and D)		
Short-term	$ 3,304	$ 3,775
Medium- and long-term	95,615	92,488
	98,919	96,263
SECURITIES SOLD UNDER AGREEMENTS TO REPURCHASE AND PAYABLE FOR CASH COLLATERAL RECEIVED	1,927	1,772
AMOUNTS REQUIRED TO MAINTAIN VALUE OF CURRENCY HOLDINGS—Note A		
Amounts payable	6	4
Amounts deferred	874	754
	880	758
OTHER LIABILITIES		
Accrued charges on borrowings	2,725	2,750
Net payables for currency swaps—Notes C and D	2,623	1,972
Payables for investment securities purchased	3,381	1,715
Due to the International Development Association and facilities administered by the International Development Association—Note E	1,204	1,013
Accounts payable and other liabilities	579	485
	10,512	7,935
ACCUMULATED PROVISION FOR LOAN LOSSES—Note B	3,324	3,150
Total liabilities	115,562	109,878
Equity		
CAPITAL STOCK (see Statement of Subscriptions to Capital Stock and Voting Power and Note A) Authorized capital (1,525,248 shares—June 30, 1994; 1,525,659 shares—June 30, 1993)		
Subscribed capital (1,409,235 shares—June 30, 1994; 1,372,648 shares—June 30, 1993)	170,003	165,589
Less uncalled portion of subscriptions	159,338	155,058
	10,665	10,531
PAYMENTS ON ACCOUNT OF PENDING SUBSCRIPTIONS—Note A	87	19
RETAINED EARNINGS (see Statement of Changes in Retained Earnings and Note E)	14,468	14,032
CUMULATIVE TRANSLATION ADJUSTMENT (see Statement of Changes in Cumulative Translation Adjustment)	1,394	541
Total equity	26,614	25,123
Total liabilities and equity	$142,176	$135,001

The Notes to Financial Statements are an integral part of these Statements.

Statement of Income

For the fiscal years ended June 30, 1994 and June 30, 1993
Expressed in millions of U.S. dollars

	1994	1993
Income		
Income from loans—Note B		
Interest	$7,707	$7,957
Commitment charges	115	124
Income from investments—Note C		
Interest	841	1,091
Securities: Net gains/(losses)		
Realized	(33)	167
Unrealized	(127)	19
Income from securities purchased under resale agreements	86	84
Other income	11	9
Total income	8,600	9,451
Expenses		
Borrowing expenses		
Interest on borrowings—Note C	6,549	6,654
Prepayment costs	31	108
Amortization of issuance costs and other borrowing costs	76	109
Interest on securities sold under agreements to repurchase and payable for cash collateral received	46	81
Administrative expenses—Notes F, G and H	731	679
Provision for loan losses—Note B	—	578
Other expenses	6	6
Total expenses	7,439	8,215
Operating Income	1,161	1,236
Less contributions to special programs—Note F	110	106
Net Income	$1,051	$1,130

Statement of Changes in Retained Earnings

For the fiscal years ended June 30, 1994 and June 30, 1993
Expressed in millions of U.S. dollars

	1994	1993
Retained earnings at beginning of the fiscal year	$14,032	$13,202
Transfer to International Development Association—Note E	(465)	(300)
Transfer to Debt Reduction Facility for IDA-Only Countries—Note E	(100)	—
Transfer to Trust Fund for Gaza—Note E	(50)	—
Net income for the fiscal year	1,051	1,130
Retained earnings at end of the fiscal year	$14,468	$14,032

Statement of Changes in Cumulative Translation Adjustment

For the fiscal years ended June 30, 1994 and June 30, 1993
Expressed in millions of U.S. dollars

	1994	1993
Cumulative translation adjustment at beginning of the fiscal year	$ 541	$378
Translation adjustments for the fiscal year	853	163
Cumulative translation adjustment at end of the fiscal year	$1,394	$541

The Notes to Financial Statements are an integral part of these Statements.

Statement of Cash Flows

For the fiscal years ended June 30, 1994 and June 30, 1993
Expressed in millions of U.S. dollars

	1994	1993
Cash flows from lending and development activities		
Loan disbursements	$(10,502)	$(13,077)
Loan principal repayments	10,350	10,186
Loan principal prepayments	970	460
Payments to International Development Association	(452)	(303)
Payments to Debt Reduction Facility for IDA-Only Countries	(23)	(29)
Net cash provided by (used) in lending and development activities	343	(2,763)
Cash flows from financing activities		
Medium- and long-term borrowings		
New issues	8,178	12,445
Retirements	(9,121)	(12,282)
Net cash flows from short-term borrowings	(504)	(1,652)
Net cash flows from currency swaps	(176)	(357)
Net cash flows from capital transactions	199	344
Net cash flows for financing activities	(1,424)	(1,502)
Cash flows from operating activities		
Net income	1,051	1,130
Adjustments to reconcile net income to net cash provided by operating activities		
Depreciation and amortization	197	244
Provision for loan losses	—	578
Changes in assets and liabilities		
Decrease in accrued income on loans and investments	92	110
Increase in miscellaneous assets	(24)	(210)
Decrease in accrued charges on borrowings	(180)	(174)
Increase in accounts payable and other liabilities	85	8
Net cash provided by operating activities	1,221	1,686
Effect of exchange rate changes on unrestricted cash and liquid investments	586	188
Net increase (decrease) in unrestricted cash and liquid investments	726	(2,391)
Unrestricted cash and liquid investments at beginning of the fiscal year	18,473	20,864
Unrestricted cash and liquid investments at end of the fiscal year	$ 19,199	$ 18,473
Composed of		
Investments	$ 21,325	19,799
Unrestricted currencies	216	68
Net payable for investment securities purchased/sold	(992)	(189)
Net payable for securities purchased/sold under resale/repurchase agreements and payable for		
cash collateral received	(1,350)	(1,205)
	$ 19,199	$ 18,473
Supplemental disclosure		
Increase resulting from exchange rate fluctuations		
Loans outstanding	$ 5,658	$ 1,210
Borrowings	3,952	525
Net payable for currency swaps	1,084	992

The Notes to Financial Statements are an integral part of these Statements.

Summary Statement of Loans

June 30, 1994
Expressed in millions of U.S. dollars

Borrower or guarantor	Total loans	Loans approved but not yet effective[1]	Undisbursed loans[2]	Loans outstanding[3]	Percentage of total loans outstanding
Algeria	$ 2,931	$ 140	$1,140	$ 1,651	1.51
Argentina	5,696	509	1,298	3,889	3.56
Armenia	12	—	11	1	*
Australia[4]	*	—	—	*	*
Bahamas, The	22	—	4	18	0.02
Bangladesh	60	—	—	60	0.05
Barbados	48	8	20	20	0.02
Belarus	172	42	91	39	0.04
Belize	49	—	25	24	0.02
Bolivia	128	—	—	128	0.12
Bosnia-Herzegovina/Federal Republic of Yugoslavia[5]	1,673	—	21	1,652	1.51
Botswana	128	—	4	124	0.11
Brazil	11,904	496	4,867	6,541	5.98
Bulgaria	612	148	216	248	0.23
Cameroon	888	—	165	723	0.66
Chile	2,491	—	527	1,964	1.80
China	11,283	2,145	3,829	5,309	4.86
Colombia	3,996	179	1,097	2,720	2.49
Congo	143	16	4	123	0.11
Costa Rica	568	148	79	341	0.31
Côte d'Ivoire[6]	1,899	—	124	1,775	1.62
Croatia	245	128	18	99	0.09
Cyprus	153	—	90	63	0.06
Czech Republic	649	—	308	341	0.31
Dominican Republic	368	—	93	275	0.25
Ecuador	1,303	35	444	824	0.75
Egypt, Arab Republic of	2,081	184	454	1,443	1.32
El Salvador	369	—	100	269	0.25
Estonia	82	50	4	28	0.03
Ethiopia	4	—	—	4	*
Fiji	74	—	31	43	0.04
Gabon	140	30	24	86	0.08
Ghana	76	—	—	76	0.07
Greece	1	—	—	1	*
Guatemala	319	—	123	196	0.18
Guyana	42	—	—	42	0.04
Honduras	504	—	12	492	0.45
Hungary	3,167	—	993	2,174	1.99
Iceland	4	—	—	4	*
India	14,325	94	4,109	10,122	9.26
Indonesia	17,334	1,054	3,988	12,292	11.24
Iran, Islamic Republic of	867	—	672	195	0.18
Iraq	48	—	—	48	0.04
Jamaica	837	48	169	620	0.57
Jordan	812	20	155	637	0.58
Kazakhstan	279	56	101	122	0.11
Kenya[7]	551	—	—	551	0.50
Korea, Republic of	3,247	—	802	2,445	2.24
Kenya, Tanzania and Uganda[8]	*	—	—	*	*
Latvia	71	—	35	36	0.03
Lebanon	269	77	151	41	0.04
Lesotho	112	—	77	35	0.03
Liberia	151	—	—	151	0.14
Lithuania	88	26	14	48	0.04
Macedonia, former Yugoslav Republic of	105	—	3	102	0.09

Borrower or guarantor	Total loans	Loans approved but not yet effective[1]	Undisbursed loans[2]	Loans outstanding[3]	Percentage of total loans outstanding
Madagascar	$ 16	$ —	$ —	$ 16	0.01
Malawi	67	—	—	67	0.06
Malaysia	1,501	70	348	1,083	0.99
Mauritania	14	—	—	14	0.01
Mauritius	224	8	61	155	0.14
Mexico	17,287	1,530	2,716	13,041	11.93
Moldova	89	—	10	79	0.07
Morocco	5,440	312	1,368	3,760	3.44
Nicaragua	84	—	—	84	0.08
Nigeria	4,630	—	1,256	3,374	3.09
Oman	49	—	6	43	0.04
Pakistan	4,106	230	1,079	2,797	2.56
Panama	349	—	118	231	0.21
Papua New Guinea[4]	410	11	119	280	0.26
Paraguay	343	115	49	179	0.16
Peru	2,024	184	404	1,436	1.31
Philippines	6,711	478	1,323	4,910	4.49
Poland	3,593	—	2,302	1,291	1.18
Portugal	177	—	48	129	0.12
Romania	1,381	401	437	543	0.50
Russia	2,919	1,590	713	616	0.56
St. Kitts and Nevis	1	—	1	*	*
St. Lucia	3	—	2	1	*
St. Vincent and the Grenadines	1	—	1	*	*
Senegal	49	—	—	49	0.05
Seychelles	9	—	4	5	*
Sierra Leone	3	—	—	3	*
Slovak Republic	296	—	118	178	0.16
Slovenia	255	—	106	149	0.14
Sri Lanka	57	—	—	57	0.05
Sudan	6	—	—	6	0.01
Swaziland	23	—	—	23	0.02
Syrian Arab Republic	418	—	—	418	0.38
Tanzania	128	—	—	128	0.12
Thailand	2,078	—	315	1,763	1.61
Trinidad and Tobago	99	—	39	60	0.05
Tunisia	2,357	116	574	1,667	1.53
Turkey	7,797	100	2,270	5,427	4.97
Uganda	13	—	—	13	0.01
Ukraine	27	—	26	1	*
Uruguay	779	67	165	547	0.50
Uzbekistan	22	—	21	1	*
Venezuela	2,741	394	701	1,646	1.51
Zaire	88	—	—	88	0.08
Zambia	232	—	—	232	0.21
Zimbabwe	803	90	155	558	0.51
Subtotal Members	163,079	11,329	43,347	108,403	99.19
Caribbean Development Bank[9]	62	20	17	25	0.02
International Finance Corporation	1,159	—	296	863	0.79
Total—June 30, 1994	$164,300	$11,349	$43,660	$109,291	100.00
Total—June 30, 1993	$158,879	$10,964	$43,464	$104,451	

* Indicates amounts less than $0.5 million or 0.005 percent.

(continued)

Summary Statement of Loans   (continued)

June 30, 1994
Expressed in millions of U.S. dollars

NOTES

1. Loans totaling $5,196 million ($5,996 million—June 30, 1993) have been approved by the IBRD but the related agreements have not been signed. Loan agreements totaling $6,153 million ($4,968 million—June 30, 1993) have been signed, but the loans do not become effective and disbursements thereunder do not start until the borrowers and guarantors, if any, take certain actions and furnish certain documents to the IBRD.

2. Of the undisbursed balance, the IBRD has entered into irrevocable commitments to disburse $1,861 million ($1,837 million—June 30, 1993).

3. Total loans outstanding as of June 30, 1994 includes $89,588 million ($80,832 million—June 30, 1993) at variable interest rates and $19,703 million ($23,619 million—June 30, 1993) at fixed interest rates.

4. In some instances loans were made, with the guarantee of a member, in countries which at the time were included in that member's territories but which subsequently became independent and separate members of the IBRD. Liabilities for these loans are shown under the name of the original member (whose guarantee continues unaffected). Loans with outstanding balances equivalent to $0.4 million ($1 million—June 30, 1993) are shown under Australia, the guarantor, but represent obligations of Papua New Guinea.

5. See Notes to Financial Statements—Notes A and B.

6. One loan with an outstanding balance equivalent to $1 million ($3 million—June 30, 1993) is shown under Côte d'Ivoire (Guarantor) but is also partially guaranteed by Burkina Faso.

7. Includes portions of loans made to corporations of the former East African Community.

8. Members are jointly and severally liable.

9. These loans are for the benefit of the Bahamas, Barbados, Grenada, Guyana, Jamaica, Trinidad and Tobago, and territories of the United Kingdom (Associated States and Dependencies) in the Caribbean Region, who are severally liable as guarantors to the extent of subloans made in their territories.

Summary of Currencies Repayable on Loans Disbursed and Outstanding

Currency	1994	1993	Currency	1994	1993
Austrian schillings	$ 189	$ 175	Luxembourg francs	$ 35	$ 63
Belgian francs	235	220	Malaysian ringgits	41	42
Canadian dollars	164	178	Netherlands guilders	2,701	2,808
Danish kroner	75	71	Norwegian kroner	65	62
Deutsche mark	26,142	23,412	Portuguese escudos	22	21
European currency units	17	19	Pounds sterling	258	245
Finnish markkaa	48	44	Saudi Arabian riyals	91	91
French francs	783	732	South African rand	41	42
Indian rupees	26	26	Spanish pesetas	116	116
Irish pounds	28	24	Swedish kronor	72	73
Italian lire	183	185	Swiss francs	11,855	12,235
Japanese yen	37,175	35,190	United States dollars	28,753	28,200
Kuwaiti dinars	154	151	Other currencies	22	26
			Loans outstanding	$109,291	$104,451

Maturity Structure of Loans Outstanding

Period	
July 1, 1994 through June 30, 1995	$ 12,278
July 1, 1995 through June 30, 1996	11,638
July 1, 1996 through June 30, 1997	11,893
July 1, 1997 through June 30, 1998	11,863
July 1, 1998 through June 30, 1999	11,245
July 1, 1999 through June 30, 2004	36,194
July 1, 2004 through June 30, 2009	12,947
July 1, 2009 through June 30, 2014	1,233
Total	$109,291

The Notes to Financial Statements are an integral part of these Statements.

Summary Statement of Borrowings

June 30, 1994 and June 30, 1993
Expressed in millions of U.S. dollars

Medium- and Long-term Borrowings and Swaps

	Medium- and long-term borrowings			Swap agreements[a]			Net currency obligations	
	Principal outstanding[b]		Weighted average cost (%)	Currency swap payables (receivables)		Weighted average cost (return) (%)		
	1994	1993	1994	1994	1993	1994	1994	1993
Australian dollars	$ 504	$ 498	13.15	$ (505)	$ (503)	(13.17)	$ (1)[g]	$ (5)
Austrian schillings	295	274	7.89	(73)	(68)	(8.44)	222	206
Belgian francs	523	483	7.39	(471)	(434)	(8.75)	52	49
Canadian dollars	1,745[d]	1,718[d]	9.05	(1,548)	(1,584)	(8.76)[c]	197	134
Danish kroner	48	122	10.30	(47)	(121)	(10.31)	1	1
Deutsche mark	11,111[d]	9,127[d]	7.05	11,848	10,129		22,959	19,207
					(49)	7.25[c]		
European currency units	2,111[d]	2,431[d]	7.25	(1,953)	(2,120)	(7.25)	158	311
Finnish markkaa	114	209	9.68	(112)	(206)	(9.70)	2	3
French francs	1,421	1,337	9.24	(857)	(807)	(9.09)[c]	564	530
Greek drachmas	63	—	15.22	(62)	—	(15.22)	1	—
Hong Kong dollars	401	271	7.84	(400)	(267)	(7.85)	1	4
Irish pounds	61	—	7.75	(60)	—	(7.75)	1	—
Italian lire	3,506[d]	3,310[d]	10.74	(3,490)	(3,298)	(10.70)[c]	16	12
Japanese yen	35,617[d]	34,173[d]	5.45	549	721	11.83[c]	34,581	33,009
				(1,585)	(1,885)	(7.41)[c]		
Kuwaiti dinars	102	99	7.65	—	—		102	99
Luxembourg francs	92	142	8.26	(60)	(84)	(8.39)	32	58
Netherlands guilders	3,087	3,184	7.35	559	584	6.80	2,251	2,497
				(1,395)	(1,271)	(7.70)		
New Zealand dollars	148	175	12.40	(148)	(174)	(12.40)	—	1
Norwegian kroner	36	34	9.55	—	—		36	34
Portuguese escudos	267	195	10.78	(264)	(194)	(10.80)	3	1
Pounds sterling	2,797[d]	2,692[d]	9.87	(1,415)	(1,381)	(9.18)[c]	1,382	1,311
Spanish pesetas	1,001	1,077	11.67	(987)	(1,064)	(11.67)	14	13
Swedish kronor	118	279	11.42	(118)	(278)	(11.43)	—	1
Swiss francs	5,758	5,692	6.08	4,442	4,680	5.40[c]	10,200	10,372
United States dollars	24,713[d,e]	25,013[d,e]	8.03	2,934	4,030	8.35[c]	24,975[g]	25,885
				(2,672)	(3,158)	(7.51)[c]		
Principal at face value	95,639	92,535	7.08[f]					
Plus net unamortized (discounts) premiums	(24)	(47)						
Total	$95,615	$92,488						

a. See Notes to Financial Statements—Note C.

b. Includes zero-coupon borrowings which have been recorded at their discounted values. The aggregate face amounts and discounted values of these borrowings at June 30, 1994 and June 30, 1993 are:

In millions of U.S.-dollar equivalents Currency	Aggregate face amount		Discounted value	
	1994	1993	1994	1993
Canadian dollars	$ 145	$ 156	$120	$117
Deutsche mark	1,260	1,169	319	278
Italian lire	64	64	51	47
Swiss francs	973	858	253	212
United States dollars	2,874	2,969	572	608

c. Includes income and expense from interest rate swaps. At June 30, 1994 and June 30, 1993, the IBRD has entered into interest rate swap agreements with respect to notional principal amounts as follows:

In millions Currency	Currency amount		U.S.-dollar equivalent	
	1994	1993	1994	1993
Canadian dollars	149	149	$ 108	$ 117
Deutsche mark	14,991	13,569	9,442	7,932
French francs	984	984	182	171
Italian lire	200,000	—	127	—
Japanese yen	152,350	97,500	1,522	922
Pounds sterling	100	100	155	149
Swedish kronor	—	300	—	38
Swiss francs	1,124	1,124	841	742
United States dollars	3,681	4,521	3,681	4,521

(continued)

Summary Statement of Borrowings   *(continued)*

June 30, 1994 and June 30, 1993
Expressed in millions of U.S. dollars

As of June 30, 1994 and June 30, 1993, 95 percent of the above notional principal amounts of these interest rate swap agreements are from floating rates into fixed rates.

d. Includes the following variable interest rate borrowings at June 30, 1994 and June 30, 1993, which through swaps have been transformed into the financial equivalent of fixed rate borrowings:

In millions

	Currency amount		U.S.-dollar equivalent	
Currency	1994	1993	1994	1993
Canadian dollars	100	100	$ 72	$ 78
Deutsche mark	425	200	268	117
European currency units	640	640	774	734
Italian lire	550,000	200,000	351	129
Japanese yen	149,500	97,500	1,494	922
Pounds sterling	25	25	39	37
United States dollars	1,602	1,377	1,602	1,377

e. Includes $175 million ($173 million—June 30, 1993) borrowed from the Interest Subsidy Fund. The Interest Subsidy Fund, which obtained its resources from voluntary contributions from member governments, was established to subsidize the interest payments to the IBRD on selected loans.

f. The weighted average cost of medium- and long-term borrowings outstanding at June 30, 1994, after adjustment for swap activities, was 6.72 percent (6.90 percent—June 30, 1993).

g. Includes borrowings of $125 million of United States dollars and $69 million of Australian dollar equivalent for which effective interest rate has not yet been fixed. These transactions are allocated to single currency loans.

Maturity Structure of Medium- and Long-term Borrowings

Period

July 1, 1994 through June 30, 1995	$10,674
July 1, 1995 through June 30, 1996	9,527
July 1, 1996 through June 30, 1997	12,685
July 1, 1997 through June 30, 1998	13,225
July 1, 1998 through June 30, 1999	7,328
July 1, 1999 through June 30, 2004	31,663
July 1, 2004 through June 30, 2009	3,182
July 1, 2009 through June 30, 2014	2,029
July 1, 2014 through June 30, 2019	3,591
July 1, 2019 through June 30, 2024	1,400
Thereafter	335
Total	$95,639

Short-term Borrowings

	Principal outstanding		Weighted average cost (%)
	1994	1993	1994
Short-term Notes (U.S. dollars)*			
Principal outstanding at face value	$ 691	$1,306	
Net unamortized discounts and premiums	(8)	(13)	
Subtotal	683	1,293	3.49
Short-term Notes (Japanese yen)*	21	—	1.35
Central Bank Facility (U.S. dollars)	2,600	2,482	5.36
Total	$3,304	$3,775	4.94

Note:
* Includes interest rate swap agreements with respect to notional principal amounts of $262 million of United States dollars and $21 million equivalent of Japanese yen.

The Notes to Financial Statements are an integral part of these Statements.

Statement of Subscriptions to Capital Stock and Voting Power

June 30, 1994
Expressed in millions of U.S. dollars

Member	Subscriptions					Voting power	
	Shares	Percentage of total	Total amounts	Amounts paid in (Note A)	Amounts subject to call (Note A)	Number of votes	Percentage of total
Afghanistan	300	0.02	$ 36	$ 3.6	$ 33	550	0.04
Albania	830	0.06	100	3.6	97	1,080	0.07
Algeria	9,252	0.66	1,116	67.1	1,049	9,502	0.65
Angola	2,676	0.19	323	17.5	305	2,926	0.20
Antigua and Barbuda	292	0.02	35	0.4	35	542	0.04
Argentina	10,052	0.71	1,213	103.8	1,109	10,302	0.71
Armenia	1,139	0.08	137	5.9	131	1,389	0.10
Australia	21,610	1.53	2,607	171.4	2,435	21,860	1.50
Austria	11,063	0.79	1,335	80.7	1,254	11,313	0.78
Azerbaijan	924	0.07	111	7.1	104	1,174	0.08
Bahamas, The	1,071	0.08	129	5.4	124	1,321	0.09
Bahrain	1,103	0.08	133	5.7	127	1,353	0.09
Bangladesh	4,854	0.34	586	33.9	552	5,104	0.35
Barbados	948	0.07	114	4.5	110	1,198	0.08
Belarus	1,865	0.13	225	17.0	208	2,115	0.15
Belgium	28,983	2.06	3,496	215.8	3,281	29,233	2.01
Belize	329	0.02	40	0.8	39	579	0.04
Benin	487	0.03	59	2.5	56	737	0.05
Bhutan	479	0.03	58	1.0	57	729	0.05
Bolivia	1,002	0.07	121	8.0	113	1,252	0.09
Botswana	615	0.04	74	2.0	72	865	0.06
Brazil	24,946	1.77	3,009	185.1	2,824	25,196	1.73
Bulgaria	5,215	0.37	629	36.5	593	5,465	0.38
Burkina Faso	487	0.03	59	2.5	56	737	0.05
Burundi	402	0.03	48	1.8	47	652	0.04
Cambodia	214	0.02	26	2.6	23	464	0.03
Cameroon	857	0.06	103	6.6	97	1,107	0.08
Canada	44,795	3.18	5,404	334.9	5,069	45,045	3.10
Cape Verde	508	0.04	61	1.2	60	758	0.05
Central African Republic	484	0.03	58	2.5	56	734	0.05
Chad	484	0.03	58	2.5	56	734	0.05
Chile	6,931	0.49	836	49.6	787	7,181	0.49
China	44,799	3.18	5,404	335.0	5,069	45,049	3.10
Colombia	6,352	0.45	766	45.2	721	6,602	0.45
Comoros	282	0.02	34	0.3	34	532	0.04
Congo	520	0.04	63	2.9	60	770	0.05
Costa Rica	233	0.02	28	1.9	26	483	0.03
Côte d'Ivoire	2,516	0.18	304	16.4	287	2,766	0.19
Croatia	1,287	0.09	155	13.6	142	1,537	0.11
Cyprus	1,461	0.10	176	8.4	168	1,711	0.12
Czech Republic	6,308	0.45	761	45.9	715	6,558	0.45
Denmark	10,251	0.73	1,237	74.6	1,162	10,501	0.72
Djibouti	314	0.02	38	0.7	37	564	0.04
Dominica	283	0.02	34	0.3	34	533	0.04
Dominican Republic	1,174	0.08	142	9.8	132	1,424	0.10
Ecuador	2,771	0.20	334	18.2	316	3,021	0.21
Egypt, Arab Republic of	7,108	0.50	857	50.9	807	7,358	0.51
El Salvador	141	0.01	17	1.7	15	391	0.03

(continued)

Statement of Subscriptions to Capital Stock and Voting Power *(continued)*

June 30, 1994
Expressed in millions of U.S. dollars

Member	Shares	Subscriptions Percentage of total	Total amounts	Amounts paid in (Note A)	Amounts subject to call (Note A)	Voting power Number of votes	Percentage of total
Equatorial Guinea.	401	0.03	$ 48	$ 1.6	$ 47	651	0.04
Estonia	518	0.04	62	2.8	60	768	0.05
Ethiopia	978	0.07	118	4.7	113	1,228	0.08
Fiji.	728	0.05	88	3.9	84	978	0.07
Finland.	8,560	0.61	1,033	61.9	971	8,810	0.61
France	69,397	4.92	8,372	520.4	7,851	69,647	4.79
Gabon.	554	0.04	67	3.6	63	804	0.06
Gambia, The	305	0.02	37	0.7	36	555	0.04
Georgia.	1,584	0.11	191	9.3	182	1,834	0.13
Germany.	72,399	5.14	8,734	542.9	8,191	72,649	5.00
Ghana.	856	0.06	103	10.3	93	1,106	0.08
Greece	945	0.07	114	11.4	103	1,195	0.08
Grenada	531	0.04	64	1.4	63	781	0.05
Guatemala.	1,123	0.08	135	9.3	126	1,373	0.09
Guinea	725	0.05	87	5.0	82	975	0.07
Guinea-Bissau.	303	0.02	37	0.6	36	553	0.04
Guyana.	1,058	0.08	128	5.3	122	1,308	0.09
Haiti.	599	0.04	72	3.7	69	849	0.06
Honduras	360	0.03	43	1.3	42	610	0.04
Hungary	8,050	0.57	971	58.0	913	8,300	0.57
Iceland	1,258	0.09	152	6.8	145	1,508	0.10
India.	44,795	3.18	5,404	333.7	5,070	45,045	3.10
Indonesia	14,981	1.06	1,807	110.3	1,697	15,231	1.05
Iran, Islamic Republic of.	23,686	1.68	2,857	175.8	2,682	23,936	1.65
Iraq	2,808	0.20	339	27.1	312	3,058	0.21
Ireland	5,271	0.37	636	37.1	599	5,521	0.38
Israel	4,750	0.34	573	33.2	540	5,000	0.34
Italy	44,795	3.18	5,404	334.8	5,069	45,045	3.10
Jamaica	2,578	0.18	311	16.8	294	2,828	0.19
Japan.	93,770	6.65	11,312	703.5	10,608	94,020	6.47
Jordan	1,388	0.10	167	7.8	160	1,638	0.11
Kazakhstan	1,675	0.12	202	15.0	187	1,925	0.13
Kenya.	2,461	0.17	297	15.9	281	2,711	0.19
Kiribati	261	0.02	31	0.1	31	511	0.04
Korea, Republic of	9,372	0.67	1,131	67.9	1,063	9,622	0.66
Kuwait	13,280	0.94	1,602	97.4	1,505	13,530	0.93
Kyrgyz Republic.	621	0.04	75	3.9	71	871	0.06
Lao People's Democratic Republic. .	100	0.01	12	1.2	11	350	0.02
Latvia	777	0.06	94	5.6	88	1,027	0.07
Lebanon	340	0.02	41	1.1	40	590	0.04
Lesotho.	372	0.03	45	1.3	44	622	0.04
Liberia	463	0.03	56	2.6	53	713	0.05
Libya	7,840	0.56	946	57.0	889	8,090	0.56
Lithuania.	846	0.06	102	6.3	96	1,096	0.08
Luxembourg	1,652	0.12	199	9.8	189	1,902	0.13
Macedonia, former Yugoslav Republic of	240	0.02	29	2.5	26	490	0.03
Madagascar.	1,422	0.10	172	8.1	163	1,672	0.12
Malawi	1,094	0.08	132	5.6	126	1,344	0.09

Member	Subscriptions					Voting power	
	Shares	Percentage of total	Total amounts	Amounts paid in (Note A)	Amounts subject to call (Note A)	Number of votes	Percentage of total
Malaysia	8,244	0.58	$ 995	$ 59.5	$ 935	8,494	0.58
Maldives	469	0.03	57	0.9	56	719	0.05
Mali	652	0.05	79	4.3	74	902	0.06
Malta	1,074	0.08	130	5.4	124	1,324	0.09
Marshall Islands, The	263	0.02	32	0.1	32	513	0.04
Mauritania	505	0.04	61	2.7	58	755	0.05
Mauritius	1,242	0.09	150	6.7	143	1,492	0.10
Mexico	18,804	1.33	2,268	139.0	2,129	19,054	1.31
Micronesia	479	0.03	58	1.0	57	729	0.05
Moldova	1,368	0.10	165	7.6	157	1,618	0.11
Mongolia	466	0.03	56	2.3	54	716	0.05
Morocco	2,791	0.20	337	26.9	310	3,041	0.21
Mozambique	522	0.04	63	3.3	60	772	0.05
Myanmar	2,484	0.18	300	16.1	284	2,734	0.19
Namibia	855	0.06	103	6.4	97	1,105	0.08
Nepal	968	0.07	117	4.6	112	1,218	0.08
Netherlands	35,503	2.52	4,283	264.8	4,018	35,753	2.46
New Zealand	7,236	0.51	873	51.9	821	7,486	0.52
Nicaragua	608	0.04	73	2.1	71	858	0.06
Niger	478	0.03	58	2.4	55	728	0.05
Nigeria	7,102	0.50	857	72.6	784	7,352	0.51
Norway	9,982	0.71	1,204	72.6	1,132	10,232	0.70
Oman	1,561	0.11	188	9.1	179	1,811	0.12
Pakistan	9,339	0.66	1,127	67.8	1,059	9,589	0.66
Panama	216	0.02	26	2.6	23	466	0.03
Papua New Guinea	726	0.05	88	5.0	83	976	0.07
Paraguay	690	0.05	83	4.7	79	940	0.06
Peru	2,992	0.21	361	29.1	332	3,242	0.22
Philippines	6,844	0.49	826	48.9	777	7,094	0.49
Poland	10,908	0.77	1,316	79.6	1,236	11,158	0.77
Portugal	5,460	0.39	659	38.5	620	5,710	0.39
Qatar	1,096	0.08	132	9.0	123	1,346	0.09
Romania	4,011	0.28	484	30.5	453	4,261	0.29
Russia	25,140	1.78	3,033	262.7	2,770	25,390	1.75
Rwanda	587	0.04	71	3.6	67	837	0.06
St. Kitts and Nevis	275	0.02	33	0.3	33	525	0.04
St. Lucia	552	0.04	67	1.5	65	802	0.06
St. Vincent and the Grenadines	278	0.02	34	0.3	33	528	0.04
São Tomé and Principe	278	0.02	34	0.3	33	528	0.04
Saudi Arabia	44,795	3.18	5,404	335.0	5,069	45,045	3.10
Senegal	1,163	0.08	140	9.7	131	1,413	0.10
Seychelles	263	0.02	32	0.2	32	513	0.04
Sierra Leone	403	0.03	49	1.8	47	653	0.04
Singapore	320	0.02	39	3.9	35	570	0.04
Slovak Republic	1,823	0.13	220	17.9	202	2,073	0.14
Slovenia	1,261	0.09	152	9.5	143	1,511	0.10
Solomon Islands	288	0.02	35	0.4	34	538	0.04
Somalia	552	0.04	67	3.3	63	802	0.06

(continued)

Statement of Subscriptions to
Capital Stock and Voting Power   *(continued)*

June 30, 1994
Expressed in millions of U.S. dollars

		Subscriptions				Voting power	
Member	Shares	Percentage of total	Total amounts	Amounts paid in (Note A)	Amounts subject to call (Note A)	Number of votes	Percentage of total
South Africa	13,462	0.96	$ 1,624	$ 98.8	$ 1,525	13,712	0.94
Spain	23,686	1.68	2,857	175.6	2,682	23,936	1.65
Sri Lanka	3,817	0.27	460	26.1	434	4,067	0.28
Sudan	850	0.06	103	7.2	95	1,100	0.08
Suriname	412	0.03	50	2.0	48	662	0.05
Swaziland	440	0.03	53	2.0	51	690	0.05
Sweden	14,974	1.06	1,806	110.2	1,696	15,224	1.05
Switzerland	26,606	1.89	3,210	197.2	3,012	26,856	1.85
Syrian Arab Republic	1,236	0.09	149	10.5	139	1,486	0.10
Tajikistan	1,060	0.08	128	5.3	123	1,310	0.09
Tanzania	727	0.05	88	7.9	80	977	0.07
Thailand	6,349	0.45	766	45.2	721	6,599	0.45
Togo	620	0.04	75	3.9	71	870	0.06
Tonga	277	0.02	33	0.3	33	527	0.04
Trinidad and Tobago	1,495	0.11	180	13.4	167	1,745	0.12
Tunisia	719	0.05	87	5.7	81	969	0.07
Turkey	7,379	0.52	890	52.9	837	7,629	0.52
Turkmenistan	526	0.04	63	2.9	61	776	0.05
Uganda	617	0.04	74	4.4	70	867	0.06
Ukraine	10,908	0.77	1,316	79.3	1,237	11,158	0.77
United Arab Emirates	2,385	0.17	288	22.6	265	2,635	0.18
United Kingdom	69,397	4.92	8,372	539.5	7,832	69,647	4.79
United States	248,893	17.66	30,025	1,940.2	28,085	249,143	17.14
Uruguay	1,578	0.11	190	14.1	176	1,828	0.13
Uzbekistan	1,399	0.10	169	12.1	157	1,649	0.11
Vanuatu	586	0.04	71	1.8	69	836	0.06
Venezuela	11,427	0.81	1,378	118.5	1,260	11,677	0.80
Viet Nam	543	0.04	66	6.6	59	793	0.05
Western Samoa	298	0.02	36	0.5	35	548	0.04
Yemen, Republic of	1,241	0.09	150	10.5	139	1,491	0.10
Zaire	2,643	0.19	319	25.4	293	2,893	0.20
Zambia	1,577	0.11	190	15.6	175	1,827	0.13
Zimbabwe	3,325	0.24	401	22.4	379	3,575	0.25
Total—June 30, 1994*	1,409,235	100.00	$170,003	$10,664.8	$159,338	1,453,485	100.00
Total—June 30, 1993	1,372,648		$165,589	$10,530.7	$155,058	1,416,648	

NOTE:

* May differ from the sum of individual figures shown because of rounding.
The Notes to Financial Statements are an integral part of these Statements.

Notes to Financial Statements

Summary of Significant Accounting and Related Policies

The IBRD's financial statements are prepared in conformity with the accounting principles generally accepted in the United States and with International Accounting Standards.

Translation of Currencies

The IBRD's financial statements are expressed in terms of U.S. dollars solely for the purpose of summarizing the IBRD's financial position and the results of its operations for the convenience of its members and other interested parties.

The IBRD is an international organization which conducts its operations in the currencies of all of its members. The IBRD's resources are derived from its capital, borrowings, and accumulated earnings in those various currencies. The IBRD has a number of general policies aimed at minimizing exchange-rate risk in a multicurrency environment. The IBRD matches its borrowing obligations in any one currency (after swap activities) with assets in the same currency, as prescribed by its Articles of Agreement, primarily by holding or lending the proceeds of its borrowings in the same currencies in which they are borrowed. In addition, the IBRD periodically undertakes currency conversions to more closely match the currencies underlying its retained earnings with those of the outstanding loans. With respect to its other resources, the IBRD does not convert one currency into another except for small amounts required to meet certain obligations and operational needs.

Assets and liabilities are translated at market exchange rates at the end of the period. Income and expenses are translated at the market exchange rate at the dates on which they are recognized or at average market exchange rates in effect during each month. Translation adjustments, with the exception of those relating to capital subscriptions described in Note A, are charged or credited to Equity.

Valuation of Capital Stock

In the Articles of Agreement, the capital stock of the IBRD is expressed in terms of "U.S. dollars of the weight and fineness in effect on July 1, 1944" (1944 dollars). Following the abolition of gold as a common denominator of the monetary system and the repeal of the provision of the U.S. law defining the par value of the U.S. dollar in terms of gold, the pre-existing basis for translating 1944 dollars into current dollars or into any other currency disappeared. The Executive Directors of the IBRD have decided, until such time as the relevant provisions of the Articles of Agreement are amended, that the words "U.S. dollars of the weight and fineness in effect on July 1, 1944" in Article II, Section 2(a) of the Articles of Agreement of the IBRD are interpreted to mean the Special Drawing Right (SDR) introduced by the International Monetary Fund as the SDR was valued in terms of U.S. dollars immediately before the introduction of the basket method of valuing the SDR on July 1, 1974, such value being $1.20635 for one SDR.

Retained Earnings

Retained earnings consists of allocated amounts (Special reserve, General reserve, and Surplus) and Unallocated net income. The IBRD has not declared or paid any dividends to its members.

The Special reserve consists of loan commissions set aside pursuant to Article IV, Section 6, of the Articles of Agreement which are to be held in liquid assets. These assets may be used only for the purpose of meeting liabilities of the IBRD on its borrowings and guarantees in the event of defaults on loans made, participated in, or guaranteed by the IBRD. The Special reserve assets are included under Investments, comprising obligations of the United States Government, its agencies, and other official entities. The allocation of such commissions to the Special reserve was discontinued in 1964 with respect to subsequent loans and no further additions are being made to it.

The General reserve consists of earnings from prior fiscal years which, in the judgment of the Executive Directors, should be retained in the IBRD's business.

Surplus consists of earnings from prior fiscal years which are retained by the IBRD until a further decision is made on their disposition or the conditions of transfer for specified uses have been met.

Unallocated net income consists of earnings in the current fiscal year. Commencing in 1950, a portion or all of the Unallocated net income has been allocated to the General reserve. Additionally, upon approval of the Board of Governors, transfers have been made out of Unallocated net income to the International Development Association (IDA) (or facilities administered by IDA), the Global Environment Trust Fund, the Technical Assistance Trust Fund for the Union of Soviet Socialist Republics, and Surplus.

Loans

All of the IBRD's loans are made to or guaranteed by members, except loans to the International Finance Corporation (IFC). The majority of the IBRD's loans have repayment obligations in various currencies determined on the basis of a currency pooling system, which is designed to equalize exchange-rate risks among borrowers. Single currency loans are being offered on a pilot basis. Except for certain loans which were converted to the currency pooling system, loans negotiated prior to July 1980 and all single currency loans are repayable in the currencies disbursed. Interest on all loans is accrued in the currencies disbursed and outstanding.

Incremental direct costs associated with originating loans are expensed as incurred as such amounts are considered immaterial.

The IBRD does not reschedule interest or principal payments on its loans or participate in debt rescheduling agreements with respect to its loans. In exceptional cases, however, such as when implementation of a financed project has been delayed, the loan amortization schedule may be modified to avoid substantial repayments prior to project completion. It is the policy of the IBRD to place in nonaccrual status all loans made to or guaranteed by a member of the IBRD if principal, interest, or other charges with respect to any such loan are overdue by more than six months, unless the IBRD management determines that the overdue amount will be collected in the immediate future. In addition, if development credits by IDA to a member government are placed in nonaccrual status, all loans to that member government will also be placed in nonaccrual status by the IBRD. On the date a member's loans are placed in nonaccrual status, unpaid interest and other charges accrued on loans outstanding to the member are deducted from the income of the current period. Interest and other charges on nonaccruing loans are included in income only to the extent that payments have actually been received by the IBRD. On the date a member pays in full all overdue amounts, its loans emerge from nonaccrual status, its eligibility for new loans is restored, and all its overdue interest and other charges including those from prior years are recognized as income in the current period.

The IBRD determines the accumulated provision for loan losses based on an assessment of collectibility risk in the total loan portfolio, including loans in nonaccrual status. The accumulated provision is periodically adjusted based on a review of the prevailing circumstances and would be used to meet actual losses on loans. Should such losses occur in amounts in excess of the accumulated provision (and of the amount of the Special reserve), the excess would be included in the determination of net income. Adjustments to the accumulated provision are recorded as a charge or credit to income.

(continued)

Notes to Financial Statements   *(continued)*

Investments

The IBRD carries its investment securities at market value. Both realized and unrealized gains and losses are included in income from investments. From time to time, the IBRD enters into forward contracts for the sale or purchase of investment securities; these transactions are recorded at the time of commitment.

Due to the nature of the investments held by the IBRD and its policies governing the level and use of such investments, the IBRD classifies the investment portfolio as an element of liquidity in the Statement of Cash Flows.

Fair Value of Financial Instruments

The IBRD carries its investments at market value; fair values of other financial instruments are not recorded in the accounts of the IBRD, but are disclosed in Note C as additional information.

The fair value of financial instruments that are short-term approximates their carrying value.

Financial instruments for which market quotations are available have been valued at the prevailing market value. Financial instruments for which market quotations are not readily available have been valued using methodologies and assumptions that necessarily require the use of subjective judgments. Accordingly, the actual value at which such financial instruments could be exchanged in a current transaction or whether they are actually exchangeable is not determinable.

Reclassifications

Certain reclassifications of the prior year's information have been made to conform to the current year's presentation.

Note A—Capital Stock, Restricted Currencies, Maintenance of Value, and Membership

Capital Stock: At June 30, 1994, the IBRD's capital comprised 1,525,248 (1,525,659—June 30, 1993) authorized shares, of which 1,409,235 (1,372,648—June 30, 1993) shares had been subscribed. Each share has a par value of 0.1 million 1974 SDRs, valued at the rate of $1.20635 per 1974 SDR. Of the subscribed capital, $10,665 million ($10,531 million—June 30, 1993) has been paid in, and the remaining $159,338 million ($155,058 million—June 30, 1993) is subject to call only when required to meet the obligations of the IBRD created by borrowing or guaranteeing loans. As to $136,002 million ($132,471 million—June 30, 1993) the restriction on calls is imposed by the Articles of Agreement and as to $23,336 million ($22,587 million—June 30, 1993), by resolutions of the Board of Governors.

Restricted Currencies: The portion of capital subscriptions paid in to the IBRD is divided into two parts: (1) $1,067 million ($1,053 million—June 30, 1993) initially paid in gold or U.S. dollars and (2) $9,598 million ($9,478 million—June 30, 1993) paid in cash or noninterest-bearing demand obligations denominated either in the currencies of the respective members or in U.S. dollars. The amounts mentioned in (1) above, and (i) $779 million ($656 million—June 30, 1993) which were repurchased by members with U.S. dollars, and (ii) $284 million ($208 million—June 30, 1993) which were the proceeds from encashments of U.S.-dollar-denominated notes which are included in the amounts mentioned in (2) above, are freely usable by the IBRD in any of its operations. The portion of the amounts paid in U.S.-dollar-denominated notes are encashed by the IBRD in accordance with the schedules agreed between the members and the IBRD. The remaining amounts paid in the currencies of the members, referred to as restricted currencies, are usable by the IBRD in its lending

operations only with the consent of the respective members, and for administrative expenses. The equivalent of $5,444 million ($5,397 million—June 30, 1993) has been used for lending purposes, with such consent.

Maintenance of Value: Article II, Section 9 of the Articles of Agreement provides for maintenance of value, as of the time of subscription, of such restricted currencies, requiring (1) the member to make additional payments to the IBRD in the event that the par value of its currency is reduced or the foreign exchange value of its currency has, in the opinion of the IBRD, depreciated to a significant extent in its territories and (2) the IBRD to reimburse the member in the event that the par value of its currency is increased.

Since currencies no longer have par values, maintenance-of-value amounts are determined by measuring the foreign exchange value of a member's currency against the standard of value of the IBRD capital based on the 1974 SDR. Members are required to make payments to the IBRD if their currencies depreciate significantly relative to the standard of value. Furthermore, the Executive Directors decided to adopt a policy of reimbursing members whose currencies appreciate significantly in terms of the standard of value.

With respect to restricted currencies out on loan, maintenance-of-value obligations become effective only as such currencies are recovered by the IBRD. The maintenance-of-value amounts relating to restricted currencies out on loan are included in Amounts required to maintain value of currency holdings—amounts deferred.

Membership: On February 25, 1993, the IBRD's Executive Directors decided that the Socialist Federal Republic of Yugoslavia (SFRY) had ceased to be a member of the IBRD and that the Republic of Bosnia and Herzegovina, the Republic of Croatia, the former Yugoslav Republic of Macedonia, the Republic of Slovenia and the Federal Republic of Yugoslavia (Serbia and Montenegro) are authorized to succeed to the SFRY's membership when certain requirements are met. Three of the five successor Republics—the Republics of Croatia and Slovenia and the former Yugoslav Republic of Macedonia—have since become members of the IBRD. The paid-in portion of the SFRY's subscribed capital allocated to the other successor Republics (the Republic of Bosnia and Herzegovina and the Federal Republic of Yugoslavia (Serbia and Montenegro)) is included under Payments on account of pending subscriptions.

Note B—Loans, Cofinancing and Guarantees

Loans: On August 3, 1993, the IBRD's Executive Directors approved a one-year interest waiver of 25 basis points on disbursed and outstanding loans for all payment periods commencing in the fiscal year ending June 30, 1994 for all eligible borrowers. For the fiscal year ended June 30, 1993, the interest waiver approved was 35 basis points. On August 3, 1993, the Executive Directors also extended the one-year commitment fee waiver of 50 basis points on undisbursed loans to all borrowers for an additional period of one year.

On February 25, 1993, the IBRD's Executive Directors decided that the Socialist Federal Republic of Yugoslavia (SFRY) had ceased to be a member of the IBRD and that the Republic of Bosnia and Herzegovina, the Republic of Croatia, the former Yugoslav Republic of Macedonia, the Republic of Slovenia and the Federal Republic of Yugoslavia (Serbia and Montenegro) (FRY) were authorized to succeed to the SFRY's membership when certain requirements were met, including entering into a final agreement with the IBRD on the IBRD's loans made to or guaranteed by the SFRY which the particular successor Republic assumed.

Three of the five successor Republics—the Republics of Croatia and Slovenia and the former Yugoslav Republic of Macedonia—have since become members of the IBRD. With respect to the FRY, in February 1993 the IBRD reached an agreement with that Republic for the apportionment and service of debt due to the IBRD on loans made to or guaranteed by the SFRY and assumed by the FRY, which confirmed a February 1992 interim agreement between the SFRY (then consisting of the Republics of Bosnia and Herzegovina, Macedonia, Montenegro and Serbia) and the IBRD pertaining, among other things, to such loans. As of the date hereof, no debt service payments have been received by the IBRD from the FRY. With respect to the Republic of Bosnia and Herzegovina, a preliminary understanding was reached in June 1993 on the loans made to or guaranteed by the SFRY to be assumed by that Republic. Until an agreement is reached, loans benefitting that Republic are included with the loans assumed by the FRY in accordance with the IBRD's above-mentioned agreement with the FRY. (Also see Note A).

At June 30, 1994, no loans payable to the IBRD other than those referred to in the following paragraphs were overdue by more than three months.

At June 30, 1994, the loans made to or guaranteed by certain member countries and two other countries—the FRY and the Republic of Bosnia and Herzegovina—with an aggregate principal balance outstanding of $2,363 million ($2,497 million—June 30, 1993), of which $1,009 million ($772 million—June 30, 1993) was overdue, were in nonaccrual status. As of such date, overdue interest and other charges in respect of these loans totaled $628 million ($509 million—June 30, 1993). If these loans had not been in nonaccrual status, income from loans for the fiscal year ended June 30, 1994 would have been higher by $149 million ($244 million—June 30, 1993). A summary of member countries and republics with loans or guarantees in nonaccrual status follows:

	In millions		
	June 30, 1994		
Country/Republic	Principal outstanding	Principal and charges overdue	Nonaccrual since
Bosnia-Herzegovina/ Federal Republic of Yugoslavia	$1,652	$ 942	September 1992
Iraq	48	43	December 1990
Liberia	151	202	June 1987
Sudan	6	1	January 1994
Syrian Arab Republic	418	425	February 1987
Zaire	88	24	November 1993
Total	2,363	1,637	

During the fiscal year ended June 30, 1994, Congo and the former Yugoslav Republic of Macedonia paid off all of their arrears and therefore loans to them came out of nonaccrual status. As a result, income from loans for the fiscal year ended June 30, 1994 increased by $52 million corresponding to income that would have been accrued in previous fiscal years. For the fiscal year ended June 30, 1993, the increase in loan income from loans to countries coming out of nonaccrual status during that fiscal year was $407 million.

An analysis of the changes to the accumulated provision for loan losses appears below:

	In millions	
	1994	1993
Balance, beginning of the fiscal year	$3,150	$2,540
Provision for loan losses	—	578
Translation adjustments	174	32
Balance, end of the fiscal year	$3,324	$3,150

Cofinancing and Guarantees: The IBRD has entered into agreements for loans syndicated by other financial institutions either by a direct participation in, or a partial guarantee of, loans for the benefit of member countries or a partial guarantee of securities issued by an entity eligible for IBRD loans. The IBRD's direct participations in syndicated loans are included in reported loan balances.

Guarantees of $1,181 million at June 30, 1994 ($1,134 million—June 30, 1993) were not included in reported loan balances. $173 million of these guarantees were subject to call at June 30, 1994 ($150 million—June 30, 1993).

The IBRD has partially guaranteed the timely payment of interest amounts on certain loans that have been sold. At June 30, 1994, these guarantees, approximating $4 million ($5 million—June 30, 1993), were subject to call.

Statutory Lending Limit: Under the Articles of Agreement, the total amount outstanding of guarantees, participations in loans, and direct loans made by the IBRD may not be increased to an amount exceeding 100 percent of the sum of subscribed capital, reserves, and surplus. On the IBRD's Balance Sheet, reserves and surplus correspond to items labelled Retained earnings, Cumulative translation adjustment, and Accumulated provision for loan losses. The IBRD's Executive Directors have issued guidelines pursuant to which all guarantees issued by the IBRD will be counted towards this limit at the time they first become callable, irrespective of the likelihood of an actual call. At June 30, 1994, such total amount was $109 billion or 58 percent (57 percent—June 30, 1993) of the Statutory Lending Limit.

Note C—Financial Instruments

Investments

The IBRD carries its investment securities, including corresponding derivative instruments, at market value. Accordingly, the carrying amount represents the fair value of the portfolio. These fair values are based on quoted market prices, where available. If quoted market prices are not available, fair values are based on quoted market prices of comparable instruments.

For both on- and off-balance sheet securities, the IBRD limits trading to a list of authorized dealers and counterparties. Credit limits have been established for each counterparty by type of instrument and maturity category.

The annualized rate of return on average investments, net of agreements to repurchase and cash collateral received, held during the fiscal year ended June 30, 1994, including both realized and unrealized gains and losses, was 3.56 percent (6.09 percent—June 30, 1993).

As part of its overall portfolio management strategy, the IBRD invests in government obligations and time deposits. These categories also include financial instruments with off-balance sheet risk, including futures, forward contracts, covered forward contracts, options, and short sales.

Government Obligations: Government obligations include marketable securities, bonds, notes, and other obligations issued or unconditionally guaranteed by governments of countries or other official entities including the agencies and instrumentalities of the government of a country or by multilateral organizations.

Time Deposits: Time deposits include certificates of deposit, time deposits, bankers' acceptances, and other obligations issued or unconditionally guaranteed by banks and other financial institutions.

Futures and Forwards: Futures and forward contracts are contracts for delayed delivery of securities or money market instruments in which the seller agrees to make delivery at a specified future date of a specified instrument, at a specified price or yield. Covered forwards are agreements

(continued)

Notes to Financial Statements   *(continued)*

in which cash in one currency is converted into a different currency and, simultaneously, a forward exchange agreement is executed providing for a future exchange of the two currencies in order to recover the currency converted.

Options: Options are contracts that allow the holder of the option to purchase or sell a financial instrument at a specified price and within a specified period of time from the seller or to the purchaser of the option. As a seller of options, the IBRD receives a premium at the outset and then bears the risk of an unfavorable change in the price of the financial instrument underlying the option.

Short Sales: Short sales are sales of securities not held in the IBRD's portfolio at the time of the sale. The IBRD must purchase the security at a later date and bears the risk that the market value of the security will move adversely between the time of the sale and the time the security must be delivered.

A summary of the currency composition of Investments, including securities purchased under resale agreements, at June 30, 1994 and June 30, 1993 is as follows:

	In millions	
Currency	1994	1993
Deutsche mark	$ 2,382	$ 774
Japanese yen	5,332	5,189
Pounds sterling	1,479	1,456
United States dollars	10,498	10,948
Other currencies	2,211	1,999
Total	$21,902	$20,366

Loans

The following table reflects the carrying and estimated fair values of the loan portfolio as of June 30, 1994 and June 30, 1993.

	In millions			
	1994		1993	
	Carrying value	Estimated fair value	Carrying value	Estimated fair value
Fixed rate	$ 19,703	$ 21,538	$ 23,619	$ 26,364
Variable rates	89,551	94,234	80,832	86,398
Single currency loan rates	37	37	—	—
Total	$109,291	$115,809	$104,451	$112,762

All of the IBRD's loans are made to or guaranteed by countries that are members of the IBRD, except for those loans made to the IFC. The IBRD does not currently sell its loans, nor is there a market of loans comparable to those made by the IBRD. The IBRD has never suffered a loss on any of its loans, although from time to time certain borrowers have found it difficult to make timely payments for protracted periods, resulting in their loans being placed in nonaccrual status. Several borrowers have emerged from nonaccrual status after a period of time by bringing up-to-date all principal payments and all interest payments, including interest and other charges on overdue principal payments. In an attempt to recognize the risk inherent in these overdue payments, the IBRD maintains a provision for loan losses. The balance of the Accumulated provision for loan losses at June 30, 1994 was $3,324 million ($3,150 million—June 30, 1993).

Fixed rate loans: On loans negotiated prior to July 1982, the IBRD charges interest at fixed rates. The estimated fair value of these loans is

based on discounted future cash flows using the rate at which the IBRD could undertake borrowings of comparable maturities at June 30, 1994 plus a 50 basis point spread.

Variable rate loans: In 1982, the IBRD mitigated its interest rate risk by moving from fixed rate to variable rate lending. The rate charged on variable rate loans is based on the IBRD's own cost of qualified borrowings plus a 50 basis point spread, resulting in a pass-through of its average borrowing costs to those members that benefit from IBRD loans. Since the interest rate for variable rate loans is based on the interest rate of the qualified borrowings, the fair value of variable rate loans has been estimated based on the relationship of the fair value to the carrying value of the underlying borrowings.

Single currency loans: In 1993, the IBRD introduced single currency loans on a pilot basis. The rates charged on single currency loans are equal to the six-month reference interbank offered rate for the applicable currency prevailing on the semiannual reset date, plus a cost margin equal to the IBRD's weighted average margin relative to the six-month London Interbank Offered Rate on its borrowings funding single currency loans, calculated for the previous semester and averaged across currencies, plus an interest spread of 50 basis points. Since the interest rates for single currency loans are based on the interest rate of qualified borrowings, the fair value of single currency loans has been estimated based on the relationship of the fair value to the carrying value of underlying borrowings.

Borrowings

The following table reflects the carrying and estimated fair values of the borrowings portfolio as of June 30, 1994 and June 30, 1993.

	In millions			
	1994		1993	
	Carrying value	Estimated fair value	Carrying value	Estimated fair value
Short-term	$ 3,304	$ 3,304	$ 3,775	$ 3,775
Medium- and long-term	95,615	101,280	92,488	99,505
Swaps				
Currency				
Net payable	2,623	2,062	1,972	1,196
Net receivable	(513)	(728)	(775)	(1,312)
Interest rate	—	893	—	1,093
	97,725	103,507	93,685	100,482
Total	$101,029	$106,811	$97,460	$104,257

The estimated fair values are based on quoted market prices where such prices are available. Where no quoted market price is available, the fair value is estimated based on the cost at which the IBRD could currently undertake borrowings with similar terms and remaining maturities, using the secondary market yield curve. The fair value of swaps represent the estimated cost of replacing these contracts on that date.

Providing liquidity and minimizing the cost of funds are key objectives to the IBRD's overall borrowing strategy. The IBRD uses swaps in its borrowing strategy to lower the overall cost of its borrowings for those members who benefit from IBRD loans. The IBRD undertakes swap transactions with a list of authorized counterparties. Credit and maturity limits have been established for each counterparty.

The average cost of borrowings outstanding, including short-term borrowings, during the fiscal year ended June 30, 1994 was 6.74 percent (7.01

percent—June 30, 1993), reflecting a reduction in interest expense of $234 million ($367 million—June 30, 1993) as a result of swaps.

Currency swaps: The IBRD has entered into currency swaps in which proceeds of a borrowing are converted into a different currency and, simultaneously, a forward exchange agreement is executed providing for a schedule of future exchanges of the two currencies in order to recover the currency converted. The combination of a borrowing and a currency swap produces the financial equivalent of substituting a borrowing in the currency obtained in the initial conversion for the original borrowing.

Interest rate swaps: The IBRD undertakes interest rate swaps, which transform a fixed rate payment obligation in a particular currency into a floating rate obligation in that currency and vice-versa.

Note D—Risk Exposure of Financial Instruments with Off-Balance Sheet Risks

In the normal course of business, the IBRD is a party to a variety of off-balance sheet financial instruments to manage its exposure to market risks. These financial instruments involve elements of credit and market risks in excess of the amount recorded on the balance sheet. Credit risk represents the maximum potential accounting loss due to possible nonperformance by obligors and counterparties under the terms of the contract. Market risk represents the potential loss due to the decrease in the value of an off-balance sheet financial instrument caused primarily by changes in interest rates or currency exchange rates. The risk exposure of financial instruments with off-balance sheet risks as at June 30, 1994 and June 30, 1993 is given below.

	In millions	
	1994	1993
INVESTMENTS		
Futures		
• Total contract value	$ 6,829	$ 9,277
• Credit exposure due to potential nonperformance by counterparties	10	13
Forward contracts		
• Total contract value	600	450
• Credit exposure due to potential nonperformance by counterparties	—	*
Covered forward contracts		
• Gross receivables	1,485	989
• Gross payables	1,503	997
• Credit exposure due to potential nonperformance by counterparties	19	12
Options sold		
• Total contract value	687	48
Short sales		
• Total contract value	994	303
BORROWINGS		
Currency swaps		
• Gross receivables	18,222	18,947
• Gross payables	20,332	20,144
• Credit exposure due to potential nonperformance by counterparties	728	1,312
Interest rate swaps		
• Notional principal	16,341	14,592
• Credit exposure due to potential nonperformance by counterparties	111	98

* Less than $0.5 million

Note E—Retained Earnings and Allocation of Net Income

Retained Earnings: Retained earnings comprises the following elements as of June 30, 1994 and June 30, 1993:

	In millions	
	1994	1993
Special reserve	$ 293	$ 293
General reserve	13,124	11,144
Surplus	—	1,465
Unallocated net income for the fiscal year	1,051	1,130
Total	$14,468	$14,032

On August 3, 1993, the Executive Directors allocated $890 million of the net income earned in the fiscal year ended June 30, 1993 to the General reserve. On September 30, 1993, the Board of Governors approved a transfer of $100 million to the Debt Reduction Facility administered by IDA, and a transfer to IDA, by way of grant, of $140 million in an equivalent amount in SDRs, out of the net income earned in the fiscal year ended June 30, 1993. On the same day, the Board of Governors also approved a transfer of $1,090 million to the General reserve from Surplus. On September 24, 1992, as amended on November 11, 1993, the Board of Governors approved a transfer of $325 million in an equivalent amount in SDRs from Surplus as a grant to IDA, when the tenth replenishment of IDA's resources would become effective, which occurred on December 17, 1993. On November 11, 1993, the Board of Governors approved a transfer, by way of grant, of $50 million from Surplus to the Trust Fund for Gaza, to be administered by IDA.

Transfers to International Development Association: The Board of Governors approved transfers to IDA totaling $3,808 million from Unallocated net income for the fiscal years ended June 30, 1964 through June 30, 1987, and June 30, 1989 through June 30, 1993. On September 30, 1993, the Board of Governors approved a transfer to IDA, by way of grant, of $140 million in an equivalent amount in SDRs. In addition on September 24, 1992, as amended on November 11, 1993, the Board of Governors approved a transfer of $325 million to IDA, when the tenth replenishment of IDA's resources would become effective, which occurred on December 17, 1993. Transfer of $1,023 million remained payable at June 30, 1994 ($960 million—June 30, 1993).

Transfers to Debt Reduction Facility for IDA-Only Countries: The Board of Governors approved transfers to the Debt Reduction Facility for IDA-Only Countries totaling $100 million through June 30, 1993. On September 30, 1993, the Board of Governors approved a further transfer of $100 million to the Debt Reduction Facility for IDA-Only Countries. At June 30, 1994, $131 million remained payable ($53 million—June 30, 1993).

Transfer to the Trust Fund for Gaza: On November 11, 1993, the Board of Governors approved a transfer to the Trust Fund for Gaza, by way of grant, of $50 million. At June 30, 1994, $50 million remained payable.

Note F—Expenses

Administrative expenses are net of the management fee of $545 million ($467 million—June 30, 1993) charged to IDA and $107 million ($95 million—June 30, 1993) charged to reimbursable programs. Included in the amounts charged to reimbursable programs are allocated charges of $21 million ($20 million—June 30, 1993) charged to IFC and $1 million ($1 million—June 30, 1993) charged to the Multilateral Investment Guarantee Agency (M.I.G.A.).

Contributions to special programs represent grants for agricultural research, the control of onchocerciasis, and other developmental activities.

Notes to Financial Statements   (continued)

As of June 30, 1994, the IBRD has provided for liabilities associated with the estimated costs of benefits provided to former or inactive employees after employment, but before retirement. The effect is not material to the financial statements.

Note G—Staff Retirement Plan

The IBRD has a defined benefit retirement plan covering substantially all of its staff. The Plan also covers substantially all the staff of IFC and M.I.G.A. Under the Plan, benefits are based on the years of contributory service and the highest three-year average of pensionable remuneration as defined in the Plan, with the staff contributing a fixed percentage of pensionable remuneration, and the IBRD contributing the remainder of the actuarially determined cost of future Plan benefits. The IBRD uses the aggregate method for determining its contribution to the Plan. The amount of that contribution approximates the net periodic pension cost as detailed below. All contributions to the Plan and all other assets and income held for the purposes of the Plan are held by the IBRD separately from the other assets and income of the IBRD, IDA, IFC and M.I.G.A. and can be used only for the benefit of the participants in the Plan and their beneficiaries, until all liabilities to them have been paid or provided for. Plan assets consist primarily of equity and fixed income securities, with smaller holdings of cash, real estate and other investments.

Net periodic pension cost for IBRD participants for the fiscal years ended June 30, 1994 and June 30, 1993, consisted of the following components:

	In millions	
	1994	1993
Service cost—benefits earned during the fiscal year	$ 185	$ 155
Interest cost on projected benefit obligation	310	295
Actual return on plan assets	(342)	(500)
Net amortization and deferral	(50)	153
Net periodic pension cost	$ 103	$ 103

The portion of this cost that relates to the IBRD and is included in Administrative expenses for the fiscal year ended June 30, 1994 is $63 million ($64 million—June 30, 1993). The balance has been included in the management fee charged to IDA.

The following table sets forth the Plan's funded status at June 30, 1994 and June 30, 1993:

	In millions	
	1994	1993
Actuarial present value of benefit obligations		
Accumulated benefit obligation		
Vested	$(3,092)	$(3,047)
Nonvested	(43)	(34)
Subtotal	(3,135)	(3,081)
Effect of projected compensation levels	(1,743)	(1,673)
Projected benefit obligation	(4,878)	(4,754)
Plan assets at fair value	5,387	4,927
Plan assets in excess of projected benefit obligation	509	173
Remaining unrecognized net transition asset	(117)	(130)
Unrecognized prior service cost	91	99
Unrecognized net gain from past experience different from that assumed and from changes in assumptions	(483)	(142)
Prepaid pension cost	$ 0	$ 0

The weighted-average discount rate used in determining the actuarial present value of the projected benefit obligation was 8.25 percent (7.5 percent—June 30, 1993). The effect of projected compensation levels was calculated based on a scale that provides for a decreasing rate of salary increase depending on age, beginning with 13.0 percent at age 20 and decreasing to 6.5 percent at age 64. The expected long-term rate of return on assets was 9 percent (9 percent—June 30, 1993).

Note H—Retired Staff Benefits Plan

The IBRD has a Retired Staff Benefits Plan (RSBP) that provides certain health care and life insurance benefits to retirees. All staff who are enrolled in the insurance programs while in active service and who meet certain requirements are eligible for benefits when they reach early or normal retirement age while working for the IBRD. The RSBP also covers the staff of IFC and M.I.G.A.

Retirees contribute a level amount toward life insurance based on the amount of coverage. Retiree contributions toward health care are based on length of service and age at retirement. The IBRD annually contributes the remainder of the actuarially determined cost for future benefits. All contributions to the RSBP and all other assets and income held for purposes of the RSBP are held by the IBRD separately from the other assets and income of the IBRD, IDA, IFC, and M.I.G.A. and can be used only for the benefit of the participants in the RSBP and their beneficiaries until all liabilities to them have been paid or provided for. RSBP assets consist primarily of fixed income and equity securities.

During the fiscal year ended June 30, 1993, the IBRD reviewed and modified certain assumptions used in calculating its accumulated postretirement benefit obligation (APBO) to reflect actual experience. These modifications resulted in an increase in the APBO, and a special one-time contribution of $343 million was made to fund this increase. The IBRD's share of this contribution was $315 million. The remainder was contributed by IFC and M.I.G.A.

Net periodic postretirement benefits cost for IBRD participants for the fiscal years ended June 30, 1994 and June 30, 1993 consisted of the following components:

	In millions	
	1994	1993
Service cost—benefits earned during the fiscal year	$ 25	$ 14
Interest cost on accumulated postretirement benefit obligation	39	26
Actual return on plan assets	(49)	(31)
Net amortization and deferral	19	15
	$ 34	$ 24

The portion of this cost that relates to the IBRD and is included in Administrative expenses for the fiscal year ended June 30, 1994 is $21 million ($15 million—June 30, 1993). The balance has been included in the management fee charged to IDA.

The following table sets forth the RSBP's funded status at June 30, 1994 and June 30, 1993:

	In millions	
	1994	1993
Accumulated postretirement benefit obligation		
Retirees	$(228)	$(219)
Fully eligible active plan participants	(119)	(101)
Other active plan participants	(297)	(283)
	(644)	(603)
Plan assets at fair value	702	624
Plan assets in excess of accumulated postretirement benefit obligation.	58	21
Unrecognized transition obligation	—	29
Unrecognized prior service costs	(16)	—
Unrecognized net loss from past experience different from that assumed and from changes in assumptions	296	293
Prepaid postretirement benefit cost	$ 338	$ 343

Of the $338 million prepaid as of June 30, 1994, $311 million is attributable to the IBRD and is included in Miscellaneous assets on the Balance Sheet. The remainder has been attributed to IFC and MIGA.

For June 30, 1994, the APBO was determined using health care cost trend rates of 12.2 to 16.4 percent, decreasing gradually to 5.8 percent in 2010 and thereafter. The health care cost trend rate used for June 30, 1993, was 11.5 to 16.2 percent decreasing gradually to 5.0 percent in 2010 and thereafter.

The health care cost trend rate assumption has a significant effect on the amounts reported. To illustrate, increasing the assumed health care cost trend rates by one percentage point would increase the accumulated postretirement benefit obligation as of June 30, 1994 by $132 million and the net periodic postretirement benefit cost for the fiscal year then ended by $16 million.

The weighted average discount rate used in determining the accumulated postretirement benefit obligation was 8.25 percent (7.5 percent—June 30, 1993). The expected long-term rate of return on plan assets was 8.25 percent (7.5 percent—June 30, 1993).

Report of Independent Accountants

Price Waterhouse (International Firm)	The Hague Beijing Hong Kong London	New York Tokyo Washington

Price Waterhouse

July 27, 1994

President and Board of Governors
  International Bank for Reconstruction
  and Development

In our opinion, the financial statements appearing on pages 174 through 193 of this Report present fairly, in all material respects, in terms of United States dollars, the financial position of the International Bank for Reconstruction and Development at June 30, 1994 and 1993, and the results of its operations and its cash flows for the years then ended in conformity with generally accepted accounting principles in the United States and with International Accounting Standards. These financial statements are the responsibility of management of the International Bank for Reconstruction and Development; our responsibility is to express an opinion on these financial statements based on our audits. We conducted our audits of these statements in accordance with generally accepted auditing standards, including International Standards on Auditing, which require that we plan and perform the audit to obtain reasonable assurance about whether the financial statements are free of material misstatement. An audit includes examining, on a test basis, evidence supporting the amounts and disclosures in the financial statements, assessing the accounting principles used and significant estimates made by management, and evaluating the overall financial statement presentation. We believe that our audits provide a reasonable basis for the opinion expressed above.

Price Waterhouse
(International Firm)

Financial Statements of the International Development Association and the Special Fund Administered by IDA

Statements of Development Resources

June 30, 1994 and June 30, 1993
Expressed in millions of U.S. dollars

	IDA		Special Fund	
	1994	1993	1994	1993
Development Resources				
NET ASSETS AVAILABLE FOR DEVELOPMENT ACTIVITIES				
Cash and investments immediately available for disbursement				
Due from banks	$ 65	$ 54	$ 2	$ 1
Obligations of governments and other official				
entities—Notes A and F	1,368	1,457	5	24
Obligations of banks and other financial institutions—Notes A and F	876	1,299	267	227
Net receivable (payable) on investment securities transactions—Notes A and F	116	(22)		
	2,425	2,788	274	252
Cash and investments not immediately available for disbursement—Note B				
Due from banks	2	4		
Obligations of governments and other official				
entities—Notes A and F	136	133		
Obligations of banks and other financial				
institutions—Notes A and F	501	127		
	639	264	—	—
Receivables on account of subscriptions and contributions				
Nonnegotiable, noninterest-bearing demand				
obligations	21,548	19,952	33	49
Subscriptions and contributions—Note C				
Amounts due	342	268		
Amounts not yet due	10,843	119		
Restricted assets	286	281		
	33,019	20,620	33	49
Receivable from the International Bank for Reconstruction				
and Development—Note D	1,023	960		
Other assets, net	98	96	—	1
Total net assets available for development activities	37,204	24,728	307	302
DEVELOPMENT CREDITS OUTSTANDING				
(see Summary Statement of Development Credits and Notes E and F)				
Total development credits	87,880	80,090	21	39
Less undisbursed balance	25,070	23,932	21	39
Total development credits disbursed and outstanding	62,810	56,158	—	—
Total development resources	$100,014	$80,886	$307	$302
Funding of Development Resources				
Member subscriptions and contributions (see Statement of				
Voting Power, and Subscriptions and Contributions,				
Note C)				
Unrestricted	$ 89,258	$72,496	$206	$218
Restricted	286	281		
	89,544	72,777	206	218
Payments on account of pending membership—Note C	9	10		
Transfer from the IBRD—Note D	4,176	3,661		
Cumulative translation adjustment on development credits	4,807	3,266		
Accumulated surplus (see Statements of Changes in				
Accumulated Surplus)	1,264	1,110	101	84
Securities sold under agreements to repurchase and payable for cash collateral				
received—Note A	214	62		
Total funding of development resources	$100,014	$80,886	$307	$302

The Notes to Financial Statements are an integral part of these Statements.

Statements of Changes in Accumulated Surplus

For the fiscal year ended June 30, 1994 and June 30, 1993
Expressed in millions of U.S. dollars

	IDA		Special Fund	
	1994	1993	1994	1993
ACCUMULATED SURPLUS				
Income from development credits—Notes E and G ...	$ 417	$ 398		
Income from investments—Note G	168	373	$ 18	$ 30
Management fee charged by the International Bank for				
Reconstruction and Development—Note G	(545)	(467)		
Amortization of discount on subscription advances	(9)	(7)		
Changes from operations	31	297	18	30
Effect of exchange rate changes on accumulated surplus	123	(446)	(1)	(50)
Net changes	154	(149)	17	(20)
Balance at beginning of the fiscal year	1,110	1,259	84	104
Balance at end of the fiscal year	$1,264	$1,110	$101	$ 84

Statements of Cash Flows

For the fiscal year ended June 30, 1994 and June 30, 1993
Expressed in millions of U.S. dollars

	IDA		Special Fund	
	1994	1993	1994	1993
Cash flows from development activities				
Development credit disbursements	$(5,520)	$(4,913)	$ (11)	$ (33)
Development credit principal repayments	420	366		
Net cash used in development activities	(5,100)	(4,547)	(11)	(33)
Cash flows from member subscriptions and				
contributions	3,960	4,112	16	37
Cash flows from other contributions	452	303		
Cash flows from operating activities				
Changes from operations	31	297	18	30
Adjustments to reconcile changes from operations to				
net cash provided by operating activities				
Amortization of discount on subscription advances	9	7		
Net changes in other assets and liabilities	163	108	—	—
Net cash provided by operating activities	203	412	18	30
Effect of exchange rate changes on cash and				
investments immediately available for disbursement .	122	(462)	(1)	(50)
Net (decrease) increase in cash and investments				
immediately available for disbursement	(363)	(182)	22	(16)
Cash and investments immediately available for				
disbursement at beginning of the fiscal year	2,788	2,970	252	268
Cash and investments immediately available for				
disbursement at end of the fiscal year	$ 2,425	$ 2,788	$274	$252

The Notes to Financial Statements are an integral part of these Statements.

Summary Statement of Development Credits

June 30, 1994
Expressed in millions of U.S. dollars

	IDA			Special Fund			Total	
Borrower or guarantor	Total development credits	Undisbursed development credits[1]	Development credits outstanding	Total development credits	Undisbursed development credits	Development credits outstanding	Development credits outstanding	Percentage of development credits outstanding
Afghanistan	$ 75	$ —	$ 75	$ —	$ —	$ —	$ 75	0.12
Albania	138	87	51	—	—	—	51	0.08
Angola	260	231	29	—	—	—	29	0.05
Armenia	29	26	3	—	—	—	3	*
Bangladesh	6,862	1,662	5,200	6	—	6	5,206	8.29
Benin	584	157	427	12	—	12	439	0.70
Bhutan	29	9	20	—	—	—	20	0.03
Bolivia	1,002	390	612	—	—	—	612	0.97
Botswana	12	—	12	—	—	—	12	0.02
Burkina Faso	773	299	474	—	—	—	474	0.75
Burundi	748	202	546	—	—	—	546	0.87
Cambodia	65	35	30	—	—	—	30	0.05
Cameroon	408	76	332	—	—	—	332	0.53
Cape Verde	48	23	25	—	—	—	25	0.04
Central African Republic	455	90	365	—	—	—	365	0.58
Chad	447	135	312	—	—	—	312	0.50
Chile	12	—	12	—	—	—	12	0.02
China	8,691	2,983	5,708	82	—	82	5,790	9.22
Colombia	12	—	12	—	—	—	12	0.02
Comoros	81	33	48	—	—	—	48	0.08
Congo	173	—	173	—	—	—	173	0.28
Costa Rica	3	—	3	—	—	—	3	*
Côte d'Ivoire	549	132	417	—	—	—	417	0.66
Djibouti	51	9	42	—	—	—	42	0.07
Dominica	12	*	12	—	—	—	12	0.02
Dominican Republic	18	—	18	—	—	—	18	0.03
Ecuador	28	—	28	—	—	—	28	0.04
Egypt, Arab Republic of	1,323	385	938	—	—	—	938	1.49
El Salvador	21	—	21	—	—	—	21	0.03
Equatorial Guinea	59	11	48	—	—	—	48	0.08
Ethiopia	1,950	653	1,297	—	—	—	1,297	2.07
Gambia, The	186	43	143	—	—	—	143	0.23
Ghana	2,904	938	1,966	49	—	49	2,015	3.21
Grenada	7	—	7	—	—	—	7	0.01
Guinea	960	220	740	—	—	—	740	1.18
Guinea-Bissau	225	38	187	6	—	6	193	0.31
Guyana	254	79	175	—	—	—	175	0.28
Haiti	474	146	328	14	—	14	342	0.55
Honduras	446	178	268	—	—	—	268	0.43
India	20,979	4,857	16,122	91	21	70	16,192	25.78
Indonesia	787	—	787	—	—	—	787	1.25
Jordan	72	—	72	—	—	—	72	0.12
Kenya	2,211	514	1,697	52	—	52	1,749	2.78
Korea, Republic of	87	—	87	—	—	—	87	0.14
Kyrgyz Republic	143	102	41	—	—	—	41	0.06
Lao People's Democratic Republic	413	173	240	—	—	—	240	0.38
Lesotho	223	82	141	—	—	—	141	0.22
Liberia	110	4	106	—	—	—	106	0.17

	IDA			Special Fund			Total	
Borrower or guarantor	Total development credits	Undisbursed development credits[1]	Development credits outstanding	Total development credits	Undisbursed development credits	Development credits outstanding	Development credits outstanding	Percentage of development credits outstanding
Macedonia, former Yugoslav Republic of .	$ 42	$ —	$ 42	$ —	$ —	$ —	$ 42	0.07
Madagascar	1,308	358	950	40	—	40	990	1.58
Malawi	1,412	304	1,108	19	—	19	1,127	1.79
Maldives	37	7	30	—	—	—	30	0.05
Mali	994	267	727	14	—	14	741	1.18
Mauritania	377	84	293	—	—	—	293	0.47
Mauritius	17	—	17	—	—	—	17	0.03
Mongolia	89	45	44	—	—	—	44	0.07
Morocco	35	—	35	—	—	—	35	0.06
Mozambique	1,531	939	592	—	—	—	592	0.94
Myanmar	818	33	785	—	—	—	785	1.25
Nepal	1,453	561	892	—	—	—	892	1.42
Nicaragua	351	142	209	—	—	—	209	0.33
Niger	686	138	548	—	—	—	548	0.87
Nigeria	953	797	156	—	—	—	156	0.25
Pakistan	4,492	1,599	2,893	—	—	—	2,893	4.61
Papua New Guinea	110	—	110	—	—	—	110	0.17
Paraguay	38	—	38	—	—	—	38	0.06
Philippines	280	109	171	—	—	—	171	0.27
Rwanda	716	242	474	—	—	—	474	0.75
St. Kitts and Nevis	2	—	2	—	—	—	2	*
St. Lucia	6	*	6	—	—	—	6	0.01
St. Vincent and the Grenadines	2	—	2	6	—	6	8	0.01
São Tomé and Principe .	70	25	45	—	—	—	45	0.07
Senegal	1,198	232	966	26	—	26	992	1.58
Sierra Leone	328	155	173	—	—	—	173	0.28
Solomon Islands	37	16	21	—	—	—	21	0.03
Somalia	555	131	424	—	—	—	424	0.68
Sri Lanka	1,838	538	1,300	—	—	—	1,300	2.07
Sudan	1,237	1	1,236	14	—	14	1,250	1.99
Swaziland	6	—	6	—	—	—	6	0.01
Syrian Arab Republic	44	—	44	—	—	—	44	0.07
Tanzania	2,887	950	1,937	—	—	—	1,937	3.08
Thailand	104	—	104	—	—	—	104	0.17
Togo	607	141	466	26	—	26	492	0.78
Tonga	6	2	4	—	—	—	4	0.01
Tunisia	53	—	53	—	—	—	53	0.08
Turkey	139	—	139	—	—	—	139	0.22
Uganda	2,361	888	1,473	—	—	—	1,473	2.35
Vanuatu	17	5	12	—	—	—	12	0.02
Viet Nam	391	335	56	—	—	—	56	0.09
Western Samoa	48	6	42	—	—	—	42	0.07
Yemen, Republic of	1,102	349	753	14	—	14	767	1.22
Zaire	1,314	22	1,292	—	—	—	1,292	2.06
Zambia	1,345	400	945	7	—	7	952	1.52
Zimbabwe	471	184	287	—	—	—	287	0.46
Subtotal members	87,306	25,007	62,299	478	21	457	62,756	99.92

(continued)

Summary Statement of Development Credits *(continued)*

June 30, 1994
Expressed in millions of U.S. dollars

	IDA			Special Fund			Total	
Borrower or guarantor	Total development credits	Undisbursed development credits[1]	Development credits outstanding	Total development credits	Undisbursed development credits	Development credits outstanding	Development credits outstanding	Percentage of development credits outstanding
West African Development Bank[2] ..	$ 64	$ 40	$ 24	$ —	$ —	$ —	$ 24	0.04
Caribbean Development Bank[3]	45	23	22	—	—	—	22	0.03
Other[4]	8	—	8	—	—	—	8	0.01
Total—June 30, 1994[5]	$87,423	$25,070	$62,353	$478	$ 21	$457	$62,810	100.00
Total—June 30, 1993[5]	$79,659	$23,932	$55,727	$470	$ 39	$431	$56,158	

* indicates amounts less than $0.5 million or 0.005 percent.

NOTES

1. Of the undisbursed balance at June 30, 1994, IDA has entered into irrevocable commitments to disburse $229 million ($277 million—June 30, 1993).

2. These development credits are for the benefit of Benin, Burkina Faso, Cote d'Ivoire, Mali, Niger, Senegal, and Togo.

3. These development credits are for the benefit of Grenada and territories of the United Kingdom (Associated States and Dependencies) in the Caribbean region.

4. Represents development credits made at a time when the authorities on Taiwan represented China in IDA (prior to May 15, 1980).

5. In the Statement of Development Resources at June 30, 1994, total development credits of $87,880 million ($80,090 million—June 30, 1993) and total development credits disbursed and outstanding of $62,810 million ($56,158 million—June 30, 1993) include development credits outstanding of $457 million ($431 million—June 30, 1993) which were originated under the Special Fund, since such amounts are repayable to IDA (see Notes to Financial Statements—Note E).

Maturity Structure of Development Credits Disbursed and Outstanding

Period	IDA	Special Fund	Total
July 1, 1994 through June 30, 1995	$ 554	$ 5	$ 559
July 1, 1995 through June 30, 1996	587	5	592
July 1, 1996 through June 30, 1997	653	5	658
July 1, 1997 through June 30, 1998	740	5	745
July 1, 1998 through June 30, 1999	902	5	907
July 1, 1999 through June 30, 2004	7,407	27	7,434
July 1, 2004 through June 30, 2009	10,098	69	10,167
July 1, 2009 through June 30, 2014	11,591	69	11,660
July 1, 2014 through June 30, 2019	10,663	69	10,732
July 1, 2019 through June 30, 2024	9,050	69	9,119
July 1, 2024 through June 30, 2029	6,583	69	6,652
July 1, 2029 through June 30, 2034	3,069	60	3,129
July 1, 2034 through June 30, 2039	456	—	456
Total[1]	$62,353	$457	$62,810

NOTE

1. In the Statement of Development Resources at June 30, 1994, total development credits disbursed and outstanding of $62,810 million ($56,158 million—June 30, 1993) include development credits outstanding of $457 million ($431 million—June 30, 1993) which were originated under the Special Fund, since such amounts are repayable to IDA (see Notes to Financial Statements—Note E).

The Notes to Financial Statements are an integral part of these Statements.

Statement of Voting Power, and Subscriptions and Contributions

June 30, 1994
Expressed in millions of U.S. dollars except vote data

Member[1]	IDA			Special Fund contributions
	Number of votes	Percentage of total	Subscriptions and contributions	
Part I Members				
Australia	131,094	1.36	$ 1,525.6	$ —
Austria	64,389	0.67	750.4	—
Belgium	103,228	1.07	1,179.2	50
Canada	295,694	3.06	3,818.5	159
Denmark	92,868	0.96	1,140.3	34
Finland	65,982	0.68	578.1	—
France	390,814	4.04	6,145.8	149
Germany	658,521	6.81	10,426.4	—
Iceland	24,316	0.25	16.4	—
Ireland	29,443	0.30	103.1	—
Italy	259,450	2.68	2,941.7	90
Japan	988,143	10.22	20,756.2	—
Kuwait	69,834	0.72	649.2	—
Luxembourg	25,517	0.26	47.6	—
Netherlands	205,959	2.13	3,365.0	—
New Zealand	29,602	0.31	100.1	—
Norway	93,414	0.97	1,075.4	40
Portugal	18,617	0.19	4.1	—
Russia	28,202	0.29	143.3	—
South Africa	29,813	0.31	83.1	—
Spain	42,462	0.44	302.3	—
Sweden	192,965	2.00	2,221.1	74
Switzerland	80,016	0.83	984.7	—
United Arab Emirates	1,367	0.01	5.6	—
United Kingdom	495,881	5.13	6,524.2	—
United States	1,490,101	15.41	21,831.5	—
Subtotal Part I Members[2]	5,907,692	61.10	86,718.9	596
Part II Members				
Afghanistan	13,557	0.14	1.0	—
Albania	19,711	0.20	0.3	—
Algeria	24,494	0.25	5.1	—
Angola	45,662	0.47	7.9	—
Argentina	96,503	1.00	58.0	—
Armenia	584	0.01	0.5	—
Bangladesh	57,640	0.60	7.3	—
Belize	1,788	0.02	0.2	—
Benin	5,297	0.05	0.6	—
Bhutan	12,233	0.13	0.1	—
Bolivia	29,552	0.31	1.4	—
Botswana	23,686	0.24	0.2	—
Brazil	158,736	1.64	92.3	—
Burkina Faso	19,065	0.20	0.7	—
Burundi	22,398	0.23	1.0	—
Cambodia	7,826	0.08	1.3	—
Cameroon	18,656	0.19	1.3	—
Cape Verde	4,948	0.05	0.1	—
Central African Republic	10,920	0.11	0.6	—
Chad	10,990	0.11	0.6	—
Chile	31,782	0.33	4.5	—
China	193,370	2.00	39.6	—
Colombia	34,350	0.36	22.5	—
Comoros	13,141	0.14	0.1	—
Congo	6,685	0.07	0.6	—
Costa Rica	12,323	0.13	0.3	—
Côte d'Ivoire	17,866	0.18	1.3	—

(continued)

Statement of Voting Power, and Subscriptions and Contributions *(continued)*

June 30, 1994
Expressed in millions of U.S. dollars except vote data

Member[1]	IDA			Special Fund contributions
	Number of votes	Percentage of total	Subscriptions and contributions	
Part II Members (continued)				
Croatia	28,087	0.29	$ 5.5	$ —
Cyprus	27,628	0.29	1.1	—
Czech Republic	38,648	0.40	23.6	—
Djibouti	532	0.01	0.2	—
Dominica	14,985	0.15	0.1	—
Dominican Republic	25,333	0.26	0.6	—
Ecuador	23,279	0.24	0.8	—
Egypt, Arab Republic of	45,364	0.47	6.7	—
El Salvador	6,244	0.06	0.4	—
Equatorial Guinea	6,167	0.06	0.4	—
Ethiopia	21,353	0.22	0.7	—
Fiji	6,755	0.07	0.7	—
Gabon	2,093	0.02	0.6	—
Gambia, The	15,151	0.16	0.3	—
Georgia	22,523	0.23	0.9	—
Ghana	22,131	0.23	3.0	—
Greece	36,429	0.38	18.2	—
Grenada	18,930	0.20	0.1	—
Guatemala	20,750	0.21	0.5	—
Guinea	27,284	0.28	1.3	—
Guinea-Bissau	4,982	0.05	0.2	—
Guyana	18,160	0.19	1.0	—
Haiti	17,143	0.18	1.0	—
Honduras	21,332	0.22	0.4	—
Hungary	73,914	0.76	37.6	—
India	300,767	3.11	55.1	—
Indonesia	94,802	0.98	14.8	—
Iran, Islamic Republic of	15,455	0.16	5.7	—
Iraq	9,407	0.10	1.0	—
Israel	20,567	0.21	2.5	—
Jordan	24,627	0.25	0.4	—
Kazakhstan	806	0.01	1.8	—
Kenya	25,760	0.27	2.2	—
Kiribati	4,777	0.05	0.1	—
Korea, Republic of	39,153	0.40	113.6	—
Kyrgyz Republic	580	0.01	0.5	—
Lao People's Democratic Republic	11,723	0.12	0.6	—
Latvia	614	0.01	0.7	—
Lebanon	8,562	0.09	0.6	—
Lesotho	23,744	0.25	0.2	—
Liberia	22,771	0.24	1.1	—
Libya	7,771	0.08	1.3	—
Macedonia, former Yugoslav Republic of	15,759	0.16	1.0	—
Madagascar	10,797	0.11	1.2	—
Malawi	27,352	0.28	1.0	—
Malaysia	39,045	0.40	3.6	—
Maldives	22,892	0.24	*	—
Mali	22,407	0.23	1.2	—
Marshall Islands, The	4,906	0.05	*	—
Mauritania	10,885	0.11	0.6	—
Mauritius	28,318	0.29	1.2	—
Mexico	68,128	0.70	124.8	—
Micronesia	18,424	0.19	*	—

	IDA			
Member[1]	Number of votes	Percentage of total	Subscriptions and contributions	Special Fund contributions
Moldova	612	0.01	$ 0.7	$ —
Mongolia	5,039	0.05	0.3	—
Morocco	45,650	0.47	4.8	—
Mozambique	5,721	0.06	1.7	—
Myanmar	35,848	0.37	2.9	—
Nepal	25,765	0.27	0.7	—
Nicaragua	24,627	0.25	0.4	—
Niger	16,541	0.17	0.7	—
Nigeria	8,257	0.09	4.2	—
Oman	24,631	0.25	0.4	—
Pakistan	89,116	0.92	13.7	—
Panama	5,657	0.06	*	—
Papua New Guinea	13,050	0.13	1.1	—
Paraguay	11,419	0.12	0.4	—
Peru	6,990	0.07	2.1	—
Philippines	16,583	0.17	6.5	—
Poland	224,289	2.32	52.1	—
Rwanda	17,371	0.18	1.0	—
St. Kitts and Nevis	4,978	0.05	0.2	—
St. Lucia	22,416	0.23	0.2	—
St. Vincent and the Grenadines	514	0.01	0.1	—
São Tomé and Principe	4,714	0.05	0.1	—
Saudi Arabia	330,314	3.42	2,033.2	—
Senegal	27,102	0.28	2.2	—
Sierra Leone	12,667	0.13	1.0	—
Slovak Republic	20,893	0.22	7.0	—
Slovenia	18,956	0.20	3.0	—
Solomon Islands	518	0.01	0.1	—
Somalia	10,506	0.11	1.0	—
Sri Lanka	42,359	0.44	4.0	—
Sudan	22,886	0.24	1.3	—
Swaziland	11,073	0.11	0.4	—
Syrian Arab Republic	7,651	0.08	1.2	—
Tajikistan	20,568	0.21	0.5	—
Tanzania	33,598	0.35	2.2	—
Thailand	42,359	0.44	4.3	—
Togo	21,847	0.23	1.0	—
Tonga	11,380	0.12	0.1	—
Trinidad and Tobago	770	0.01	1.6	—
Tunisia	2,793	0.03	1.9	—
Turkey	64,045	0.66	75.9	—
Uganda	21,093	0.22	2.2	—
Uzbekistan	746	0.01	1.5	—
Vanuatu	13,670	0.14	0.2	—
Viet Nam	8,889	0.09	1.9	—
Western Samoa	13,061	0.14	0.1	—
Yemen	24,658	0.26	2.1	—
Zaire	12,164	0.13	3.8	—
Zambia	26,868	0.28	3.4	—
Zimbabwe	7,368	0.08	5.0	—

(continued)

Statement of Voting Power, and Subscriptions and Contributions (continued)

June 30, 1994
Expressed in millions of U.S. dollars except vote data

Member[1]	IDA			Special Fund contributions
	Number of votes	Percentage of total	Subscriptions and contributions	
Subtotal Part II Members[2]	3,760,349	38.91	$ 2,948.5	$ —
Total—June 30, 1994[2, 3]	9,668,041	100.00	$89,667.4	$596
Total—June 30, 1993[3]	8,862,437	100.00	$72,911.3	$596

* Indicates amounts less than $0.05 million.

NOTES

1. See Notes to Financial Statements—Note C for an explanation of the two categories of membership.

2. May differ from the sum of individual figures shown because of rounding.

3. In the Statements of Development Resources at June 30, 1994, member subscriptions and contributions of $89,544 million ($72,777 million—June 30, 1993) does not include $512 million ($512 million—June 30, 1993) of Switzerland's subscription and contributions and includes Special Fund contributions of $389 million ($378 million—June 30, 1993).

$512 million ($512 million—June 30, 1993) of Switzerland's subscription and contributions have not been included since this represents the difference between the total cofinancing grants of $580 million provided by Switzerland directly to IDA borrowers as cofinancing grants between the fourth and the ninth replenishments of IDA resources, and the July 1992 contribution by Switzerland of $68 million representing the present value of future reflows on these grants if they had been made through IDA on IDA's repayment terms.

Special Fund contributions of $389 million ($378 million—June 30, 1993) have been included, since the development credits that were funded using these resources are repayable to IDA (see Notes to Financial Statements—Note C).

The Notes to Financial Statements are an integral part of these Statements.

Notes to Financial Statements

Summary of Significant Accounting and Related Policies

IDA's financial statements are prepared in conformity with the accounting principles generally accepted in the United States and with International Accounting Standards.

Organization and Operations

IDA: IDA was established on September 24, 1960 to promote economic development, increase productivity, and raise the standard of living of its developing country members.

Special Fund: On October 26, 1982, IDA established the Special Fund constituted by funds to be contributed by members of IDA and administered by IDA, to supplement the regular resources available for lending by IDA. The arrangements governing the Special Fund may be amended or terminated by IDA's Executive Directors subject to the agreement of a qualified majority of the contributors to the Special Fund. The resources of the Special Fund are kept separate from the resources of IDA.

Translation of Currencies

IDA's financial statements are expressed in terms of U.S. dollars solely for the purpose of summarizing IDA's financial position and the results of its operations for the convenience of its members and other interested parties.

IDA: IDA is an international organization which conducts its operations in the currencies of all of its members. Assets and liabilities are translated at market rates of exchange at the end of the accounting period. Subscriptions and contributions are translated in the manner described below. Income and expenses are translated at the market rates of exchange at the dates on which they are recognized or at an average of the market rates of exchange in effect during each month. Translation adjustments relating to the revaluation of development credits denominated in Special Drawing Rights (SDRs) are charged or credited to Cumulative translation adjustment on development credits. Other translation adjustments are charged or credited to the Accumulated surplus.

Special Fund: Assets of the Special Fund are translated at market rates of exchange at the end of the period. Contributions are translated in the manner described below. Income is translated at market rates of exchange on dates of recognition of income. Translation adjustments are charged or credited to the Accumulated surplus.

Valuation of Subscriptions and Contributions

IDA: The subscriptions and contributions provided through the third replenishment are expressed in terms of "U.S. dollars of the weight and fineness in effect on January 1, 1960" (1960 dollars). Following the abolition of gold as a common denominator of the monetary system and the repeal of the provision of the U.S. law defining the par value of the U.S. dollar in terms of gold, the pre-existing basis for translating 1960 dollars into current dollars or any other currency disappeared. The Executive Directors of IDA have decided, until such time as the relevant provisions of the Articles of Agreement are amended, that the words "U.S. dollars of the weight and fineness in effect on January 1, 1960" in Article II, Section 2(b) of the Articles of Agreement of IDA are interpreted to mean the SDR introduced by the International Monetary Fund as the SDR was valued in terms of U.S. dollars immediately before the introduction of the basket method of valuing the SDR on July 1, 1974, such value being equal to $1.20635 for one SDR (the 1974 SDR), and have also decided to apply the same standard of value to amounts expressed in 1960 dollars in the relevant resolutions of the Board of Governors.

The subscriptions and contributions provided through the third replenishment are expressed on the basis of the 1974 SDR. Prior to the decision of the Executive Directors, IDA had valued these subscriptions and contributions on the basis of the SDR at the current market value of the SDR.

The subscriptions and contributions provided under the fourth replenishment and thereafter are expressed in members' currencies or SDRs and are payable in members' currencies. Beginning July 1, 1986, subscriptions and contributions made available for disbursement in cash to IDA are translated at market rates of exchange on the dates they were made available. Prior to that date, subscriptions and contributions which had been disbursed or converted into other currencies were translated at market rates of exchange on dates of disbursement or conversion. Subscriptions and contributions not yet available for disbursements are translated at market rates of exchange at the end of the accounting period.

Special Fund: Beginning April 1, 1989, subscriptions and contributions received but not yet disbursed, as well as subscriptions and contributions disbursed or converted into other currencies, are translated at market rates of exchange on the dates they were made available for disbursement in cash to the Special Fund. Prior to that date, subscriptions and contributions which had been disbursed or converted into other currencies were translated at market rates of exchange on dates of disbursement or conversion. Subscriptions and contributions receivable are translated at market rates of exchange at the end of the accounting period.

Development Credits

All development credits are made to member governments or to the government of a territory of a member (except for development credits which have been made to regional development banks for the benefit of members or territories of members of IDA). It is the policy of IDA to place in nonaccrual status all development credits made to a member government or to the government of a territory of a member if principal or charges with respect to any such development credit are overdue by more than six months, unless IDA management determines that the overdue amount will be collected in the immediate future. In addition, if loans by the IBRD to a member government are placed in nonaccrual status, all development credits to that member government will also be placed in nonaccrual status by IDA. On the date a member's development credits are placed in nonaccrual status, charges that had been accrued on development credits outstanding to the member which remained unpaid are deducted from the income of the current period. Charges on nonaccruing development credits are included in income only to the extent that payments have actually been received by IDA. On the date a member pays in full all overdue amounts, the member's credits emerge from nonaccrual status, its eligibility for new credits is restored, and all overdue charges (including those from prior years) are recognized as income in the current period.

In projecting the repayments of principal which would be available for new commitments, IDA takes into consideration any collectibility risks that may exist in principal receivable from development credits. No provision has been established for credit losses. Should losses occur arising from principal receivable from development credits, they would be charged against IDA's Development Resources. To date, IDA has not suffered any losses on receivables from development credits, nor are any losses anticipated.

IDA: The repayment obligations of IDA's development credits funded from resources through the fifth replenishment are expressed in the development credit agreements in terms of 1960 dollars. In June 1987, the Executive Directors decided to value those development credits at the rate of $1.20635 per 1960 dollar on a permanent basis. Development credits funded from resources provided under the sixth replenishment and thereafter are denominated in SDRs; the principal amounts disbursed under such development credits are to be repaid in currency amounts currently equivalent to the SDRs disbursed.

(continued)

Notes to Financial Statements   *(continued)*

Special Fund: Special Fund development credits are denominated in SDRs. The principal amounts disbursed under such development credits are to be repaid in currency amounts currently equivalent to the SDRs disbursed.

Special Fund development credits are made on the same terms as regular IDA development credits except that the proceeds of Special Fund development credits may be used only to finance expenditures for goods or services from (a) Part II members of IDA; (b) Part I members contributing to the Special Fund; and (c) Part I members contributing to the regular resources of IDA through IDA's FY84 Account who have notified IDA that such contributions are to be treated in the same manner as contributions to the Special Fund for purposes of any future adjustment of the voting rights of the members of IDA.

Investments

IDA carries its investment securities at market value. Both realized and unrealized gains and losses are included in income from investments.

Reclassifications

Certain reclassifications of the prior year's information have been made to conform to the current year's presentation.

Note A—Investments

A summary of the currency composition of the Investments at June 30, 1994 and June 30, 1993 is as follows:

In millions of U.S.-dollars equivalent

Currency	IDA 1994	IDA 1993	Special Fund 1994	Special Fund 1993
Belgian francs	$ 61	$ 60	$ 14	$ 12
Canadian dollars	—	43	73	69
Danish kroner	—	—	13	9
Deutsche mark	1,342	1,184	—	—
French francs	230	197	37	45
Japanese yen	327	305	—	—
Italian lire	80	85	91	80
Netherlands guilders . .	56	146	—	—
Pounds sterling	151	155	—	—
Swedish kronor	67	75	44	36
United States dollars .	683	744	—	—
Total	$2,997	$2,994	$272	$251

As part of its overall portfolio management strategy, IDA is party to financial instruments with off-balance sheet risk, including futures, covered forward contracts, options, and short sales. Futures are contracts for delayed delivery of securities or money market instruments in which the seller agrees to make delivery at a specified future date of a specified instrument, at a specified price or yield. At June 30, 1994 the total contract value of futures contracts was $1,161 million ($211 million—June 30, 1993) and IDA's exposure to credit loss on futures contracts due to potential nonperformance of counterparties was $1 million ($7 million—June 30, 1993).

Covered forwards are agreements in which cash in one currency is converted into a different currency and, simultaneously, a forward exchange agreement is executed providing for a future exchange of the two currencies in order to recover the currency converted. At June 30, 1994, IDA had gross receivables from covered forward agreements of $323 million ($119 million— June 30, 1993) and gross payables from covered forward agreements of

$317 million ($125 million—June 30, 1993). At June 30, 1994, IDA's exposure to credit loss on covered forwards due to potential nonperformance by counterparties was $6 million (nil—June 30, 1993).

Options are contracts that allow the holder of the option to purchase or sell a financial instrument at a specified price and within a specified period of time from the seller or to the purchaser of the option. As a seller of options, IDA receives a premium at the outset and then bears the risk of an unfavorable change in the price of the financial instrument underlying the option. The total contract value of options sold at June 30, 1994 was $216 million ($29 million—June 30, 1993).

Short sales are sales of securities not held in IDA's portfolio at the time of the sale. IDA must purchase the security at a later date and bears the risk that the market value of the security will move adversely between the time of the sale and the time the security must be delivered. The total contract amount of short sales at June 30, 1994 was $13 million ($7 million—June 30, 1993). This amount is included in Net payable on investment security transactions.

Note B—Cash and Investments Not Immediately Available for Disbursement

Under the Articles of Agreement and the arrangements governing replenishments, IDA must take appropriate steps to ensure that, over a reasonable period of time, the resources provided by donors for lending by IDA are used on an approximately pro rata basis. Donors sometimes contribute resources substantially ahead of their pro rata share. Unless otherwise agreed, IDA does not disburse these funds ahead of donors' pro rata shares. Cash and investments not immediately available for disbursement represents the difference between the amount contributed and the amount available for disbursements on a pro rata basis.

Note C—Member Subscriptions and Contributions

Restricted Assets and Subscriptions: For the purposes of its financial resources, the membership of IDA is divided into two categories: (1) Part I members, which make payments of subscriptions and contributions provided to IDA in convertible currencies which may be freely used or exchanged by IDA in its operations and (2) most Part II members, which make payments of ten percent of their initial subscriptions in freely convertible currencies, and the remaining ninety percent of their initial subscriptions, and all additional subscriptions and contributions in their own currencies or in freely convertible currencies. Certain Part II members provide a portion of their subscriptions and contributions in the same manner as mentioned in (1) above. IDA's Articles of Agreement and subsequent replenishment agreements provide that the currency of any Part II member paid in by it may not be used by IDA for projects financed by IDA and located outside the territories of the member except by agreement between the member and IDA.

Maintenance of Value: Article IV, Section 2(a) and (b) of IDA's Articles of Agreement provides for maintenance-of-value payments on account of the local currency portion of the initial subscription whenever the par value of the member's currency or its foreign exchange value has, in the opinion of IDA, depreciated or appreciated to a significant extent within the members' territories, so long as and to the extent that such currency shall not have been initially disbursed or exchanged for the currency of another member. The provisions of Article IV, Section 2(a) and (b) have by agreement been extended to cover additional subscriptions and contributions of IDA through the third replenishment, but are not applicable to those of the fourth and subsequent replenishments.

The Executive Directors decided on June 30, 1987, that settlements of maintenance-of-value obligations, which would result from the resolution of the valuation issue on the basis of the 1974 SDR, would be deferred until the Executive Directors decide to resume such settlements.

Tenth Replenishment: On March 31, 1993, the Board of Governors of IDA adopted a resolution authorizing the tenth replenishment of IDA's resources. The tenth replenishment provides IDA with resources to fund credits committed during the period July 1, 1993 to June 30, 1996. The amount of the replenishment, including supplementary contributions provided by certain members, is equivalent to SDR 13,000 million (at the exchange rates determined pursuant to a formula agreed by IDA and contributing donors). The tenth replenishment became effective on December 17, 1993.

Subscriptions and Contributions Not Yet Due: At June 30, 1994, unrestricted subscriptions and contributions not yet due will become due as follows:

In millions

Period	June 30, 1994
July 1, 1994 through June 30, 1995	$ 5,362
July 1, 1995 through June 30, 1996	5,366
Thereafter	115
Total	$10,843

Contributions to Special Fund: Member contributions to the Special Fund totaling $596 million at June 30, 1994, ($596 million—June 30, 1993) are reflected as Member subscriptions and contributions in the Statements of Development Resources. At June 30, 1994, the Special Fund total is reflected net of $389 million ($378 million—June 30, 1993), which represents development credit disbursements that are repayable to and included in Member subscriptions and contributions of IDA.

Membership: On February 25, 1993, the IBRD's Executive Directors decided that the Socialist Federal Republic of Yugoslavia (SFRY) had ceased to be a member of the IBRD and that the Republic of Bosnia and Herzegovina, the Republic of Croatia, the former Yugoslav Republic of Macedonia, the Republic of Slovenia and the Federal Republic of Yugoslavia (Serbia and Montenegro) are authorized to succeed to the membership of the SFRY in the IBRD when certain requirements are met. In accordance with the Articles of Agreement of the Association, on February 25, 1993, the SFRY ceased to be a member of IDA due to the cessation of its membership in IBRD. Three of the five successor Republics—the Republics of Croatia and Slovenia and the former Yugoslav Republic of Macedonia—have since become members of IDA. As of June 30, 1994, the subscription and contributions allocated to the other successor Republics (the Republic of Bosnia and Herzegovina, and the Federal Republic of Yugoslavia (Serbia and Montenegro)) are included under Payments on account of pending membership.

On May 29, 1992, Switzerland became a member of IDA. Before that date, Switzerland had contributed to IDA an equivalent of $51 million. As agreed between the Swiss Confederation and IDA, these grant contributions were converted to an IDA subscription. Further, during the commitment periods between the fourth and the ninth replenishments of the IDA resources, Switzerland had cofinanced projects by making available to IDA borrowers untied grants in the aggregate amount of Swiss francs 1,055 million (historical U.S. dollar amount of $580 million). On July 7, 1992, as agreed between the Swiss Confederation and IDA, these grant contributions were converted to an IDA subscription and contribution when Switzerland contributed a further $68 million, representing the present value of future reflows of the cofinancing grants if they had been made through IDA on IDA's repayment terms. At June 30, 1994, $512 million ($512 million—June 30, 1993), representing the difference between the total cofinancing grants of $580 million and the present value of future reflows of $68 million, have not been included in the Member subscriptions and contributions in the Statements of Development Resources.

Note D—Transfers from the International Bank for Reconstruction and Development (IBRD)

IDA: The IBRD's Board of Governors approved transfers to IDA totaling $3,808 million through June 30, 1993. Of the total amount, $80 million has been disbursed for grants for agricultural research, the control of onchocerciasis, and other developmental activities. On September 30, 1993, the IBRD's Board of Governors approved a transfer of $140 million to IDA by way of grant. On September 24, 1992, as amended on November 11, 1993, the IBRD's Board of Governors authorized a transfer of an amount equivalent to $325 million by way of a grant to IDA when the tenth replenishment would become effective, which occurred on December 17, 1993.

Note E—Development Credits

Special Fund development credits disbursed and outstanding of $457 million at June 30, 1994 ($431 million—June 30, 1993) are included in the Statements of Development Resources of IDA since principal repayments on these development credits will become part of the general resources of IDA, unless otherwise provided in a decision of IDA's Executive Directors to terminate administration of the Special Fund by IDA.

At June 30, 1994, principal installments of $0.6 million and charges of $0.5 million payable to IDA on development credits were overdue by more than three months. At June 30, 1994, the aggregate principal amounts outstanding on all development credits to any borrower, other than those referred to in the following paragraph, with any development credit overdue by more than three months was $474 million.

At June 30, 1994, the development credits made to or guaranteed by certain member countries with an aggregate principal balance outstanding of $3,533 million ($1,046 million—June 30, 1993), of which $42 million ($18 million—June 30, 1993) was overdue, were in nonaccrual status. As of such date, overdue charges in respect of these development credits totaled $46 million ($21 million—June 30, 1993). If these development credits had not been in nonaccrual status, income from development credits for the year ended June 30, 1994 would have been higher by $31 million ($7 million—June 30, 1993), which is net of charges received from such members during the year. A summary of member countries with credits or guarantees in nonaccrual status follows:

In millions

Borrower	June 30, 1994		
	Principal Outstanding	Principal and Charges Overdue	Nonaccrual Since
Afghanistan	$ 75	$ 3	June 1992
Haiti	342	13	April 1992
Liberia	106	11	April 1988
Somalia	424	19	July 1991
Sudan	1,250	17	January 1994
Syrian Arab Republic . . .	44	7	April 1988
Zaire	1,292	18	November 1993
Total	$3,533	$88	

During the fiscal year ended June 30, 1994, Congo paid off all of its arrears and therefore credits to it came out of nonaccrual status. As a result, income from credits for the fiscal year ended June 30, 1994 increased by $2 million corresponding to income that would have been accrued in previous fiscal years. For the fiscal year ended June 30, 1993, no credits came out of nonaccrual status.

(continued)

Notes to Financial Statements   *(continued)*

Note F—Disclosures about Fair Value of Financial Instruments

Investments: Since IDA carries its investments at market value, the carrying amount represents the fair value of the portfolio. These fair values are based on quoted market prices, where available. If quoted market prices are not available, fair values are based on quoted market prices of comparable instruments. The fair value of financial instruments that are short term approximate their carry value.

Credits: All of IDA's credits are made to or guaranteed by countries that are members of IDA. These credits are made to provide concessional assistance to low-income developing countries. While the principal amount is fully repayable, no interest is charged to the borrower. A service fee of 0.75% of the disbursed and outstanding balance is charged, however, to cover the costs of administering the credits. Due to the concessional nature of these credits, it is not meaningful to calculate a fair value for outstanding credits.

Note G—Income and Expenses

IDA: IDA pays a management fee to the IBRD representing its share of the administrative expenses incurred by the IBRD.

Special Fund: The service and commitment charges payable by borrowers under Special Fund development credits are paid directly to IDA to compensate it for services as administrator of the Special Fund. Income from investments of the Special Fund becomes part of the resources of the Special Fund.

Report of Independent Accountants

Price Waterhouse The Hague   New York
(International Firm) Beijing   Tokyo
Hong Kong   Washington
London

Price Waterhouse

July 27, 1994

President and Board of Governors
  International Development Association and the
  Special Fund Administered by the International Development Association

In our opinion, the financial statements appearing on pages 196 through 208 of this Report present fairly, in all material respects, in terms of United States dollars, the financial position of the International Development Association and the Special Fund Administered by the International Development Association at June 30, 1994 and 1993, and the changes in their accumulated surplus and their cash flows for the years then ended in conformity with generally accepted accounting principles in the United States and with International Accounting Standards. These financial statements are the responsibility of management; our responsibility is to express an opinion on these financial statements based on our audits. We conducted our audits of these statements in accordance with generally accepted auditing standards, including International Standards on Auditing, which require that we plan and perform the audit to obtain reasonable assurance about whether the financial statements are free of material misstatement. An audit includes examining, on a test basis, evidence supporting the amounts and disclosures in the financial statements, assessing the accounting principles used and significant estimates made by management, and evaluating the overall financial statement presentation. We believe that our audits provide a reasonable basis for the opinion expressed above.

Price Waterhouse
(International Firm)

IBRD/IDA Appendices

Governors and Alternates of the World Bank

Appendix 1

June 30, 1994

Member	Governor	Alternate
Afghanistan	Abdul Karim Khalili	Mohammad Ehsan
Albania	Piro Dishnica	Adrian Xhyheri
Algeria	Ahmed Benbitour	Kacim Brachemi
Angola	José Pedro de Morais	Sebastião Bastos Lavrador
Antigua and Barbuda[a]	Molwyn Joseph	Ludolph Brown
Argentina	Domingo Felipe Cavallo	Roque Benjamin Fernández
Armenia	Hrant A. Bagratian	Armen Yeghiazarian
Australia	Ralph Willis	Gordon Bilney
Austria	Ferdinand Lacina	Hans Dietmar Schweisgut
Azerbaijan[a]	Galib A. Agayev	Vagif K. Akhmedov
Bahamas, The[a]	Hubert A. Ingraham	Luther E. Smith
Bahrain[a]	Ibrahim Abdul Karim	Rasheed M. Al-Maraj
Bangladesh	M. Saifur Rahman	Muhammad Lutfullahil Majid
Barbados[a]	L. Erskine Sandiford	George Reid
Belarus[a]	Nikolai Filippovich Rumas	Nikolai K. Lisai
Belgium	Philippe Maystadt	Alfons Verplaetse
Belize	Dean O. Barrow	Joseph D. Waight
Benin	Robert Tagnon	Rigobert Ladikpo
Bhutan	Dorji Tshering	Yeshey Zimba
Bolivia	Fernando Alvaro Cossio	Gaby Candia de Mercado
Botswana	Festus G. Mogae	Goldie John Stoneham
Brazil	Rubens Ricupero	Pedro Sampaio Malan
Bulgaria[a]	Stoyan I. Alexandrov	Mileti Mladenov
Burkina Faso	Zephirin Diabre	T. Celestin Tiendrebeogo
Burundi	Toyi Salvator	Nestor Ntungwanayo
Cambodia	Sam Rainsy	Cham Prasidh
Cameroon	Augustin Frederic Kodock	Esther Dang Belibi
Canada	Paul Martin	Huguette Labelle
Cape Verde	José Tomás Veiga	Alexandre Vieira Fontes
Central African Republic	Thierry Bingaba	Gregoire Zowaye
Chad	Ibni Oumar Mahamat Saleh	Hassan Adoum Bakhit
Chile	Eduardo Aninat	José Pablo Arellano
China	Liu Zhongli	Jin Renqing
Colombia	Rudolf Hommes	Armando Montenegro
Comoros	Assoumany Aboudou	Chabane Abdallah Halifa
Congo	Clement Mouamba	Antoine Banvidi
Costa Rica	Fernando Herrero Acosta	Leonardo Garnier Rimolo
Côte d'Ivoire	Niamien N'Goran	Victor Kouame
Croatia	Zoran Jasic	Josip Kulisic
Cyprus	Phaedros Economides	Michael Erotokritos
Czech Republic	Ivan Kocarnik	Jan Vit
Denmark	Helle Degn	Ole Loensmann Poulsen
Djibouti	Ahmed Aden Youssouf	Ibrahim Kassim Chehem
Dominica	Mary Eugenia Charles	Gilbert Williams
Dominican Republic	Mario Read Vittini	Eligio J. Bisono B.
Ecuador	Cesar Robalino Gonzaga	Modesto Correa
Egypt, Arab Rep. of	Kamal Ahmed El-Ganzoury	Yousef Boutros Ghali
El Salvador	Ramon Gonzalez Giner	José Roberto Orellana Milla
Equatorial Guinea	Manuel-Enrique King Somo	Felipe Hinestrosa Ikaka
Estonia[a]	Heiki Kranich	Martin Poder
Ethiopia	Alemayehu Daba	Abdulmejid Hussein
Fiji	Paul F. Manueli	Rigamoto Taito
Finland	Iiro Viinanen	Toimi Kankaanniemi

Member	Governor	Alternate
France	Jean-Claude Trichet	Christian Noyer
Gabon	Andre Dieudonne Berre	Richard Onouviet
Gambia, The	Bakary B. Dabo	Alieu M. N'gum
Georgia	David Iakobidze	Tengiz Geleishvili
Germany	Carl-Dieter Spranger	Gert Haller
Ghana	Kwesi Botchwey	Kwesi Amissah-Arthur
Greece	Yannos Papantoniou	George Romeos
Grenada	Nicholas Brathwaite	Nolan K. Murray
Guatemala	Ana Ordonez de Molina	Willy W. Zapata Sagastume
Guinea	Soriba Kaba	Kerfalla Yansane
Guinea-Bissau	Filinto Barros	Issufo Sanha
Guyana	Asgar Ally	Michael Sheer Chan
Haiti	Marie Michele Rey	Jean-Marie Cherestal
Honduras	Juan Ferrera	Hugo Noe Pino
Hungary	Ivan Szabo	Almos Kovacs
Iceland	Sighvatur Bjorgvinsson	Fridrik Sophusson
India	Manmohan Singh	Montek Singh Ahluwalia
Indonesia	Mar'ie Muhammad	Boediono
Iran, Islamic Rep. of	Morteza Mohammad-Khan	Mehdi Navab Motlagh
Iraq	Tarik T.M. Al Tukmachi	Hashim Ali Obaid
Ireland	Bertie Ahern	Paddy Mullarkey
Israel	Jacob A. Frenkel	Aaron Fogel
Italy	Antonio Fazio	Mario Draghi
Jamaica[a]	Omar Davies	Marjorie Henriques
Japan	Hirohisa Fujii	Yasushi Mieno
Jordan	Hisham Khatib	Marwan Awad
Kazakhstan	Erkeshbay Zh. Derbisov	Mars Urkumbayev
Kenya	W. Musalia Mudavadi	Benjamin Kipkoech Kipkulei
Kiribati	Taomati Iuta	Ntiua Tetinaniku
Korea, Republic of	Jae-Hyong Hong	Myung-Ho Kim
Kuwait	Nasser Abdullah Al-Roudhan	Bader Meshari Al-Humaidhi
Kyrgyz Republic	Kamchybek Shakirov	Askar I. Sarygulov
Lao People's Democratic Republic	Khamxay Souphanouvong	Pany Yathotou
Latvia	Ojars Kehris	Uldis Osis
Lebanon	Fuad A.B. Siniora	El-Fadl Chalak
Lesotho	Selometsi Baholo	E.M. Matekane
Liberia	Amelia A. Ward	Wilson K. Tarpeh
Libya	Mohamed A. Bait El Mal	Bashir Ali Khallat
Lithuania[a]	Julius Veselka	Eduardas Vilkelis
Luxembourg	Jean-Claude Juncker	Yves Mersch
Macedonia, former Yugoslav Republic of	Dzevdet Harjredini	Hari Kostov
Madagascar	Tovonanahary Rabetsitonta	Rajaona Andriamananjara
Malawi	Louis Joseph Chimango	Charles D. Nthenda
Malaysia	Anwar Ibrahim	Mohd. Sheriff Kassim
Maldives	Fathulla Jameel	Mohamed Ahmed Didi
Mali	Soumaila Cisse	Issaga Dembele
Malta[a]	John Dalli	Albert A. Attard
Marshall Islands	Ruben R. Zackhras	Michael Konelios
Mauritania	Taki Ould Sidi	Mohamed Lemine Ould Deidah
Mauritius	Paramhamsa Nababsing	Dharam Dev Manraj
Mexico	Pedro Aspe Armella	Guillermo Ortiz
Micronesia, Federated States of	Aloysius J. Tuuth	Asterio Takesy

(continued)

Governors and Alternates
of the World Bank   *(continued)*

Appendix I

June 30, 1994

Member	Governor	Alternate
Moldova	Valeriu Sergiu Kitsan	Dumitru Ursu
Mongolia	Demchigjavyn Molomzhamts	Dalrain Davaasambuu
Morocco	M'Hammed Sagou	Omar Kabbaj
Mozambique	Eneas da Conceição Comiche	Adriano Afonso Maleiane
Myanmar	Win Tin	Thein Aung Lwin
Namibia[a]	Zedekia Ngavirue	Godfrey Gaoseb
Nepal	Mahesh Acharya	Thakur Nath Pant
Netherlands	Wim Kok	J.P. Pronk
New Zealand	Murray Horn	John Whitehead
Nicaragua	Emilio Pereira Alegria	José Evenor Taboada Arana
Niger	Abdallah Boureima	Kane Aichatou Boulama
Nigeria	Kalu Idika Kalu	Gidado Idris
Norway	Sigbjoern Johnsen	Kari Nordheim-Larsen
Oman	Qais Abdul-Munim Al-Zawawi	Mohammed Bin Musa Al Yousef
Pakistan	V.A. Jafarey	Aftab Ahamd Khan
Panama	Delia Cardenas	Luis H. Moreno, Jr.
Papua New Guinea	Masket Iangalio	Gerea Aopi
Paraguay	Crispiniano Sandoval	Julio Gonzalez Ugarte
Peru	Jorge Camet Dickmann	Alfredo Jalilie Awapara
Philippines	Roberto F. de Ocampo	Gabriel C. Singson
Poland	Hanna Gronkiewicz-Waltz	Witold Kozinski
Portugal	Eduardo de Almeida Catroga	F. Esteves de Carvalho
Qatar[a]	Mohammed bin Khalifa Al-Thani	Abdullah Khalid Al-Attiyah
Romania[a]	Florin Georgescu	Vladimir Soare
Russian Federation	Aleksandr N. Shokhin	Viktor V. Gerashchenko
Rwanda	Marc Rugenera	Felicien Ntahondi
St. Kitts and Nevis	Kennedy A. Simmonds	William V. Herbert
St. Lucia	John G.M. Compton	Zenith James
St. Vincent and the Grenadines	James F. Mitchell	Dwight Venner
São Tomé and Principe	Arlindo Afonso de Carvalho	Adelino Castelo David
Saudi Arabia	Mohammad Abalkhail	Hamad Al-Sayari
Senegal	Papa Ousmane Sakho	Awa Thiongane
Seychelles[a]	Danièlle de St. Jorre	Emmanuel Faure
Sierra Leone	John A. Karimu	Nathaniel S.B. Wellington
Singapore[a]	Richard Hu Tsu Tau	Ngiam Tong Dow
Slovak Republic	Brigita Schmognerova	Vladimir Masar
Slovenia	Mitja Gaspari	Bozo Jasovic
Solomon Islands	Andrew G.H. Nori	Manasseh Sogavare
Somalia	(vacant)	(vacant)
South Africa	Christian Lodewyk Stals	Andries Benjamin La Grange
Spain	Pedro Solbes Mira	Alfredo Pastor Bodner
Sri Lanka	D.B. Wijetunga	R. Paskaralingam
Sudan	Mohamed Khair El Zubair	A. Mohamed Hassan
Suriname[a]	Humphrey S. Hildenberg	Stanley B. Ramsaran
Swaziland	T.N. Masuku	Musa D. Fakudze
Sweden	Anne Wibble	Alf Svensson
Switzerland	Jean-Pascal Delamuraz	Flavio Cotti
Syrian Arab Republic	Mohammed Khaled Al-Mahayni	Adnan Al-Satti
Tajikistan	Kayum K. Kavmidinov	Normat I. Iounoussov
Tanzania	Horace Kolimba	Peter J. Ngumbullu

Member	Governor	Alternate
Thailand	Tarrin Nimmanahaeminda	Aran Thammano
Togo	Yandja Yentchabre	Kwassi Klutse
Tonga	James Cecil Cocker	(vacant)
Trinidad and Tobago	Wendell Mottley	T. Ainsworth Harewood
Tunisia	Mohamed Ghannouchi	Taoufik Baccar
Turkey	Osman Birsen	Ayfer Yilmaz
Turkmenistan[a]	Hudaiberdy A. Orazov	Annadurdy Khadjiev
Uganda	Jehoash Mayanja-Nkangi	Emmenuel T. Mutebile
Ukraine[a]	Viktor Yushchenko	Michael O. Goncharuk
United Arab Emirates	Hamdan bin Rashid Al-Maktoum	Ahmed Humaid Al-Tayer
United Kingdom	Kenneth Clarke	Baroness Chalker of Wallasey
United States	Lloyd M. Bentsen	Joan E. Spero
Uruguay[a]	Ignacio de Posadas	Javier de Haedo
Uzbekistan	Bakhtiyar S. Hamidov	Vyasheslav A. Golyshev
Vanuatu	Willie Jimmy	Antoine Pikoune
Venezuela[a]	Julio Sosa Rodriguez	Enzo del Bufalo
Viet Nam	Cao Sy Kiem	Le Van Chau
Western Samoa	Tuilaepa S. Malielegaoi	Epa Tuioti
Yemen, Republic of	Abdul Karim Al-Eryani	Anwar Rizq Al-Harazi
Zaire	Celestin Tshibwabwa Kanyama	Kakese Mulume-Nda-Mumi
Zambia	Ronald Damson Siame Penza	James M. Mtonga
Zimbabwe	B.T.G. Chidzero	Leonard Ladislas Tsumba

a. Not a member of the IDA.

Executive Directors and Alternates of the World Bank and Their Voting Power

Appendix 2

June 30, 1994

			IBRD		IDA	
Executive director	Alternate	Casting votes of	Total votes	% of total	Total votes	% of total
Appointed						
Jan Piercy	(vacant)	United States	249,143	17.42	1,490,101	15.67
Yasuyuki Kawahara	Kiyoshi Kodera[b]	Japan	94,020	6.58	988,143	10.39
Fritz Fischer	Harald Rehm	Germany	72,649	5.08	658,521	6.93
Marc-Antoine Autheman	Jérôme Haas	France	69,647	4.87	390,814	4.11
Huw Evans	David Stanton	United Kingdom	69,647	4.87	495,881	5.22
Elected						
Walter Rill (Austria)	Nurcan Akturk (Turkey)	Austria, Belarus,[a] Belgium, Czech Republic, Hungary, Kazakhstan, Luxembourg, Slovak Republic, Turkey	71,048	4.97	391,440	4.12
Eveline Herfkens (Netherlands)	Ileana Ionescu (Romania)	Armenia, Bulgaria,[a] Cyprus, Georgia, Israel, Moldova, Netherlands, Romania,[a] Ukraine[a]	68,189	4.77	277,873	2.92
Robert R. de Cotret (Canada)	Hubert Dean (The Bahamas)	Antigua and Barbuda,[a] The Bahamas,[a] Barbados,[a] Belize, Canada, Dominica, Grenada, Guyana, Ireland, Jamaica,[a] St. Kitts and Nevis, St. Lucia, St. Vincent and the Grenadines	61,511	4.30	406,908	4.28
Angel Torres (Spain)	Gabriel Castellanos (Guatemala)	Costa Rica, El Salvador, Guatemala, Honduras, Mexico, Nicaragua, Panama, Spain, Venezuela[a]	58,848	4.12	201,523	2.12
Bimal Jalan (India)	M.A. Syed (Bangladesh)	Bangladesh, Bhutan, India, Sri Lanka	54,945	3.84	412,999	4.34
Enzo Grilli (Italy)	Helena Cordeiro (Portugal)	Albania, Greece, Italy, Malta,[a] Portugal	54,354	3.80	334,207	3.51
Jorunn Maehlum[c] (Norway)	Helga Jonsdottir (Iceland)	Denmark, Estonia,[a] Finland, Iceland, Latvia, Lithuania,[a] Norway, Sweden	49,166	3.44	470,159	4.94
Mohamed Benhocine (Algeria)	Abdul Karim Lodhi (Pakistan)	Afghanistan, Algeria, Ghana, Iran (Islamic Republic of), Morocco, Pakistan, Tunisia	48,693	3.41	213,196	2.24
Marcos Caramuru de Paiva (Brazil)	Marcela Cartagena (Ecuador)	Brazil, Colombia, Dominican Republic, Ecuador, Haiti, Philippines, Suriname,[a] Trinidad and Tobago	46,593	3.26	276,194	2.90
Wang Liansheng (China)	Zhang Shengman (China)	China	45,049	3.15	193,370	2.03
Ibrahim A. Al-Assaf (Saudi Arabia)	Ibrahim M. Al-Mofleh (Saudi Arabia)	Saudi Arabia	45,045	3.15	330,314	3.47
John H. Cosgrove (Australia)	Bong-Hee Won (Republic of Korea)	Australia, Kiribati, Korea (Republic of), Marshall Islands, Mongolia, New Zealand, Papua New Guinea, Solomon Islands, Vanuatu, Western Samoa	43,606	3.05	254,870	2.68
Jean-Daniel Gerber (Switzerland)	Jan Sulmicki (Poland)	Azerbaijan,[a] Kyrgyz Republic, Poland, Switzerland, Turkmenistan,[a] Uzbekistan	42,484	2.97	305,631	3.21

Executive director	Alternate	Casting votes of	IBRD		IDA	
			Total votes	% of total	Total votes	% of total
Faisal A. Al-Khaled (Kuwait)	Mohamed W. Hosny (Arab Republic of Egypt)	Bahrain,[a] Egypt (Arab Republic of), Jordan, Kuwait, Lebanon, Libya, Maldives, Oman, Qatar,[a] Syrian Arab Republic, United Arab Emirates, Yemen (Republic of)	42,047	2.94	237,357	2.50
Aris Othman (Malaysia)	Jannes Hutagalung (Indonesia)	Fiji, Indonesia, Lao People's Democratic Republic, Malaysia, Myanmar, Nepal, Singapore,[a] Thailand, Tonga, Viet Nam	37,494	2.62	276,566	2.91
O.K. Matambo (Botswana)	Harry M. Mapondo (Malawi)	Angola, Botswana, Burundi, Ethiopia, The Gambia, Guinea, Kenya, Lesotho, Liberia, Malawi, Mozambique, Namibia,[a] Nigeria, Seychelles,[a] Sierra Leone, Sudan, Swaziland, Tanzania, Uganda, Zambia, Zimbabwe	32,022	2.24	404,692	4.26
Andrei Bugrov (Russian Federation)	Alexander N. Doumnov (Russian Federation)	Russian Federation	25,390	1.78	28,202	.30
Nicolás Flaño (Chile)	Julio Nogues (Argentina)	Argentina, Bolivia, Chile, Paraguay, Peru, Uruguay[a]	24,745	1.73	176,246	1.85
Jean-Pierre Le Bouder (Central African Republic)	Ali Bourhane (Comoros)	Benin, Burkina Faso, Cameroon, Cape Verde, Central African Republic, Chad, Comoros, Congo, Côte d'Ivoire, Djibouti, Equatorial Guinea, Gabon, Guinea-Bissau, Madagascar, Mali, Mauritania, Mauritius, Niger, Rwanda, São Tomé and Principe, Senegal, Togo, Zaire	23,537	1.65	293,488	3.09

In addition to the executive directors and alternates shown in the foregoing list, the following also served after June 30, 1993:

Executive director	End of period of service	Alternate director	End of period of service
Boris G. Fedorov (Russian Federation)	October 30, 1993	Ahmed M. Al-Ghannam (Saudi Arabia)	December 28, 1993
Jean-Pierre Landau (France)	August 3, 1993	Fernando S. Carneiro (Portugal)	September 2, 1993
Pedro Malan (Brazil)	October 30, 1993	Mark M. Collins, Jr. (United States)	December 3, 1993
David Peretz (United Kingdom)	February 18, 1994	Arshad Farooq (Pakistan)	March 22, 1994
Frank Potter (Canada)	August 19, 1993		
Bernard Snoy (Belgium)	February 28, 1994		

NOTE: Cambodia (464 votes in IBRD and 7,826 votes in IDA), Iraq (3,058 votes in IBRD and 9,407 votes in IDA), Somalia (802 votes in IBRD and 10,506 votes in IDA) and South Africa (13,712 votes in IBRD and 29,813 votes in IDA) did not participate in the 1992 Regular Election of Executive Directors. Croatia (1,537 votes in IBRD and 28,087 votes in IDA), former Yugoslav Republic of Macedonia (490 votes in IBRD and 15,759 votes in IDA), Federated States of Micronesia (729 votes in IBRD and 18,424 votes in IDA), Slovenia (1,511 votes in IBRD and 18,956 votes in IDA) and Tajikistan (1,310 votes in IBRD and 20,568 votes in IDA) became members after that election.

a. Member of the IBRD only.

b. To be succeeded by Rintaro Tamaki (Japan) effective July 1, 1994.

c. To be succeeded by Ruth Jacoby (Sweden) effective August 2, 1994.

Officers and Department Directors of the World Bank

Appendix 3

June 30, 1994

President	Lewis T. Preston
Managing Director	Attila Karaosmanoglu
Managing Director	Sven Sandstrom
Managing Director	Ernest Stern
Vice President, Africa	Edward V.K. Jaycox
Vice President, Cofinancing and Financial Advisory Services	Koji Kashiwaya
Vice President and Controller	Stephen D. Eccles
Vice President and Chief Economist, Development Economics	Michael Bruno
Vice President, East Asia and Pacific	Gautam S. Kaji
Vice President, Environmentally Sustainable Development	Ismail M. Serageldin
Vice President, Europe and Central Asia	Wilfried P. Thalwitz
Vice President, Finance and Private Sector Development	Jean-François Rischard
Vice President, Financial Policy and Risk Management	Johannes F. Linn
Vice President, Human Resources Development and Operations Policy	Armeane M. Choksi
Vice President, Latin America and Caribbean	S. Javed Burki
Vice President and General Counsel	Ibrahim F.I. Shihata
Vice President, Management and Personnel Services	S. Shahid Husain
Vice President, Middle East and North Africa	Caio K. Koch-Weser
Director-General, Operations Evaluation	Robert Picciotto
Vice President and Secretary	Timothy T. Thahane
Vice President, South Asia	Joseph D. Wood
Vice President and Treasurer	Jessica P. Einhorn

External Affairs

Director, External Affairs Department	Alexander Shakow
Director, European Office	Hans Wyss

Legal

Assistant General Counsel, Administration and General Affairs	Eva L. Meigher
Assistant General Counsel, Finance...	Stephen A. Silard
Assistant General Counsel, Operations	Andres Rigo

Secretary's

Deputy Secretary, General Operations	Arnold J. Clift

Africa Regional Office

Director, Occidental and Central Africa Department: Benin, Cameroon, Central African Republic, Congo, Côte d'Ivoire, Equatorial Guinea, Gabon, Guinea, Togo	Olivier Lafourcade
Director, Eastern Africa Department: Eritrea, Ethiopia, Kenya, Somalia, Sudan, Tanzania, Uganda ...	Francis X. Colaco
Director, South-Central and Indian Ocean Department: Angola, Burundi, Comoros, Djibouti, Madagascar, Mauritius, Rwanda, Seychelles, Zaire	F.J. Aguirre-Sacasa
Director, Western Africa Department: Ghana, Liberia, Nigeria, Sierra Leone	Ian M. Hume
Director, Sahelian Department: Burkina Faso, Cape Verde, Chad, The Gambia, Guinea-Bissau, Mali, Mauritania, Niger, São Tomé and Principe, Senegal	Katherine Marshall
Director, Southern Africa Department: Botswana, Lesotho, Malawi, Mozambique, Namibia, South Africa, Swaziland, Zambia, Zimbabwe	Stephen M. Denning
Director, Africa Technical Department	Kevin M. Cleaver

Asia Technical Department

Director	Harold W. Messenger

East Asia and Pacific Regional Office

Director, Country Department I: Cambodia, Republic of Korea, Lao PDR, Malaysia, Mekong Committee, Myanmar, Philippines, Thailand, Viet Nam	Callisto E. Madavo
Director, Country Department II: China, Mongolia	Nicholas C. Hope
Director, Country Department III: Fiji, Indonesia, Kiribati, The Marshall Islands, Micronesia, Papua New Guinea, Solomon Islands, Tonga, Vanuatu, Western Samoa	Marianne Haug

South Asia Regional Office

Director, Country Department I: Bangladesh, Bhutan, Nepal	Ann O. Hamilton
Director, Country Department II: India	Heinz Vergin
Director, Country Department III: Afghanistan, Maldives, Pakistan, Sri Lanka.................	Paul Isenman

Europe and Central Asia, Middle East and North Africa Regions Technical Department
Director . . . . Anil Sood

Europe and Central Asia Regional Office
Director, Country Department I: Bulgaria, Cyprus, FYR of Macedonia, Portugal, Romania, Turkey . . Michael H. Wiehen
Director, Country Department II: Albania, Republic of Bosnia and Herzegovina, Croatia, Czech
    Republic, Hungary, Poland, Slovak Republic, Slovenia . . . . Kemal Dervis
Director, Country Department III: Azerbaijan, Kazakhstan, Kyrgyz Republic, Russia, Tajikistan,
    Turkmenistan, Uzbekistan . . . . Russell J. Cheetham
Director, Country Department IV: Armenia, Belarus, Estonia, Georgia, Latvia, Lithuania, Moldova,
    Ukraine . . . . Basil G. Kavalsky
Director, Resource Mobilization and Private Sector Development . . . . Ghassan El-Rifai

Middle East and North Africa Regional Office
Director, Country Department I: Algeria, Islamic Republic of Iran, Libya, Malta, Morocco, Tunisia . . Daniel Ritchie
Director, Country Department II: Bahrain, Egypt, Iraq, Jordan, Kuwait, Lebanon, Occupied
    Territories, Oman, Qatar, Saudi Arabia, Syrian Arab Republic, United Arab Emirates,
    Republic of Yemen . . . . Ram Kumar Chopra

Latin America and the Caribbean Regional Office
Director, Country Department I: Brazil, Peru, Venezuela . . . . Rainer B. Steckhan
Director, Country Department II: Costa Rica, El Salvador, Guatemala, Honduras, Mexico, Nicaragua,
    Panama . . . . Edilberto L. Segura
Director, Country Department III: The Bahamas, Barbados, Belize, Bolivia, Caribbean Development
    Bank, Colombia, Dominican Republic, Guyana, Haiti, Jamaica, OECS Member States, Suriname,
    Trinidad and Tobago . . . . Yoshiaki Abe
Director, Country Department IV: Argentina, Chile, Ecuador, Paraguay, Uruguay . . . . Ping-Cheung Loh
Director, Technical Department . . . . M.G. Sri-Ram Aiyer

Cofinancing and Financial Advisory Services
Director . . . . Inder Sud

Development Economics
Director, Development Policy . . . . Mark W. Baird
Director, Economic Development Institute . . . . Amnon Golan
Director, International Economics Department . . . . Masood Ahmed
Director, Policy Research Department . . . . Lyn Squire
Administrator, Research Advisory Staff . . . . Shahid Yusuf (Acting)

Environmentally Sustainable Development
Director, Agriculture and Natural Resources Department . . . . Michel J. Petit
Chief Environmental Advisor to the President and Director, Environment Department . . . . Mohamed T. El-Ashry
Director, Transportation, Water, and Urban Development Department . . . . Louis Y. Pouliquen
Executive Secretary, Consultative Group On International Agricultural Research . . . . Alexander von der Osten

Finance and Private Sector Development
Director, Financial Sector Development Department . . . . Gary L. Perlin
Director, Industry and Energy Department . . . . Richard D. Stern
Director, Private Sector Development Department . . . . Magdi R. Iskander

Human Resources Development and Operations Policy
Director, Education and Social Policy Department . . . . K.Y. Amoako
Director, Operations Policy Department . . . . James W. Adams
Director, Population, Health and Nutrition Department . . . . Janet de Merode
Director, Public Sector Management . . . . Alberto de Capitani

(continued)

Officers and Department Directors of the World Bank *(continued)*

Appendix 3

June 30, 1994

Financial Policy and Risk Management
Director, Resource Mobilization Department . . . .   Paula Donovan
Director, Risk Management and Financial Policy Department . . . .   Mieko Nishimizu

Treasurer's
Director, Cash Management Department . . . .   Walter Peyerl
Director, Financial Operations Department . . . .   Kenneth G. Lay
Director, Investment Department . . . .   Veronique Lavorel
Director, Pension Department . . . .   Nestor V. Santiago
Director, Tokyo Office . . . .   Shinichiro Kawamata

Controller's
Director, Accounting Department . . . .   Michael E. Ruddy
Auditor General, Internal Auditing Department . . . .   Allan D. Legg
Director, Loan Department . . . .   V.S. Raghavan
Director, Planning and Budgeting Department . . . .   Richard B. Lynn

Management and Personnel Services
Director, General Services Department . . . .   Pilar J. San Jose
Director, Headquarters Construction Department . . . .   Ernesto E. Henriod
Director, Health Services Department . . . .   Bernhard H. Liese
Director, Organization and Business Practices Department . . . .   Ian A. Scott
Director, Personnel Management Department . . . .   Peter Karp
Director, Personnel Services and Compensation Department . . . .   Everardo Wessels

Operations Evaluation
Director, Operations Evaluation Department . . . .   Hans-Eberhard Kopp

Offices of the World Bank

June 30, 1994

Headquarters: 1818 H Street, N.W., Washington, D.C. 20433, U.S.A.

New York Office	Carlston B. Boucher Special Representative to the United Nations	The World Bank Mission to the United Nations/New York Office 809 United Nations Plaza, Suite 900 New York, N.Y. 10017, U.S.A.
European Office	Hans Wyss Director	The World Bank 66, avenue d'Iéna 75116 Paris, France
London	(vacant) Resident Administrative Officer	World Bank New Zealand House, 15th Floor Haymarket London, SW1 Y4TE, England
Tokyo Office	Shinichiro Kawamata Director	The World Bank Kokusai Building (Room 916) 1-1, Marunouchi 3-chome Chiyoda-ku, Tokyo 100, Japan
Regional Mission in Eastern Africa	F. Stephen O'Brien Chief, Resident Mission	The World Bank View Park Towers Monrovia Street Nairobi, Kenya (mailing address: P.O. Box 30577)
Regional Mission in Western Africa	Robert A. Calderisi Chief, Resident Mission	The World Bank Corner of Booker Washington and Jacques AKA Streets Cocody, Abidjan 01 Côte d'Ivoire (mailing address: B.P. 1850)
Regional Mission in Thailand	Bradley O. Babson[a] Chief, Resident Mission	The World Bank 14th Floor, Tower A, Diethelm Towers 93/1 Wireless Road, Bangkok, 10330 Thailand
Regional Mission in Latvia	Lars Jeurling Chief, Resident Mission	The World Bank Kalku Street, 15 Riga, Latvia 1050
Baltics Regional Mission Satellite in Estonia	Hillar Lauri Operations Officer	The World Bank/Maailmapank Kohtu 8 Tallinn EE0001 Estonia
Baltics Regional Mission Satellite in Lithuania	Ramune Zabuliene Operations Officer	The World Bank Gedimino Avenue 11 Vilnius 2039 Lithuania
Albania	Kutlay Ebiri Resident Representative	The World Bank Deshmoret e 4 Shkurtit, No. 34 Tirana, Albania
Angola	Florent Agueh Resident Representative	Banco Mundial Rua Alfredo Troni (Edificio BPC) 14° Andar CP 1331, Luanda, Angola
Argentina	Patricio Millan Resident Representative	Banco Mundial Piso 12 Avenida Leandro N. Alem 628-30 Buenos Aires, Argentina

(continued)

Offices of the World Bank   *(continued)*   Appendix 4

June 30, 1994

Bangladesh	Christopher Willoughby[b] Chief, Resident Mission	The World Bank 3A Paribagh Dhaka 1000, Bangladesh (mailing address: G.P.O. 97)
Belarus	(vacant)[c] Chief, Resident Mission	The World Bank 6A Partizansky Avenue, 5th Floor Minsk 220033 Republic of Belarus
Benin	(vacant) Resident Representative	The World Bank Zone Résidentielle de la Radio Cotonou, Benin (mailing address: B.P. 03-2112)
Bolivia	Constance A. Bernard Resident Representative	Banco Mundial Edificio BISA, Piso 9 16 de Julio 1628 La Paz, Bolivia (mailing address: Casilla 8692)
Brazil	Braz Menezes (Acting) Resident Representative	Banco Mundial Setor Comercial Sul, Quadra 1, Bloco H Edifício Morro Vermelho—8 Andar Brasília, DF 70399-900, Brazil
Brazil	Braz Menezes (Acting) Representative	Banco Mundial Rua Visconde de Piraja No. 351, Sala 1206, Ipanema 22410-003 Rio de Janeiro, RJ, Brazil
Brazil	Tulio Barbosa Acting Head of Field Office	Banco Mundial, S/127 Edifício SUDENE Cidade Universitária 50.738 Recife PE. Brazil
Bulgaria	John Wilton Resident Representative	The World Bank World Trade Center—Sofia 36 Dragan Tsankov Boulevard Sofia, Bulgaria
Burkina Faso	Albert D. Osei Resident Representative	The World Bank Immeuble BICIA (3ème étage) Ouagadougou, Burkina Faso (mailing address: B.P. 622)
Burundi	Jacqueline R. Damon Resident Representative	The World Bank Avenue du 18 Septembre Bujumbura, Burundi (mailing address: B.P. 2637)
Cameroon	Joseph K. Ingram Resident Representative	The World Bank Immeuble Kennedy Avenue Kennedy Yaoundé, Cameroon (mailing address: B.P. 1128)
Central African Republic	Lucien E. Moreau Resident Representative	Banque Mondiale Rue des Missions Bangui, C.A.R. (mailing address: B.P. 819)
Chad	(vacant) Resident Representative	The World Bank P.O. Box 146 N'djamena, Chad

China	Pieter Bottelier Chief, Resident Mission	The World Bank No. 2 Fu Cheng Lu Diaoyutai, State Guest House Building No. 5 Beijing 100830, China (mailing address: P.O. Box 802)
Colombia	Kristin Hallberg Resident Representative	Banco Mundial Carrera 10, No. 86-21, Piso 3 Apartado Aéreo 10229 Bogotá, D.E., Colombia (mailing address: Apartado Aéreo 10229)
Congo	(vacant) Resident Representative	Banque Mondiale Immeuble Arc (5ème étage) Avenue Amilcar Cabral Brazzaville, Congo (mailing address: B.P. 14536)
Ecuador	John Panzer Resident Representative	Banco Mundial Calle Juan Leon Mera 130 y Ave. Patria Edifico Corporation Financiera Nacional 6to Piso Quito, Ecuador
Egypt	Sven Burmester Resident Representative	The World Bank World Trade Center 1191 Corniche El-Nil 15th Floor Cairo, Egypt

Ethiopia	Abhay Deshpande
	Resident Representative
		The World Bank
		Africa Avenue
		    Bole
		Addis Ababa, Ethiopia
		    (mailing address: P.O. Box 5515)

Ghana	Ravi Kanbur Resident Representative	The World Bank 69 Eighth Avenue Extension Northridge Residential Area Accra, Ghana (mailing address: P.O. Box M27)
Guinea	Eduardo Locatelli Resident Representative	Banque Mondiale Immeuble de l'Archevêche Face Baie des Anges Conakry, Guinea (mailing address: B.P. 1420)
Guinea-Bissau	Yves J. Tencalla Resident Representative	World Bank Apartado 700 1041, Guinea-Bissau
Hungary	Andrew P. Rogerson Resident Representative	World Bank Suba Trade Center, 4th Floor Nagymezo Utca 44 Budapest 1065, Hungary

India	Oktay Yenal[d]
	Chief, Resident Mission
		The World Bank
		70 Lodi Estate
		New Delhi 110003, India
		    (mailing address: P.O. Box 416,
		    New Delhi 110001)

(continued)

Offices of the World Bank   *(continued)*   Appendix 4

June 30, 1994

Indonesia	(vacant)[e] Director, Resident Staff	The World Bank Jalan Rasuna Said, Kav. B-10, 3rd floor Kuningan, Jakarta 12940, Indonesia (mailing address: P.O. Box 324/JKT)
Jamaica	Robert Ban Pulley Resident Representative	World Bank Island Life Center 6 St. Lucia Avenue Suite 8, South Kingston 5, Jamaica
Kazakhstan	David Pearce Resident Representative	The World Bank c/o Ministry of Economy 115 Zheltokson Str. Almaty 480091, Kazakhstan
Kyrgyz Republic	(vacant)[f] Resident Representative	Bishkek, Kyrgyz Republic
Madagascar	Michel Palein Resident Representative	Banque Mondiale 1, Rue Patrice Lumumba Antananarivo 101, Madagascar (mailing address: B.P. 4140)
Malawi	Arif Zulfiqar Resident Representative	The World Bank Development House Capital City Lilongwe 3, Malawi (mailing address: P.O. Box 30557)
Mali	Linda McGinnis Resident Representative	The World Bank Immeuble SOGEFIH Avenue Moussa Travele Quartier du Fleuve Bamako, Mali (mailing address: B.P. 1864)
Mauritania	Claude Delapierre Resident Representative	The World Bank Villa No. 30, Ilot A Quartier Socofim Nouakchott, Mauritania (mailing address: B.P. 667)
Mexico	Eugene D. McCarthy Resident Representative	Banco Mundial Plaza Nafin Insurgentes Sur 1971 Nivel Paseo, Locales 71 y 72 Col. Guadalupe Inn 01020 México, D.F.
Mozambique	Roberto Chavez Resident Representative	World Bank Ave. Kenneth Kaunda, 1224 2-Andar Maputo, Mozambique (mailing address: Caixa Postal 4053)
Nepal	Joseph Manickavasagam Resident Representative	The World Bank Jyoti Bhawan, Kantipath Kathmandu, Nepal (mailing address: P.O. Box 798)

Nicaragua	Ulrich Lachler Resident Representative	The World Bank Edificio Malaga, Modulo A-1 Plaza España Managua, Nicaragua C.A.
Niger	Abdul Haji Resident Representative	Banque Mondiale Rue des Dallols Niamey, Niger (mailing address: B.P. 12402)
Nigeria	Gerald F. Flood Resident Representative	The World Bank 1st Floor, Plot PC-10 Engineering Close, off Idowu Taylor Street Victoria Island Lagos, Nigeria (mailing address: P.O. Box 127)
Pakistan	Philippe Nouvel Chief, Resident Mission	The World Bank 20 A Shahrah-e-Jamhuriat, Islamabad, Pakistan (mailing address: P.O. Box 1025)
Philippines	Thomas W. Allen Resident Representative	The World Bank Central Bank of the Philippines Multi-Storey Building, Room 200 Roxas Boulevard Manila, Philippines
Poland	Paul Knotter Resident Representative	The World Bank INTRACO I Building 17th Floor 2 Stawki Street 00-193 Warsaw, Poland
Romania	Arntraud Hartman Resident Representative	The World Bank Boulevard Dacia 83 Sector 2 Bucharest, Romania
Russia	Everardus Stoutjesdijk Resident Representative	The World Bank Moscow Office Sadovo-Kudrinskaya No. 3 Moscow 123242 Russian Federation
Rwanda	Julio Gamba Resident Representative	The World Bank Blvd. de la Révolution SORAS Building Kigali, Rwanda (mailing address: P.O. Box 609)
Saudi Arabia	Mohsin Alikhan Resident Representative	The World Bank Resident Mission UNDP Building, King Faisal Street Riyadh, Saudi Arabia 11432 (mailing address: P.O. Box 5900)
Senegal	(vacant) Resident Representative	The World Bank Immeuble S.D.I.H. 3 Place de l'Indépendance Dakar, Senegal (mailing address: B.P. 3296)

(continued)

Offices of the World Bank   *(continued)*   Appendix 4

June 30, 1992

South Africa	Isaac Sam Resident Representative	World Bank Grosvenor Gate, First Floor Hyde Park Lane Hyde Park 2196 Johannesburg, South Africa
Sri Lanka	J. Roberto B. Bentjerodt Resident Representative	The World Bank Development Finance Corporation of Ceylon (DFCC) Building, 1st Floor 73/5 Galle Road Colombo 3, Sri Lanka (mailing address: P.O. Box 1761)
Tanzania	Motoo Konishi Resident Representative	The World Bank N.I.C. Building (7th Floor, B) Dar-es-Salaam, Tanzania (mailing address: P.O. Box 2054)
Togo	Jacques Daniel Resident Representative	The World Bank 169 boulevard du 13 Janvier Immeuble BTCI (8ème étage) Lomé, Togo (mailing address: B.P. 3915)
Turkey	Frederick Thomas Temple Chief, Resident Mission	The World Bank Ataturk Bulvari, No. 211 Gama-Guris Building Kat 6 06683 Kavaklidere, Ankara, Turkey
Uganda	Brian Falconer Resident Representative	The World Bank P.O. Box 4463 Kampala, Uganda
Ukraine	Daniel Kaufmann Chief, Regional Mission	World Bank 26, Shovkovychna St. (Ex. K Liebknecht St.) Suites Two and Three Kiev 252024, Ukraine
Uzbekistan	Parvez Hasan Regional Representative	43, Academician Suleimanova St. Tashkent, Uzbekistan
Venezuela	Bruce D. Carlson Resident Representative	Banco Mundial Edificio Parque Cristal Torre Oeste, Piso 15 Oficína 15-05 Avenida Francisco de Miranda Los Palos Grandes Caracas, Venezuela
Viet Nam	(vacant)[g] Resident Representative	World Bank Suite 301/302, 4th floor Binh Minh Hotel 27 Ly Thai To St. Hoan Kiem District Hanoi, Viet Nam
Zaire	(vacant) Liaison Office	World Bank Liaison Office c/o UNDP P.O. Box 7248 Kinshasa, Zaire

| Zambia | Gedion B. Nkojo
Resident Representative | The World Bank
Red Cross House, 2nd Floor
Long Acres
Lusaka, Zambia
(mailing address: P.O. Box 35410) |
| Zimbabwe | Christiaan J. Poortman
Resident Representative | The World Bank
CABS Centre (11th Floor)
Jason Moyo Avenue
Harare, Zimbabwe
(mailing address: P.O. Box 2960) |

a. To be succeeded by Arnaud Guinard as of July 1, 1994.
b. To be succeeded by Pierre Landell-Mills as of July 1, 1994.
c. Christopher Willoughby, Chief as of July 1, 1994.
d. To be succeeded by Javad Khalilzadeh-Shirazi as of July 1, 1994.
e. Dennis N. de Tray, Chief as of July 11, 1994.
f. Michael R. Rathnam, Chief as of September 5, 1994.
g. Bradley O. Babson, Chief as of July 1, 1994.

IBRD and IDA Cumulative Lending Operations, by Major Purpose and Region

Appendix 5

June 30, 1994
(millions of US dollars)

Purpose[b]	Africa	IBRD loans to borrowers, by region[a]					Total
		East Asia and Pacific	South Asia	Europe and Central Asia	Latin America and the Caribbean	Middle East and North Africa	
Agriculture							
Agriculture sector loan	1,805.7	3,423.6	1,398.0	2,878.1	9,634.9	2,251.4	21,391.7
Agroindustry	30.0	620.2	61.4	894.1	1,228.4	224.2	3,058.3
Fisheries	—	92.7	14.0	7.0	16.2	41.0	170.9
Forestry	372.0	78.0	—	408.9	155.0	190.5	1,204.4
Irrigation and drainage	110.2	4,205.7	814.6	1,421.4	2,989.5	1,661.4	12,202.8
Livestock	170.7	80.0	248.0	179.5	1,042.0	46.5	1,766.7
Other—agriculture	297.0	85.1	190.0	847.0	225.5	224.5	1,869.1
Perennial crops	634.5	1,595.4	—	50.0	123.0	58.0	2,460.9
Research and extension	154.2	423.4	25.0	209.9	735.0	77.5	1,625.0
Total	3,574.3	10,604.1	2,751.0	6,895.9	16,149.5	4,775.0	44,749.8
Education	542.5	4,262.9	55.0	1,105.3	4,162.8	1,719.2	11,847.7
Energy							
Oil, gas, and coal	400.2	1,522.9	3,710.0	3,069.5	1,413.5	771.2	10,887.3
Power	1,872.1	11,480.2	9,334.6	4,413.2	11,610.7	2,053.8	40,764.6
Total	2,272.3	13,003.1	13,044.6	7,482.7	13,024.2	2,825.0	51,651.9
Environment	—	331.5	—	92.0	429.5	6.0	859.0
Financial sector	1,299.0	5,179.0	2,902.2	4,206.3	10,123.1	2,686.8	26,396.4
Industry	667.6	3,317.2	2,919.9	3,760.7	4,287.6	1,700.7	16,653.7
Mining and other extractive	541.1	484.1	793.5	—	1,043.3	264.2	3,126.2
Multisector	2,162.6	4,042.3	610.0	6,824.2[c]	7,051.2	2,112.3	22,802.6
Population, health, and nutrition	289.4	767.9	31.3	446.0	1,772.8	421.6	3,729.0
Public sector management	15.2	147.0	150.0	690.2	2,397.6	172.9	3,572.9
Social sector	—	—	—	—	158.0	—	158.0
Telecommunications	510.2	1,534.7	712.5	545.3	530.3	691.5	4,524.5
Transportation							
Aviation	59.0	9.2	5.6	19.0	218.5	—	311.3
Highways	1,817.8	6,393.9	738.9	2,702.2	7,608.5	1,356.1	20,617.4
Other—transportation	4.5	—	—	295.0	17.8	30.0	347.3
Ports and waterways	285.9	1,558.5	437.2	625.8	523.7	967.0	4,398.1
Railways	733.5	2,970.8	1,500.4	1,093.0	1,938.5	237.5	8,473.7
Transportation sector loan	61.6	677.2	184.0	137.0	301.8	—	1,361.6
Urban transport	—	342.0	25.0	40.0	1,555.5	116.0	2,078.5
Total	2,962.3	11,951.6	2,891.1	4,912.0	12,164.3	2,706.6	37,587.9
Urban development	933.7	2,915.3	294.1	767.2	4,119.6	1,525.1	10,555.0
Water supply and sewerage . . .	1,169.8	1,832.4	103.0	1,301.8	4,539.2	2,237.5	11,183.7
Grand total	16,940.0	60,373.1	27,258.2	39,029.6	81,953.0	23,844.4	249,398.3

— Zero

a. Except for the total amount shown in footnote d, no account is taken of cancellations subsequent to original commitment. IBRD loans to the IFC are excluded.

b. Operations have been classified by the major purpose they finance. Many projects include activity in more than one sector or subsector.

	East Asia and Pacific	South Asia	Europe and Central Asia	Latin America and the Caribbean	Middle East and North Africa	Total	IBRD and IDA
Africa							

IDA credits to borrowers, by region							
Africa	East Asia and Pacific	South Asia	Europe and Central Asia	Latin America and the Caribbean	Middle East and North Africa	Total	IBRD and IDA
3,352.5	2,476.7	3,152.8	22.4	280.4	309.3	9,594.1	30,985.8
364.5	218.0	716.9	—	16.5	45.0	1,360.9	4,419.2
55.7	70.0	217.3	—	—	67.3	410.3	581.2
391.0	728.9	828.9	—	38.9	—	1,987.7	3,192.1
871.0	1,221.1	6,164.9	80.0	18.5	396.5	8,752.0	19,954.8
479.7	88.1	267.1	20.5	67.5	5.0	927.9	2,694.6
338.9	424.5	405.0	—	—	6.9	1,175.3	3,044.4
488.9	300.5	283.0	15.0	3.2	—	1,090.6	3,551.5
713.0	120.5	767.8	—	21.0	20.4	1,642.7	3,267.7
7,055.2	5,648.3	12,803.7	137.9	446.0	850.4	26,941.5	71,691.3
3,049.6	1,421.9	2,495.3	9.6	176.9	391.5	7,544.8	19,392.5
638.3	66.0	371.4	—	148.2	86.0	1,309.9	12,197.2
1,572.1	308.8	3,745.5	25.7	201.7	252.9	6,106.7	46,871.3
2,210.4	374.8	4,116.9	25.7	349.9	338.9	7,416.6	59,068.5
2.6	50.0	14.7	—	4.8	—	72.1	931.1
2,382.5	302.8	829.0	35.0	155.1	74.8	3,779.2	30,175.6
987.5	137.2	1,616.5	—	27.5	97.9	2,866.6	19,520.3
74.2	16.0	19.0	—	49.5	—	158.7	3,284.9
5,425.5	217.7	3,999.7	141.1	499.5	35.0	10,318.5	33,121.1
1,235.2	597.9	2,549.6	—	185.0	303.6	4,871.3	8,600.3
801.8	145.7	171.8	64.0	115.1	13.7	1,312.1	4,885.0
—	9.7	—	10.9	—	—	20.6	178.6
441.2	101.8	882.2	18.0	—	83.0	1,526.2	6,050.7
14.0	—	10.0	—	—	—	24.0	335.3
3,661.7	778.7	1,264.4	—	338.3	180.2	6,223.3	26,840.7
8.5	32.0	267.2	18.0	—	—	325.7	673.0
423.2	161.2	262.0	—	16.0	9.2	871.6	5,269.7
628.6	206.7	1,017.5	—	45.0	38.5	1,936.3	10,410.0
624.1	17.8	47.5	—	—	30.0	719.4	2,081.0
—	60.0	176.0	—	—	7.0	243.0	2,321.5
5,360.1	1,256.4	3,044.6	18.0	399.3	264.9	10,343.3	47,931.2
1,274.9	432.4	1,592.3	45.3	174.2	66.0	3,585.1	14,140.1
1,004.2	494.2	1,847.6	11.6	91.1	203.2	3,651.9	14,835.6
31,304.9	11,206.8	35,982.9	517.1	2,673.9	2,722.9	84,408.5	333,806.8[d]

c. Includes $497 million in European reconstruction loans made before 1952.

d. Cancellations amount to $23,507.3 million for the IBRD and $4,755.5 million for IDA, totaling $28,262.8 million.

IBRD and IDA Cumulative Lending Operations, by Borrower or Guarantor

Appendix 6

June 30, 1994
(millions of US dollars)

Borrower or guarantor	IBRD loans		IDA credits		Total	
	Number	Amount	Number	Amount	Number	Amount
Afghanistan	—	—	20	230.1	20	230.1
Africa region	1	15.0	1	45.5	2	60.5
Albania	—	—	10	132.6	10	132.6
Algeria.	54	4,560.5	—	—	54	4,560.5
Angola.	—	—	8	248.8	8	248.8
Argentina	58	8,741.8	—	—	58	8,741.8
Armenia.	1	12.0	1	28.0	2	40.0
Australia	7	417.7	—	—	7	417.7
Austria.	9	106.4	—	—	9	106.4
Bahamas, The.	5	42.8	—	—	5	42.8
Bangladesh	1	46.1	141	6,729.9	142	6,776.0
Barbados	11	103.2	—	—	11	103.2
Belarus	3	170.2	—	—	3	170.2
Belgium.	4	76.0	—	—	4	76.0
Belize	6	53.3	—	—	6	53.3
Benin.	—	—	40	534.3	40	534.3
Bhutan.	—	—	6	28.2	6	28.2
Bolivia.	14	299.3	40	948.1	54	1,247.4
Botswana	20	280.7	6	15.8	26	296.5
Brazil.	206	21,689.7	—	—	206	21,689.7
Bulgaria.	7	593.0	—	—	7	593.0
Burkina Faso	—	1.9	44	746.3	44	748.2
Burundi	1	4.8	44	658.1	45	662.9
Cambodia	—	—	1	62.7	1	62.7
Cameroon	44	1,294.4	17	429.0	61	1,723.4
Cape Verde	—	—	7	44.9	7	44.9
Caribbean region	4	83.0	2	43.0	6	126.0
Central African Republic	—	—	23	386.9	23	386.9
Chad	—	—	29	444.1	29	444.1
Chile.	54	3,255.4	—	19.0	54	3,274.4
China	82	11,759.4	59	7,795.7	141	19,555.1
Colombia.	137	8,047.6	—	19.5	137	8,067.1
Comoros	—	—	12	73.2	12	73.2
Congo.	10	216.7	9	174.6	19	391.3
Costa Rica	38	888.9	—	5.5	38	894.4
Côte d'Ivoire	62	2,887.9	7	522.2	69	3,410.1
Croatia.	1	128.0	—	—	1	128.0
Cyprus.	30	418.8	—	—	30	418.8
Czech Republic.	2	326.0	—	—	2	326.0
Czechoslovakia.	1	450.0	—	—	1	450.0
Denmark	3	85.0	—	—	3	85.0
Djibouti	—	—	8	51.6	8	51.6
Dominica	—	—	3	11.0	3	11.0
Dominican Republic	21	566.9	3	22.0	24	588.9
East African Community	10	244.8	—	—	10	244.8
Eastern Africa region	—	—	1	45.0	1	45.0
Ecuador.	54	1,912.9	5	36.9	59	1,949.8
Egypt.	56	3,955.8	31	1,376.5	87	5,332.3
El Salvador	25	485.6	2	25.6	27	511.2
Equatorial Guinea	—	—	9	45.0	9	45.0
Estonia	3	80.4	—	—	3	80.4
Ethiopia.	12	108.6	52	1,860.6	64	1,969.2

Borrower or guarantor	IBRD loans		IDA credits		Total	
	Number	Amount	Number	Amount	Number	Amount
Fiji	13	152.9	—	—	13	152.9
Finland	18	316.8	—	—	18	316.8
France	1	250.0	—	—	1	250.0
Gabon	11	206.8	—	—	11	206.8
Gambia, The.	—	—	23	160.2	23	160.2
Ghana	9	207.0	73	2,499.2	82	2,706.2
Greece	17	490.8	—	—	17	490.8
Grenada	—	—	1	5.0	1	5.0
Guatemala	23	725.1	—	—	23	725.1
Guinea	3	75.2	41	854.5	44	929.7
Guinea-Bissau	—	—	18	186.9	18	186.9
Guyana	12	80.0	12	247.8	24	327.8
Haiti	1	2.6	31	453.0	32	455.6
Honduras	33	717.3	13	438.5	46	1,155.8
Hungary	32	3,634.9	—	—	32	3,634.9
Iceland	10	47.1	—	—	10	47.1
India	153	21,838.2	202	21,284.1	355	43,122.3
Indonesia	188	20,411.7	46	931.8	234	21,343.5
Iran, Islamic Republic of	39	2,058.1	—	—	39	2,058.1
Iraq	6	156.2	—	—	6	156.2
Ireland	8	152.5	—	—	8	152.5
Israel	11	284.5	—	—	11	284.5
Italy	8	399.6	—	—	8	399.6
Jamaica	58	1,228.1	—	—	58	1,228.1
Japan	31	862.9	—	—	31	862.9
Jordan	37	1,198.4	15	85.3	52	1,283.7
Kazakhstan	4	273.7	—	—	4	273.7
Kenya	46	1,200.0	62	2,202.2	108	3,402.2
Korea, Republic of	107	8,324.0	6	110.8	113	8,434.8
Kyrgyz Republic	—	—	3	138.0	3	138.0
Lao People's Democratic Republic	—	—	20	383.6	20	383.6
Latvia	2	70.0	—	—	2	70.0
Lebanon	7	368.7	—	—	7	368.7
Lesotho	1	110.0	23	224.2	24	334.2
Liberia	21	156.0	14	114.5	35	270.5
Lithuania	2	86.4	—	—	2	86.4
Luxembourg	1	12.0	—	—	1	12.0
Macedonia, FYR of	1	40.0	—	40.0	1	80.0
Madagascar	5	32.9	59	1,191.5	64	1,224.4
Malawi	9	124.1	55	1,269.8	64	1,393.9
Malaysia	83	3,446.6	—	—	83	3,446.6
Maldives	—	—	5	33.9	5	33.9
Mali	—	1.9	49	912.0	49	913.9
Malta	1	7.5	—	—	1	7.5
Mauritania	3	146.0	1	320.8	34	466.8
Mauritius	27	354.2	4	20.2	31	374.4
Mexico	146	23,418.6	—	—	146	23,418.6
Moldova	2	86.0	—	—	2	86.0

(continued)

IBRD and IDA Cumulative Lending Operations, by Borrower or Guarantor

Appendix 6

(continued)

June 30, 1994
(millions of US dollars)

Borrower or guarantor	IBRD loans		IDA credits		Total	
	Number	Amount	Number	Amount	Number	Amount
Mongolia	—	—	4	85.0	4	85.0
Morocco	104	7,089.7	3	50.8	107	7,140.5
Mozambique	—	—	27	1,401.3	27	1,401.3
Myanmar	3	33.4	30	804.0	33	837.4
Nepal	—	—	64	1,394.1	64	1,394.1
Netherlands	8	244.0	—	—	8	244.0
New Zealand	6	126.8	—	—	6	126.8
Nicaragua	27	233.6	9	340.4	36	574.0
Niger	—	—	37	572.5	37	572.5
Nigeria	84	6,248.2	14	902.9	98	7,151.1
Norway	6	145.0	—	—	6	145.0
Oman	11	157.1	—	—	11	157.1
Pakistan	78	5,163.2	95	4,420.6	173	9,583.8
Panama	33	876.3	—	—	33	876.3
Papua New Guinea	27	542.0	9	113.2	36	655.2
Paraguay	31	625.1	6	45.5	37	670.6
Peru	69	3,437.7	—	—	69	3,437.7
Philippines	133	9,050.9	5	294.2	138	9,345.1
Poland	19	3,657.0	—	—	19	3,657.0
Portugal	32	1,338.8	—	—	32	1,338.8
Romania	41	3,534.9	—	—	41	3,534.9
Russia	10	2,890.0	—	—	10	2,890.0
Rwanda	—	—	44	644.4	44	644.4
São Tomé and Principe	—	—	8	58.9	8	58.9
Senegal	19	164.9	54	1,052.2	73	1,217.1
Seychelles	2	10.7	—	—	2	10.7
Sierra Leone	4	18.7	18	312.0	22	330.7
Singapore	14	181.3	—	—	14	181.3
Slovak Republic	2	135.0	—	—	2	135.0
Slovenia	1	80.0	—	—	1	80.0
Solomon Islands	—	—	6	33.9	6	33.9
Somalia	—	—	39	492.1	39	492.1
South Africa	11	241.8	—	—	11	241.8
Spain	12	478.7	—	—	12	478.7
Sri Lanka	12	210.7	61	1,862.0	73	2,072.7
St. Kitts and Nevis	1	1.5	—	1.5	1	3.0
St. Lucia	1	2.5	—	5.2	1	7.7
St. Vincent and the Grenadines	1	1.4	1	6.4	2	7.8
Sudan	8	166.0	48	1,352.9	56	1,518.9
Swaziland	11	75.8	2	7.8	13	83.6
Syria	17	613.2	3	47.3	20	660.5
Tanzania	18	318.2	81	2,691.5	99	3,009.7
Thailand	100	4,734.1	6	125.1	106	4,859.2
Togo	1	20.0	35	535.7	36	555.7
Tonga	—	—	2	5.0	2	5.0
Trinidad and Tobago	17	216.5	—	—	17	216.5
Tunisia	93	3,394.7	5	74.6	98	3,469.3
Turkey	112	12,057.9	10	178.5	122	12,236.4
Uganda	1	8.4	54	2,116.9	55	2,125.3

Borrower or guarantor	IBRD loans		IDA credits		Total	
	Number	Amount	Number	Amount	Number	Amount
Ukraine	1	27.0	—	—	1	27.0
Uruguay.	38	1,231.6	—	—	38	1,231.6
Uzbekistan	1	21.0	—	—	1	21.0
Vanuatu	—	—	4	15.4	4	15.4
Venezuela.	29	2,984.7	—	—	29	2,984.7
Viet Nam	—	—	4	384.5	4	384.5
Western Africa region	1	6.1	3	52.5	4	58.6
Western Samoa	—	—	8	46.6	8	46.6
Yemen.	—	—	99	1,088.4	99	1,088.4
Yugoslavia	90	6,114.7	—	—	90	6,114.7
Zaire	7	330.0	59	1,151.5	66	1,481.5
Zambia	28	679.1	31	1,234.5	59	1,913.6
Zimbabwe	24	893.2	6	443.4	30	1,426.6
Other[a]	14	329.4	4	15.3	18	344.7
Total	3,660	249,398.3	2,445	84,408.5	6,105	333,806.8

— Zero

NOTE: Joint IBRD/IDA operations are counted only once, as IBRD operations. When more than one loan is made for a single project, the operation is counted only once. Details may not add to totals because of rounding.

a. Represents IBRD loans and IDA credits made at a time when the authorities on Taiwan represented China in the World Bank (prior to May 15, 1980).

Statement of IBRD Loans Approved during Fiscal Year 1994

Appendix 7

Borrower or guarantor/project name	Date of approval	Maturities	Principal amount (US$ millions)
Algeria			
Water Supply and Sewerage Rehabilitation Project	02-Jun-94	1999/2011	110.0
Emergency Desert Locust Control Project................	23-Dec-93	1999/2011	30.0
Argentina			
Capital Market Development Project	01-Mar-94	2001/2009	500.0
Capital Market Development Technical Assistance Project	01-Mar-94	1999/2009	8.5
Maternal and Child Health and Nutrition Project...........	03-Aug-93	1999/2008	100.0
Barbados			
Human Resources Project	01-Jul-93	1998/2008	7.8
Belarus			
Forestry Development Project	26-May-94	1999/2009	41.9
Rehabilitation Loan	16-Nov-93	1999/2008	120.0
Institution Building Project	29-Jul-93	1999/2008	8.3
Belize			
Belize City Infrastructure Project	30-Nov-93	1998/2011	20.0
Brazil			
Third Northeast Basic Education Project	23-Nov-93	1999/2008	206.6
AIDS and STD Control Project	09-Nov-93	1999/2008	160.0
Brazil (Guarantor)			
Basic Education Quality Project—State of Paraná..........	28-Jun-94	2000/2009	96.0
Water and Coastal Pollution Management Project—State of Espírito Santo	28-Jun-94	2000/2009	154.0
Basic Education Quality Improvement Project—State of Minas Gerais	17-May-94	1999/2009	150.0
State Highway Management II Project— State of Piauí...............................	15-Mar-94	1999/2009	54.0
State Highway Management II Project— State of Tocantins............................	15-Mar-94	1999/2009	87.0
State Highway Management II Project— State of Maranhão	15-Mar-94	1999/2009	79.0
Municipal Management and Environmental Infrastructure Project—State of Minas Gerais	20-Jul-93	1999/2008	150.0
Bulgaria			
Agricultural Development Project.....................	29-Jun-94	1999/2011	50.0
Water Companies Restructuring and Modernization Project	26-May-94	1999/2011	98.0
Caribbean Development Bank (Guarantor)			
Sixth Caribbean Development Bank Project	29-Jun-94	1999/2011	20.0
Chile			
Municipal Development Pilot Project	07-Dec-93	1999/2011	10.0
China			
National Highway Project	07-Jun-94	2000/2014	380.0
Xiaolangdi Multipurpose Project	14-Apr-94	2002/2014	460.0
Yangzhou Thermal Power Project	22-Mar-94	1999/2014	350.0
Sichuan Gas Development and Conservation Project........	17-Mar-94	1999/2014	255.0
Shanghai Environment Project	08-Mar-94	1999/2014	160.0
Telecommunications Project	21-Dec-93	1999/2014	250.0
Fujian Provincial Highway Project.....................	14-Dec-93	1999/2014	140.0

Borrower or guarantor/project name	Date of approval	Maturities	Principal amount (US$ millions)
China *(continued)*			
Second Shanghai Metropolitan Transportation Project.......	14-Oct-93	1999/2014	150.0
Colombia			
Natural Resource Management Program	23-Dec-93	1999/2013	39.0
Secondary Education Project	16-Dec-93	1999/2014	90.0
Public Financial Management Project	07-Dec-93	1999/2014	30.0
Costa Rica			
Health Sector Reform Social Security System Project	21-Oct-93	1998/2011	22.0
Croatia			
Emergency Reconstruction Project....................	21-Jun-94	1998/2011	128.0
Czech Republic (Guarantor)			
Telecommunications Project	09-Sep-93	1999/2008	80.0
Ecuador			
Irrigation Subsector Technical Assistance Program.........	10-May-94	1999/2014	20.0
Third Social Development Project— Social Investment Fund	22-Feb-94	1999/2013	30.0
Mining Development and Environmental Control Technical Assistance Project	21-Oct-93	1999/2013	14.0
Egypt (Guarantor)			
Agricultural Modernization Project	24-Mar-94	1999/2014	54.0
El Salvador			
Technical Assistance Project	14-Sep-93	1999/2013	2.5
Second Structural Adjustment Loan...................	14-Sep-93	1999/2013	50.0
Estonia			
District Heating Rehabilitation Project	26-May-94	2000/2009	38.4
Highway Maintenance Project	12-May-94	1999/2009	12.0
Gabon			
Economic Recovery Loan	21-Jun-94	1999/2009	30.0
Hungary			
Tax Administration Modernization Project...............	08-Jul-93	1998/2008	29.0
Hungary (Guarantor)			
Energy and Environment Project	17-Feb-94	1999/2009	100.0
India (Guarantor)			
Container Transport Logistics Project	09-Jun-94	2000/2014	94.0
Indonesia			
Sumatera and Kalimantan Power Project	21-Jun-94	2000/2014	260.5
Java Irrigation Improvement and Water Resources Management Project	21-Jun-94	2000/2014	165.7
University Research for Graduate Education Project	14-Jun-94	2000/2014	58.9
Integrated Swamps Development Project	14-Jun-94	2000/2014	65.0

(continued)

Statement of IBRD Loans Approved during Fiscal Year 1994 *(continued)*

Appendix 7

Borrower or guarantor/project name	Date of approval	Maturities	Principal amount (US$ millions)
Indonesia *(continued)*			
Semarang-Surakarta Urban Development Project	07-Jun-94	2000/2014	174.0
Dam Safety Project	31-May-94	1999/2014	55.0
Fifth Kabupaten Roads Project	17-May-94	2000/2014	101.5
Surabaya Urban Development Project	12-Apr-94	1999/2014	175.0
Skills Development Project	25-Mar-94	1999/2014	27.7
Second Highway Sector Investment Project	10-Mar-94	1999/2014	350.0
National Watershed Management and Conservation Project	09-Nov-93	1999/2013	56.5
Jamaica			
Tax Administration Reform Project	16-Jun-94	2000/2011	13.2
Private Investment and Export Development Project	25-Mar-94	1999/2011	35.0
Jordan			
Energy Sector Adjustment Loan	07-Oct-93	1999/2013	80.0
Jordan (Guarantor)			
Telecommunications Project	26-May-94	1999/2014	20.0
Kazakhstan			
Petroleum Technical Assistance Project	02-Jun-94	1999/2011	15.7
Urban Transport Project	07-Apr-94	1999/2011	40.0
Rehabilitation Loan	16-Sep-93	1999/2010	180.0
Technical Assistance Project	03-Aug-93	1999/2010	38.0
Korea, Republic of			
Science and Technical Education Project	06-Jan-94	1999/2009	190.0
Environmental Technology Development Project	06-Jan-94	1999/2008	90.0
Financial Intermediation Project	23-Dec-93	1999/2009	100.0
Latvia			
Agricultural Development Project	11-Jan-94	1998/2011	25.0
Lebanon			
Irrigation Rehabilitation and Modernization Project	29-Jun-94	2000/2011	57.2
Revenue Enhancement and Fiscal Management Technical Assistance Project	29-Jun-94	1999/2011	19.9
Lithuania			
Power Rehabilitation Project	24-May-94	1998/2011	26.4
Macedonia, FYR of			
Economic Recovery Loan	08-Feb-94	1999/2014	40.0
Malaysia			
Health Development Project	14-Dec-93	1999/2011	50.0
Second Rubber Industry Smallholders Development Authority (RISDA) Project	25-Jan-94	1999/2009	70.0
Mauritius			
Technical Assistance to Enhance Competitiveness Project	24-May-94	2000/2009	7.7

Borrower or guarantor/project name	Date of approval	Maturities	Principal amount (US$ millions)
Mexico (Guarantor)			
Northern Border Environment Project	09-Jun-94	2000/2009	368.0
Second Water Supply and Sanitation Sector Project	09-Jun-94	1999/2009	350.0
Second Solid Waste Management Project	09-Jun-94	1999/2009	200.0
Second Primary Education Project.	31-Mar-94	1999/2009	412.0
On-Farm and Minor Irrigation Networks			
Improvement Project	17-Feb-94	1997/2008	200.0
Moldova			
Rehabilitation Loan	21-Oct-93	1999/2013	60.0
Morocco			
Second Agricultural Sector Investment Loan.	23-Jun-94	2000/2014	121.0
Irrigated Areas Agricultural Services Project	21-Dec-93	1999/2014	25.0
Fifth Water Supply Project	23-Nov-93	1999/2014	128.0
Environmental Management Project.	14-Sep-93	1999/2013	6.0
Morocco (Guarantor)			
Fifth Water Supply Project (ONEP)	23-Nov-93	1999/2014	32.0
National Rural Finance Project	23-Nov-93	1999/2013	100.0
Pakistan			
Power Sector Development Project	23-Jun-94	1999/2014	230.0
Public Sector Adjustment Loan	14-Sep-93	1999/2013	150.0
Panama			
Roads Rehabilitation Project	21-Dec-93	1999/2011	60.0
Papua New Guinea			
Petroleum Exploration and Development			
Technical Assistance Project	09-Dec-93	1999/2013	11.0
Paraguay			
Natural Resources Management Project	22-Feb-94	1999/2013	50.0
Eighth Highway Project	21-Dec-93	1999/2013	65.0
Peru			
Transport Rehabilitation Project.	17-Mar-94	1999/2014	150.0
Basic Health and Nutrition Project	03-Feb-94	1999/2014	34.0
Social Development and Compensation Fund			
(FONCODES) Project	16-Dec-93	199/2013	100.0
Philippines (Guarantor)			
Leyte-Luzon Geothermal Project—			
National Power Corporation (NPC)	07-Jun-94	1999/2014	113.0
Leyte-Luzon Geothermal Project—			
Philippine National Oil Company (PNOC)	07-Jun-94	1999/2014	114.0
Subic Bay Freeport Project	02-Jun-94	2000/2014	40.0
Leyte-Cebu Geothermal Project	03-Feb-94	1999/2013	211.0
Poland			
Forest Development Support Project	29-Jul-93	1999/2010	146.0

(continued)

Statement of IBRD Loans Approved during Fiscal Year 1994 *(continued)*

Appendix 7

Borrower or guarantor/project name	Date of approval	Maturities	Principal amount (US$ millions)
Romania			
Industrial Development Project	19-May-94	2000/2014	175.0
Petroleum Sector Rehabilitation Project	05-Apr-94	1999/2014	175.6
Education Reform Project	05-Apr-94	1999/2014	50.0
Russia			
Second Oil Rehabilitation Project	29-Jun-94	1999/2011	500.0
Enterprise Support Project	21-Jun-94	2000/2011	200.0
Land Reform Implementation Support Project	16-Jun-94	1999/2011	80.0
Agriculture Reform Implementation Support Project	16-Jun-94	1999/2011	240.0
Financial Institutions Development Project	19-May-94	1999/2011	200.0
Highway Rehabilitation and Maintenance Project	17-Feb-94	1999/2011	300.0
Slovenia			
Enterprise and Financial Sector Adjustment Loan	15-Jul-93	1999/2008	80.0
Slovak Republic			
Economic Recovery Loan	30-Nov-93	1999/2011	80.0
Slovak Republic (Guarantor)			
Telecommunications Project	15-Jul-93	1998/2010	55.0
Tunisia			
Northwest Mountainous Areas Development Project	23-Dec-93	1999/2011	27.5
Agricultural Sector Investment Loan	18-Nov-93	1999/2011	120.0
Private Investment Credit Project	09-Dec-93	1999/2011	50.0
Tunisia (Guarantor)			
Private Investment Credit Project—Arab Tunisian Bank (ATB)	09-Dec-93	1998/2011	6.0
Private Investment Credit Project—Banque de Développement Economique de Tunisie	09-Dec-93	1998/2010	12.0
Private Investment Credit Project—Banque Internationale Arabe de Tunisie (BIAT)	09-Dec-93	1998/2011	8.0
Private Investment Credit Project—Banque de Tunisie et des Emirats d'Investissement (BTEI)	09-Dec-93	1999/2011	10.0
Private Investment Credit Project—Crédit Foncier Commercial de Tunisie (CFCT)	09-Dec-93	1998/2011	7.0
Private Investment Credit Project—Société Tuniso-Séoudienne d'Investissement et de Développement (STUSID)	09-Dec-93	1999/2011	10.0
Private Investment Credit Project—Tunisie Leasing (TL)	09-Dec-93	1998/2011	6.0
Private Investment Credit Project—Union Bancaire pour le Commerce et l'Industrie (UBCI)	09-Dec-93	1999/2011	7.0
Private Investment Credit Project—Union Tunisienne de Leasing (UTL)	09-Dec-93	1998/2011	4.0
Turkey			
Privatization Implementation Assistance and Social Safety Net Project	03-May-94	1999/2011	100.0
Uruguay			
Basic Education Quality Improvement Project	03-May-94	2000/2009	31.5
Natural Resources Managment and Irrigation Development Project	25-Jan-94	1999/2009	41.0
Private Sector Development Project	25-Jan-94	1999/2009	35.0
Uzbekistan			
Institution Building/Technical Assistance Project	07-Oct-93	1999/2013	21.0

Borrower or guarantor/project name	Date of approval	Maturities	Principal amount (US$ millions)
Venezuela			
Basic Education Project	04-Nov-93	1999/2008	89.4
Urban Transport Project	04-Nov-93	1999/2008	100.0
Zimbabwe (Guarantor)			
Third Power Project	18-Jan-94	1999/2014	90.0
Total			14,243.9

NOTE: All loans approved in fiscal 1994 are at variable interest rates.

Statement of IDA Credits Approved during Fiscal Year 1994

Appendix 8

Country/project name	Date of approval	Maturities	Principal amount (millions) SDR	US$ equivalent
Albania				
School Rehabilitation and Capacity Building Project	23-Jun-94	2004/2034	6.9	9.6
Durres Water Supply Rehabilitation Project	10-May-94	2004/2034	8.4	11.6
Technical Assistance Project for Social Safety Net Development	14-Sep-93	2004/2033	3.9	5.5
Labor Market Development Project	14-Sep-93	2004/2033	3.9	5.4
Housing Project	08-Jul-93	2003/2033	10.6	15.0
Armenia				
Earthquake Reconstruction Project	01-Feb-94	2004/2028	20.1	28.0
Bangladesh				
Second Road Rehabilitation and Maintenance Project	28-Jun-94	2004/2034	103.9	146.8
Jute Sector Adjustment Credit	20-May-94	2004/2034	2.4	3.3
Jute Sector Adjustment Credit	17-Feb-94	2004/2034	175.0	247.0
Jamuna Bridge Project	17-Feb-94	2004/2034	143.6	200.0
Benin				
Rural Water Supply and Sanitation Project..............	07-Jun-94	2004/2034	7.0	9.8
Third Education Project	17-May-94	2004/2034	13.2	18.1
Community-Based Food Security Project...............	12-Apr-94	2004/2033	7.1	9.7
Economic Management Project	09-Nov-93	2004/2033	3.7	5.2
Bhutan				
Third Forestry Development Project...................	06-Jul-93	2004/2033	3.9	5.4
Bolivia				
Municipal Sector Development Project.................	08-Feb-94	2004/2033	30.1	42.0
Structural Adjustment Credit	14-Jan-94	2001/2031	6.7	9.4
Burkina Faso				
Population and AIDS Control Project..................	31-May-94	2004/2034	19.0	26.3
Health and Nutrition Project	31-Mar-94	2004/2034	21.2	29.2
Economic Recovery Credit	29-Mar-94	2004/2034	18.0	25.0
Cambodia				
Emergency Rehabilitation Project	26-Oct-93	2004/2033	45.2	62.7
Cameroon				
Economic Recovery Credit	16-Jun-94	2004/2034	53.1	75.0
Structural Adjustment Credit	22-Mar-94	2004/2034	37.1	51.0
Structural Adjustment Program	10-Mar-94	2004/2034	36.3	50.0
Cape Verde				
Public Sector Reform and Capacity Building Project........	08-Feb-94	2004/2033	5.7	8.1
Caribbean Development Bank				
Sixth Caribbean Development Bank Project	29-Jun-94	2004/2034	7.8	11.0
Chad				
Health and Safe Motherhood Project..................	14-Jun-94	2004/2034	13.1	18.5
Public Works and Capacity Building Project..............	19-May-94	2004/2033	12.4	17.4
Economic Recovery Credit	29-Mar-94	2004/2034	14.4	20.0
China				
Forest Resource Development and Protection Project	07-Jun-94	2004/2029	141.7	200.0

Country/project name	Date of approval	Maturities	Principal amount (millions) SDR	US$ equivalent
China *(continued)*				
Loess Plateau Watershed Rehabilitation Project	26-May-94	2004/2029	106.3	150.0
Xiaolangdi Resettlement Project.	14-Apr-94	2004/2029	79.9	110.0
Songliao Plain Agricultural Development Project.	17-Feb-94	2004/2029	148.5	205.0
Second Red Soils Area Development Project	03-Feb-94	2004/2029	108.4	150.0
Rural Health Workers Development Project.	03-Aug-93	2003/2028	79.3	110.0
Comoros, The				
Small Enterprise Development Project	21-Jun-94	2004/2034	3.7	5.1
Population and Human Resources Project	14-Dec-93	2004/2033	9.2	13.0
Congo				
Economic Recovery Credit	28-Jun-94	2004/2029	70.0	100.0
Côte d'Ivoire				
National Agricultural Services Support Project	28-Jun-94	2004/2034	15.7	21.8
Labor Force Training Support Project	28-Jun-94	2004/2034	12.1	17.0
Rural Savings and Loans Rehabilitation and Promotion Project	05-Apr-94	2004/2033	1.5	2.2
Human Resources Adjustment Program	24-Feb-94	2002/2026	62.0	85.0
Competitiveness and Regulatory Reform Project	08-Feb-94	2002/2026	36.2	50.0
Human Resources Adjustment Program	08-Feb-94	2002/2026	72.4	100.0
Financial Sector Adjustment Program	08-Feb-94	2001/2026	72.4	100.0
Egypt				
Agricultural Modernization Project.	24-Mar-94	2004/2029	48.7	67.0
Ethiopia				
Calub Gas Development Project	29-Mar-94	2004/2034	53.7	74.3
Structural Adjustment Credit	14-Jan-94	2003/2033	0.3	0.5
Gambia, The				
Capacity Building for Environmental Management Technical Assistance Project	12-Apr-94	2004/2033	1.9	2.6
Public Works and Capacity Building Project.	14-Dec-93	2004/2033	7.9	11.0
Ghana				
Community Water and Sanitation Project	14-Apr-94	2004/2034	15.9	22.0
Local Government Development Project	17-Feb-94	2004/2034	27.7	38.5
Agricultural Sector Adjustment Credit	14-Jan-94	2002/2031	4.1	5.7
Agricultural Sector Investment Project	14-Dec-93	2004/2033	15.3	21.5
Guinea				
Health and Nutrition Sector Project	01-Mar-94	2004/2033	17.4	24.6
Guyana				
Second Structural Adjustment Credit	14-Jan-94	2000/2030	2.0	2.8
Sugar Industry Restructuring and Privatization Project	16-Sep-93	2004/2033	10.9	15.0
Water Supply Technical Assistance and Rehabilitation Project .	21-Dec-93	2004/2033	12.5	17.5
Honduras				
Agricultural Sector Adjustment Credit	14-Jan-94	2003/2033	20.1	27.9
Agricultural Sector Adjustment Credit	05-Aug-93	2003/2033	43.3	60.0

(continued)

Statement of IDA Credits Approved during Fiscal Year 1994 (continued)

Country/project name	Date of approval	Maturities	Principal amount (millions) SDR	US$ equivalent
India				
Family Welfare (Assam, Rajasthan and Karnataka) Project ...	16-Jun-94	2004/2029	62.7	88.6
Cataract Blindness Control Project	12-May-94	2004/2029	85.3	117.8
Maharashtra Emergency Earthquake Rehabilitation Project ...	31-Mar-94	2004/2029	177.0	246.0
Haryana Water Resources Consolidation Project...........	29-Mar-94	2004/2029	187.3	258.0
Forestry Research Education and Extension Project.........	24-Feb-94	2004/2029	33.8	47.0
Andhra Pradesh Forestry Project......................	24-Feb-94	2004/2029	55.6	77.4
Kenya				
Micro and Small Enterprise Training and Technology Project .	05-Apr-94	2004/2034	15.7	21.8
Education Sector Adjustment Credit....................	14-Jan-94	2001/2031	30.3	42.2
Kyrgyz Republic				
Privatization and Enterprise Sector Adjustment Credit	29-Jun-94	2004/2029	42.5	60.0
Telecommunications Project	23-Jun-94	2004/2029	12.8	18.0
Lao People's Democratic Republic				
Second Highway Improvement Project..................	14-Apr-94	2004/2034	21.8	30.0
Forest Management and Conservation Project	25-Mar-94	2004/2034	6.3	8.7
Luang Namtha Provincial Development Project............	15-Mar-94	2004/2034	7.1	9.7
Lesotho				
Privatization and Private Sector Development Assistance Project	17-May-94	2004/2034	7.9	11.0
Macedonia, FYR of				
Economic Recovery Credit	08-Feb-94	2004/2029	29.0	40.0
Madagascar				
Cyclone Emergency Rehabilitation Project...............	09-Jun-94	2004/2034	9.3	13.1
Antananarivo Urban Works Project	29-Mar-94	2004/2033	13.3	18.3
Petroleum Sector Reform Project	29-Jul-93	2003/2033	36.7	51.9
Malawi				
Second Institutional Development Project	09-Jun-94	2004/2034	16.0	22.6
Entrepreneurship Development and Drought Recovery Program Credit	14-Jan-94	2002/2034	3.1	4.3
Mali				
Transport Sector Project	26-May-94	2004/2034	46.1	65.0
Economic Recovery Credit	17-Mar-94	2004/2033	18.2	25.0
National Agricultural Research Project..................	16-Dec-93	2004/2033	14.2	20.0
Mauritania				
Agricultural Services Project	08-Mar-94	2000/2030	13.1	18.2
Public Enterprise Sector Adjustment Credit	14-Jan-94	2004/2033	1.0	1.3
Mongolia				
Transport Rehabilitation Project	24-May-94	2004/2034	21.6	30.0
Economic Transition Support Project	28-Oct-93	2004/2033	14.2	20.0
Mozambique				
Second Economic Recovery Program	16-Jun-94	2004/2034	141.7	200.0
Gas Engineering Project	16-Jun-94	2004/2034	21.3	30.0
Financial Sector Capacity Building Project...............	14-Apr-94	2004/2033	6.6	9.0

Country/project name	Date of approval	Maturities	Principal amount (millions)	
			SDR	US$ equivalent
Mozambique *(continued)*				
Second Roads and Coastal Shipping Project	07-Apr-94	2004/2034	136.2	188.0
Nepal				
Population and Family Health Project	12-Apr-94	2004/2034	19.4	26.7
Road Maintenance and Rehabilitation Project	15-Mar-94	2004/2034	36.6	50.5
Higher Education Project	21-Dec-93	2004/2033	14.2	20.0
Nicaragua				
Second Economic Recovery Credit	21-Jun-94	2004/2034	42.5	60.0
Second Economic Recovery Credit	21-Jun-94	2004/2034	5.4	7.6
Health Sector Reform Project	16-Dec-93	2004/2033	10.8	15.0
Agricultural Technology and Land Management Project	20-Jul-93	2004/2033	31.1	44.0
Niger				
Basic Education Sector Project	31-May-94	2004/2034	29.3	41.4
Economic Recovery Credit	17-Mar-94	2004/2034	18.2	25.0
Pakistan				
Social Action Program Project	31-Mar-94	2004/2034	145.2	200.0
Balochistan Natural Resource Management Project	22-Mar-94	2004/2029	10.7	14.7
Sindh Special Development Project	16-Dec-93	2004/2028	33.3	46.8
Public Sector Adjustment Credit	14-Sep-93	2004/2028	71.8	100.0
Rwanda				
Second National Agricultural Research Project	14-Oct-93	2004/2033	10.9	15.0
Private Sector Development	09-Sep-93	2004/2033	8.7	12.0
Senegal				
Economic Recovery Credit	17-Mar-94	2004/2034	18.2	25.0
Transport Sector Adjustment Credit	14-Jan-94	2001/2031	2.7	3.7
Sierra Leone				
Structural Adjustment Credit	14-Jan-94	2004/2033	0.1	0.2
Structural Adjustment Credit	14-Oct-93	2004/2033	35.9	50.0
Tanzania				
Second Integrated Roads Project	07-Apr-94	2004/2034	123.3	170.2
Agricultural Sector Management Project	20-Jul-93	2003/2033	17.3	24.5
Togo				
Togo Urban Development Project	31-May-94	2004/2033	18.6	26.2
Uganda				
Second Structural Adjustment Credit	10-May-94	2004/2034	57.8	80.0
Cotton Subsector Development Project	10-May-94	2004/2034	10.0	14.0
Sexually Transmitted Infections Project	12-Apr-94	2004/2034	36.3	50.0
Transport Rehabilitation Project	25-Mar-94	2004/2034	54.5	75.0
Small Towns Water and Sanitation Project	17-Mar-94	2004/2033	30.4	42.3
Financial Sector Adjustment Credit	14-Jan-94	2003/2033	0.8	1.1
Viet Nam				
Agricultural Rehabilitation Project	25-Jan-94	2004/2033	69.4	96.0

(continued)

Statement of IDA Credits Approved during Fiscal Year 1994 *(continued)*

Appendix 8

Country/project name	Date of approval	Maturities	Principal amount (millions) SDR	Principal amount (millions) US$ equivalent
Viet Nam *(continued)*				
Primary Education Project	26-Oct-93	2004/2033	49.6	70.0
Highway Rehabilitation Project	26-Oct-93	2004/2033	112.2	158.5
Yemen				
Education Sector Investment Project	17-Feb-94	2004/2033	23.9	33.0
Zambia				
Petroleum Sector Rehabilitation Project	31-May-94	2004/2034	21.6	30.0
Economic and Social Adjustment Credit................	10-Mar-94	2004/2034	108.9	150.0
Privatization and Industrial Reform Credit...............	14-Jan-94	2002/2032	12.1	16.8
Second Privatization and Industrial Reform Credit	09-Aug-93	2003/2033	7.0	10.0
Financial and Legal Management Upgrading Project	13-Jul-93	2003/2033	12.8	18.0
Total...			4,733.6	6,592.1

NOTE: Starting with the sixth replenishment of IDA, credits are expressed in special drawing rights (SDRs). The US-dollar equivalent of the original principal amount of credits denominated in SDRs is shown at the rate approved by the executive board. All credits approved in fiscal 1994 have a service charge of 0.75 percent on the disbursed and outstanding balance. Details may not add to totals because of rounding.

Current IBRD, IDA, and Blend Borrowers   Appendix 9
(based on fiscal years 1994–97 lending program)

June 30, 1994

IBRD only

Algeria	Ecuador	Lebanon	Russian Federation
Argentina	El Salvador	Lithuania	Slovak Republic
Azerbaijan	Estonia	Mauritius	Slovenia
Barbados	Fiji	Malaysia	South Africa
Belarus	Gabon	Mexico	Swaziland
Belize	Guatemala	Morocco	Thailand
Brazil	Hungary	Moldova	Trinidad and Tobago
Bulgaria	Indonesia	Panama	Tunisia
Chile	Iran, Islamic Republic of	Paraguay	Turkey
Colombia	Jamaica	Papua New Guinea	Turkmenistan
Costa Rica	Jordan	Peru	Ukraine
Croatia	Kazakhstan	Philippines	Uruguay
Czech Republic	Korea, Republic of	Poland	Uzbekistan
Dominican Republic	Latvia	Romania	Venezuela

IDA only

Albania	Congo	Lao People's Democratic Republic	Senegal
Armenia	Côte d'Ivoire	Madagascar	Sierre Leone
Bangladesh	Djibouti	Malawi	Solomon Islands
Benin	Eritrea	Maldives	Sri Lanka
Bhutan	Ethiopia	Mali	Tajikistan
Bolivia	Gambia, The	Mauritania	Tanzania
Burkina Faso	Georgia	Mongolia	Togo
Burundi	Ghana	Mozambique	Uganda
Cambodia	Guinea	Nepal	Vanuatu
Cameroon	Guinea-Bissau	Nicaragua	Viet Nam
Cape Verde	Honduras	Niger	Western Samoa
Central African Republic	Kenya	Nigeria	Yeman, Republic of
Chad	Kiribati	Rwanda	Zambia
Comoros		São Tomé and Principe	

Blend countries

Angola	Egypt	Kyrgyz Republic	Pakistan
Caribbean Region	Guyana	Lesotho	Zimbabwe
China	India	Macedonia, FYR of	

Development Committee Communiqués, Fiscal Year 1994

Forty-seventh meeting, Washington, September 27, 1993

1. The 47th meeting of the Development Committee was held in Washington DC on September 27, 1993 under the chairmanship of Mr. Rudolf Hommes, Minister of Finance and Public Credit of Colombia.[1] The Committee extended its thanks to the retiring Chairman, Mr. Ricardo Hausmann of Venezuela.

2. GAZA AND THE WEST BANK. The Committee welcomed the outstanding contribution to the Middle East Peace Process made by the World Bank in preparing the ground for a coordinated program of financial support for Gaza and the West Bank.

3. WORLD ECONOMY. The Committee reviewed the impact on developing countries of recent trends in the world economy. It renewed its call for a fresh impetus to growth in the industrial countries, and for a successful conclusion of the Uruguay Round by the end of 1993 on the basis of a comprehensive and balanced agreement; this is crucial to the growth prospects for industrial and developing countries alike. It therefore welcomed the joint statement by Mr. Sutherland, Mr. Preston, and Mr. Camdessus, issued on the morning of its meeting.

4. ADJUSTMENT EXPERIENCE OF LOW-INCOME COUNTRIES AND THEIR FINANCING NEEDS. The Committee recognizes that many low-income countries have found it hard to make the economic adjustment necessary to achieve economic and social progress. There are several reasons: the main ones are poor initial conditions; lack of domestic savings; lack of adequate institutional and administrative capacity; inappropriate policies which take time to correct; and an unfavorable external environment. Progress in most directions has been slower than among the middle-income countries, but the preliminary evidence suggests that countries which sustain strong adjustment policies do better than the rest. In these countries there has been significant progress with macro-economic stabilization and outwardly orientated policies, and in decontrolling domestic prices, particularly in agriculture. But even there, financial-sector and public-enterprise reforms have lagged behind, and private investment has responded only with a considerable lag. As a result, improvements have not yet led to a sustained increase in income per capita, and success in reducing poverty and in protecting the environment has been uneven.

5. The Committee welcomes the broadening political consensus on adjustment strategies which stress stabilization and market-friendly measures, combined with human resource development and poverty alleviation. It believes such strategies will succeed over time, if implemented consistently and backed up by structural reforms consistent with long-term sustainable development. It therefore urges countries which have not yet embarked on the adjustment process to formulate and implement their own programs accordingly. The design of adjustment programs and of external assistance needs to reflect the socio-political background and institutional capacity of the countries concerned. It follows that the best programs are those which are home-grown. The Bank and the Fund (as appropriate) in their relations with the borrowing countries, will do more to address the impact of macro-economic and adjustment measures and their sequencing on poverty, employment, investment and the environment. Some of the lessons of the East-Asian experience may be relevant to today's low-income countries, particularly those of macro-economic policy, export orientation, human resource development and the training of a professional civil service.

6. In many cases, low-income countries will need to supplement domestic savings with foreign investment and with substantial and timely concessional financial support, together with necessary and appropriate relief of bilateral debt. To sustain the required levels of external support and investment, they will have to maintain their commitment to economic reform, poverty alleviation, environmental soundness, public participation and good governance. Donors should focus concessional assistance on the low-income adjusting countries. They should complete ratification of IDA-10 as early as possible, agree to the broad-

[1] Mr. Lewis T. Preston, President of the World Bank, Mr. Michel Camdessus, Managing Director of the International Monetary Fund, Mr. Peter Sutherland, Director-General of the GATT, Mr. Mohammed Imady, Minister of Economy and Foreign Trade of Syria and Chairman of the Group of 24, and Mr. Peter Mountfield, Executive Secretary, took part in the meeting. Observers from a number of international and regional organizations also attended.

est possible spectrum of contributors to the ESAF successor, work for its rapid implementation, and make significant bilateral contributions to the SPA.

7. SOCIAL SECURITY REFORM AND SOCIAL SAFETY NETS. The Committee looked at the continued need for social support, both to meet life hazards and to help those hurt by necessary adjustment measures. Many existing insurance structures have created unsustainable burdens on the government budget and the competitiveness of the formal sector, while failing to cover important groups of the population. Existing entitlements may now have to be reviewed. In many countries, including economies in transition, a system combining elements of public and private provision will be appropriate, but the mix will vary from case to case. The international institutions can help by continuing to provide technical assistance and policy advice.

8. In addition to these classical social security systems, countries engaged in adjustment or systemic transformation may require well-designed extra social safety nets, integrated into their poverty-reduction strategy, involving schemes such as labor-intensive public works, nutrition programs, targeted food subsidies, retraining of dismissed workers, and "social funds." But governments should avoid creating new long-term entitlements which might build up future budgetary problems. The appropriate mix of measures depends on data availability, administrative capacity, and financial resources. Budget outlays should where necessary be reallocated to provide financial resources, both for safety nets and for other pro-poor social spending. The poorest among them may require continued technical and financial support for such schemes from the World Bank and from donors. The Committee welcomes the constructive part played by the Bank and the Fund in their respective roles, in supporting social security system reforms and establishing and financing safety nets as part of their adjustment lending.

9. WORLD BANK WOMEN-IN-DEVELOPMENT STRATEGY. The Committee welcomed a report on the World Bank's attempts to integrate gender issues into its overall development strategy. It commends the progress made, and welcomes the President's commitment to a further strengthening of the Bank's

operations in this area. It notes that the Bank's Executive Board will be reviewing the strategy in the Spring of 1994.

10. THE COST-EFFECTIVENESS OF AID. The Committee believes it is more than ever important to enhance the effectiveness of development assistance, welcomes recent steps taken by the World Bank in this context, and proposes to address this matter next year. In order to provide maximum help to recipients, donor agencies and multilateral institutions need to maintain and improve their cost-effectiveness.

11. NEXT MEETING. The Committee will meet again in Washington DC on April 26, 1994, when it will discuss population and migration issues.

Forty-eighth meeting, Washington, April 26, 1994

1. The 48th meeting of the Development Committee was held in Washington DC on April 26, 1994, under the chairmanship of Mr. Rudolf Hommes, Minister of Finance and Public Credit of Colombia.[1]

2. RESOURCE FLOWS. Ministers welcome the increased flows of resources to developing countries; 1993 was another record year. Particularly noteworthy was the sustained growth in private flows, which went mainly to the faster-growing and outwardly oriented countries which have implemented successful reforms. Similarly, much of the increase in official flows has been concentrated on nonconcessional loans to middle-income countries. Much of the concessional official development assistance has been targeted on poorer countries, although its total increased only modestly in 1993 and the outlook continues to be unfavorable. In that connection, Ministers welcome the progress made and the increased amounts pledged at last week's meeting on the Special Program of Assistance for Africa, and the recent extension and enlargement of the IMF's Enhanced Structural Adjustment Facility.

---

[1] Mr. Lewis T. Preston, President of the World Bank, Mr. Michel Camdessus, Managing Director of the International Monetary Fund, Mr. Willy W. Zapata, President of the Banco de Guatemala and Chairman of the Group of 24, and Mr. Peter Mountfield, Executive Secretary, took part in the meeting. Observers from a number of international and regional organizations also attended.

Development Committee
Communiqués, Fiscal Year 1994

3. POPULATION. The Committee reviewed some of the issues which will be raised at the forthcoming United Nations Conference on Population and Development to be held in Cairo in September 1994. They welcomed the Secretary-General of the Conference, Dr. Nafis Sadik, who addressed their meeting.

4. *Trends.* The world's population has grown by 1.7 billion in the past two decades. Almost all the increase was in the developing countries. The total population now stands at nearly 5.7 billion, about a billion of whom still live in poverty. Although the rate of growth is now slowing down, another 2.8 billion will be added to the total by 2025, on the current United Nations "most likely" projections. On this basis, world population will probably double in less than 50 years. Ministers agree that the massive economic, social, political and environmental consequences of these changes cannot be ignored.

5. *Policies.* Ministers believe that an integrated population policy in developing countries must recognize the links between economic growth, population, poverty reduction, health, investment in human resources and environmental degradation. All couples and individuals have the right to decide freely and responsibly on the number and spacing of their children. Family planning is only one of the available instruments and needs to be seen in the broader context of changing social patterns and the increased awareness of women's role. Population programs are therefore becoming increasingly diverse, depending on the stage of the demographic transition in each country. Moreover, experience demonstrates that improved education and employment prospects (particularly for girls), improved health, and increased income all tend to reduce the birth rate. Institutional arrangements for the delivery of services may need to be strengthened, and must be tailored to local conditions and needs, taking full advantage of available nongovernmental and private sector organizations. They must pay full regard to the social and cultural traditions of each country.

6. *Priorities.* Ministers note that the Cairo Conference will seek to establish clear and realistic objectives for future population policy. Without prejudging the outcome of the Conference, they agree that three objectives in particular deserve special attention:

First, improvements in the primary school enrollment rate in low-income countries to achieve universal primary education;

Second, improving access to family planning and related health services, estimated by UNFPA to require a doubling of investments by the year 2000;

Third, reductions in maternal and child mortality in developing countries.

7. *Developing countries.* In general, the resource requirements are affordable, compared with other major expenditure programs. Many developing economies can meet the costs. In some cases costs are already covered by user fees. But for the poorest people, continued public support will be essential, and is justified by the benefits. Ministers agreed that developing countries should consider giving these three objectives priority within total budgets.

8. *Donors.* The poorest countries will still need help from donors. Bilateral and multilateral donors currently contribute about $1 billion a year to population programs in developing countries. Ministers hope that many individual bilateral donors will be able to improve the present average 1.25% share of existing aid budgets allocated to population programs, as well as their support for health and education.

9. *The World Bank.* At the multilateral level, Ministers welcome the increasing share of the World Bank's social sector programs which have risen from 6% to 16% of the total portfolio in the past five years. Within this program, about $1.8 billion annually is currently allocated to population, health and nutrition, and $1.9 billion to education. Much of this affects the demand for population services indirectly. There are currently ten or more projects a year with significant direct population components, costing $200 million, concentrated mainly in the poorest developing countries. Ministers welcome the Bank's readiness to respond rapidly to requests for more assistance in this field. Ministers recognize that the Bank is not the principal organization concerned with population, but that its policy dialogue and wider operations give it a unique opportunity to promote population policies. They therefore call on the Bank, other donors, the other multilaterals such as UNFPA, and the borrowing governments to collaborate fully in operations and in mobilizing the institutional and financial re-

sources needed; and re-evaluate their efforts following the Cairo Conference.

10. *Migration*. Ministers discussed the related issue of international migration, and its social, political and financial consequences for importing and exporting countries alike. They note that relatively little is known about the nature of these issues. Ministers noted the need for policies addressing these issues. They call for more policy-oriented research on migration and closer collaboration between the different international agencies concerned.

11. TRADE. Ministers greatly welcome the successful conclusion of the Uruguay Round and the agreements reached at Marrakesh and call for their rapid ratification and full implementation. These agreements reduce the risk of a relapse into protectionism, which would have greatly damaged many developing countries and countries in transition. They open up the prospect of faster economic growth for the world as a whole. All countries stand to gain. For countries to reap the full benefits from the Round, it is essential that they maintain stable macroeconomic environments and intensify their structural reform programs and trade liberalization, while improving their access to world markets.

12. Ministers note that some developing countries may be adversely affected in the transition to the new world trading system, by the loss of preferences or by higher prices for food imports, although these effects will only be felt gradually, leaving time for adjustment. They urge the Bank and the Fund to take account of these possible adverse effects in designing country assistance strategies and operational support for the affected countries.

13. Ministers welcome the creation of the new World Trade Organization. They urge the WTO, the Bank and the Fund to cooperate fully and, within their own areas of responsibility, to help developing countries and countries in transition to take advantage of the new market opportunities. They also hope that all developing countries and countries in transition will soon join, so as to increase market access for their exports. They note that both Bank and Fund are engaged in fuller study of the impact of the Round, of future trade policy, and of their own future activities in the trade area. Ministers will resume discussion of these questions at their next meeting.

14. *Commodities*. Ministers also reviewed recent work in the Bank and the Fund on commodity prices. They agree that despite signs of a modest recovery in the short term, prices are unlikely to return to the levels of the 1970s and early 1980s. Given these uncertainties, Ministers agree it would be prudent not to assume an improvement in the long term, and wise to err on the side of caution.

15. Ministers agree that if price shocks are expected to be only temporary, then provision of compensatory finance may be appropriate. But if the fall in prices is expected to be permanent, then an adjustment-oriented response should not be deferred in the hope of a recovery. Ministers therefore believe that developing country governments should continue to diversify their economies. They will need the ongoing support of the World Bank, the Fund and the donor community. Ministers call on the Bank to explore additional measures in its investment work in this area. The continuing volatility of prices also requires the maintenance of contingency measures to safeguard programs supported by the Fund.

16. Ministers note that few international commodity agreements have maintained price levels in the face of falling demand, increased production, and lower costs. Government price stabilization schemes do not generally work well when commodity prices are expected to fall further or remain low; they tend to create distortions and place considerable strain on government budgets. For many countries and products, hedging instruments in commercial futures markets now permit private agents to protect themselves against price fluctuations, although there remain a number of legal, financial and technical barriers. Ministers welcome the technical assistance being given by UNCTAD, the World Bank and other agencies, to help smaller producers overcome these obstacles and take advantage of such markets. They welcome the studies being undertaken by the Bank of new guarantee mechanisms which would permit these poorer and less creditworthy countries to undertake market-based hedging operations.

17. DEVELOPMENT BANKS. The Committee agreed in principle to establish a small Task Force to review the development role being played by the Multilateral Development Banks, including the World Bank, and the four

Development Committee
Communiqués, Fiscal Year 1994

main regional banks . This Task Force, whose Chairman, terms of reference, and composition will be agreed after consultation with the governments, will aim to complete its work by October 1995.

18. CHAIRMAN. The Committee selected Mr. M'Hamed Sagou of Morocco to be its next Chairman in succession to Mr. Rudolf Hommes of Colombia. The Committee expressed its warmest thanks to Mr. Hommes at the end of his period in the Chair.

19. NEXT MEETING. The Committee agreed to meet again in Madrid, Spain, on October 3, 1994, when it will discuss the question of Aid Effectiveness and the work of the World Bank and IMF in the light of the Uruguay Round.

Index